Sailor Without a Boat

Reading this book is like gorging on candy. Once you begin, you won't want to stop.
    Raymond Ouellet, Gatineau, QC

Sailor Without a Boat was so interesting, that I virtually gobbled it up within a few days! Let's hope that Robert Bériault will produce more books like this one.
    Mario Boileau, Rockland, Ontario

From start to finish, we were carried away with Robert's book, especially with his manner of relating the stories (my husband and I read the book together in bed at night). What an adventurer! What a writer! We were particularly impressed with his descriptions and especially with his positive spirit and his sense of observation and analysis. It is a wonderful lesson about our world, which he describes so well.
    Michèle Lavallée, Gatineau, Quebec

I received *Sailor Without a Boat* at Christmas and I was not able to put it down! It's filled with interesting experiences and adventures.
    Garry Cooke, Grimsby, Ontario

Robert gives readers a street-smart common sense approach to sailing on other people's yachts. He draws on years of experience to outline the challenges of blue water sailing with noteworthy consideration to Caribbean waters. The book kept me hanging in suspense at times and laughing at others. Interesting, informative, exciting – A must read for those with a lust for adventure. I hope *Sailor Without a Boat* will not be his last offering.
    Jim Keith, Fernandina Beach, Florida

At times, I laughed to tears when reading *Sailor Without a Boat*! Robert wields a skilful pen and he knows how to say things with humility, passion and humour.
    Dominique Champeau, Gatineau, Quebec

It is a good story that engages the reader while meeting a practical need for those aspiring sailors who prefer not to take on the considerable expense of maintaining a pleasure craft. What a pleasure to read about Robert's adventures and his voyages of discovery!
    Tony Cassils, Ottawa, Ontario

Throughout the book, the descriptions are rich, original and personal. Robert's unusual resilience makes him worthy of being called a true adventurer. His stories reveal what cruising life is like and how this lifestyle can lead to the discovery of the world and other cultures. This book is not simply a story, but also a learning experience about many elements of sailing, geography and humanity.
    Richard Groleau, Gatineau, Quebec

This is an amazing account of Robert's second life after a career in scientific research.
    Douglas Mitchell, Lethbridge, Alberta

Sailor Without a Boat is a well-written, remarkable collection of stories, anecdotes and musings about the wonders of sailing, about the environment and about life in general. – Fun to read and full of really good stuff!
    David Delaney, Ottawa, Ontario

Sailor Without a Boat proves that there is no age to start living the adventure of your dreams. The book relates details of daily life on boats in the middle of the ocean and ashore in distant places. Robert reminds us that the risks of sailing on great oceans in small vessels don't always come from the sea or the mechanics of the boat, but also from one's shipmates. A great read, full of excellent insights, advice and contacts for anyone interested in imitating him.
    Normand Bergevin, Embrun, Ontario

Sailor Without a Boat

How I Sailed on Other People's Yachts and Lived to Tell About It.

Robert Bériault

Copyright © 2011 Robert A. Bériault

All rights reserved

ISBN 978-1466436138

Contents

Preface ……………………………………………..	6
Acknowledgements ……………………………..……	8
Chapter 1. Pirates of Margarita………..……………....…	11
Chapter 2. Beginnings……………………………….…	19
Chapter 3. Learning the Ropes………………………….	31
Chapter 4. More Than I Bargained For……...……………	55
Chapter 5. A Brush With Death of Another Kind……….	87
Chapter 6. Searching for an OPY………………………...	97
Chapter 7. A Small Ocean for Starters……………..……	107
Chapter 8. Teaching and Learning………………………	173
Chapter 9. Margarita, Here We Come……………..……	199
Chapter 10. Life After Margarita…………………………	219
Chapter 11. A Whole Ocean At Last………..………..…	251
Chapter 12. Transatlantic on an Open 60! ………..……	281
Annex 1. Advice for Finding an OPY……………….…...	320
Annex 2. Checklist for Sailing on an OPY..………….....	330
Annex 3. OPY Search Web sites..……………………....	332
Annex 4. Canadian and American Sailing Standards…..	333
Annex 5. Checklists for Successful Bareboating ……….	335
Annex 6. The Nautical Mile Explained……………..……	338
Annex 7. Musings on Piracy……………………….……	339
Glossary……………………………………………...……	341

Preface

Maybe you're an aspiring adventurer who dreams of exploring the great oceans, or of sailing from island to island or of discovering distant lands and peoples, but never did so because you couldn't make the giant commitment of buying a sailboat. Maybe you're an experienced sailor, puzzled by the title of this book and want to find out how a person can acquire any meaningful sailing experience without owning a boat. *Sailor Without a Boat* tells the story of my dream to sail around the world and how I sailed for the last thirteen years on other people's yachts without the burdens of boat ownership.

And as you might have deduced from the subtitle, during my short history of sailing I sometimes met with more excitement than anticipated. Much of the drama you will find in these pages came from the vicissitudes of the wind and seas, the intricacies of navigation, the idiosyncrasies of my shipmates and the continual scourge of things that break on a boat. The following chapters also tell the story of how at an advanced age I took up a sport that is usually learned in youth, but then earnestly tried to make up for lost time. They disclose how the world of sailing has allowed me to learn the technical skills needed to navigate in relative safety, to establish many new friendships, to enjoy the wonders of being at sea and to discover fascinating corners of the world.

The storyteller in me wanted this to be primarily a collection of entertaining anecdotes and stories about my sailing adventures and the people who befriended me, accompanied me, mentored me, amused me, supported me, frustrated me and enchanted me. The stories recounted in this book are all based on real-life experiences of mine and are true even if some of them might seem hard to believe. In many cases I found myself with the obligation to change names to protect the innocent or the guilty, or to prevent hurting someone's feelings. In a few instances I was compelled to omit interesting facts that might have reflected unfavourably on certain characters in my story, including myself.

Since sailing is so complex and its vocabulary so rich, the opportunist and the teacher in me couldn't let a perfect occasion slip by without sneaking in some pedagogy. You will see that most of the time when the story leads to a technical aspect of sailing, I assume that you're new to the activity and explain the concept in plain language, all the while respecting the nautical terminology. For the same reason, I've included a glossary of sailing terms at the back of the book, which covers all the terms you will find as the story develops.

Preface

This isn't meant to be a "How To" book, but I think that reading Annex 1, Advice for Finding an OPY (Other People's Yachts), Annex 2, Checklist for Sailing on an OPY and Annex 3, OPY Search Web sites would be a good start if you ever entertain the notion of emulating me in sailing on other people's yachts. Should you decide that you want to learn to sail or to improve your sailing knowledge, you might check out Annex 4, which describes the courses offered by the Canadian and American sailing associations. And if you reach the stage where you are ready to rent a boat, bareboating in nautical parlance, you might find it useful to consult Annex 5, Checklists for Successful Bareboating.

You will find that I have expressed time of day in terms of the 24-hour clock, known as military time, as it is the appropriate thing to do in the nautical world. In this way, for example, nine thirty five at night will read 2135 and is expressed as twenty-one thirty-five hours. The unit of distance used in the nautical domain, as in the world of aeronautics, is the nautical mile, which is equal to 1.85 kilometres or 1.15 statute or road miles. So from now on, when you see "miles", you'll know what I'm talking about. Likewise, the unit of speed used in this book will be the knot, which is one nautical mile per hour. We must never say, "The boat is doing 10 knots per hour", as the word knot implies "per hour". For a ballpark estimate in kilometres or kilometres per hour, just multiply miles or knots by 2. If you wish to find out where this bizarre unit comes from, you might want to read my attempt at an explanation in Annex 6.

What I hope to accomplish by publishing this book is to amuse and entertain, but more importantly, to communicate my love of the sea and if you have never sailed before, to convince you to give it a try. Whether you are a seasoned sailor, a novice sailor, a future sailor or a confirmed landlubber, I hope there will be something for you in this book and that you will enjoy the read.

Acknowledgements

Since I am not given to spending my days sitting down, *Sailor Without a Boat* would not have been possible had a personal disaster not befallen me. Upon returning from a hike in the Guatemalan jungle, I was stricken with a blinding eye infection caused by a tropical fungus never diagnosed before in Ottawa. Because I could not tolerate sunlight, I was confined to my lounging chair for five months, forced into a state of immobility that was very unnatural for me. While away on that fateful trip, which started out as a passage across the Pacific Ocean, I had written to my friends and family about my adventures and misadventures. Upon my return, several of my readers complimented me on my writing style and suggested that I write a book about my sailing experiences. Without their prompting, the idea would never have crossed my mind. One day, after taking my painkiller and my hourly eye drops, I booted my laptop and was pleased to discover that my light-sensitive eye was able to tolerate the low illumination of the small screen. Heeding my friends' advice, I began putting down in writing recollections of my sailing experiences. I quickly discovered what a pleasure it is to turn ideas and memories into written words. As a bonus, the effort needed to maintain my concentration took my mind off the pain, and the activity of writing helped carry me through the terrible ordeal. I'd like to start by thanking those who instilled in me the idea.

This book, of course, would not have been possible had I not learned to sail in the first place. For this I am indebted to my mentors and teachers who patiently coached me during my years of sailing apprenticeship: Maureen Adamache, Grant Reader, Gilles Séguin and Éric Simard. I would probably be a poorer teacher today had I not learned from the example of Warren Chafe, my Intermediate level teacher. And I would never have become a sailing instructor had Kim Moffat not have faith in me and had Ron Schute not provided me the chance to teach with his fine sailing school.

Since sailing is a social activity, I would have few stories to tell had it not been for my friends with whom I've sailed as crew or as captain on numerous outings and trips. For this I owe a great deal of gratitude to my sailing friends Jim Burgess, Rachel Gauthier, Denis Ouellet, Carole Pilon, Gilles Racette, Jacques Sorel, and Jacquie Thériault. I wish to thank Dominique Champeau for having kept me abreast of sailing opportunities that have led to some of the stories in this book. Also, I'm thankful that mylucky stars have conspired for me to meet Anthony Johnson who has provided me with so many sailing adventures on the Caribbean and for having reviewed my book in its embryonic stage. A big "thank you" to David Delaney and my two sailing friends Raymond Ouellet and Don Bedier for having reviewed my book and for their numerous suggestions.

I am highly gratified by my brother-in-law Nigel Berrisford's generous rating of the book and for his encouragement, without which I might not have decided to publish.

I owe special thanks to Gillian Kennedy Higenbottam for her thorough, professional editing of the final version of the manuscript, where she uncovered a surprising number of mistakes, typos, inconsistencies and missing transitions. I guess that's what an editor if for!

Finally, I could not have done this without the encouragement of my family. My dear wife Micheline, who has lived my experiences vicariously through my stories and pictures, was unconditionally supportive in the two years I spent writing this book; she has patiently sifted through the manuscript four times and provided me with much needed constructive criticism. Hats off to my son Philippe who has also reviewed the book twice and offered his sharp critique. Merci to my daughter Natalie, my granddaughter Gabrielle and son-in-law Serge for their support and their love.

Rough sea outside the bay in sight of village

Calm water inside the bay out of sight of village

Chapter 1

Pirates of Margarita

Tuesday, July 27, 2004.

Anthony had sailed the Caribbean for thirty years and had never closed the companionway hatch for the night. Nevertheless, once he did close the entrance to the cabin, we felt secure and it never dawned upon us to discuss what we'd do if our sailboat were to be boarded by pirates.

My friend Anthony, a very fit, 64-year-old Trinidadian sailor, had invited me on this sailing trip aboard *Ventus*. He was of medium build and sported a salt and pepper chin curtain style of beard with an extra tuft under the lower lip. Although his curly, greying hair assumed a distant African origin, his rather pale complexion made him look Caucasian. Jacqui, who was also from Trinidad, had sailed with Anthony on many occasions. She was a petite, energetic, 70-year-old grandmother with brown complexion, Asian traits and curly, black hair. She had a passion for sailing and was an accomplished cook.

The three of us had spent the previous night at anchor in the bay outside the Chacachacare boat yard and had slept wretchedly. Near the entrance to the wide Boca del Rio bay, we had been exposed to a considerable swell that made *Ventus* pitch and roll incessantly. To prevent a repeat of that uncomfortable night we left the exposed anchorage and re-anchored in more sheltered waters, further into the bay. We were then out of sight of the Boca del Rio village, surrounded by mangrove. The boatyard owner had suggested that we might want to join an ecotour of the mangroves. He told us not to leave the boat unattended, as Venezuela was experiencing increasing problems with theft. However, he assured us that there had been no history of aggression on Margarita, this island province of the economically devastated country.

Having waited till after the siesta for the stores to reopen, Anthony and I motored the dinghy into the Boca del Rio village to pick up some eggs, bread and ice, leaving Jacqui to guard the ship.

We locked the dinghy to the main dock under the scrutiny of a dozen curious children. The dock was attached to a beach that was hardly twenty feet wide, littered with fragments of wood, old tires, scrap metal and broken concrete. A solid wall of decrepit row houses made of cement blocks obstructed our access to the street. We walked along the beach to the right, looking for a passageway to the street. To no avail. We turned around and walked the other way for the same purpose, only to come to another dead end.

A thin, barefoot girl of no more than nine had spotted us and asked us where we wanted to go. We wanted to find the supermarket recommended in the Boating Guide, "El supermercado" we told her in our best Spanish. She led us to the open door of one of the homes, said something in Spanish to a woman, and to our surprise she led us through the house to the street. Walking ahead of us, the little girl guided us along the broken sidewalks, past the disintegrating church and bank. She walked with assurance, as if she owned the place and as if guiding strange men were a daily occurrence. The dusty, dimly lit supermarket had eggs and mostly bare shelves. We bought a tray of eggs, but there was no bread nor ice. "Una paneteria", we told our diminutive guide and she led us silently through a maze of streets lined with deteriorating concrete block houses abutting the sidewalk. The bakery offered two kinds of bread and we bought a few of each. We still hadn't found our ice. "¿Adonde podemos comprar hielo?" we asked the little girl. And she confidently led us through grubby streets to a corner store that featured meat, frozen products and a row of pinball machines. Anthony bought her an ice cream bar, which she consumed with the panache of a connoisseur. Once we had bought the ice our little escort led us back to the house that provided our link with the beach and we then broke company.

While we were away, Jacqui was resting in the aft cabin. She heard a motorboat approaching. Through the portlights she saw two young men in a motorized gondola typical of the area's tourist boats. They did a complete circle around our yacht, apparently without noticing Jacqui, then motored towards the mangrove and vanished.

When Anthony and I returned to *Ventus* with our purchases we found Jacqui in the cockpit in the company of a young Venezuelan man of perhaps 18 or 19. We joked that we can't leave Jacqui for an hour without her seducing some handsome man, humour that struck a sour note.

While she had been resting in the quarter cabin Jacqui heard footsteps on the deck. She bolted for the companionway and saw a young man in a bathing suit coming down, soaking wet. She stood on the bottom step to block his way. He appeared surprised to discover someone on board. When she demanded to know what he was doing there, he signalled he was thirsty and said "Agua, agua!" Without abandoning her vantage point in front of the intruder she reached for the galley faucet just next to her and poured the unwanted visitor a glass of water and motioned him back into the cockpit. In a colloquial and incomprehensible Spanish he told us his name was Che and from his gesturing we gathered that he came from the fishing boat we could see anchored further in the bay. He was of average height, Hispanic in appearance, and had his right leg fully tattooed. He asked many questions about our origin and destination but offered no explanation for what the heck he was doing on our boat. After a while he dove into the water and swam, not towards the fishing boat, but towards the distant mangrove, into which he disappeared.

These events left us with a feeling of unease. If it hadn't been so late in the afternoon, we would have weighed anchor and sailed to Robledal, the closest anchorage, 14 miles away around the west tip of the island. These disturbing events prompted us to close the companionway hatch before preparing for bed. We couldn't lock it as it was only equipped to be locked from the outside, but having it closed made us feel safer. As usual for the Caribbean, we had hoisted the dinghy up to deck level and locked it to the mast with a wire cable.

The peaceful atmosphere of the Hallberg Rassy 39, with its beautiful, rich teak woodwork and its warm, indirect lighting imparted a sense of calm. Jacqui was in bed in the aft cabin, Anthony was at the chart table writing on his laptop and I was reading in bed, in the fore cabin, oblivious of the chaos that was about to take place.

Suddenly we heard booming footsteps on the deck, accompanied by loud shouts ordering us to open the door! I bolted to the salon. Three brown faces peered through the salon portlights and a pair of feet appeared through the main hatch, hanging down above the salon table. Anthony yelled at the top of his lungs, "GO AWAY, LEAVE US ALONE!"

The man in the hatch leaned over and grabbed onto Anthony's T-shirt. A hand brandishing a big pistol jutted through a portlight ahead of the chart table. I saw the brown face of the gunman who was aiming at Anthony. Jacqui screamed:

"They're going to kill us all. Oh my God!"

The hand pulled the trigger and the weapon just made a loud SCHLICK! At the same time Anthony lost his balance and fell onto the starboard settee on his back, leaving a chunk of his T-shirt in the hand of the intruder in the hatch. My heart sank, as I wasn't sure if my captain was dead. But he immediately rebounded, roaring orders at the attackers to go away.

I rushed to the fore cabin and closed the hatch and portlights. I then opened the door of the head (toilet), which was located immediately aft of the fore cabin. To my surprise, a boy of no more than sixteen was crawling through the tiny hatch headfirst and grabbed me by my pajama top. I attempted to punch him on the nose but he was swifter than I and warded off my offense, but released his grip on me. Then I screamed at him with as much authority as I could muster:

"Va! Va! Va! Go home! Leave us alone. Va en casa!"

To my astonishment and relief, the boy heeded my command and backed off, allowing me to reach up over the deck and swing the hatch closed. During this time, a hand grabbed Anthony's laptop through the portlight above the chart table. Jacqui quickly grabbed the keyboard end and a tug of war ensued. Unfortunately she lost her grip and the computer disappeared into the night. However three of the keys from the keyboard came off and fell back onto the cabin floor. At the same time, we could hear winching sounds resonating from the mast. They were trying to steal the dinghy!

By then I had gone around and closed all the portlights and Anthony had managed to beat back the intruder in the salon hatch and close the cover. He picked up the VHF radio and called for help. One of the attackers grabbed a dinghy oar and pounded on the Plexiglass hatch cover, trying to break it. Anthony got through to the *Guardia Nacional*. He called out in Spanish,

"This is sailing vessel *Ventus*! We are being attacked by pirates! We need immediate assistance!"

He gave our position and turned the volume up loud so the attackers could hear the response. Anthony then turned on all the navigation and deck lights in the hope of intimidating the attackers. Meanwhile, I launched a rocket flare through one of the portlights. It made a muffled "woosh", exuded a stream of warm gas and filled the cabin with smoke. Suddenly, the companionway hatch slipped opened and a face appeared. Anthony launched himself onto the sliding hatch cover and flung it closed with a loud slam. We heard an unintelligible answer on the radio in colloquial Spanish, but later a boater in a nearby location translated for us that the *Guardia Nacional* was coming to our rescue. Mercifully, when the aggressors heard the *Guardia Nacional* respond, they got scared and took off.

After waiting half an hour in the smoke-filled cabin for the *Guardia Nacional* to come, we decided to leave Boca del Rio. We had originally planned on sailing a clockwise circumnavigation of the island but we didn't have the heart for that anymore. Anyhow, we would have to register a police report and it just seemed to make sense to return to the familiar Bahía la Mar of Porlamar, our port of entry and the largest city of the Nueva Esparta state of which Margarita is the largest island. A cursory inspection above decks revealed only a small chip in the main hatch Plexiglass and a few scratches on the hull where the thieves had partially lowered the dinghy. We raised the dinghy back to deck level, weighed anchor and motored off. To extricate ourselves from the bay we had to steer around two reefs without the help of the computer charts, eyes glued to the depth sounder. After we had passed the submerged hazards the *Guardia Nacional* hailed us on the radio. The sailor who was within radio range translated that they were on their way, but by road – as they didn't have a boat! Once in the village, they would commandeer a boat to come to our rescue, they said. Anthony responded not to bother and that we were leaving Boca del Rio. The wind was too light for sailing so we motored for five hours under an ink-black sky.

At 0430 we lowered anchor in the Bahía la Mar, just near Marina Juan and went to sleep. At 0600 we were wide-awake, our biological clocks having sounded their alarm. Juan, the owner of the marina, pleaded with us to file a police report without which, he said, there would be no chance of nabbing and convicting the bandits. It was vitally important for Margarita's economy that sailors not be dissuaded from visiting. He assured us that the local authorities would be very keen to track down and punish the perpetrators.

Thus began a two-day odyssey of depositions, police reports, interrogation and fingerprinting. Anthony hired Juan's brother, a taxi driver who spoke English, to ferry us around and to act as interpreter. An officer at the State police station in Porlamar inputted our story into a computer as our interpreter translated, in turn, each of our versions. At the end, the officer interrogated us and recorded our responses. He printed a hardcopy of the depositions and under our signature he had us stamp our fingerprints!

At Juan's insistence, Anthony decided to file another report, with the local police in Boca del Rio, an hour and a half's drive from Porlamar. For $50 Juan's brother would drive us to Boca del Rio and act as our interpreter. There was nothing in it for Anthony, but he felt that he owed his fellow islanders an expression of solidarity, which meant he should do what he could to help Margarita save its tourist industry.

The desk of the chief of police sat squarely in the main entrance of the police station, in full view of passers-by on the sidewalk. He sat us on chairs in front of him and listened to the story as related by our interpreter who by now knew the whole narrative by heart.

After listening attentively to our tale, the chief asked us if we could wait 20 minutes. We said, "Of course." He rattled off an order to four of his underlings. The men disappeared briefly into the back room and each returned to the office sporting a big gun. A paddy wagon pulled up to the door, the posse climbed aboard and the vehicle sped off in a cloud of dust under the eyes of a gathering crowd. Twenty minutes later the cops returned with two manacled suspects. Neither of them resembled in the least the faces we had seen through the portlights, Che or the fellows who had circled *Ventus* in the gondola. The police then locked up the two hapless chaps in the slammer and left again. Meanwhile, another officer made us look through a big book of mug shots of shirtless, sweaty, tattooed, mean-looking convicts, all for naught. The paddy wagon returned after a long absence, but this time without suspects. The chief claimed that his men knew who the guilty were but that the boys had gone into hiding. His officers would be mounting an operation during the night. Would we phone tomorrow, as they would have them in custody by then? It would be necessary for us to come back to Boca del Rio to identify the suspects.

During the next days at anchor, I had time to reflect on my near-death experience. Three extremely improbable events contributed to our still being alive. First, had we not closed the companionway – for the first time ever – the bandits would have just walked into the cabin and who knows what would have been the result of the fight. Two old men and an old woman would have been easy pickings for four strong men in the prime of their lives. Second, had the gun not jammed, Anthony would have been killed. Then would the intruders have wanted to leave two witnesses? Third, what were the chances of our being able to reach the National Guard by radio and immediately get an answer? – Probably the closest thing there is to winning the lottery.

Anthony and Jacqui had taken the dinghy ashore to do some shopping downtown. I desisted, preferring to be on my own for a while. I was lounging on the deck without a book or magazine or newspaper. I needed to relax and release some of the pent up tension. The scenery that lay before me was a world of contrasts and contradictions. As I looked around the anchorage, I felt the calm of the enchanting Bahía la Mar. I beheld the mirror clear water, the sickle-shaped white sand beach that stretched for miles, the Porlamar skyline against the background of mountains and sapphire sky. Within the downtown that my shipmates were visiting, the marble and tile sidewalks were lined with upscale stores that catered to a small elite, including a dwindling number of tourists.

In contrast, beyond the beautiful streets and elegant stores was a maze of substandard houses where working people were struggling in underpaid, dead-end jobs to feed their families, where unemployed youths had no employable skills, where barefoot children wandered underfed, where innocent people slept fitfully in fear of attack from roaming gangs. These conditions had been exacerbated by the deteriorating economic conditions of the country over the previous ten years.

I lived on the same planet as they, yet I had the luxury of relaxing on a well-equipped yacht, with lockers full of fine food and drink. I had the means of flying across the globe to exotic destinations to enjoy my passion. My home was in a country where those living below the poverty line were rich by comparison with the poor of Venezuela.

I counted my blessings and was thankful I was still alive and in good health. My thoughts parted with the present and drifted back to my very first sailing experience.

First sail

A canoe ain't a sailboat

Where's the brake on this thing?

Chapter 2

Beginnings

Summer, 1955

"The sail's dragging in the water, mate! Secure the starboard mast!" came the command from Michel as he was wrestling with the makeshift helm.

The rowboat was ploughing through the waves under the thrust of our improvised sail, a groundsheet suspended between two oars (two makeshift "masts") jammed into the gunwales. We had left the cottage at Jessups Falls, Ontario, and rowed down the South Nation River towards Baie Noire, our favourite fishing hole on the opposite side of the Ottawa River on the Québec side. Upon reaching the middle of the giant river, we realized that a powerful east wind was blowing upstream towards our left. Like many opportunistic canoeists, rafters and kayakers had done in the past, Michel and I pooled the ingenuity of our 15-year-old minds and figured a way of harnessing the energy of the wind to spare our muscle energy. It was simply a matter of assembling the basic elements at hand:

Nature's wind, my mother's brand new plywood rowboat, an old tarp, two oars to support the tarp and a long piece of driftwood for a tiller and rudder.

Having abandoned the plan of going fishing, we decided to enjoy the ride wherever the wind would take us. The motion, the sound of the wind, the waves coming within centimetres of the freeboard, all contributed to the fun. This was at least three times faster than rowing! Before we knew it, we'd passed the Wendover Church, at the top of the hill to our port.

Michel had told me the story of the old captain who was observed by his crew, through the window of his cabin, carrying out a nightly ritual. He would take out a small piece of paper from his chart table, unfold it carefully, and read its contents diligently, nod his head, then fold it and put it away. The men were intrigued as to what might have been the content of the mysterious little note. One day, when the captain was safely out of his quarters, his first mate retrieved the small piece of paper from its hiding place, unfolded it and finally the secret was revealed. The message read: "Port is left, starboard is right."

With our sail bulging from the wind, and spray flying off the crest of the waves, we forged ahead westward, upriver, past Clarence, past Rockland. This was fun! No question of turning around! Wow! We took turns at the helm, playing the role of "Captain", holding the boat on course in the middle of the river where the wind was at its fiercest and the waves were at their highest. We didn't know, nor did it matter, that a captain's job is to care for his boat and crew, not necessarily to steer the boat.

In spite of our very French names, Michel de Saint Georges and Robert Bériault, we had always spoken in English together. Michel had been raised by his anglophone mother in the absence of his French Canadian father, so was more at ease with the English language, whereas I was just as comfortable with one or the other. Born of two French speaking parents, I was raised in the English neighbourhood of Sandy Hill, in Ottawa, so at a very young age I learned to speak the language of Shakespeare on the street and that of Molière in the house and at school. I was always thankful that I had had the chance to become fluent in both languages, especially in a country where a working knowledge of both official languages can open many doors.

As the wind increased in strength, the little rowboat, cum sailboat, would pitch and roll and a wave would flop over the side, sending a couple of inches of unsteady, shifting water to the bottom of the boat, adding to the danger (fun). The newly acquired load provided some needed work for the appointed mate, in the way of several minutes of frantic bailing.

We were oblivious to the fact that we were sailing in wind conditions that should require small craft to keep off the water. Wind is considered light if it's blowing less than twelve knots, and moderate up to

19 knots. However, when it reaches twenty knots, it generates dangerous waves that can easily upset small boats. In the twenty-first century Environment Canada and the Coast Guard consider such conditions grounds for a "Strong Wind Warning".

We were minimalist sailors by today's standards, as we didn't have life jackets, or a buoyant heaving line, or a sound-signalling device, or a waterproof flashlight, all misdemeanours that would generate severe fines in today's age of government paternalism. But this was the year 1955, the good old days of laissez-faire, those lazy, hazy days when bicycle helmets and air bags were inventions of the distant future. If my father had known what Michel and I had been up to that day, he wouldn't have been worried in the least – the boat, being built of wood, was unsinkable, both boys knew how to swim and they knew well enough to stay with the vessel in case of capsize. So Dad would have driven his '49 Chevrolet back to the cottage that evening with complete equanimity.

I'm not saying that it was wise not to have been wearing lifejackets under those wind conditions. When the weather gets rough, you should always don a floating device. We just didn't have the money for that safety item in those days. Safety is a luxury of the rich. Just look at how many Haitian fishermen own a lifejacket.

The weather was definitely calming when suddenly the cry "Ahoy, mate! Unidentified floating object 15 degrees to port", came from my Captain. It was an oval-shaped, flexible mass of brown-grey matter, perhaps six to twelve inches thick, about six feet across, seemingly a matt of fibrous matter that undulated with the movement of the waves. Upon closer examination bubbles appeared at the surface and upon poking with a paddle, chunks would break off from the main mass, releasing a malodorous smell like a mixture of rotten eggs and the contents of a sceptic tank. "It's a shitberg, my friend", Michel exclaimed, having found an apt neologism for this strange apparition.

The mighty Ottawa River, a jewel of Central Canada, has been intimately involved with the history and development of the Ottawa Valley. Finding its source in Lake Capimitchigama in the Laurentian Mountains, the 1271 km long river drains 146,000 square kilometres of land, and forms a divide between much of the provinces of Québec and Ontario. The river was an important trade route for early European settlers. In the early 19th century, the Ottawa River and its tributaries were used to gain access to large virgin forests of giant white pine. A booming trade in squared timber was developed to supply the efforts of British expansionism, and large rafts of logs were floated down the Ottawa and the St. Laurence rivers to Québec City from where they were shipped to Britain. By the middle of the 19th century, demand for sawn lumber in New York and Boston launched a new industry of cut lumber, which increased the demand for the river as the transportation route. The disappearance of the white pine forests gave rise to a new pulp and paper industry in the early 1900s and the river continued being the main transportation route for wood until log driving was prohibited in the 1960s.

Over the course of two centuries of log driving, a tremendous amount of wood debris from floating logs and from saw mills accumulated in the river bed, I am told up to 60 feet thick. Bacterial decomposition worked away at the mostly lignin and cellulose-containing mass, impregnating it with methane and hydrogen sulphide gasses. This eventually raised massive matts of the fibrous material to the surface of the water, creating a subject of great interest, amazement, intrigue and experimentation for inquisitive boys who would be happening upon the water.

As we progressed upstream, the sightings of these strange masses became more frequent. Some of the shitbergs were only two or three feet across, whereas the larger ones measured up to ten feet and perhaps more. We observed that these little floating islands of stinking muck were loosely held together by their fibrous components, therefore they would break up into smaller pieces if they were beyond a critical size when they rose from the depths of the riverbed. The interesting thing was that just by smashing one in the middle with the blade of a paddle, you could easily split it in half, creating two shitbergs where there was formerly one.

The wind started to die down when the Masson-Cumberland ferry terminal came into view in the distance. We landed on the Québec side of the river and reluctantly lowered our drooping sail, in view of a gaggle of admiring little boys dangling fishing lines off the pier. A single, three-vehicle ferry criss-crossed the river as it carried its tiny load of vehicles and foot passengers across the inter-provincial border between Ontario and Quebec. As fifteen-year-old boys are apt to enjoy doing in such circumstances, we spent a long time watching every step of the procedure: The crabbing of the boat's course into the current, the deceleration on its approach of the shore, the swift 180 degree turn before reversing to the dock, the teamwork between the helmsman and Mr. Bourbonnais handling the docklines, the orderly backing out of the debarking vehicles, the boarding of the next round of cars or light trucks, the collection of the 50 cent fee, the sound of the whistle and casting off with the next load.

The cottage on the South Nation was a long way behind by now. We took turns rowing back, allowing our muscles time to recover between shifts. With the current nudging us along and the complete absence of a headwind slowing us down, the return trip was nevertheless quite a long haul. During my breaks at rowing I basked in the warmth and the calm, as the sun lowered itself below the western horizon.

We arrived at the cottage after dark and had supper by the bonfire. My muscles felt heavy and tired, but my spirits were light and high, since I had enjoyed the exhilaration of my very first experience at sailing.

Summer, 1970

"It would be best if you would come back by three since John and Pary arrive for dinner at four".

"Don't worry", I assured my better half, Micheline, as I stepped off the dock into my Grumman aluminum canoe, "There's lots of time".

I had bought this silvery, 17-foot marvel of craftmanship a few years previously and it had provided me with many exciting white water excursions as well as countless peaceful rides at my Father's cottage on Lac St-Pierre de Wakefield. One of the features of this American-made canoe, aside from its remarkable strength, was the availability of an accessory that resonated with my environmental propensity, a full sailing rig that consisted of a mast, lateen mainsail, a set of two side daggerboards and a rudder with tiller. Since it seemed like such a brilliant idea, I sank almost as much money in buying this paraphernalia as the boat itself had cost me. I assembled the rig at the cottage the previous weekend but wasn't able to try it out for the usual reason why sailors stay ashore – there was no wind. This weekend, my parents were away and we had the run of the place to ourselves. There was a good wind and I was testing my new sailing rig for the first time.

The cottage was near the south end of the main bay, which ran north south and was about half a mile wide and five long. I was granted a strong south wind, just about the maximum that I'd want to experience in an open canoe. I hoisted the sail, let it out to fill it with wind and immediately the canoe sprung to life. Contrary to my intuition, the canoe became very stable once the sail was up. The north end of the lake was out of view in the distance. The going was good, so I just kept on sailing downwind.

I knew that sailboats couldn't forge their way directly into the wind, but that they could work their way upwind by zigzagging at 45-degree angles to the path of the wind. All you have to do to reach an upwind destination is to tack from one side to the other until you get there. But what I hadn't been told was that a canoe is not a sailboat, no matter how you dress it up.

I heedlessly kept going with the wind in my back, basking in the exhilaration of being effortlessly carried away. It was thrilling to be skimming along on the water without the noise and smell of an outboard engine. I revelled in the satisfaction that I wasn't contributing to polluting the lake like the 500 local motorboats that plied its waters.

In what seemed like too little time, I came to the north end of the lake and I turned the boat around; now I was positioning myself to head upwind towards the cottage.

Let me explain the tacking procedure with a concrete example. And here I will use the words left and right instead of risking confusing you with the terms even the old captain had trouble with. We start by sailing as close to the wind as possible, what sailors call close-hauled. Let's suppose the wind is coming from the front right, so you feel it on your right cheek. Then the boat will be heeling to the left side, with the mainsail filled with air, and the boom will be a little left of the centreline. You're approaching shallower water on the left bank, so before you run aground, you come about, or tack. Therefore you'll do a 90-degree turn to the right, across the path of the wind. This will put you at 45 degrees to the wind on the other side of the path of the wind and now you will have the wind on your left cheek. I hope this makes sense to you. As the boat carries through its 90-degree turn, the sail flips over to the right of the centreline. If you've followed this so far, you've figured that the wind is now coming from the front left and the boat is heeling towards the right.

"It took me just over half an hour to get here and I have an hour and a half to return to the cottage, so there's no problem", I thought.

But something was wrong. I couldn't quite manage that 45-degree heading to the wind. I reached the left shore of the bay, then tacked across the wind, directing the boat towards the opposite shore, but with very little upwind angle. Before I knew it I had almost reached the right shore and checking my position, realized that I had made no windward progress. Tacked again. This time I tried steering tighter into the wind, but all that happened was that the boat would slow down, then come to a stop. This is known in the sailing world as being "in irons". Bearing away, the boat would pick up speed, but then I would only be heading for the shore, not the required south end of the bay.

"I know what the problem is!" I knew nothing about centre of effort and centre of lateral resistance, but my intuition led me to reason, "What I need to do is to move the daggerboards further forward. This will place the force of the wind further behind the daggerboards, bringing the bow more into the wind."

So I tacked again and brought the boat to a stop on the right shore where the water was shallow and I stepped out onto the muddy bottom. The modification was quite simple. The rig had been designed so that you can easily realize such fine-tuning adjustments. I unscrewed the wingnuts holding the daggerboard unit, pushed it further forward, reset the wingnuts and voilà!

I was talking to myself at this point,

"Now we'll see what this sucker will do!" with the faith of a four-year old child in the existence of Santa Claus.

Back into the boat, I headed towards the middle of the bay, steering her close to the wind. Something was wrong. The angle of the boat to the wind seemed about right. Checking it out with my informed eye, I could make out my angle to the path of the wind at 45 degrees, just like by the book! The problem, though, was that the daggerboard adjustment had caused the boat speed to plummet to almost nothing. The only way I could get the boat to move was to enlarge my angle to the wind to 70 or 80 degrees by bearing away. As I was making so little headway, the wind and the waves were effectively carrying me sideways and backwards, a phenomenon that I would later learn is called leeway. The long and the short of it, I wasn't moving forward at all.

Back to shore again. I adjusted the daggerboards aft, in case I had misunderstood the hydraulic forces that make a sailboat move forward. But to no avail. I had come to the realization that this rigging system just couldn't work for sailing upwind and that I'd better find an alternate way of getting back to the cottage in time to greet my guests.

To my chagrin, I had to lower the sail and stow the mast, the steering gear and the daggerboards aboard the canoe and paddle the boat back to the cottage like a canoe – after all, that's what it is. As it turned out, stowing the sail was one of those things that is easier said than done.

Here I will explain what is a lateen sail rig. Unlike the more common sloop rig the lateen rig allows for the mast to be quite short, making it easy to carry on top of a car. Two sides of the triangular sail are lashed to aluminum poles, the top one being the gaff and the bottom one the boom. The poles act as a two-sided frame that holds the sail. Close to where the two poles join, they are attached to the mast, allowing the top of the sail to extend way above the mast. It is a very nice system until you try to lower the sail in the middle of a lake in a gale.

Then the fun begins. As I lowered the sail, the gaff and the boom began swinging wildly in the wind, risking knocking me unconscious. Once I was able to grab hold of the two lurching poles, I still had to contend with the sail that was flopping wildly between them. Before I could grab hold of it, the sail landed in the water, dragging the canoe to one side. As I tried to gather the submerged sail, I had to gradually ease it out of the lake to allow the ton of water it contained to slowly drain off. By then the canoe was abeam to the waves, rocking wildly without the stabilizing force of the wind in the sail.

In the end, I managed to make a loose roll by wrapping the fabric around the gaff, the boom and the mast, with plenty of residual sail flapping in the wind. Then I had to remove the two daggerboards. I started by raising them both, as Grumman had designed them so they could swivel up out of the water. But when I removed the starboard one the weight of the port one, along with the force of the wind, swung the canoe swiftly around. I didn't have bungees for tying everything down, so I had to improvise a lashing system with my docklines. Finally everything was secure and I was ready to paddle. In hindsight, all of this should have been done ashore.

By then, half an hour had elapsed and the wind had blown me into the weeds at the very end of the lake, adding another half mile to the trip back. I then picked a course along the shore where the wind was calmer and began the arduous paddle back against wind and waves.

All the poles and canvass tied on top of the gunwales created too much windage. I quickly realized that there was no way I could reach the cottage in time by paddling against that powerful wind. I had to resort to the most embarrassing of choices. I pulled over onto the public boat launch ramp, dumped my canoe and its paraphernalia on the side of the road and walked the eight kilometres to the cottage.

By the time I arrived at the cottage my better half and our guests were seated on the dock enjoying a cool drink. Micheline was surprised to see me coming towards her from behind and on foot,

"My gosh, what happened to your canoe?"

"Let me fix myself a drink and I'll tell you all about it."

As an epilogue to this little tale, I kept the sailing rig for three summers and tried it many times. Never was I able to sail upwind. The best I ever succeeded was to sail back and forth on a beam reach, that is, with the wind at 90 degrees to the side of the boat. A few years later Grumman took the sailing rig off its list of accessories. They never said why.

November 1975

White sails appeared in my peripheral vision as we were driving down the road along Biscayne Bay, Florida, causing my head to swivel briskly towards shore. "Hey, Roger, look at those Catamarans!"

"Lets go see." responded Roger.

So I hung a left at the first exit and brought the car to a stop just short of a dozen Hobie Cats pulled up on the beach.

Beginnings

"Wowie! They're for rent, guys!" exclaimed Marielle.

"Looks like fun, but I've never sailed in my life." interjected Roger.

"But I've sailed." I added, without telling a lie. "There's really nothing mysterious about it. You'll love it Roger; the Hobie Cat is the fastest boat on the water."

Micheline and I were breaking loose from looking after the house and kids for a week. We had joined up with Micheline's sister Marielle and her husband Roger for our first visit to the Sunshine State, the point of convergence for hundreds of thousands of Canadians who seek to escape the hardships of their northern winter.

We heard whishing and swishing sounds, which drew our gaze towards the little harbour, a circular basin, less than the size of a football field, protected from the open water by a stone jetty about fifteen feet high, leading to a narrow opening to the sea. One of the Hobie Cats was sailing around the perimeter of the basin, very fast, a few feet from the edge. At the helm was a young man, actually a boy of perhaps fifteen or sixteen, slim and muscular, sporting a Florida tan and a mane of blond hair flying in the wind. He handled the tiller and the sheet with expertise and precision, sailing the boat with the same ease and accuracy as if it had been a motorboat. When he saw us approach, he brought the boat to a stop by beaching it and introduced himself as Harry.

Our prodigious sailor confirmed that the boats were available for rent by the hour. From the answers that he provided to my questions I gathered that the main qualification for renting one was the ability to pay the hourly fee and the $2000 refundable deposit by credit card. He advised me to read the disclaimer, which stipulated that in case of accident I was responsible for any injury to the boat should I smash it on a rock, any damage I might cause to other property and any personal harm should I maim or kill somebody.

Roger and I decided to go for it and agreed to rent one for two hours. So without hesitation I signed on the dotted line and proffered my credit card.

We donned our bathing suits and regulation life jackets then Harry gave us a short briefing on where to go and not to go and reminded me that I was responsible for any damages. Actually, his reminder resonated as a warning or a threat!

As I mentioned, the Hobie Cat is a catamaran – a sport boat made for people who don't mind getting wet. It is one of those fast boats you've seen skimming across the water with one of the pontoons in the air. It is basically a rectangular trampoline attached to two narrow pontoons, called amas. At the aft end of each ama is a retractable rudder, both of which are linked to a tiller. There is one tall mast to which is attached a horizontal boom. The mainsail is attached to the mast and the boom and its angle to the wind can be controlled with the aid of a rope called a sheet. On some models there is a second sail at the front.

Since I was *de facto* captain I had Roger climb onto the trampoline, gave the boat a light shove to bring her into water deep enough to lower the rudders and climbed aboard. I ordered Roger to hold onto the sheet while I manned the helm.

"Pull the sheet in, Roger!" I ordered.
Nothing.
"OK, Roger, the sail is in too close to the midline. Let it out a bit."
Nothing.
"Hold it like that, and I'll turn the tiller the other way."
Still nothing.
"The wind seems to be coming from that direction." Roger said, pointing ahead of us.
"Right. I'll just turn the tiller this way to fill the sail ... Oh, wow! ... Hey, we're off! ... Oh, shit! Gaaaaawd! WE'RE HEADED FOR THE JETTY!"

I never imagined a boat could accelerate like this! We were headed strait for the fifteen-foot high jetty at the speed of light! In the split second that followed I had a mental flash: I could see our boat striking the stone wall and Roger and me flying over it in our bathing suits with legs and arms flailing every which way. I could see the catamaran smashed to smithereens at the bottom of the big barrier. And then in my mind's eye I saw the waiver and the $2000 deposit and I could hear Harry's ominous warning echoing in my mind.

Micheline had witnessed our predicament and called out to Harry for help. He ran as fast as he could atop the jetty towards our catamaran and yelled at the top of his voice,

"LET GO THE ROPE, LET GO THE ROPE!"

Roger released the sheet as directed and miraculously the boat came to a smooth stop a few inches from the jetty just as a lightweight catamaran does when the wind is let out of the sail. Then he started giving me further instruction. I thought at first he wanted me to surrender the boat and get the heck out of his marina, but no, he was advising me as to how to set the boat on a course out of the harbour,

"OK, now push the tiller the other way and hold the sail the opposite way against the wind."

With the sail back-winded and the rudders pointing to one side, the boat miraculously reversed while turning, after which the sail filled up and our craft proceeded uneventfully forward towards the exit.

I was a tad shaken by what had just occurred and quite relieved to have escaped unscathed. I was convinced that had I been a cat, I would have lost one of my nine lives. However, as I usually like to put a positive spin on things, without referring to the near-death aspect of the incident, I asked, "That was fun, eh Roger?"

After two hours of manoeuvring by trial and error we returned the boat intact, having enjoyed a great sail. Upon entering the harbour, I saw the high stone jetty to my port, and felt fortunate that my body parts weren't scattered across it. I felt relieved to have my damage waiver deposit returned to me.

To my profound embarrassment and humiliation, in the car the conversation turned to the heart-thumping near-miss with the stone jetty. Snickers, guffaws and belly laughs proliferated beyond what I felt was reasonable, considering that we had brought the boat back intact. The bright side of this ordeal was that the only damage was to my faltering ego.

&&&&&&&

I heard a splash right next to where I was resting on *Ventus*. I sat up and turned towards the sound to discover a pelican floating with its beak in the water, filtering its catch in its large beak. One of its buddies was gracefully circling Bahía la Mar and dove head first, landing with an awkward splash, then surfacing with an empty beak. Petrels were skimming the surface of the sea for their sustenance, wings almost touching the water. I returned to my meditation…and recalled the day when I discovered a way to enjoy a more subdued kind of sailing, and without having to buy a boat.

First live-aboard in Georgian Bay

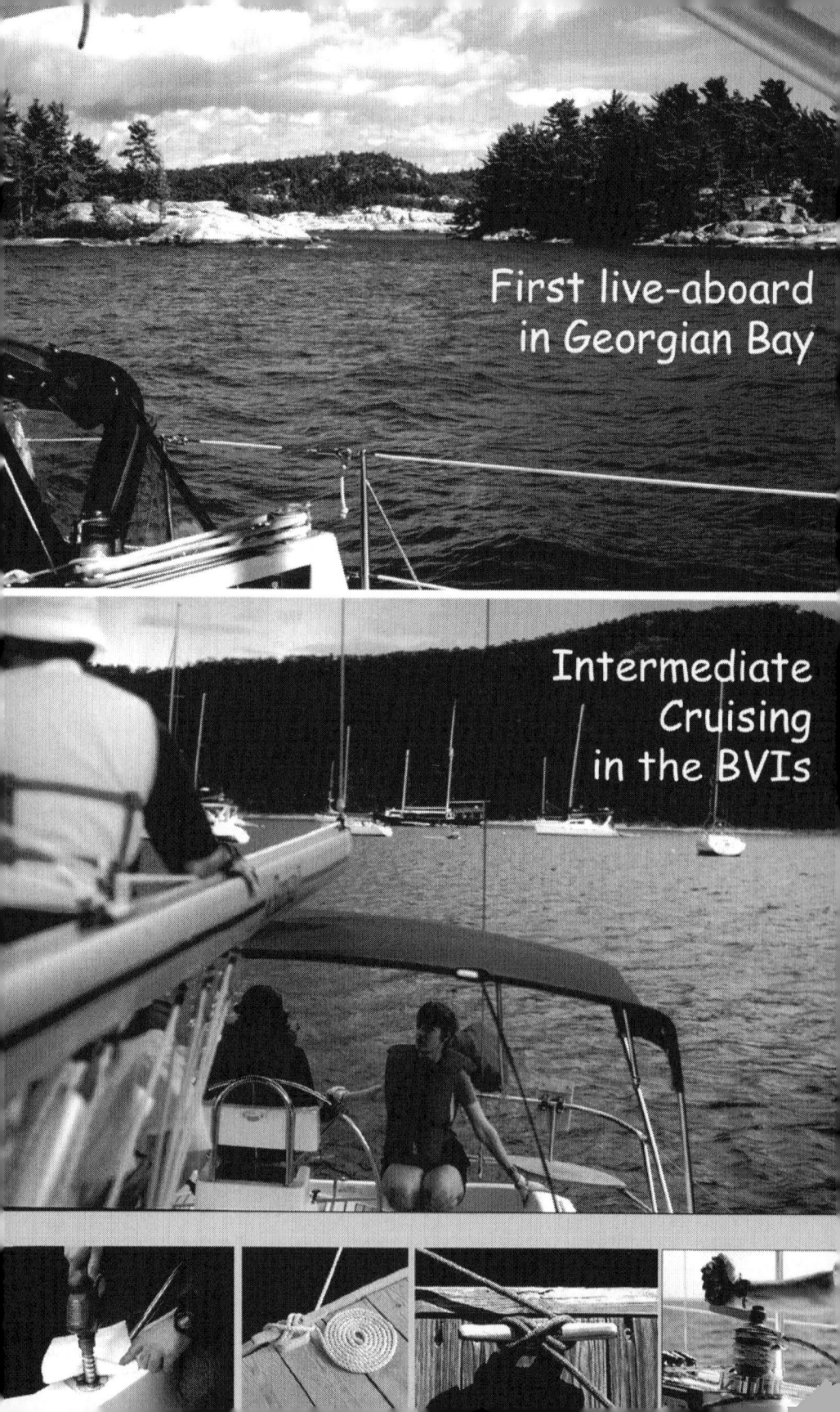

Intermediate Cruising in the BVIs

Chapter 3

Learning the Ropes

Back in the olden days of 1998 when you were searching for a phone number you consulted the yellow pages, as the Internet had not quite reached the point of being the resource of first choice. I was looking for a sailing school.

All my life, I had dreamt of sailing around the world. The discovery of distant places and the mysteries they reveal, the encounters with different cultures, the recounting of the stories of civilizations past through their monuments, hiking in spectacular scenery in many corners of the globe, the excitement of discovery and the adventure of crossing oceans held a powerful spell over me.

Now I was retired and could no longer conjure up any excuse for not carrying out my dream. However, out of a judicious dose of caution, I thought it would be wise to learn how to sail, and perhaps live on a sailboat for a few weeks before forging ahead into a life I knew nothing about. After all, maybe I wouldn't like living in the cramped quarters of a boat, or maybe I would find long passages boring, or heaven forbid, I might get seasick!

So why not start by taking a sailing course? I was leafing through the Ottawa phone book when I came across the "North Channel Sailing School". I later discovered that this body of water is actually a large expanse in the northern end of Georgian Bay, which itself lies in the northern reaches of Lake Huron.

A male voice on the answering machine announced: "Hello you've reached Rick and Shawn" We can't come to the phone now, but leave us a-CLICK Hello, hello, hello, this is Rick".

"Oh, I wanted the North Channel Sailing School. I must have misdialed."

"No, this *is* the North Channel Sailing School. What can I do for you?"

I explained what I was looking for and Rick began his spiel about his sailing club. He started by saying that the NCSS was founded in 1980, that it was non-profit, run entirely voluntarily by its 22 members, that it had one 23-foot boat in Aylmer and just sold its last boat in Georgian Bay.

Here I must digress and say something about the geography of the greater Ottawa area. I've already given you some history of the Ottawa River, but what is important here is that just at the west end of the city of Ottawa there is a marked widening in the river forming a lake of two miles in width by five in length known as Lake Deschênes. Navigation is limited by a set of rapids at the Ottawa end of the lake and Chat Falls dam 25 miles farther upriver.

The lake, being in an urban area, is a popular sailing venue, with three marinas harbouring about 1000 sailboats. Two of them are on the Ontario side of the river and one on the Québec side in Aylmer.

Rick went on to explain that most of the club's members lived in greater Ottawa and became tired of driving nine hours to Georgian Bay to end up doing more boat maintenance than sailing. Furthermore, all of the founding members had set themselves other goals and abandoned the organization. Consequently the remaining members kept only one boat and brought it to Aylmer. So now, once or twice a season the School will rent boats in the North Channel of Georgian Bay for weeklong, live-aboard cruises.

For $25 I could become a member and for a flat fee of $375 I could join the Sail-All-You-Want program, which allowed me to sail out of Aylmer as often as I wanted during the season. And if I wanted a live-aboard experience under the direction of a competent captain I could join one of the week-long charters NCSS was organizing in Georgian Bay for about $600. What could be more perfect?

The club had established a reservation system for the use of the boat in Aylmer. A calendar was published every month on which the qualified skippers put down their names against the day or evening they wished to sail. Regular members would phone the skipper to reserve a place for themselves on the days or evenings they wanted to go sailing.

"One day you might want to become a qualified skipper if you achieve the required qualifying knowledge and skills," Rick added.

It kept getting better: If I wanted I could take the Basic Cruising Standard course by the Canadian Yachting Association (CYA), recognized worldwide, *for free*! Rick finished with, "Would you like to join me for a complimentary outing on our sailboat next Saturday? – No obligation."

Non-scuffing shoes afoot, knapsack in hand, hat atop, I met Rick at dock C of the Aylmer Marina. He was a young-looking, tall man in his early thirties, whose round, smiling face wore a permanent five o'clock shadow. He inspired confidence without showing any pretension.

He led me to *Iniskip*, a beautiful little 23-foot long sloop, an Edel 665 with a red hull. He showed me how to board the boat safely by grabbing onto one of the shrouds, those strong wire cables that tie the mast to the sides of the hull. He then showed me around the boat, pointing out the safety equipment, and introduced Raphaël, a regular member, and Gaston, a new member who like myself, was going out for the first time.

Rick and Raphaël got busy preparing the boat, giving the neophytes instructions and explaining what was going on. Everything happened like clockwork: The life ring and heaving line were attached to the pushpit. The jib was bent onto the forestay. In layman language: The front sail was attached to the front wire cable that ties the mast to the front of the boat. The sheets were uncoiled and placed at the ready. Battery voltage was verified. The VHF radio was turned on and the weather forecast jotted down in the log. The mainsail cover and the compass cover were removed and stowed inside. The bilge was checked for the presence of water. The red key for the dead man switch was attached to the engine, the fuel level checked, the fuel line plugged into the engine and the air vent opened. The engine was started, the flow of cooling water observed visually and the forward and reverse gears were checked to make sure they were operational. I didn't know there was so much to check on a small boat.

It's important that you understand the docking facilities at the Aylmer Marina, as you will later appreciate. There are four big, long parallel docks attached to the shore, sticking out into the harbour. On each side of each dock at regular intervals are attached narrow passageways about 30 inches wide by 20 feet long, called mooring fingers. Each finger holds two boats, one on either side. On this day, there was no boat tied to the other side of our finger, just an empty space.

Then to my surprise – because I didn't think that I'd be put to work the first time out – Rick took Gaston and me aside to explain how we were to cast off the docklines, in what order, and how to get back on the boat.

Then he explained in minute detail how we were to carry out the reverse operation upon our return. Rick wanted to make it clear:

"My job will be to bring the boat to a stop within a foot from the finger. Remember, guys, you're getting off on the starboard side. Before stepping off, you position yourself holding onto the shroud with your left hand and your dockline in your right hand, you wait for my command to step off, and *don't jump* onto the finger, simply step onto it, then put one turn of your line around the dock cleat."

I picked a good day for my first day sailing on a keelboat. A keelboat, by the way, is a boat that has a fin-like protrusion under the hull, somewhat like a dead fish floating upside down. The keel does two things. It helps the boat steer in a straight line and it reduces leeway, or sideways drift.

Environment Canada Weather granted us glorious sunshine, a blue sky dotted with white cumulus clouds, calm waters and a brisk wind. Our captain-instructor took the time to explain every manoeuvre and its reason for being. What appealed to me most was his hands-on approach. He allowed Gaston and me to have a go at every manoeuvre.

In order to enjoy a relaxing lunch, Rick put the boat into the hove-to position, a brilliant manoeuvre that "parks" the boat in the middle of the lake. The procedure results in the rudder attempting to turn the boat one way while the headsail tries to make it go the opposite way. In consequence, the boat doesn't know where it should go, so it just sits there, in a state of confusion, drifting slowly, but very stable in the waves.

During lunch Rick and Raphaël raised the difficulties the club was undergoing. Whereas in its heyday the School boasted of 200 members and four boats, now it was down to a dismal 22 members and one boat. On the positive side, it enjoyed a well-padded bank account. The sale of three of its boats allowed the club to pay off its significant debts but left it with a nice surplus. The members were aging, as Rick was the youngest of the group. They were no longer content with sleeping aboard a small, cramped boat like the Edel. They had acquired a taste for the comforts provided by an enclosed head, separate staterooms, walking headroom, inboard engine and wheel steering, none of which little *Iniskip* provided. The club now had the money. Should it look for a bigger, more comfortable boat for cruising on Lac Deschênes? In view of the continually diminishing membership, the Board of directors was in a quandary: If the club buys a bigger boat, there would not be enough demand to justify keeping two boats, nor enough manpower to maintain two boats. If we bought a new boat, would we then dispose of *Iniskip*?

I enjoyed the sailing, the Edel, the lake, the people. I knew after the first hour that I wanted to join this organization and that I'd want to get involved directly. There were interesting challenges ahead in addition to learning how to sail.

At the end of the afternoon, Rick had us lower the sails and he steered through the long channel into the harbour under engine alone. By then we had the fenders and docklines in place. Rick positioned Gaston and me at the level of the shrouds, standing on the footrail, outside the lifelines, ready to disembark with our respective docklines. "Remember to wait for my command to step off."

Gaston was a large man, especially in circumference, and had tattoo-covered arms the size of the boat's fenders. He bore a million dollar smile behind a stiff, handlebar moustache, his blue eyes beaming under his captain's cap.

The two of us were facing forward with Gaston ahead of me with the forward dockline in his right hand. Rick had taken into account that the wind was beam to the boat and brought us to a stop about two feet away, parallel to the finger, waiting for the wind to gently push the boat sideways into position. Gaston was eying the finger nervously, fidgeted for a bit, repositioned himself and took a giant leap off the boat, skidding on the deck of the finger, and landing with a monumental splash, head first into the water, still grasping his dockline! He scrambled towards the deck, hanging onto his precious rope, and with the help of three pairs of hands, he flopped onto the deck, soaked like a wet sponge. He was uninjured, except for the embarrassment he must have felt as the object of uncontrolled and unmitigated laughter and the subject of an interesting story that passed around all of the marina.

I sailed at least twice a week for the remainder of the season. Summer went and fall came. I had learned a lot and still had a lot to learn. But I was hooked. I joined evening classes with the Canadian Power and Sail Squadron, a non-profit organization that provides classroom instruction about boating and navigation. On the weekend in October when the boat was hauled out of the water for the winter, I assisted with every step of the winterizing procedures and felt a twinge of regret when we finally covered the boat with the tarp for her winter rest.

In November came the Annual General Meeting (AGM). Two items worthy of mention:

1) Robert Bériault was voted member of the Board. I was delighted to join this terrific group of people.

2) A resolution was passed, earmarking $30,000 towards the purchase of a larger sailboat and a search committee was appointed.

One day in August of the following summer, Brent approached the dock, absolutely beaming, and with his Kiwi accent,

Learning the Ropes

"We found our byebie, guys!"

Brent was one of the more senior members of the club and had undertaken the leadership of the boat selection committee. With the excitement of a young boy babbling about his new electronic game, he recounted the steps he and his committee had taken to find the perfect boat, how she passed the marine survey with flying colours, and how the price was negotiated.

The Tanzer 29 is a Canadian-made boat built in 1986. As the model name implies, she was 29 feet long, six more than *Iniskip*, but having twice the weight and volume. Our new baby had all the features we were looking for and was in impeccable shape. To top it off, Brent had skilfully whittled the price down from the asking forty grand to thirty.

The seller had bought her two years previously from an aging man who rarely sailed her but kept her in pristine condition. Our seller had just started a fledging prefab home company in Masson and needed to inject both more time and more money to get the business off the ground.

The fibreglass hull was a spotless cream-white with a blue stripe along the sides, the sails were crisp (like new), the woodwork well polished, the engine compartment so clean you would have thought it was new. She came with many accessories that you would have to pay extra for on a new boat, including a refrigerator. Another plus: She was located only a short distance from her future home, as she was berthed at a private dock in Masson, a small town 40 km downriver from Aylmer. Our boat would have to be transported by road because she couldn't climb Chaudière falls and Deschênes rapids, but that would be a minor cost. We were taking possession on October 1st.

This season the club gained a few members, lost just as many former ones, but was comfortably afloat financially. A few years back, before selling off its boats, the club had no money and the Board had to make the difficult decision that the skippers would no longer have the privilege of sailing for free. From then on they would pay the same price as the regular members, a critical decision that prevented the club from foundering.

Another major change in the organization was to transition away from the Glénan teaching method to adopt the Canadian Yachting Association standards. The former is a philosophy of teaching that transforms a neophyte into a seasoned offshore sailor through live-aboard experience. There is no strict curriculum with this approach to teaching and the student receives no certificate of any kind. However, times have changed, the Board members realized. In this age of immediate gratification people demand something concrete to show for their learning efforts – a piece of paper, a certificate. And Bingo! The CYA method offers just that. In fact, the CYA provides several levels of proficiency depending on the person's needs. If the person wants to putter around on a small lake with his own sailboat, he can get by with the Basic Cruising Standard. If he wants to qualify to rent a sailboat to cruise along coastlines during daylight hours he would want to be holder of the Intermediate certificate. If his ambition is to navigate more difficult waters in places where there are tides and currents to deal with, he would need the Advanced Cruising Standard. And finally, if his goal is to explore the world's oceans, he might want to complete the Offshore Standard. These certifications are recognised by sailing clubs around the world – a good selling point from a merchandising point of view. The Board members came to the decision that the club would position itself to award CYA certification and it was convenient that at least one member of the organization, in the person of Doreen, was qualified to teach the basic level. A diminutive, bubbly woman, a lawyer working for the Federal government, she had mingled with Advantage Boating, (previously named Ottawa Sailing School) racing enthusiasts and eventually had worked through the gruelling classroom, dockside and afloat training to become instructor.

During my first complete summer with the club I sailed to my heart's content, passed the Basic Cruising Standard exam with Doreen and was awarded my first certification.

The crowning sailing event for me that summer was my seven-day cruise in the North Channel of Georgian Bay with five other members of the club. The boat was a CS36, a well designed and comfortable sloop equipped with all the amenities of a boat its size, except that in 1999 we didn't have electronic chart plotters that show the position of the boat with respect to the navigation hazards. Navigation was mainly by an ancient method called dead reckoning, with the aid of GPS to pinpoint our position on a paper chart.

Our captain was Serge, a tall man with salt and pepper hair in his early forties, a senior member of the club who had made several excursions in Georgian Bay. Amongst the crew were a couple from Chicoutimi, Québec, Louis and Linda, both in their mid-forties. There was another couple, Rachel and her husband Bob from Ottawa. Louis and Linda had sailed with NCSS when it was in its prime, and still kept in touch with the present-day members. Rachel, an energetic brunette with an engaging, smiling round face, was a nurse, in her mid-fifties, who had recently taken to sailing. She was to become a frequent sailing companion for me, in spite of our divergences with regards to the occult and scientific thought. More on this later.

Georgian Bay was just as beautiful as I had been led to believe, if not more so. The North Channel is a wide expanse of water north of

Manitoulin Island. The latter is so large that 108 lakes have formed on it, some of which have their own islands and in turn several of these islands within the island have their own ponds. Lake Manitou, (104 sq. km or 40 sq. miles) is the largest lake on a fresh water island in the world! Georgian Bay features more than 30,000 islands and hundreds of beautiful anchorages from which sailors can go ashore to explore the natural wonders. Everywhere we turned our gaze, we were served a magnificent tapestry of green, windswept pines against majestic towering hills of white granite plunging into clear blue water. It featured a rich marine heritage and lighthouses that dotted the coastline, making it an excellent venue for putting into practice the navigation principles I had garnered through reading and through my off-season night courses.

We had planned the provisions ahead of time and taken them with us from Ottawa, so we just had to unload them upon arrival at the boat. The manager of the boat rental company gave the skipper a briefing, and in turn Serge gave us a detailed introduction to a large keelboat before casting off.

Every day, after a hearty breakfast, we sailed for four to six hours, lunching on sandwiches while underway, and in the latter part of the afternoon, we anchored in one of the magnificent bays, sheltered from wind and waves. If there were time, we would take the dinghy to shore to explore the territory or go for a swim. For supper each person had planned a meal for the group and brought all the ingredients necessary, including, it goes without saying, an appropriate wine. After supper the captain and any of those interested would plan the next day's cruise and would select an anchorage while the others took care of the dishes. When there was time, we would play a card game or a board game or simply sit around sipping a *digestif* or an after-supper tea while exchanging philosophical opinions, sailing stories and jokes.

One evening, I had reserved a surprise for my cruising friends. I had promised them a session of tea reading. Not that I had any experience in this form of voluntary deception, although experience is certainly a good thing. But since Rachel was a great fan of spiritualism, astrology, psychic reading and paranormal events, I decided I would provide her (and the crew) with a free Tea-Reading experience. In the way of preparation, I experimented to find a type of tealeaves that produced interesting shapes when settled in the bottom of a cup and to determine the amount of leaves to use per cup. The main skills I practiced at home before the trip were how to swirl the cup convincingly, how to look spiritual while the leaves sank to the bottom, how to gaze into the cup while appearing to be reading something, and how to look surprised, concerned, sad or happy.

Since I had already mastered the physical side of the reading, I made a list of standard fail-safe phrases that could apply to my shipmates: To Serge who had just started a new job with the City of Ottawa: "I sense that you will be up for promotion"; to Louis, an engineer who was working in high tech: "The leaves tell me that you will have to cope with problem resolution at work"; to Linda who was raising pre-teen kids: "I read that you will soon have to deal with conflicts with the children; to Bob, who worked as a financial advisor for a large firm: "You will soon meet a very rich customer, and I see that you will increase your personal finances in the near future"; as for Rachel, who was the main object of this exercise, and who was to retire in the near future, my line was easily chosen: "The tea leaves are clear on this: I see that there will be much travel in your life in the years to come."

A few years later, as we sat drinking margaritas in a boat cockpit with a group of friends, Rachel, beaming with contentment said, "Robert, you were right when you read my tea leaves in Georgian Bay. You predicted that there would be lots of travel in my life, and it turned out to be right on!"

As a member of the Board, I attended a special meeting to discuss the agenda for our upcoming AGM in November. We would, of course announce the purchase of the Tanzer, but would refrain from discussing selling the Edel for the time being. We had enough funds to support both boats for a few years. It was proposed and seconded that the said agenda be submitted along with the financial report and the invitation to the AGM.

Two weeks later, Rick phoned, voice filled with angst, "Robert, we're having an emergency meeting tomorrow afternoon at my place and everybody has to be there. Can you come?"

"Sure, but what's up?"

"It's a special meeting about the future of NCSS. I can't tell you any more about it and I have several more calls to make. Everybody will be here at one thirty."

All of the members of the Board were present, seated in a circle, waiting, silently, as if attending the wake of a dear friend. Being a new member of the committee, I felt it was better not to ask any questions and wait and see what would transpire.

Suddenly, footsteps at the door. I felt a flash of tension amongst my peers. In barrelled a couple in their early fifties – a tall, slim woman followed by a thin, bespectacled man sporting a salt and pepper moustache and goatee. The woman was wearing a navy blouse with a sailor collar. She beheld some of the beauty and some of the fearsomeness of the Snow White

Queen, with her thin face and hands, her dark, piercing eyes and her fierce and determined stance.

"What is this I hear about selling *Iniskip*?" she bellowed in a rapid, France French accent.

"That's unacceptable!" she screamed.

She looked around the room, nostrils flaring, pausing for effect. My mind swirled and I was asking myself, "Who *is* this person, how does she know we had ever discussed the possibility of selling *Iniskip*? What business does she have coming here?"

"You won't destroy the school that the founders have worked so hard at establishing! The constitution has to be respected!" her voice mounting to a crescendo.

She was pacing back and forth in the middle of the floor, hands clasped behind her back.

"What do you expect to do with a Tanzer 29?" she bellowed, her voice trembling with rage, "Are you trying to turn my school into a club of elite seniors?"

No one spoke. The man who had followed her in stood silently at the back of the room, impassive. Between the woman's rants you could have heard a pin drop.

"The founders have poured their *lives* into making this school one of world renown. We've adopted the Glénan method, and what have *you* done with this? You've turned it into a mockery of proper sailing with your populist CYA standard. Only the Glénans teach proper technique," speaking very rapidly.

She puffed herself up and continued her tirade, "And now you want to throw all of that away like a discarded rag. We had three Edels custom-built and used these in Georgian Bay as our main teaching boats and they served us perfectly well," thrusting her index finger forward in a stabbing motion to emphasize her point.

"You're turning this school into a club for old people by selling *Iniskip* and spending the summers making circles around Lac Deschênes in a vacationer's boat. I want you to know that this is not acceptable!" her fists tightly closed and shaking.

"The Tanzer 29 isn't a teaching boat. It's a boat for weekend sailors, a floating cottage, a party boat," her voice dripping with disgust. "This just won't pass, understand?"

She yelled at the man at the back of the room,

"Viens-t-en!" turned around and bellowed to the group:

"You won't get away with this, understand?" and she left, with the man at her trail.

Complete stupefaction reigned in the room, every face white as a sheet. Lips quivering, Doreen was on the verge of bursting into tears. The silence was broken by our President, Serge, who was pale as a ghost, and in a low, stammering voice he proposed that we hold a meeting the following week to discuss what to do next. I then learned that the woman was Catherine and the man, her husband Alexandre, the founders of the School, who once in a blue moon show up unexpectedly when they come back to Canada from the Caribbean to visit friends and family.

I couldn't make it to that meeting, but found out that the Board decided to push the date of the AGM forward to the end of October to accommodate the woman and her husband, as they were scheduled to leave for the South on November 1st.

It was with a sense of trepidation that I anticipated the AGM...

We had decided to hold the annual meeting in the Masson primary school gymnasium so that the members would have a chance to view our pride and joy on her supporting cradle in the town's boatyard before the meeting. We posed for photographs in front of our yet unnamed boat. Most of the members were present but I noticed as well a few strangers I had never seen before.

After the review of the boat, we congregated at the school. We took our places in silence and apprehension, the members of the board at the head table at the front and the others on chairs facing the Board. After the members were all seated, in strutted Catherine and Alexandre with, in tow, a dozen *Strangers* that I had never seen before, including those who had posed for pictures by the boat. She marched in with the confidence of a German general, and directed her troop to be seated around her at the back of the room.

Serge, in his position of President announced the opening of the meeting with a stroke of his hammer and welcomed everybody to the 1999 NCSS Annual General Meeting. A Meeting chairperson and secretary were nominated.

When came the verification of the quorum, Catherine sprang up, brandishing a sheaf of papers in one hand and a bundle of cash in the other. She spoke at machine gun speed,

"I have twenty-one applications for membership at $25 each and twelve proxies. The Constitution allows any person to apply for membership anytime during the fiscal year and any member in good standing can have up to five proxies."

A current of tension rippled through the hall. It was apparent that this expert in constitutional matters had spent the past weeks plotting a diabolical scheme. As I was to learn later, she recruited old cronies and ex-members of NCSS and convinced them of the impending collapse of "their" sailing school and that it was their duty to help her rig the voting in favour of righteousness.

As the meeting was proceeding, I was asking myself: Who *are* these people? Did they want to get rid of the new boat? Was it a coup to oust the current Board members and take over the club? Why else would they spend $25 each for one evening? – For the sadistic pleasure of gruesome intimidation? – For the sake of pleasing that angry woman? It didn't make sense to me.

When came the approval of the agenda, Catherine spoke up again and said she wanted to table two items: A presentation by herself and one by Alexandre.

In presenting his report the president spoke of the purchase of the Tanzer, colouring his speech with a positive spin. Brent described the boat and talked about the plans for next summer. The treasurer then gave his report, and spoke of the club's healthy bottom line with its $18,000 cash reserve after the purchase of the boat.

Then came the item "Presentation by Catherine". Catherine jumped up, took over the floor and spoke rapidly but without the sense of panic that she had exhibited the first time I had encountered her. Over the next ten minutes she reiterated the importance of preserving the school's original objectives and the necessity of having a proper teaching boat. Then, in a change of heart, she acknowledged the value of having a larger boat for complementing the advantages of the smaller one.

"Whew! At least we're keeping the Tanzer!" I thought.

Still speaking at machine-gun speed, she put forth a motion to preserve the teaching vocation of the club, and without further discussion a resolution was unanimously passed. She then handed the microphone to Alexandre.

In a slow, monotone speech, he began by describing the minutiae of the Centre's constitution. Then he told the story about how the Centre was started by a group of sailors from Montreal, Hull and Ottawa, who won an Ontario Lotto grant to buy three Edels at $15,000 each, how they had them custom-designed, how they berthed the boats on Georgian Bay, how they slept five people to a boat. He recounted how they recruited hundreds of new members, how they respected proper teaching methods, how they imparted the love of the sea to their students, how everybody respected the Glénan method, how their students became accomplished sailors.

What made my ears perk was his disclosure that in their wisdom, the founders decided to name an Honour Member every year. All told, five of the pioneers, including his truly, had been granted a lifetime appointment as an Honour Member. Their duty was to oversee the functions of the club and to ensure that the constitution was respected. The Honour Members didn't need to pay the annual membership fee, but had all the powers and rights of regular members and had the power to advise the Board of Directors on constitutional matters and to set them straight if they felt the Board was out of line. Then, after forty minutes of colourless speech, he proposed that the Directors who were to be elected tonight be bound by the rules of the Constitution.

This wasn't too extreme a suggestion in my way of thinking, but Brent was so incensed by the underhanded way these people had commandeered the meeting, that he got up and said, "I'm not going to have anything to do with this charade. I'm leaving. Goodnight!" and barrelled out of the hall.

Doreen was so upset, that she burst into tears and rushed out after Brent, forgetting that she was supposed to drive my friend Don home after the meeting. A vote was carried out, with a show of hands, and all hands went up with the exception of a few abstentions from my peers who were too incensed by the devious way the meeting had been overtaken.

Then came the elections to renew the Board of directors. I wondered how many of the *Strangers* would be nominated. This would be their chance to get rid of the "negligent directors" who had purportedly turned a school of world renown into an old people's club. The elections chair called for nominations and started by asking the current members if they accepted nomination. All of those present did. "Any more nominations from the floor?"

Silence, except for some uncomfortable shuffling at the back of the room. "Last call for nominations."

At this point, Catherine got up and said: "I nominate Rolland Laliberté, Camille Thériault, Dolores Chaput and Hyacinthe Rouleau."

"Rolland Laliberté, do you accept the nomination?"

A negative answer with a muffled apology.

"Camille Thériault, do you accept the nomination?"

Another embarrassed, negative answer followed by a hollow excuse.

As it turned out, the two women *Stranger* nominees accepted to become Directors, and since there were two vacancies on the Board, all were elected by acclamation.

What threatened to be a bloodbath, in the end, turned out to be a minor skirmish. The wounds that my peers and I sustained that evening healed into scars of mistrust and resentment of the founding members. Fortunately, the evening battle resulted in little real change except for the addition of two board members, which was not even going to affect the balance of power.

As for the other *Strangers*, all except the angry woman and her husband disappeared from our lives, never to be seen again.

The turn of the millennium came and went and the Y2K computer bug that was to cause planes to fall out of the sky and bring the end of civilization just fizzled out and the North Channel Sailing School directors were making plans for rejuvenating their club.

However, all work and no play makes Jack a dull boy. The phone rang. Serge at the other end, "Robert, how would you like to take a break and do your Intermediate Sailing Standard and *at the same time* spend a week cruising in the British Virgin Islands?" his voice filled with excitement.

"Is the Pope Catholic?" was my response.

Serge was telling me that Advantage Boating offered an all-inclusive package that comprised the return flight to the British Virgin Islands (BVI), the Intermediate sailing course with certification, a week of sailing amongst those magnificent islands and all the food we could eat. Warm, sunny weather thrown in as a bonus!

The BVIs are a British territory, part of the British West Indies, lying about 60 miles east of Puerto Rico. There are about 50 islands in this country, many of them uninhabited. When sailing amongst these gems of the Caribbean we come across names like Tortola, the main island, Virgin Gorda, Jost Van Dyke, Ginger Island and Anegada. Not to be confused with their Yankee sisters, they offer a more subdued quality of tourism, as the country is free from golf courses or shopping malls. Nightlife is quiet by contrast with that of its neighbouring US Virgin Islands. You might see a couple riding on horseback through the surf, or partaking in a croquet game, or just sipping a happy hour cocktail on a terrace.

Four other members of our club joined us for a total of six students, four of whom were Francophone. Our instructor Warren Chafe, an anglophone, was a calm, competent pedagogue who had the skill of bringing out the best in his students. I mention the language because this cultural difference turned out to be of significance at the grocery store, as you will see. I should also mention, to his credit, that this boatload was divided between Rachel and Viviane who were doing their Basic Cruising Standard and the other four who were doing the Intermediate Standard. Amongst those four, in addition to Serge and me, there were our CYA Basic instructor Doreen and my frequent sailing friend Don.

The basic course teaches not only the rudiments of sailing technique, but also how to become a captain on a small boat, how to navigate during daylight hours on familiar waters, the captain's responsibilities vis-à-vis the boat and crew, how to communicate effectively and how to deal with certain emergencies.

The intermediate level is intended for managing a 30 to 40 foot boat, one that is large enough for living and partying on for days at a time. Warren would teach us how to navigate without running aground, sinking or ramming other boats, how to use the equipment germane to bigger boats, simple adjustments and maintenance of the diesel engine, the art of provisioning (actually, Warren learned one or two things about this from his French crew), the management of the galley and advanced techniques of anchoring and recovering a man overboard. I might point out that feminists and human rights activists don't object to the discrimination inherent in "*man* overboard". At the end of the course, the successful student qualifies for bareboat chartering, that is, renting a large sailboat and taking charge of the boat and crew. This entails sailing safely without scaring the living daylights out of one's crew and other boaters, bringing the boat and crew back to port without damage and with the crew eager to do it again.

January 23, 2000.

Our plane landed in Charlotte Amalie, in the neighbouring US Virgin Islands from where we took a ferry to Soper's Hole, Tortola, the largest of the BVIs. The immigration and customs people cleared us in without subjecting us to the usual indignities that border people learn to perform during their training. We headed for the dock and found *Princess of Whales* (spelling intentional), our 40-foot, French-built Beneteau. Warren was waiting for us, sporting his Advantage Boating T-shirt and sailor's cap. First thing, he suggested, was to choose our berths and unpack.

Let me help you visualize the amount of living space there is inside a 40-foot keelboat. Keep in mind that I'm talking about monohulls, or single hull boats, not catamarans that are made with two hulls joined together by a royal ballroom. The Beneteau 400 has a beam of 12 feet and about 6'6" headroom. Before you do a volume multiplication, remember that a boat is not a rectangular box like a Greyhound bus. A keelboat is pointed at the bow and with a substantial rocker or upward curve at both ends, design traits that make the boat efficient at advancing through the water, but that reduce the inside space. Furthermore, much of the volume of the boat is taken up by the engine room, cockpit, cockpit lockers, chain locker, propane locker, water tanks, fuel tanks, sewage holding tanks, the refrigerator, and the bilge.

Learning the Ropes

It's a wonder there's any room left for people! In spite of the advances in computer boat design, naval architects haven't yet managed to build boats that are small on the outside and big on the inside. Our boat featured three small staterooms with wall-to-wall double berths, a compact galley, a miniature head with shower and a large central salon, with a table surrounded by a u-shaped settee capable of accommodating seven merry guests with elbow room to spare.

The next item on Warren's schedule was provisioning. There was a small, well-stocked supermarket within walking distance. There is an old saying that the English eat to live but the French live to eat. Rachel is the world's finest gourmet and lover of food. Her culinary imagination and creativeness are as big as her heart. Cooking is her passion, if not her obsession. She will always let someone else take over, out of respect, but given the choice, she would rather plan and prepare every meal herself. As I mentioned, the food was included in our package, so Warren was picking up the tab at the expense of the school. When asked for his preferences, our instructor replied that he would eat whatever we put in front of him. He admitted he was not a gourmet, but that on one of his courses he got bored with the food when his all-male class fed him hot dogs for the entire week.

We assured him that would not be the case with us and he began catching on to what we meant when he saw what was going into the shopping cart: Foie gras, smoked oysters, shrimp, scallops, capers, sun-dried tomatoes, sesame oil, pine nuts, Portobello mushrooms, artichoke hearts, mint pesto, herbal teas, ground coffee, every fresh fruit and vegetable in the produce department, Camembert, Brie, goat cheese, in addition to the basics such as flour, baking powder, olive oil, butter and eggs. His eyebrows raised a notch with each addition to the cart and with each addition of *a shopping cart*. In the end, we had filled four carts and ran up the largest bill Advantage Boating had ever faced. Each meal was a Babette's Feast, judging by the expressions of delight on Warren's face. Each time I've run into him in the ensuing years, he would reminisce about the meals he savoured with his French group.

The next day we were up early and had a simple breakfast of pancakes, fresh fruit and maple syrup. Then we sailed away on my first experience in the Caribbean. Here I must point out a particularity of Advantage Boating. It is a strict policy of the school that its students wear lifejackets at all times when the boat is underway. In the Caribbean I have never seen *anybody* wearing such a device. It just isn't done, even when riding an overloaded dinghy surrounded by sharks in a hurricane in the dark. Caribbean sailors wouldn't be caught dead wearing a lifejacket, as they're convinced that wearing one is a self-fulfilling prophecy of disaster. So whenever other boaters encountered our sailboat with seven people wearing big, fat, orange lifejackets, they craned their necks for a second look and they instinctively steered away to keep a respectable distance from this bizarre apparition.

Mind you, I'm not pooh-poohing the wearing of lifejackets. To the contrary, safety should always be at the forefront for any responsible captain. The law requires that your boat carry one approved lifejacket of the right size for each person on board, but doesn't mandate wearing it. Donning the lifejacket then becomes a judgement call. I insist that non-swimmers and young children wear one when they are outside the cabin and that everybody who goes on deck wear one in heavy seas. When the movement of the boat reaches the point when it is tricky to walk on the deck, then it is time to put on a harness and clip onto the boat. At night you should always clip on when you venture out onto the deck and when you're alone in the cockpit. I found that the best kind of lifejacket for a swimmer is the self-inflatable type with built-in harness. It is lightweight, unobtrusive and comfortable and you are much more likely to be wearing it when needed. Should it fail to automatically inflate when you fall overboard, you can inflate it by mouth.

I was enchanted with the scenery: green hilly islands within view of each other, surrounded by clear, warm water, under a permanently blue sky. Each island was skirted by a scalloped coastline with postcard-pretty coves of lustrous white sand, perfect for anchoring for the night.

We had chosen to join the throngs of Northerners who were escaping from their frozen landscapes to find respite from shovelling snow, scraping windshields, spreading salt on driveways and bundling up against arctic gales. In other words this was high season in the BVIs and the anchorages tended to fill up rapidly towards mid-afternoon.

On this very first day Warren put his students through their paces to determine each person's level. We then carried through many manoeuvres, which, with six students on a boat, took forever to practice. Consequently, it was late by the time we were ready to call it quits and search for an anchorage. As we entered a bay called The Bight, around 1800, Warren discovered that every spot was taken up. We circled around, weaving between the anchored boats under the apprehensive stares of lounging cruisers, searching for a little nook that might have been overlooked for us to appropriate. The rule about anchoring is that the last boat to drop the hook has to keep clear of the ones that have arrived before her. Generally (unless there is a current) when there is a change of direction of the wind, all the boats remain bow into the wind, so they all swing in the same direction, thereby keeping clear of each other. After having circled the bay a couple of times without finding a space for anchoring, Warren decided to do the only thing possible. That was to practice a bow and stern anchoring amongst the boats. In other words, he put down an anchor at the bow as is normally done, reversed the boat to twice the normal distance, put down a second anchor at the stern, then motored halfway between the two anchors and took up the slack on the rodes. Since *Princess of Whales* was thus tied at both ends, she couldn't swing. According to Warren's practiced eye, should the wind shift, the adjacent boats would stay clear of us.

We hadn't even settled in, than one of the neighbours, standing on the deck of his boat, called out to us. He appeared upset and warned us that he would hold us responsible if the boats collided in the middle of the night. Warren assured him that there was no danger of collision and not to worry. I hoped my instructor was right, as I wasn't so sure myself.

One particularity of this boat is that she had in-mast furling. This means that instead of lowering the mainsail and of flaking it onto the boom as is done on most boats, the sail was rolled up inside the mast with a cranking mechanism, leaving the aluminum boom bare. One feature of the boom with such a furling system is that there is a slot along its entire topside, through which a mechanism slides to pull the mainsail out to the end of the boom as it is unfurled. Keep in mind how a flute is made (the musical instrument).

I awoke suddenly in the middle of the night with the sound of an approaching train, which was bearing down on us at a terrific speed! The sound increased to a thundering vibration as it neared. My heartbeat picked up, as the fearsome noise and throbbing were right above us. Almost as suddenly as it came, it started to dissipate and then disappeared into the distance.

I soon realized, once shaken out of my slumber that there were no trains in this anchorage, and I figured out what it was. I got out of bed, climbed the companionway and my eyes met Warren's who had chosen to sleep in the cockpit. He silently motioned towards the anchorage. I saw that all the boats except ours were lined up 90 degrees to their original orientation. Since our boat couldn't swing, the wind was coming right across the side of the boat and boom instead of streaming the length of the vessel. In physics, resonance is the tendency of a system to oscillate at larger amplitude at some frequencies than at others. When a gust reached a certain strength, it would blow the "giant horizontal flute" attached to the mast at just the right frequency to generate a harmonic vibration that caused the boat to vibrate. This phenomenon has been known to knock the wings off airplanes as happened in the case of Lockheed's Electra. *Princess of Whales* didn't have wings that fall off to worry about, so I went back to sleep. I was awakened several times, however, every time a gust reached the critical velocity. By the way, Warren's estimation was correct; none of the neighbouring boats came close to touching us, or we them.

The wind was blowing at a comfortable, steady 15 knots and the boat heeled moderately under full sails. Of course, that's what a keelboat does in windy conditions. Nevertheless, this didn't go well with Viviane, who, to the surprise and bewilderment of everybody, burst out into tears, "I don't like it when it heels!" Warren, as a good captain will, acquiesced to the sensitivities of his nervous student, and gave the command to reduce sail in order to reduce heeling. This was a good lesson for me, as now when I have new crew I watch their hands. If their grip on the helm is tight like a vice and their knuckles white as death, I will ask them how they feel and reassure them that there is no danger. If that fails, I reduce sail correspondingly.

I have to admit that I find nothing more disquieting than a woman crying. I'm a very fortunate man, because in my 46 years of marriage, my better half never cried except for the death of a loved one. Yet, before the week was over another woman on the boat would turn on the waterworks. We were sailing along the coast of one of the larger islands and Warren was having us practice dead reckoning. In the days of ancient mariners, that is, prior to *1986*, when sailors navigated without GPS, they had to rely on visual landmarks, lights and buoys, to determine their position. They used the tools of the trade: compass, charts (nautical maps), rulers, dividers, pencils and eraser. Today, modern navigation still encompasses the old techniques. You never know, you might break your GPS, or heaven forbid, the US defence department could decide to switch off the Global Positioning System. Warren had us plot our planned course in pencil on the chart, as is customary. Dead reckoning (DR) is simply a matter of using the boat's speed and heading to calculate where the boat should be every hour along the plotted line. If the speed changes along the way, then you have to erase all your DR marks and start your calculations over from where you estimate you are at the time. Because of a wind shift, our speed changed, so Warren had Doreen erase all the DR points from here on. For some reason I couldn't fathom, Doreen suddenly blurted out:

"I was never taught to do it this way!"

And to everybody's consternation, she burst out crying. Warren was quite taken aback, as there was no call for this at all. Doreen isn't even French! Besides, she was not only an experienced sailor but was the only NCSS member qualified for teaching the CYA Basic Cruising Standard at the time. I will always be at a loss to understand the emotional responses of a woman.

We dropped anchor for a few hours off Virgin Gorda to experience one of the Caribbean's greatest natural oddities: a shoreline cluster of gigantic boulders called the Baths, where sailors and tourists clamber through crannies between and under the giant rocks and bathe in stone basins of crystalline water.

One of the main evening activities in this enchanting sailing venue was to help Rachel prepare supper; it took a crew of two full-time dishwashers to clean up after her, as she joyously used every pot, pan and utensil on the boat at least once per meal. Of course, the crowning event was sitting down at the table and enjoying the fruits of her culinary art along with the appropriate wines. After supper, there would usually be a lesson of sailing theory and planning the next day's sail. On the fifth day, all of the practical course material had been covered so instead of sailing we did the written part of the test, which Warren corrected on the spot. To everybody's relief, we all passed our respective levels. The last day was spent lackadaisically sailing back to Soper's Hole to return *Princess of Whales* to her berth.

Back in Ottawa, late that year, we held our first Board meeting with the two *Strangers* who had joined the Board of Directors the night of the AGM. My peers and I realised that Dolores and Hyacinthe weren't our enemies after all, but were just two former sailors who had reached their late forties and were eager to get back into sailing. These two, in turn, realized that the "negligent" members of the Board who had been operating the club did so with the best of intentions, and furthermore, had valiantly kept it afloat for several years in spite of financial difficulties and the abandonment by its founders. Bygones were bygones and now the time had come to work together to put NCSS back on its feet.

The solution centered around increasing the membership, which was essential to supporting two boats on a continuous basis. Many *ad hoc* advertisement strategies had been used in the past, but none brought about the level of recruitment we were aiming for. We needed to double the membership this year. In order to attract the undecided would-be sailors, we decided to create an additional category of membership that would consist of an Initiation Program at $150, comprising one learning session at the dock followed by three outings. After the course, they could apply the entire fee towards the more expensive Sail-All-You-Want program if they wished.

Since I was the only retired member at the time, I was granted the dubious honour of being appointed Recruitment Director. I would have preferred Happy Hour Director, or Director of Après Sailing Activities, but somebody had to do the groundwork. After some intensive cogitation I cooked up a plan.

The bulk of our recruitment would be accomplished through one major yearly membership drive, culminating in a Public Information

Evening (PIE) in early April of each year. During the winter we would announce the upcoming PIE by placing adds in local newspapers and sailing magazines, putting up posters everywhere and writing to people who had previously indicated an interest in sailing. The PIE would be held in a public hall in Aylmer, consisting of two rooms. On one side we would provide a number of exhibits and on the other, a multimedia presentation. In the way of exhibits, we would have a signing-in table, a display of maps and charts of our sailing venues, an arrangement of pictures showing happy sailors in multifarious poses on sailboats, wearing everything from full rain gear to the flimsiest of swimsuits, a marine safety exhibit by the Canadian Coast Guard, an exhibit describing the CYA sailing course and a recruitment table. To add a bit of piquant to the evening, we'd hold draws for a free Introduction to Sailing course and a variety of door prizes. The presentation would consist of a slide show of pictures of irresistible sailing places, girls & guys with ear-to-ear smiles on sailboats, as well as a description of the club's different programs.

The Board went for the idea and allotted a budget of $1200 for the project. I spent the next three months preparing for the event. With the help of fifteen volunteers on the night of the PIE, 93 prospects showed up and stayed for the slide show. To our delight, we ended up with 50 members.

The NCSS was off the ground! There was an enthusiasm that I had not felt in my two previous seasons. The addition of the Tanzer generated much interest, helping to make 2000 an excellent sailing season. Tallying up the logs at the end of the season we calculated that the two boats combined enjoyed a total of 823 person-outings.

Naming a boat is part of a long tradition in the maritime world. The reason why boat naming has survived the ages is that every boat has a personality, a character, and even though I don't believe in the supernatural, I would even go as far as saying a spirit or a soul. Under sail, a boat is a living, pulsating organism, the fruit of the imagination and calculations of its designer, but also the nurtured, adopted child of the owner who has lovingly dressed her up with accessories, equipment, and aesthetic refinements. Even before the buyer takes possession of his new boat, he begins searching his brain for a name that expresses something of personal significance, or wit or humour or a philosophical thought.

There is an old naval superstition relating to boat names. It is said that changing the name of a boat can bring ill health and bad luck. There are still people who decide to play it safe and keep the name used by the previous owner. Nevertheless, many boat buyers today will rename a used boat and choose a name that suits their own personality or life circumstances.

Learning the Ropes

Our Tanzer had lived until now without ever having been named, a very unusual and improper state of affairs. We therefore launched a contest for the choice of a name. Carmen, the youngest of our members at the age of 28 was an attractive, well proportioned brunette. An enthusiastic sailor, she had sailed 50 times during the season – a record for our club – and had given much thought to naming the boat. Her spiritual asceticism led her to coining the winning entry "Namaste", a Hindi word that signifies a greeting of deep reverence and appreciation, expressed by "The divine in me recognises and honours the divine in you". Not exactly my choice, since I'm not given to spirituality and can't even recognise the divine in myself! But I liked it nevertheless, as it expresses generosity and it has a nice ring to it. And I suppose one could substitute something else for the word *divine*, such as *goodness*, or *humanity*, or *sailor*, or *boozer*.

One day, as I was carrying out a repair on *Namaste*, an unexpected woman visitor appeared on the finger dock next to the boat. I have to admit, upon seeing her, my heart rate picked up – and not for the reason you're thinking. Who was greeting me by name? – But my nemesis, that angry woman of the AGM, Catherine!

"Congratulations, Robert on your successful recruiting effort. That's what the school needed." she said before anything else.

This person might have her failings, but she does have great qualities. She's a very knowledgeable sailor and captain and has a reputation for being a stickler for detail. She knows the Glénan method of sailing to a T and likes to remind one that she took a course in diesel engine repair and can carry out any engine maintenance herself. She oversees the chores that she gives to any crew that might have accepted an invitation to join her. When they're on her boat, whether underway or at anchor, *she's* the captain and she alone makes all the decisions, including, it is widely rumoured, what size to cut the potatoes.

However, here was a side of her that I hadn't suspected. She was actually capable of greeting another person in a civil fashion. In hindsight, I can understand how Catherine and Alexandre must have felt when apprised of the discussion centring on disposing of the Edel and how "their" school risked diverging from its original purpose. Bearing this in mind, I can forgive the highly unusual and confrontational measure they adopted to protect the organization of their creation.

We exchanged a few casual words and then she invited me for a lesson in advanced docking procedures the next day. Taken aback by the unexpectedness and generosity of her offer, I accepted. The following day we spent a couple of hours at the dock, putting the boat in a variety of situations at the main dock and at the finger dock. She taught me some of the tricks of docking short-handed, getting in and out of a tight berth, how to dock and undock with a strong beam wind and more. From then on, whenever we meet, we remain civil towards each other, but warmth still remains to be achieved, even after ten years.

Fall came, the boats were hauled out of the water and prepared for the winter…and I was looking for an adventure.

&&&&&&&

I went down to the galley to mix myself a rum and soda and then returned to the deck to reflect on the events that had led me here, in Bahía la Mar. Anthony and Jacqui were still not back from their shopping excursion into Porlamar, so I still had time for myself. I recalled my first offshore sailing experience – which granted me far more than what I'd bargained for…

Fun to steer!

Damage to the boa = a holiday in Bermud

Beautiful Martinique at last!

Chapter 4

More Than I Bargained For

September, 2000

  I wasn't ready for sailing around the world yet. I had learned the basics of sailing. I had trained in navigation. I had experienced what it's like to live in a confined space with other people. I had gained experience in boat maintenance. But before sailing around the world, there were two other aspects of life at sea that I would need to experience. So far the largest seas I'd encountered were three or four foot waves in Georgian Bay. And because they were so well protected, I didn't encounter large waves in the BVIs either. So, would I get seasick in heavy seas? Moreover, I had never sailed beyond sight of land. Would I find it unpleasant or threatening? I had to correct these deficiencies in my sailing record by pulling off an offshore passage, or bluewater sailing. It was a matter of finding a high seas sailor who needed crew.

"Have you tried the Centre marin des Aventures? They take boats down to the Caribbean every year. You should talk to René, the director", suggested Dolores, who had become the NCSS communications director.

I'd heard the name des Aventures and knew they were a sailing school in Montreal whose main sailing grounds are the lower St. Laurence. I didn't know their reputation, but had not heard anything negative about them.

As it turned out, they were looking for crew to deliver a boat from Halifax to St. Martin, a Caribbean island about 90 miles east of the BVIs, near the top of the long necklace of islands that curves southwards to the eastern tip of Venezuela. It was part of their seasonal north-south, south-north transfer of boats for teaching in the St. Laurence during the summer and in the Caribbean during the winter.

René wasn't returning my calls. After many unfruitful attempts I managed to speak with Marie, his wife *et* secretary, who explained that the boat would cast off around the end of October and the passage would take three weeks, sailing offshore all the way. The cost would be $500 plus my food and incidentals. Since the Centre was registered with Revenue Canada as an educational institution, it would issue a tax receipt that would qualify for an income tax deduction – an unexpected bonus! I would be sailing with two other experienced men and a woman crew, led by a highly competent captain. What she failed to tell me, among other important facts, was that because the regular captain was unavailable the school had hired a substitute they had never met.

Since I was a day ahead of time in Halifax I rented a car at the airport, so I'd be free to visit a friend on the morrow. It was midnight when I reached the marina. I grabbed my gear, located the boat, *Tulip One*, a Jeanneau Sun Fizz 40. I rapped on the hull to alert the captain. A very sleepy, shirtless man with long hair opened the hatch. I introduced myself, he said he was Henri, pointed to the port aft cabin, mumbled something and disappeared into the starboard aft cabin.

The next morning, Henri was up and significantly more alert and welcoming than the night before. I estimated his age at 45, he wore an earring, and bore an anchor and a compass rose tattooed on his arms. It is said that ancient pirates wore an earring to pay for their burial if they died at sea and their body washed ashore. Perhaps I should get one too.

When I inquired, Henri told me the two men were asleep in the forepeak cabin. After our coffee, the forepeak cabin door opened and to my shock and dismay, two very young boys crawled out, rumpled and bleary-eyed. I had expected two *men*. Vincent and Jean-Michel, 18, were pals from

Montreal. Vincent had sailed dinghies but never a keelboat. Jean-Michel was sailing for the first time.

A while later, knock knock.

"Anybody there?" called a young female voice.

A gorgeous, 27-year-old brunette with long, curly hair and deep, brown eyes, introduced herself as Marie-Madeleine. She flung her packsack into the cockpit and stepped aboard with all the confidence of an old salt. She had taken a week-long sailing course with a Québec City school during the summer, and later confided that she had steered only once during the entire course. It's difficult to imagine what kind of course that could be.

The crew and captain were in jovial spirits, everybody chomping at the bit to go. We would be free the rest of the day, but tomorrow we would take care of provisioning, prepare the boat and go through a briefing with the captain.

That evening I went for supper with my Halifax friend and decided to keep the car for the following day for provisioning, since the nearest supermarket was five kilometres from the marina.

The boat was equipped with a refrigerator and a deep freezer, so we weren't limited in what we could stock for the weeks to come. I mention this because it will be relevant later. The next day we all went to the store in my rental car, filled up several carts of food, stowed the bags in the trunk and the back seat and the kids walked back to the marina for lack of space.

After we unloaded the provisions I returned the car to the rental agency and walked back to the boat for the captain's pre-departure briefing. He explained that the four crewmembers would take turns doing two-hour watches, meaning that each of us would have two hours on and six hours off. During our shift we would steer, look out for traffic and advise Henri if we felt there was a problem with the sails. We could not use the auto helm, the automatic steering device, because "there was not enough electricity" (I would only understand why a week later). The captain would not participate in watches but would be on call in the aft cabin at all times for course changes, sail changes and emergencies. We would have to wear our harness and tether and clip onto the boat whenever we were alone in the cockpit at night (which was to be expected). Men would have to use the seated position for all performances in the head to prevent urine messes, and no toilet paper should go in the head (normal procedures). Fresh water was to be used sparingly and we were to use seawater for washing dishes. The crew would take turns preparing meals and cleaning up. If we wanted to listen to CDs, there was a stereo system with loud speakers under the dodger. There would be no drugs permitted on board, "…should you have any, get rid of them before coming aboard. I don't want the Martinique authorities to impound the boat."

I interrupted Henri, "You mean, St. Martin – you said Martinique."

"No, I meant Martinique, our destination."

"What do you mean Martinique, our destination? We're going to St. Martin, aren't we? Otherwise I'm on the wrong boat."

"Robert, this boat is going to Martinique…but come to think of it, originally René planned for the boat to go to St. Martin. But that has been changed months ago. Do you have a problem with that?"

"I guess not. I haven't bought my return airline ticket."

Henri finished his speech, "And don't stay up late, don't eat too much, don't drink too much, because you want to avoid being seasick tomorrow and if you tend to be seasick, take Gravol twelve hours before setting sail."

I was quite nonplussed with the stupid error of the school administration. On the positive side, I would be getting more for my money, since Martinique is 250 miles farther south, past Guadeloupe and Dominica. Nevertheless, I had no inkling or foreboding at all about the catastrophic way *Tulip One* would end her days.

We had time to spare, so I started walking around the boat, performing the checks I had been trained to carry out. I asked Henri if he wanted me to repair the gap in the seam of the U/V protector on the leech and foot (aft and bottom edges) of the jib. The jib on most larger boats uses what is called roller reefing to reduce the amount of exposed sail. Along the leech and the foot there is a band of sacrificial canvass about 8 inches wide, which, when the sail is rolled up, hides the entire sail, thereby protecting the Dacron fabric from ultraviolet rays. About seven inches of the stitching were undone.

"I can sew." I offered.

Henri answered, "No, don't bother, that won't cause a problem."

The propane wouldn't flow to the stove and I discovered that the solenoid valve at the tank was corroded. Henri agreed that I clean the contacts to restore the system to operational mode.

I couldn't find the emergency grab bag. Whenever a boat sails out of sight of land, it should carry a lifeboat, which ours did, but also a bag containing supplies to keep the crew alive and in communication for several days while waiting to be rescued. The grab bag usually contains a spare VHF radio, GPS and flares, food, water or a manual water maker, a powerful flashlight, a signalling mirror, fishing line and hooks, a first aid kit, paper and pencil, as well as each person's money, valuables and passport. Should we have to abandon ship, it would be a simple matter of throwing the emergency grab bag into the lifeboat. The reason why I couldn't find it was simple: The school didn't provide one.

Normally, before undertaking a passage, a sailor consults a long-term weather forecast. If the weather threatens to be rough, the wise sailor will wait for a suitable "weather window" before leaving. For example, Catherine, the NCSS founder, has once had to wait two weeks for an appropriate weather window before crossing the Atlantic. The weather forecast called for 35-knot winds over the next three days. I suggested to Henri that we postpone our departure until the weather calmed, but he answered, "This is a big boat. It's made for this kind of weather."

That answer didn't impress me. For one thing, heavy seas can take a toll on a boat's rigging and more important, I didn't think our inexperienced crew was up to the task.

I discovered that the radar was non-functional, though not a problem once away from coastal traffic, but I mention it because there will be an issue with this apparatus later. A fibreglass sailboat is invisible to other boats' radar because the material the hull is made of doesn't reflect radar waves. All the metal parts being curved, they just scatter the beams all around, thus the reception components of the other boat's radar can't detect them. So in order to be seen, a sailboat must have a radar reflector in place, a simple and inexpensive device that was absent on *Tulip One*.

The engine had been completely overhauled before the boat was brought from Montreal to Halifax, so there shouldn't be any problem in that regard, or so I thought. I pointed out to Henri that there was a smell of diesel in the engine compartment, but he answered, "Every boat this age has a diesel smell. It's normal." I wasn't sure of that.

That night, I reflected about our situation. There were some aspects of this trip that didn't seem quite right. However, I felt that I was committed at this point, so I decided to go ahead as planned.

The next day at ten o'clock sharp we cast off, on my watch. I felt jubilant at the helm, as I had not sailed since the end of the NCSS sailing season a month ago. I enjoyed seeing the shoreside docks, buildings, warehouses, silos, boatyards and marinas come into view as we progressed out of the long, narrow harbour. Once out in the open, the sea had formed six-foot waves, the largest I had ever experienced. Henri called out compass course changes, which I readily made. Towards the end of my watch at noon, the waves had increased to eight feet in height. Our boat carried herself very elegantly in these conditions. On the ocean the waves are much longer than high, so the boat just rises effortlessly on a passing wave and follows its up and down movement obediently without any fuss.

When my two-hour watch was up, Marie-Madeleine took the helm. We were sailing on a broad reach, flying full sails. I took a place on the port seat, but started feeling queasy. Yet, I had heeded all of Henri's advice to prevent seasickness. Before I had a chance to think about it my stomach made the decision to expel its contents, so I thrust myself to the side and let it all out overboard. Some people throw up discretely, emitting no more noise than that of a reverse burp. When I'm sick, discretion isn't part of the picture. I put my whole heart into it. In fact, it feels as if my entire gut will be expelled. The sound of my retching can be heard miles around, overpowering the crashing of the wind and waves. And I don't stop after just one little effort. No, when I start, I can continue retching non-stop for several minutes at a go.

Henri was very sympathetic. He went below to the galley and came back with a box of soda crackers and encouraged me to eat a little and drink a little water.

"You must keep something in your stomach, Robert."

"Why, I thought to myself, so I can vomit again?" and lo and behold, there I went again.

Henri kept on feeding me crackers and I kept on vomiting. Every five or ten minutes I would lean over the side and retch for several minutes. At first, I *thought* I would die, but after a few hours of this never-ending agony, I *hoped* I would die! By four o'clock I was completely exhausted. The frequency of vomiting had diminished, so I felt confident that I could crawl down the companionway to my berth, trailing a bucket along. I lay down on the bed and managed to sleep a few minutes between salutes to the bucket.

Of all the hardships that the sea can wreak upon a sailor, seasickness is by far the most atrocious. This condition is the result of a disagreement between the movement that the eyes perceive and the position that the inner ear's balance system senses. The sensation it produces affects not only the stomach, but the entire body, producing an intolerable, overwhelming, overall sensation of nausea. It can last from a few hours to several days and when on a long passage, the victim eventually returns to a normal condition. The feeling can be so unbearable, that some stricken people are reputed to have committed suicide rather than putting up with the torment.

At six o'clock, it was already dark and I heard Henri's voice calling, "Robert, it's your watch."

I thought to myself, "The bastard, can't he see that I'm dying? How can he be so heartless?"

And he added, "Sometimes when a seasick person takes the helm he stops being sick. It's quite remarkable, you know."

And I thought, "*Stops* being sick? At this time nothing sounded better than *to stop* being sick. So through a superhuman effort, I dragged myself out of bed, and while being thrown about inside the jostling boat, I pulled on my foul weather gear. As I was pulling on my first boot, the boat lurched sideways and was propelled upwards on a huge wave. When the boat fell off the wave, lurching in the opposite direction, I was sent in the air and landed, smashing my ribs on the hard edge of the berth. It was only later that I would realize I had broken two ribs, and every movement of the boat caused me untold pain during the remainder of the trip. I put on my second sailing boot and my foul weather jacket, strapped on my harness, and crawled up the companionway into the cockpit.

As if by miracle, the moment I took the wheel in my hands I stopped being sick, just as Henri had said. And I never vomited again – not even felt queasy – for the entire trip.

At 0200 it was my turn again to take over steering. For the first time since my childhood, I saw the sky as had the aboriginals of centuries ago. It was blackness, punctuated by millions of twinkling dots of light, a spectacle of awesome beauty. The Milky Way was clearly visible as a wide band of tiny, powdery, luminescent specks spanning the sky in the form of a gigantic arch, stretching from one horizon to the other. The sky had a depth to it that is never perceptible in modern urban agglomerations. The sensation of being on a tiny boat in the centre of an immense pool of shiny black water extending to the horizon all around me, with a gargantuan black dome covering the whole of my universe, impressed upon me the insignificance of the human animal in the scheme of things – and allowed me to ignore the pain of the broken ribs.

I should explain the sleeping arrangements that are *de facto* inescapable on a small boat underway in heavy seas. First, when the boat is bouncing and falling off the crest of waves, it is impossible to lie down in the forepeak berth without being airborne half the time. Under such circumstances if you insisted on persisting you would find yourself being thrown from mattress to ceiling like a ping-pong ball. You wouldn't sleep and you would get hurt. Consequently, in our case, the two boys were looking for a bed. The second limitation with regard to the available beds results from the boat's heeling angle, making one side of the boat low and the other high, with the settees on either side of the salon leaning at an angle of up to 20 degrees. The person sleeping on the low side would be comfortably snuggled up against the wall, but the person on the high side would have nothing preventing him from rolling off the settee onto the floor. This is where a leecloth comes in handy. It is simply a piece of canvas fastened under the mattress and suspended from the ceiling, acting as a "wall" to prevent the sleeper from falling out. Henri had his own dedicated berth, so the four mates effectively had to share three berths. The solution was to adopt the old naval tradition of hot bunking; that is, when one mate finishes his watch, he takes the berth, still warm, of the one replacing him.

Each crewmember has his own bed sheet and pillow, which he deploys or stows as needed.

The next morning when I awoke, I could see a glorious beam of sunshine illuminating the walls of the cabin. I climbed up the companionway and saw a blue sky overhead, splattered with puffy cumulus clouds. And suddenly, behind the boat, an enormous wave appeared, like a threatening wall of water, looking as though it might swamp the entire boat. But almost by magic, the wave gently lifted the boat like a rubber duck in a bathtub, then *Tulip One* slid gently down the watery hill, the wave passed underneath and proceeded without us. Twenty-four foot waves are a mighty impressive sight from the vantage point of the cockpit of a 40-foot boat. You might be interested to know that the height of waves is a factor of wind strength and fetch, fetch being the distance the wind has been able to blow over the water before it reaches the point being measured. On a lake there is very little fetch, but on the ocean there can be thousands of miles of fetch, generating very large waves.

"What the heck?" ...I was suddenly assaulted by a loud, aggressive, ugly, rhythmic sound, accompanied by a hoarse male voice uttering nonsensical twaddle and fatuous words, which I recognized as...horrors! – French rap! The hair-raising noise was emanating from the boat's loud speakers under the dodger. African-American rap is bad enough, but when this form of scrappy, primitive cacophony is rendered in my mother tongue it never fails to arouse my ire and to launch me into a state of hostility...Fear hit me like a ton of bricks. My mind was reeling,

"How could I cope with this for three weeks? How many hours would I be subjected to it per day? How many CDs of this garbage do the kids have with them? How could I negotiate my way out of listening to this crap? Then I thought, Darn! If only I had brought my Nat King Cole CDs, I'd have a bargaining tool!"

I hated to arrive at the inevitable conclusion, but I would just have to grin and bear it.

Vincent was of average build, had reddish blond hair with long, swept bangs, dark eyes dominating a triangular face with generous lips and a stamped-in-place smile. Of the two boys, Vincent was the leader – outgoing, confident and gregarious. Jean-Michel was the same height, but thin, perhaps for having replaced full meals with inhaled substances. His oval face wore a blondish Hitler-style moustache above a small mouth and his head was dominated by very short, almost brush-cut, pale brown hair. He was the exact opposite of his pal – quiet, focused and reclusive. As for our pretty brunette, she had been a primary school teacher, but two years ago had left that profession to care for children with mental deficiencies.

Her most astonishing characteristic was her unparalleled ability to swear. Whereas in English swear words revolve mostly around sex, in French Canada curse words comprise sacred, church objects. It is a terrible offence and it rings as being extremely rude to utter the words for tabernacle, sacred host, holy chalice, Calvary, Virgin, etc. You can add emphasis by adding the qualifier maudit (damn) to any of these words or by stringing several of these together. As in English it is considered socially unacceptable to take the name of the Son of God in vain. Marie-Madeleine's swearing could have put a Quebec construction labourer to shame. It was incongruent and quite disconcerting to hear such coarse language coming from such a pretty mouth.

The wind was shifting somewhat, veering closer towards north, placing the boat closer to a run, that is, the wind was coming more from the back than from the side, generating a potentially dangerous situation. I could see that since the wind had picked up, Marie-Madeleine was struggling with the wheel. Under heavy seas, maintaining a straight course is difficult because each wave that passes under the boat tends to make it yaw (deviate from its course). Under these circumstances the helmsman must exercise a lot of concentration to prevent an accidental gibe. A gibe happens when the boat crosses the path of the wind from the back and the mainsail swings over to the other side. In this case the wind was hitting the boat on the aft starboard quarter, roughly 35 to 40 degrees from the back, so the mainsail was way out over the port side, swung out almost as far as it could go. If the boat suddenly turns further downwind due to the action of an unexpected wave, there is a distinct danger that the wind will grab the opposite side of the mainsail and swing it and the boom hard over to the other side. When this occurs by accident it imposes a tremendous stress on the rigging, and can cause serious damage.

There is a saying in the sailing world, that when you *think* of reducing sail, then *it's time* to reduce sail. I suggested to Henri that in view of the increased wind we might be safer to take a third reef. He turned down the idea. I have to admit the captain had the support of the kids, as when I made the suggestion I got a frown from the youngsters. So I suggested that we might change course slightly upwind to make an accidental gibe less likely. That was also turned down on the grounds that this would increase our time at sea. Since I had joined the crew to be at sea, I couldn't understand what was his point.

Suddenly, KABOOM! Marie-Madeleine had a moment of distraction and failed to keep the boat on course when a large wave made the boat yaw and the mainsail gibed, causing the boom to swing violently to starboard, to the end of the main sheet. Upon inspection, we found some of the mainsail sheet blocks (pulleys) were slightly bent, but no more damage.

My night shift was in the dead of night, from 0200 to 0400. The constant movement of the boat caused the broken ends of my fractured ribs to rub together, generating sleep-robbing pain. Nevertheless, once I took my place behind the wheel, the adrenalin rush dissolved away the pain. I never felt more alive than when I was steering in heavy seas under a star-lit sky. Nights at sea hold a singular spell on me. I feel as if I'm at the confluence of the ocean and the vault of heaven, as though the firmament and the sea meet at the exact spot that my little boat occupies at the moment, as though all of what is within my view from horizon to horizon to horizon to horizon has been put there for *me*, as if I belong there, as though I'm part of it and it is part of me.

One of the amazing features of a nighttime sea is the presence of bioluminescent plankton. These are tiny organisms that give off light whenever they are stimulated by a sudden movement. They are present by the billions, and give off bluish light when disturbed by a moving fish, boat, or even a splashing hand in the water. They appear as sparkling waves on either side of the bow, or as an illuminated ring if you throw a rock in the water, or as a broadening flash if you throw a pail of water into the sea. When dolphins come to visit at night, they liven up their spectacle by leaving long trails of light in their paths.

Steering at night is a particular experience. When at sea and navigating by compass, one has to steer according to a compass heading, which is expressed as a number from 0 to 360 degrees corresponding to the compass rose. Say the navigator, in my case, Henri, has calculated that the heading to steer is 175 degrees; the helmsman then has to keep the centre line of the boat as close as possible to the 175 mark on the compass. Since we are steering for two hours at a time, it is impossible to keep our eyes riveted to the compass continuously. It would be physically and mentally too tiring and besides we have to watch for traffic and we have to make the time pleasant. The trick then is to line up the desired compass heading with the lubber line (the line on the compass representing the centre line of the boat), look ahead and line up the forestay or one of the shrouds with one of the low lying stars. As long as you keep the forestay or shroud lined up with your guiding star, you will be on the correct heading. Because of the rotation of the Earth, the stars aren't fixed, so you must take a new bearing on another star every ten minutes or so. When the sky is completely clouded over you have to look at the compass more often and use the wind on your face as your guiding instrument.

On the first and second days we had worn long johns, woollen sweaters, foul weather gear, woollen socks and rubber boots, toque and gloves. On this third day out at sea, something seemingly miraculous happened. Almost from one minute to the next, the bone chilling, damp sea wind was supplanted by warm, semitropical air. We had suddenly run into the powerful, warm current called the Gulf Stream, even though it doesn't all come from the Gulf of Mexico. Hence, we were able to divest ourselves of our heavy garb for the rest of the trip. By the way, the Gulf Stream actually takes its root with the North Equatorial Current, which starts near Africa and the Canaries, then crosses the Atlantic westward and curves northward along the chain of Caribbean islands to form the Antilles Current. This north current melds with the less important Loop Current coming from the Gulf of Mexico at the Straights of Florida to form the famous Gulf Stream that runs north along the US East Coast to then curve eastward towards Europe.

The kids were revelling in the thrill of steering in heavy seas. This was our third day and the seas were still very big, rendering the steering more demanding than ever. Since the boat was still over-canvassed (too much sail) another gibe was an accident waiting to happen. Furthermore, Henri had given nobody any coaching in steering, as if he assumed this came as a natural instinct.

It was no surprise when the first gibe of the day occurred in the hands of Jean-Michel, five minutes before the end of his watch. Steering in weather as heavy as this is hard work and by the end of one's watch, fatigue sets in, reducing one's attention. The noise from the sheet ripping two of the traveller blocks apart resonated with a ringing sound from the standing rigging. Fortunately, there were two spares of similar size, which I replaced quite easily.

Henri was angry and admonished us to be more vigilant, and rolled in a little bit of jib, still leaving too much sail exposed to the wind, in my estimation. If I had had my druthers, I would have taken that third reef. Yet, another gibe was to occur... In the afternoon, towards the end of Vincent's watch, again, a violent gibe, with the result that another block was broken and the force of the wind on the sail ripped the five top slides out of the mainsail. I wasn't able to find another replacement for the block so I had to jury-rig it to work temporarily. The damage to the sail could not be repaired with the equipment we had on board, so we risked ripping more slides out of the mainsail. Except when it came to climbing the mast, I almost always ended up carrying out the repairs since the boys weren't mechanically versed, I enjoyed the challenge and Henri was always happy to delegate the work.

It is important to mention that during the night we experienced a marked wind shift, from a broad reach to a close haul. We were now sailing against the waves, which caused delightful splashing over the deck. As the boat approached the uphill side of a wave, the bow rose above the crest, and then the boat descended the downhill side until it hit the trough. Then the bow would dig into the water and a wonderful spray of warm water would splash over us in the cockpit. Occasionally a wave would be bigger than average and instead of producing a splash, it would flop onto the deck and run down over the sides.

As an aside, there is an interesting phenomenon about waves. About every seventh wave will be significantly bigger than its sisters. It can be as much as one and a half times as large, as you discover when you're walking along the beach in your shoes, trying to keep them dry. Related to this is the less frequent occurrence of the rogue wave, also known as freak wave, monster wave, killer wave or extreme wave. Very rarely, one wave will be much larger than the others, three to five times as large as the average wave of its surroundings. The scientific explanation for this is still hotly contested. As you can imagine, a displacement of water of this magnitude, when striking a boat, can result in disaster. And disaster fell upon the boys.

Vincent was at the helm, savouring the early afternoon sun and the occasional warm splash, and he echoed the French Canadian rap blaring out of the cockpit speakers. The rest of the crew and captain were below. Henri was sleeping, Jean-Michel recovering from his seasickness, Marie-Madeleine and I preparing sandwiches for lunch. Suddenly the boat made a jarring, downward movement, we heard a staggering splash, the entire vessel shuddered as if in an earthquake, and a cascade of water came rushing down the companionway into the cabin. I charged up the stairs to find the cockpit filled with water and Vincent hanging onto the wheel, soaked like a wet cat. I looked astern just in time to see part of the dodger and the two loud speakers floating away on the wave behind the boat, rapidly disappearing in the distance! I must have been in the good graces of the Sea Gods, as a salutary rogue wave had saved me from the intolerable dissonance of French Canadian rap for the rest of the passage! The boys were almost in tears.

That night, during my watch the sky became particularly dark. Suddenly the air felt chilly. I suspected this was a sign of a coming squall. I rapped on the cockpit wall and called out to Henri to come. He immediately appeared at the companionway, went back inside to fetch his harness and climbed into the cockpit with his headlamp on. By then a very strong wind had picked up, heeling the boat more than I would have liked, even though I had eased the mainsheet to bleed off some air in the sail. He instructed me to steer the boat into the wind and he climbed onto the deck with the agility of an athlete. He lowered the sail to the third row of reefing cringles, slipped the tack grommet onto the metal reefing hook, tightened the luff, then the reefing line. I wished the autohelm had worked so I could have helped, but Henri was managing quite well without my input. By then the wind was blowing so hard that it made a deafening whistling sound in the shrouds. Then the rain came pelting down – so hard that the drops striking my face were like stinging needles. Some sailors equip themselves with goggles for this situation, a good idea. Henri came back into the cockpit as though there was nothing to it, pulled out the furling line to roll up the jib until it was scarcely the size of a beach towel. By then the boat was stable and moving quite fast considering she carried very little sail. It was obvious that this sailor had spent a lot of time at sea and had experienced stormy weather before. Within ten minutes, the excitement was over and the wind was back to its "normal" 30 to 35 knots. I asked the captain what he estimated the wind had been at its strongest and he responded that according to the intensity of the screeching, we had encountered a wind of "only" 55 knots, or 100 kilometres an hour.

The modern sailboat is equipped with a panoply of instruments and appliances that run on electricity. Although *Tulip One* was modestly equipped in comparison with her counterparts, she nevertheless had cabin lighting, a compass light, instrument lights, a bilge pump, galley and head sink pumps, navigation lights, radio and GPS that are essential for safety, not counting the unused autohelm and radar.

On *Tulip One* the refrigeration compressors were not electric, but mechanically connected to the boat's diesel engine, so the engine had to be run an hour in the morning and an hour in the evening to keep the food cold. While the engine was running, the batteries were getting recharged. Every sailing yacht has two sets of batteries: a single starting battery for the engine and a bank of two or more deep cycle batteries, called the house batteries, for running everything else. By keeping the starting battery isolated from the others you increase the chances of having power when comes the time to start the engine. There is no manual way of starting an engine this size.

As a matter of routine, every morning we performed a battery voltage test. This morning, on our fourth day, when Henri and I checked the instrument panel for the battery voltage I noted that both batteries were a little low. Henri told me not to worry and claimed that the voltage was within normal range. Then we started the engine to recharge the refrigeration and batteries.

Suddenly, a cry from Jean-Michel in the cockpit:
"Henri, the jib is coming apart, come and see!"

The jib had started to unwind itself at the top of the forestay. Its halyard (rope) had gotten untied and disappeared into the mast. First, we had to take down the sail, flake it and tie it along the lifelines.

Usually a sailboat will have one or two spare halyards in place, which can be used in such an emergency, but not *Tulip One*. Someone had to go up the mast in the bosun chair to feed the end of the halyard back onto its sheave. It is simply a matter of attaching a small weight to a length of fishing line, dropping it down the inside the mast cavity, retrieving it at the bottom, attaching the halyard to the end of the fishing line and pulling it through.

"Who wants to go up the mast?" called out Henri.

"Me!" volunteered Vincent with glee.

The problem was that we did not have any fishing line or any small diameter rope we could fish the halyard with. So Henri attached a weight directly to the end of the halyard. We took down the staysail (the smaller foresail at the front of the mast) attached its halyard to the bosun chair, wound the other end around a winch at the bottom of the mast, and Jean-Michel winched Vincent up to the top. We were at sea in six-foot waves, making it very difficult for Vincent to hold onto the mast with one hand and work with the other. Because the halyard was so stiff, the weight wasn't sufficient to overcome the friction, so it wouldn't go down the cavity in the mast. He tried and tried, to no avail, and gave up. I preferred not to volunteer, since there were other people who could take Vincent's place. Henri added more weight to the end of the halyard and climbed up the mast himself. With much effort and time, he managed to coax the halyard down to the bottom of the mast, where it was retrieved. A few minutes later, we were sailing once again, flying our full complement of sails.

Life aboard a small boat with two teenagers was a bit of a challenge. Since the captain did none of the cooking, most of the cuisine was accomplished by Marie-Madeleine and me, either separately or through a joint effort. I didn't mind cooking, since I enjoy eating. Besides, it was understood that those who didn't cook would do the dishes. One day, Jean-Michel volunteered to prepare supper. He proudly presented us with the fruit of his labour at the stove, a spartan fare of hot dogs made from boiled wieners, cold buns, mustard and ketchup. I didn't have many dishes to wash.

What I found remarkable, yet somewhat disturbing was how my young shipmates' conversations revolved around sex and marijuana. What they lacked in number of years, they made up with the measure of their social success, which was the quantity of encounters and the number of partners. Sex was simply a cold, calculated tool with which to boost their self-esteem. The closer we came to land, the more excited the conversation came about the prospect of finding a source of cannabis. They were intent on initiating me in smoking marijuana and couldn't believe that I couldn't care less whether the stuff existed or not. I do have unconventional ideas regarding the criminalization of the drug, but no desire to choke my lungs with it.

Between the daily chores, carrying out three watches per day, sleeping and making frequent repairs, there wasn't much time left to read.

Sometimes an idle moment would be punctuated by the visit from a pod of dolphins, or the landing of a stray bird, or the sight of pelagic birds diving for fish. After a few days we settled into a routine and time seemed to whiz by.

CLING CLANG THUD! CLING CLANG THUD! CLING CLANG THUD! A loud, ringing, banging, metallic noise resonated from somewhere around the mast. It was a very strange noise, unlike any I'd ever heard on a boat. Vincent, who was at the helm cried out, "The radar's broken!" We all congregated on the deck to look in disbelief at the radome.

Radome is a contraction of radar and dome for describing a radar antenna in its protective dome. The radar antenna itself is a rapidly rotating horizontal arm connected to a transmitter and a receiver, and to protect this equipment against the elements, it is encased inside a flying saucer-like container about two feet in diameter. The radome is attached to the mast near the spreaders by means of a strong bracket. Linking the radome to the radar screen inside the boat is a very substantial wiring harness, comprising about 25 separate wires. This big cable goes through the inside of the mast, runs between the deck and the salon ceiling, down behind the walls into the control panel then to the radar monitor. So you don't want to have to replace that wire if you can possibly help it.

The radome was dangling down, suspended at the end of its wiring harness, swinging wildly from side to side with the movement of the boat, banging itself senseless on the mast, its supporting bracket lost at sea. It was impossible to put it back in place without obtaining a new bracket. Henri did the only thing he could do under the circumstances. He climbed up the mast, carrying a small line with him and tied the radome solidly to the mast and spreaders. There is a lesson for me here as a sailor. When doing your walk-around the boat to carry out your daily verifications, don't just look down – look up too.

The five torn out slides at the top of the mainsail had resulted in a twelve-inch rip near the top of the sail. We could not go on another 1100 miles to Martinique with a torn sail. This is when Henri decided that we would stopover in Bermuda to have an emergency repair done. As for that little gap in the stitching of the solar protector of the jib, it had now become a large flap of loose fabric about seven feet long, menacing to rip apart. The old adage "A stitch in time saves nine", is just as true on the sea as on land.

There was another thing worrying me. The batteries were getting lower and any amount of running the engine failed to get them up to more than 12.2 volts. Normally you would expect a fully charged battery to read around 12.7 volts. This is something we'd have to look into once in Bermuda. Furthermore, each time we opened the engine compartment for our daily checks, there was more water in the engine bilge. The origin of the leak wasn't evident, but we'd have to check this out once at the dock

"Land ahoy!" Henri called out for all to hear. At the horizon, one could just make out the form of low hills. What a thrill to see land after six and a half days at sea, out of sight of land! The mood on the boat was one of jubilation.

Bermuda is a solitary British overseas territory out in the Atlantic, 560 nautical miles from Cape Hatteras, North Carolina. It consists of 138 islands occupying a surface area of only 53 square kilometres. It has a very affluent economy, with finance as its largest sector followed by tourism, giving it the world's highest GDP per capita in 2005. It enjoys a subtropical climate, making it a pleasant destination at all times of the year.

All vessels entering Bermudian waters are required to make contact with the Bermuda Harbour by radio to advise the authorities that they are approaching and to provide their estimated time of arrival. The port captain ran through a long questionnaire, which identified the minutest details of our vessel, our flag, homeport and registration number. Henri gave him the crew list and enumerated the safety equipment on board including the registration number of our Emergency Position Indicator Beacon. The port captain then advised that once we passed the St. David's lighthouse and had the spit buoys in sight, we should radio and request permission to enter St. George's harbour.

We were now within a mile of the entrance to St. George's Harbour and Henri turned on the engine and ordered the crew to roll up the jib, lower the mainsail, put the fenders and dock lines in place. He then ordered me to raise the yellow "Q" signal flag below the starboard spreader as is required when one enters any foreign port and which remains in place until the captain has cleared customs and immigration.

The island was hilly and green and fragrant and sunny and inviting. The sight of it made my heart rush.

When we arrived abreast of St. David's lighthouse Henri radioed the port. He was told to come into the harbour, but to wait, as there wasn't room at the dock for us. So while we waited, we circled around under engine power.

Marie-Madeleine went down to fetch something from the cabin and in her usual colourful language cried out, "*Maudit tabarnac de câlisse*! There's water all over the floor! And its slippery *en sacrament*!"

Leaving Vincent at the wheel, Henri went down with me in tow. There was a small amount of water swishing across the floor, with a film of diesel mixed in with it, making our footing very tenuous. We opened the engine compartment and saw a small leak at the water pump outlet hose connection. Henri said to keep an eye on the water level and that we'd deal with the problem once at the dock and not to run the bilge pump here in the harbour.

We circled around for fifteen minutes and were enjoined to dock by the Immigration office on Ordnance Island. The customs people were very friendly and whisked us through the paperwork. We then lowered the yellow flag and put up the courtesy flag of our host country. We then motored towards the town's seawall, adjacent to the park, where we could dock free of charge.

As we were approaching the wall, Henri exclaimed, "Would I ever toke a good one now!"

The expression of longing wasn't lost on the boys. In fact, their eyes illuminated. They were itching to step ashore and explore, but Henri set them straight. The first thing was to clean up the mess left by the water leak. We lifted all the diesel-impregnated floorboards, washed them with detergent and laid them out on the park lawn to dry. Next job was to pump out the diesel-contaminated water that had accumulated in the bilge. Since environmental laws prohibited us from dumping the mess into the harbour, our ever-resourceful captain had us transfer the smelly water-fuel mixture into half a dozen large plastic garbage bags and surreptitiously place them in the park's garbage bin without puncturing them. Henri said he would repair the water leak later, since as long as the engine wasn't running there wouldn't be any ingression of seawater. The next task was to remove the mainsail and flake it, ready for sending for repairs. Our boat was the object of curiosity on the part of other sailors. With half of the green band of solar protection torn and dangling, the radome hanging from a rope, the torn dodger, the missing mainsail, wet sleeping bags draped over the boom and lifelines, our vessel was a veritable mess.

The boys were finally granted leave, and off they went! To my surprise they were back ten minutes later beaming with satisfaction. Jean-Michel blurted out excitedly, "WE'VE GOT SOME, Henri!"

They jumped aboard and darted down into the cabin, Henri and Marie-Madeleine at their trail. Jean-Michel had found a Rasta who readily sold him a bag of grass. After six and a half days of abstinence, it was time to revel. I felt somewhat ill at ease about all that pot smoke wafting within a few feet of a park sidewalk in a foreign country, but there was not much I could do to dissociate myself from the crime, should a policeman decide to make a fuss about it.

Supper was followed by another pot-smoking get-together. The kids pestered me about not participating and after much pressuring, persuaded me to acquiesce. I had only had one opportunity to try marijuana before, and this was on a skiing trip with a work colleague and two schoolteachers. I inhaled and kept the smoke deep in my lungs as was prescribed, but felt no effect, to the dismay of my skiing friends.

Whatever Jean-Michel paid for his bag of nondescript grass was money utterly wasted on me. The only effects it was having was the production of an itchy throat and a dry mouth as I tried to experience a high. Nonetheless, I could see it was having an effect on the kids and particularly on Henri.

After nightfall we started to walk down a secluded road towards Blackbeard's, a bar a couple of kilometres away, that had been recommended by another sailor. Henri was becoming increasingly giddy. As we progressed, he swayed markedly and began singing like a drunken sailor. Next, I found him lying on his back reciting poetry, speaking to an unseen vision in the sky and laughing fatuously, slapping his knees. Then he rolled over several revolutions from back to belly, slaphappy. Vincent and I helped him get up and he staggered, accompanying his poetry with grandiose gestures and exaggerated intonations, like an inebriated politician pronouncing the speech of his career. By the time we reached the bar Henri was a little more subdued. After two or three drinks, he sobered up and walked back to the boat unassisted, completely alert and coherent.

First thing next morning was to take the mainsail to the sailmaker for an estimate. Henri needed authorization before he could spend any money on repairs. He phoned René, but the director of the school could not give the OK, since the Centre marin des Aventures no longer owned the boat. They had sold it to Gilbert Gindeau, a recently retired administrator who bought the boat as a business venture. Under the terms of his contract, he would rent his vessel to the school for the winter and the summer sailing seasons, take full responsibility for maintenance and repairs; the school would be responsible for delivering the boat to the appropriate sailing venue fall and spring; Gilbert would have the boat for his own pleasure six months per year and would spend a nice tax-deductible holiday down south every year. Gilbert, a novice sailor, would have very much liked to join Henri and be part of the crew to deliver his boat to Martinique. But as life surreptitiously issues hard knocks, he was the victim of a heart attack the previous summer. Under the orders of his doctor he had to refrain from the exigencies of offshore sailing. As a consolation prize, he decided to fly to Martinique to greet *Tulip One* and spend a leisurely month aboard his new sailboat before handing her over to the school for the teaching season. Authorization was granted and the sailmaker promised that the repairs would be completed in two days.

This morning we got a visit from the Harbour Master. He had noticed a film of oil on the water behind *Tulip One*, and asked Henri if he had an engine problem. My captain assumed a puzzled, innocent look and replied that everything was fine with the boat, but, on thinking it over, he claimed, he had seen an oil spill on his way in yesterday.

"The wind must have blown the oil towards the sea wall."

He didn't see any advantage in mentioning the garbage bags of diesel-contaminated water he ordered the boys to put in the waste bin the day before.

Henri gave the kids and me the day off. There is no point in stopping over in such a beautiful place as Bermuda and not seeing anything. Upon their cannabis shopping trip the previous day the boys had seen a cycle company that rented motor scooters. They had decided then and there that their goal would be to ride one of those machines since no licence was required to drive a scooter and the minimum age was sixteen.

So the four of us took off on two machines, Vincent at the helm of one with Jean-Michel as co-pilot and me at the handlebars of another with Marie-Madeleine as my passenger. Bermudians drive on the left and they need to respect a 35 km/h speed limit throughout the entire nation. This is not a terrible hardship as there's really nowhere to go on this little island. If you drove from Somerset to Hamilton you would only have covered 15 km. Vincent's aim was to remain above the speed limit as much of the time as possible, which was a challenge with a 49 cc engine. To the regret of Marie-Madeleine my driving wasn't up to that of Vincent and I fell behind the boys in the numerous, sharp curves. I never made it up in the straight stretches, forcing the boys to stop at the curb and wait for us. No sooner had I caught up with them, than they would be whizzing along again at a vertiginous 40 km/h!

Most of the island is inhabited and beautifully landscaped, with pink sand beaches everywhere you rest your eyes. There are no favellas, no beggars, no itinerant jewellery salesmen, no bums pushing their services as "guides". The only drawback is that everything is very expensive. The average price of a house, should you entertain the notion of emigrating there, is just under a million dollars.

On our third day in Bermuda, to the displeasure of the boys, the captain ordered a complete cleanup of the boat interior, washing of the deck and reprovisioning at a local farmer's market. While the crew was slaving away, Henri went to Customs and Immigration to clear us out for the next day. We would then have 24 hours to leave the country.

I happened to lift my eyes from a stubborn spot I was scrubbing away at on the deck when I discerned Henri in the distance, accompanied by a woman and a man. The woman was gesticulating like a typical Frenchwoman trying to make a point…"Well I'll be damned!" That was my reaction when it dawned upon me who the couple was. It's indeed a small sailing world. It was no other than Catherine and Alexandre. They were on their annual pilgrimage to the warm waters of the south and had planned to stopover in beautiful Bermuda to break up the long passage to the Caribbean. They were clearing in when this man with an earring, tattoos and long hair was enumerating the names of his crew and called out the name Robert Bériault. Catherine picked up on this familiar name and asked the tattooed man if this Robert was from Ottawa and "Yes" and then "He must be the one I know. Where's your boat?"

She bore her customary corner-of-the-lips smile when she greeted me at the boat. When in a foreign country, far from home, it is always a thrill to meet a compatriot by happenstance. So it was with mixed feelings that I returned her greeting with the traditional double cheek kiss. We exchanged on our respective destinations and plans. She asked me when we had left and I told her October 28th.

"Nobody was leaving Halifax until three days later. Do you mean to say you sailed through those 35 knot winds?"

Her look was drawn to different parts of our boat, her eyes narrowed and turned into a frown.

"Now I see...But you can't sail to Martinique in this!" she said, motioning to the boat with both hands palms up.

I shrugged and glanced sideways toward the captain. She went on to lecturing our hapless captain at machine gun speed like a drill captain in the Foreign Legion,

"Mon Dieu! Look at that U-V protector! If you don't repair that before leaving, you're going to rip the whole sail to shreds."

She poised her index finger on Henri's chest, motioned to the forestay, then her finger went poke poke poke on the chest and she exclaimed, "Look at the curvature in that forestay. Every movement of the boat causes the forestay to bounce, putting a strain on the sheave at the top of the mast. If you don't take up the slack, you'll find the whole forestay, foil and sail in the water. It will *never* make it to Martinique."

Then, looking at the radome dangling under the spreaders like a big, fat piñata waiting to be struck down, she went, "Oh la la! And that radar antenna. It would be catastrophic if it fell on one of your crew. And if it fell overboard, it would be very expensive to replace a radome like that."

I was tempted to ask her what she would advise us to do about our run down batteries, but thought the better of it. I didn't want to antagonize my captain any more than necessary. Catherine's greatest asset is her knowledge of sailboats. She can be of great help to any sailor who has the patience and I should even say, the wisdom, to listen to her.

Her advice didn't fall on deaf ears. After she left, Henri began attending to the deficiencies Catherine pointed out, but in his very special way. First, he attacked the solar protector. Instead of sending the jib to the sailmaker to have it repaired, he took out his pocketknife and cut off the pieces that were dangling then ordered us to finish removing the solar protector completely with a seam ripper. Once that was taken care of, he gathered a few tools and began the task of taking up the slack in the forestay. I wasn't of much help since I wasn't familiar with the mechanics of a furler, the drum that serves to roll up the sail. When he was done, he rubbed his hands together with satisfaction, but if you had given me the waterboard treatment, I couldn't have shown you any difference in the curvature of the forestay. Then the good captain tackled the radome. He got one of the boys to winch him up to the spreaders, he tied a second rope to the unit. I didn't know what he had in mind, but then to my horror, he took a large pair of cutting pliers, severed that expensive wiring harness, then lowered the radome down to the deck.

I was very concerned with the low voltage of the batteries. Both the starting battery and the house batteries were around 11.8 to 12 volts, which indicated that they were almost discharged. Henri insisted that this was normal and not to worry. I had to find a way to prove to him that we had a problem that needed to be addressed. So I went to the nearest "petrol station" and borrowed a hygrometer. This is an apparatus that measures the specific gravity of the battery acid. A fully charged battery shows a specific gravity of 1.265 and a fully discharged one 1.11. Fortunately, I didn't have to remember these figures because the hygrometer was graduated in idiot-proof colours, green, yellow and red. Even if you know nothing about batteries, you can guess what red means. I was now able to prove to Henri that all the batteries were discharged.

His riposte was, "Robert, you're worrying too much, remember that we're not connected to shore power and we've been using the cabin lights every night."

Whenever we prepare to cast off for the open sea, there is in the air a feeling of welcome apprehension, of feverish elation, of an unfolding drama. This time, though, I was calling into question the whole idea of taking part in the second leg of the trip. Catherine was certainly right to be concerned about the sagging forestay. And now the charging system wasn't working. It was very imprudent, to put it mildly, to set out to sea without lights, radio, refrigeration, nor even GPS since ours worked directly off the boat's house battery. Should I put in effect my Plan B, and abandon ship? Then I thought of the kids and the perilous situation they might find themselves in and that it might be safer for them to have another adult with some sort of experience along the trip. Then I thought, "Robert, you're worrying for nothing. With a discharged battery the engine won't start and Henri will have to face the music."

My decision was made. I would stay on for the rest of the trip. I watched with suspense as Henri put the key in the starter switch. I crossed my fingers with tense expectation. He turned the key and to my surprise…vroom!

We were sailing outside the channel entrance with a wonderful, fifteen-knot wind behind us. My resignation had turned into qualified enthusiasm. There's nothing like being at sea on a sunny day in a brisk tail wind to lift one's spirits. I could tell that in the distance the sea had formed and that it would not be smooth sailing. Within ten minutes we were already into heavy swell. Marie-Madeleine went below for a visit to the head, but readily cried out, "*Maudit tabarnac*, There's water in the *câlisse de* boat again!"

Henri was busy taking bearings in the cockpit and asked me to check below. There was about an inch of diesel-impregnated water sloshing about above the floorboards. The boat was bashing around wildly, making it impossible to get a secure footing on the slimy floor, let alone open the engine compartment, locate the source of the leak and carry out a repair. It was obvious this was the same leak that Henri had purportedly fixed while we were on our scooter excursion. I called up to him, "Henri, we'll have to turn around!"

That wasn't well received by my captain. After all, crewmembers don't make decisions of that sort. The boys, having spent a good hour scrubbing the floorboards on terra firma, were interested in assessing the situation for themselves. They both shared my opinion. Henri responded, "Well, get on with it, run the manual bilge pump."

Yes, it was necessary to pump, but it was even more important to settle the problem and this could only be done at port. He was intent on continuing. So I was left no choice but to adopt the ultimate measure. I went up into the cockpit, stared Henri in the eye and said, "Henri, I'm not going on this trip with you. Take me back to Bermuda."

This he understood and reluctantly gave the command to head up into the wind for the return. We had to beat back to weather and Jean-Michel was having trouble keeping the boat close hauled, having had little experience with this point of sail against a strong wind and a short chop. Seeing that Jean-Michel was making little headway, the captain put Vincent at the helm. Regrettably, our sailing dinghy expert couldn't master steering a keelboat under these conditions either. When the wind is gusting the trick is to head up a little with each gust just enough so as to not lose speed, and when the gust subsides to bear away just enough not to lose what was gained. Henri got impatient and yelled, "Doesn't anybody on this boat know how to steer?"

Since I wanted to reach dry land as soon as possible, I volunteered to take the boat back to the harbour. Maybe Henri had felt uncomfortable asking me anything after our confrontation.

Two hours later, we were back at the public dock. It was déjà vu with the cleaning of the floorboards. While the kids toiled away with detergent and brushes and garbage bags of contaminated bilge water, Henri and I turned our attention to dealing with the unwanted influx of water. With the engine running, we examined each hose connection. It wasn't for naught, as we found three that were loose, one of which was leaking profusely. The hose clamp of the seawater intake hose was also loose, a mortal sin on a sailboat. It was just a matter of time before it popped off and sank the boat. It would appear that when des Aventures put the overhauled engine back in place they forgot to tighten some of the hose clamps. By then everybody was tuckered out, so Henri decided that we would delay the departure till the following day.

The next morning was like the movie Groundhog Day, where Phil repeats every movement of the previous 24 hours. Henri took the key out of his pocket. Again, I watched with bated breath as he introduced the key into the starter keyhole. Ditto for crossing my fingers with tense expectation. He turned the key and...CLICK, turned again and...CLICK. My wish was fulfilled.

His face drew a blank expression. Then a gleam of inspiration lit up his eyes as if he had just had a eureka moment. He scuttled down into the cabin and emerged with tools in hand. He promptly started dismantling the engine starter switch.

It then dawned upon me what he was up to. As with other sailboats I've seen, the engine control panel is stupidly located on the cockpit wall about 6 to 8 inches above the floor. So when that rogue wave filled up the cockpit with seawater some of the salt water seeped into the electronics behind the panel. This would inevitably result in corrosion around the wire terminals. A simple cleaning with sandpaper would cure the problem. But you can't start an engine with a dead battery.

While Henri sanded the switch terminals, I cleaned their corresponding wires and in no time the switch was put back into place, like new. The moment of truth had arrived. Henri would have to come to grips with the root of the problem – a defective charging system – and we would have to call in a qualified marine mechanic to resolve the issue. Once again, Henri fished the key out of his pocket, reintroduced it in the starter switch. We were all watching his hand in anticipation as he poised his fingers on the key, at the ready. He turned the key and, to my dismay, the engine slowly turned over one single turn and… vroom!

"If we're lucky," I thought, "we'll run the engine a couple of hours and maybe have enough charge to start it again tomorrow for the refrigeration and batteries."

We had been sailing for half an hour with the engine running, when Henri rose from his perch at the transom, heading for the companionway. Instead of going down into the cabin, he bent over and to my disbelief, switched off the engine! A simple calculation would have told him to run the engine at least two hours before switching it off. I was flabbergasted, but didn't say anything, since it was *fait accompli* and we'd just have to wait until tomorrow to see if the engine would start. I recommended to Henri that we sail without our running lights at night because the batteries were so low. He acquiesced to engaging in this illegal manoeuvre.

The next morning when came time to start the engine, as I had suspected, it wouldn't even kick over once. We were already 75 miles out at sea, downwind from the closest land, Bermuda, so we were committed to our projected destination. Eight to ten days. So when everybody was in the cockpit I opened the discussion about our predicament.

We were already outside of VHF radio range from land, so it wouldn't be much of a problem to be out a radio, except that in case of emergency, we wouldn't have the benefit of another ship hearing and relaying a distress message. As for our extinct running lights, we could still see any ship that had its lights on, so it would be a matter of staying alert for other boats and keeping our distances. We would just have to hope there wasn't another boat without lights in our path. We could do without cabin lights if we all used our flashlights or headlamps. The electric fresh water pump for the sink could be supplanted by the foot pump. The crucial things we had to save power for would be the compass light for night navigation and the GPS for determining our position at least once a day. The other serious problem was that of refrigeration. If we transferred all our frozen meat into the refrigerator, the combined cold mass would extend the time it remained cold for another 48 hours. After that, all the frozen food would become fodder for the sharks.

We thus embarked upon a rationing program unlike anything I had ever experienced. On our fourth day out, just before dumping the last of the smelly meat, I cooked the beef roast well done and we enjoyed the last of the fresh meat. We had saved the pepperoni and sausages for the post-refrigeration period, the eggs could be kept without refrigeration, we could use powdered milk and feed the soured stuff to the plankton. We were well on the way to survival. Many of the vegetables that had survived till now were not long for this world, but carrots, potatoes, onions and cabbage would last for the duration of the trip.

I got an idea. We had a 35-watt solar panel that didn't seem to be doing anything, even after four days. Since the batteries had not picked up any charge in all this time, my plan was to disconnect the starting battery from the rest of the boat wiring, connect the solar panel directly to the battery's terminals and charge it during daylight hours. At night we would disconnect it in case the diode that keeps it from discharging in the dark was defective. We would get maybe five effective hours of charging per day, and within a few days we'd be able to start the engine. Henri endorsed this plan and I put it in motion. Alas, even by our last day at sea the battery still hadn't gained any power.

It was noon when I finished my solar panel bypass and suddenly, everything went quiet and there was a strange feeling in the air. Henri called out, "Come and see this!" The sails were limp as a boned fish, as the wind had deserted us altogether. *Tulip One* just sat there, immobile in the middle of the great blue sea, rocking gently in the slight swell. And he asked, "Anybody want to go swimming?" to which there was unanimous assent.

He threw the life ring in the water, trailing behind the boat with its fifteen meters of floating line, to act as a lifeline in case a swimmer couldn't catch up with the drifting boat. Bathing in the pristine blue water of the world's largest swimming pool was a thrilling novelty. The boys practiced diving off the top of the pulpit railing. The thought of a Great White shark nibbling at my limbs came to mind, but recalling a statistic set me at ease: The National Geographic had published an article about shark attacks. Each year around the world there are about 50 to 70 confirmed shark attacks resulting in 5 to 15 fatalities. If you consider that hundreds of millions of people swim in the ocean every year, the chances of being on the menu of a man-eating shark are of the order of being struck by lighting or winning the lottery.

Without an engine, our only option was to wait for the wind to return. In the meantime, Henri pulled out the boat's sextant from the bottom of a cupboard and set himself up in the cockpit for taking a sun sight. By reading the precise angle of the sun to the horizon at noon sharp, Henri could calculate the boat's exact latitude, which is useful, but doesn't give the exact position on a chart. To calculate the intersecting coordinate, the longitude, one needs the Nautical Almanac, a book of tables published yearly, that gives the corrections for every hour of every day of the year. *Tulip One* didn't have a copy on board, so our sextant would be of only limited use should there not be enough battery power to run the GPS. Three hours later a breeze came up and we were back in business.

Henri and I were alone in the cockpit and as is often the case on a long passage, each of us was lost in his respective thoughts. After a long period of silence, I asked Henri how he liked his job. He had done this type of delivery every year for the past two decades for different organizations and it was not unusual for him to be given totally inexperienced people as crew. He was satisfied with his crew and even enjoyed the boys' vivacity and enthusiasm. He confided that this particular experience with des Aventures had not been a good one. He did not get paid for the time that the boat was held up in Rivière du Loup for the engine overhaul and he had expected the school to cover his return trip home, which it refused to do. He claimed that when he calculated all the hours he had spent on this delivery his salary came to barely one dollar an hour.

It was our seventh day at sea. The day after tomorrow at daybreak, the upper portions of the Martinique mountains should come into view like an indistinct row of bumps on the horizon. We had managed so far without power and weren't any the worse for it – except that last night, the compass light was very dim and Marie-Madeleine who had the 0400 to 0600 shift found it very difficult to see her compass heading. I embarked upon another project that day, and rigged up a flashlight above the compass so it could be easily turned on at will. On the last two nights of the passage there wasn't enough power in the house batteries to run the compass light, so we steered by flashlight and the stars.

Just as I was returning to the cabin to put away my tools, we all heard a clanging and crashing sound and a scream from the kids in the cockpit, *"Maudit, tabarnak!* The jib is in the water!"

Henri and I ran up the companionway to take stock of this new disaster. Not only was the sail dragging in the water, but also the entire forestay and foil. After all these days of bouncing and twisting, the sheave that held up the forestay worked itself loose and managed to pop out of the top of the mast. At that point all the forces of the forestay and the jib were on the halyard, causing it to chafe and sever on the sharp top edge of the mast, thus sending the whole shebang into the sea. Just as Catherine had predicted. We were lucky that the boat was rigged as a cutter, as the baby stay prevented the mast from falling. We struggled to retrieve the wet sail, roll it up around the foil and stow it on board. This job was especially challenging because the forestay and foil unit was ten feet longer than the boat itself and protruded a long way behind the pushpit. It was an unusual sight indeed. We sailed the last two days to destination with staysail and mainsail alone.

For millennia the human seafaring creature has been venturing on the earth's oceans. *"Terre!"* or *"Land ahoy!"* These simple words have stirred the seaman's passion when making landfall after a protracted term out of sight of land.

Henri was the first to perceive the faint outline of a landmass through forty miles of hazy atmosphere. Even though the sun had just risen, everybody was in the cockpit to savour the moment. Save for Henri, this trip was the first time that any of us had ever sailed offshore, hundreds of miles from land. It was the first time we had ever been underway for so long. None of us had ever steered a 16,000-pound boat in 24-foot waves. For fifteen days, we had shared bunks, drank and ate together, shared hardships, met adversity, overcame crises and enjoyed the delights of nights, days, wind, spray, visiting birds and dolphins. In spite of our differences in age and culture, we shared a common bond through the experiences we had lived together.

I reconnected the starting battery and made a last, but unfruitful attempt at starting the engine. Consequently, we would have to sail into Le Marin harbour instead of going in under engine power and we would have to anchor under sail. Le Marin is a large harbour, well protected from wind and swell. The docks can hold 660 boats and over a hundred were anchored in the bay. Henri knew Le Marin Bay like the back of his hand, as he had spent many winters there. For the first time since leaving Halifax Henri took the helm and the crew actually had to work the sails. We executed several short tacks to navigate the channel between the reefs on either side, avoid the islands in the bay and find a suitable spot for anchoring.

By happenstance, we arrived while one of Martinique's famous Yole races was underway. The most unseaworthy open boats imaginable are equipped with huge sails and are manned by more people that they can safely hold. All of the crewmembers except those mandated to bail hang on to long poles that protrude from the windward side to miraculously prevent their craft from capsizing.

"Mouillez l'ancre!" (Drop the anchor) are the final words that marked the end of the sailing adventure.

Now for the first time, we were to inflate the dinghy. It was red, with grey and green patches that had been used for mending numerous holes. Flaps of rubber that held the transom had been stuck in place with duct tape. The floorboards, once we solved the puzzle for assembling them, would work themselves loose and create a hazard to anyone bold enough to stand up. We found out that it had to be re-inflated every half hour. The connections between the transom and the rubber pontoons was so tenuous that I thought the back of the boat would cave in with the force of the 4 horse power motor, but my fear didn't pan out.

We would spend a few hours cleaning *Tulip One* and sleep one last night aboard before handing her over to her owner. Now I needed to reserve a hotel room in Le Marin for the following night, rent a car for the following week and buy an airline ticket for my return home. At last, I discovered why Henri pushed the boat so hard to make time. He had reserved his airline ticket months in advance, and his departure date was in two days.

The next day Gilbert arrived and came aboard with a worried expression on his face. We exchanged greetings, and Henri drove the kids and me and our baggage to shore in two trips. I looked back at poor *Tulip One*, and felt a twinge of nostalgia for not only had she been my home for the past three weeks, she had been my transportation and my school, as I did learn a lot while in her presence. I was saddened and somewhat embarrassed that we were handing her over to her owner in such a dismal state. Poor Gilbert, he thought he would be spending a month of leisure on his new boat but instead, would need to spend every minute of it scrambling for parts and seeing to the repairs before handing her over to the school as dictated his contract.

Henri had told us that Gilbert was financially strapped because the partner with whom he had bought the boat backed out of the deal at the last minute, leaving Gilbert holding the bag, financially speaking. Just as bad as missing his holiday, the new owner would be out of pocket by about $10,000 to bring the boat up to snuff. Thus Gilbert would not be a happy camper under these unexpected circumstances.

The kids found themselves a suitable drug dealer and took off hitchhiking with their tents. We had agreed that after we'd settled into our regular lives we would meet for a meal in Montreal. I was happy to be totally on my own to enjoy peace and quiet after three weeks of forced togetherness.

One of the virtues of Martinique is that it is part of France. In 1946, the French government transformed this island from a colony into a department. Restaurants in Martinique are either Créole, French or a delightful combination of the two styles. A tourist brochure boasts that Martinique's capital city Fort de France is backed by luxuriant hills while it oversees a yacht-filled harbour. It claims that the town, with its bustling streets shaded by overhanging balconies, is picturesque. For me, the capital had little appeal. I hate to be negative, but I found it run down, filthy, noisy, smelly and hot. In fact, I couldn't escape fast enough! Fortunately, the rest of the island was quite the opposite.

Martinique is 83 km long from top to bottom. As I was to discover, the island is rich with contrasts. The southern areas are more or less dry and flat with magnificent golden sand beaches. There are charming fishing villages and commercial developments, tiny guesthouses and large, upscale resorts. The northern part of the island features dense rain forest, mountain peaks and dark, volcanic sand beaches.

Driving was the best way to discover this little part of France. It is the lush vegetation of the "Island of Flowers" that makes it so beautiful. Hibiscus, frangipani, bougainvillea, anthuriums, poinsettias, orchids as well as exotic hardwoods are found throughout the island. There are rich plantations of guava, mango and papaya as well as bananas, pineapple, sugarcane, cinnamon and coffee. In the tropical rainforests of Martinique, ferns grow as tall as trees and green comes in a hundred different shades. Every island in the Caribbean claims to have the best rum, so it's normal that Martinique too lays claim to its superiority in this field.

Of particular interest in the northern part is Mont Pelée, a volcano that erupted in 1902, killing 30,000 persons in the west coast town of St-Pierre. Today it is dormant and a popular tourist attraction for those who have the agility and stamina to climb it to the summit. During the two days I was in the vicinity the mountain was cloud-covered. On the second day, on the chance that it might clear up I started the ascension. The lower part of the mountain was rich in tropical vegetation. It wasn't long before I was enveloped in cloud. The moss-covered rocks were dripping with moisture, making the handholds and footholds tricky. After an hour of climbing and seeing nothing, I took the decision to abandon the trek and to be content with buying postcards.

As I was waiting for my flight at the Fort-de-France International Airport, I pondered the events of the past weeks. I was returning home with answers to the two questions that had prompted this trip. I was terribly seasick on the first day. But after five days on land in Bermuda I wasn't sick at all when I returned to sea for the second time. It would appear that I have a good chance of acquiring my sea legs. As for being out of sight of land for protracted periods, I was able to adapt to a routine and found the experience agreeable. There were many exciting moments, some of them resulting from unnecessary risks. It was an unparalleled learning experience, even if it was very much based on the teaching theory of what not to do. This trip gave me the opportunity to visit two beautiful islands to which I would like to return. All in all, *Tulip One* had given me much more than I had bargained for – in more ways than one.

To top it all off, once I got back home *Tulip One* was to provide me with the shock of my sailing life.

As always when returning home from a trip abroad, I rejoice for the advantages of beautiful Greater Ottawa, the familiarity of spoken Canadian

French, the safety of the streets and the lack of corruption, the comfort of a loving family and the smell of my home.

I phoned Marie-Madeleine, as planned, to organize a post-trip get-together. She was her cheerful self, except that she paused and asked me, with a grave tone in her voice, "Have you heard about *Tulip One*?"

"No, what about her?"

"You don't know about the explosion?"

"What are you talking about, Marie-Madeleine?"

"Well it seems that while Gilbert was alone working on the boat at anchor in Le Marin Bay, there was a terrible propane gas explosion. *Tulip One* caught fire and the flames consumed the whole boat. Apparently there were only the metal rigging and the engine left in the bottom of the water."

My heart sank to the floor! The first thought that came to my mind was how lucky we were that the accident didn't happen a few days earlier when we were still at sea. There is no worse disaster at sea than an explosion followed by a fire. If the detonation doesn't kill you outright and the conflagration doesn't bake you on the spot, then how much time would you have, if any, to deploy the liferaft and get hold of the grab bag? There wouldn't even be time to put out a Mayday call on the VHF radio.

I was trembling and stammering, I asked, "What about Gilbert?"

"They say that Gilbert swam to a neighbouring boat and was unhurt. Poor guy. Thank goodness he had the boat insured."

&&&&&&&

The sudden rattling and rumbling of an anchor chain being loudly lowered startled me and tore me out of my daydream. I was a little jittery after my life-threatening boarding experience. A Beneteau 400 had quietly snuck into Bahía la Mar and was gearing up to become a nearby neighbour of *Ventus*. The husband and wife team noisily went about the business of anchoring their boat. After discretely observing their actions for a few minutes I drifted back in reflection and recalled a brush with death of another kind...

Hairless but not dead ↓

My Georgian Bay crewmembers

Chapter 5

A Brush With Death of Another Kind

April 2001

The nurse started my intravenous and made sure I was comfortable. The hustle and bustle of the hospital personnel, the comings and goings of patients, the conversations between patients in their recliner chairs with their intravenous drips, the volunteers passing around cookies and beverages every ten minutes, all contributed to a poor ambiance for reading.

Being treated for cancer makes one appreciate the fragility of life. My oncologist reassured me that if I were to choose a form of cancer, Non-Hodgkin's Lymphoma was the best in the way of response to treatment and prognosis.

Unable to concentrate on my reading, I retrieved the pamphlet I had slipped into the back cover of my book. It was from Advantage Boating, a description of an Instructor Clinic that was to take place in May, two months down the road: A two-weekend course to become a CYA Basic Cruising Standard instructor.

In 1958 when I opted out of high school there were two career choices that tempted me: Research or teaching. I applied for a job as technician. I was 17 when I got a call from the personnel department of Canada Agriculture:

"Would you like to work in a laboratory with animals?"

This was the nineteen fifties, in the throes of the baby boom, before globalization madness, before Canada exported her industrial and manufacturing jobs overseas, when a degree was an unnecessary luxury and employers grabbed 17 year-old kids off the street to train them on the spot.

I accepted this job as an interim solution while I qualified for entering Normal School, the college that trained teachers in Ottawa. However, the job turned out to be interesting and to offer chances of advancement for anyone willing to work and continue their education. Eventually I got promoted to Chief Technician and later to Laboratory Manager for a large biotechnology lab with the University of Montreal and later with the University of Guelph. I didn't have a teaching position, but I was often called upon to teach various techniques or procedures to technicians, graduate students or visiting scientists. This was a challenge I enjoyed and took seriously. I would sometimes sit and think what words to use in trying to explain to someone how to detect and determine the stage of a *corpus luteum* or an ovarian follicle by rectal palpation or how to pass an embryo transfer pipette through a cow's cervix. I always found it satisfying when my students' faces illuminated upon succeeding.

After I took retirement there were no more opportunities to teach, except after I had reached the stage that I knew more about sailing than my crew. Once I qualified as captain for NCSS, I found that whenever I had a new member with me I automatically assumed the role of teacher. One of the marvellous things about sailing is that it is a continual learning opportunity, as you can never reach the stage of knowing everything. That's why I had kept this pamphlet about the Instructor Clinic and now I was ready to register for the course.

There were prerequisites I had to obtain before the clinic took place. First and foremost, a good instructor must avoid running aground or bumping into other ships. So a good knowledge of the Collision Regulations is at the top of the list. Even though there are no large commercial ships plying the waters of Lac Deschênes, the CYA instructor qualification assumes that we will teach anywhere in Canada, so we had to learn the lights and day shapes that characterize every type and size of vessel. The importance of this can be illustrated by the story of a tragic accident that took place near Vancouver at the 1999 Symphony of Fire Festival. Hundreds of boaters were in English Bay jockeying for position to watch the fireworks show. The captain of *Sunboy*, a 40-foot cabin cruiser with 14 people on board didn't recognize the light pattern on a tugboat with a tow, which is different from that of a tugboat without a tow. His boat flipped over after becoming snared by the underwater cable connecting the towboat to its barge, and five people drowned as a result. As is often the case, there was another factor contributing to the accident. The tugboat captain had replaced a defective sidelight with a temporary lantern that was visible over the distance of only a quarter mile instead of the regulation 3 miles.

It's preferable that an instructor knows what he's talking about, otherwise he might get caught too often in a lie. So to test our knowledge we had to rewrite the Basic Cruising Standard test and the Coastal Navigation test in half the normal time with a 95% mark.

Once these preliminaries were out of the way, five of the NCSS skippers including myself attended the clinic, which consisted of classroom, dockside and on-the-water demonstrations. Since the instructor could quite conceivably need to sail the boat unassisted, he must show that he is capable of single-handed sailing. This was the last item on the last day of the clinic. I was quite nervous and felt a little out of sorts, having had a chemo treatment a few days before. I made a complete fool of myself, having made every mistake not in the book, so I asked to be retested at a later date.

So when the time was appropriate, Kim, my Instructor Evaluator, took me out for my single-handed test. I made a terrible mess of my man overboard recovery technique and was sure she was going to send me home to see my mother, when at the end, she asked, "Would you be available for a class next week?" I embarrassedly acquiesced, thinking that she wanted to give me private remedial instruction. What a relief and a joy when I realized that I had passed and she was offering me to teach a class the following week!

The previous month my surgeon had broken the bad news. The biopsy from the enlarged lymph node she had excised from my underarm showed the presence of cancerous cells. The CT scan revealed adenopathies in both the abdominal and the chest cavities, which, on a one to four scale, placed my cancer at a stage III, making me a candidate for chemotherapy. I was very lucky my family doctor referred me to a surgeon in such short time and had me promptly scheduled for a scan. I was also thankful that I had one of the best oncologists in the area, a 71-year-old doctor who would be retiring in a year – and to live in a country with a public health system. I never had to spend one cent for all the tests and treatments that I underwent.

Being struck with cancer is in a roundabout way the same as being passenger in an airliner. The captain is the one who knows how to fly the aircraft. He has seen many different weather conditions, landing strips with sheer cliffs on either side, and with open water at both ends, and he's dealt with wind shear and deicing and mechanical problems. He knows which protocol to apply in which circumstance. Likewise, the oncologist is the one who knows how to treat cancer. He has seen many different types of the affliction, has dealt with many different patients, and he knows which protocol to apply in which circumstance. When you're a passenger in a plane, you put your life in the hands of the captain, knowing that you have a better than even chance of making it alive to destination. Likewise, when you're a cancer patient you entrust your life to the wisdom and know-how of your doctor, confident that you have a good chance of making it alive when your treatment is over. One does what one must do in the circumstances. In the airplane you sit back, relax, and maybe have another stiff drink. In the oncology treatment centre, you sit back, relax and maybe have another Styrofoam cup of juice proffered by the patient services volunteer.

I adopted the approach to teaching that my intermediate instructor, Warren had used in the BVIs. He perched himself in a pushpit seat to signify that he would not be doing the sailing but would let the students learn by *doing*. I decided that I would commandeer the tiller only if the student at the helm was putting us on an imminent collision course. I have my students repeat a procedure until they get it right. I created my own flip charts and cue cards to illustrate difficult concepts. I treat my students with respect and I try to work within their limits. I try not to take anything for granted and not assume that they can read my mind.

An important aspect of learning to sail is to learn the ability to communicate between captain, helmsman and crew. The one ability that has made the human species so successful in spite of its small teeth, quasi absence of claws and its slow, naked body is its unique ability to use language. Mariners have for centuries known the importance of language for the collaborative operation of a boat. Out of this necessity was born an elaborate vocabulary specific to boating. It is for avoiding confusion, for instance, that ropes on a boat are named according to their function; for example, a halyard is used for raising and lowering a sail, and we have sheets, outhauls, reefing lines, and others.

I try to show my students that sailing is fun, even the learning part. No sailing course is complete without laughter and good-natured banter. I would work hard at making my students succeed, not at making them fail. The challenge I relish most is finding the right combination of words to explain a difficult concept, like how the wind affects the boat or how to steer. Teaching is the process of transferring knowledge from one brain to another, either through action, symbols or words. It is indeed one of mankind's most remarkable qualities.

I had read stories of chemo patients suffering from thrush, bleeding mouth lesions, abdominal cramps, constipation, numbness or tingling of fingers and toes, jaw pain or double vision, sore, red, hot, dry and itchy skin, red sores on hands and feet and nausea for days on end. Perhaps it was my constitution or my outlook on life, I'll never know, but most of those common side effects passed me by. I lost all of my hair within the first 14 days, but that doesn't hurt (I concede that it might be distressing for a woman). For 24 hours after a treatment I felt a little nauseous, but that went away when I quit taking the anti-nausea drug! I felt generally tired and listless for three or four days after a treatment. Throughout the whole ordeal water tasted like liquid metal, as did any other liquid and all food tasted bland. There was no pleasure or satisfaction in drinking or eating. And, as you would guess, happy hour consisted of fruit juice. But for the other 27 days of the month, I was reasonably fit. Since chemotherapy wasn't so intolerable I decided that I wouldn't let my health condition prevent me from enjoying life.

That year, when Gaëtan called me to organize our annual white water canoe trip, I had to abstain. I wasn't up to the hard paddling and portaging. But Gaëtan, as resourceful as ever, suggested that we all go sailing in Georgian Bay instead. This would be my first time bareboating, that is renting a boat without a captain and I eagerly embraced the challenge.

Amongst our crew was his partner Denise, a music teacher, his brother-in-law Denis, an electronics engineer who is also a competent sailor, Charles, a litigation lawyer who enjoys any new challenge and Georges, a councillor for the City of Ottawa, a man who was used to navigating stormy waters in the figurative sense. With my 59 years I was a decade older than any member of my crew, but none of them held that against me.

To mitigate any difficulties resulting from my health problem, we planned the trip for the week before a chemo treatment, so I would have sufficient time to recover from the previous course of treatments.

Citadel II, our C&C 38 sloop, was fully provisioned and I had completed my briefing with Ken, the owner of the Yacht Charter company in Gore Bay. As is usual for a sailor renting a boat for the first time, Ken took me out for a short trial run. No sooner had we left the dock than he told me to head back, satisfied that I hadn't just invented the sailing résumé I had sent him with the cheque. The weather forecast was for two-metre waves and winds gusting to 33 knots. As these were borderline conditions for me, I decided to consult some good old local knowledge and asked Ken his opinion and he responded, "The weather report refers to the main bay, not the North Channel. Go out there and have fun."

As we were sailing out of the bay, one motor yacht after another was scooting in, to escape conditions that sailors ardently pursue. And Ken was right, the wind was more like 20 to 23 knots and waves only one metre. We sailed the 10 miles across the North Channel and the swells failed to claim any victims to seasickness. We tucked the boat in a little cove behind Beardrop Island. We dropped the anchor away from shore and tied a line from the transom to a large boulder on shore. It was 2045 by the time we'd finished our more complex than usual anchoring procedure.

Our first supper was supplied by Denis, who had created a five-course Tunisian dinner starting with Omek Houria (carrot salad) followed by Chackchouka (vegetable and egg dish), Hlalem bil Lahn (pasta with chickpeas and lamb), merguez (sausage) and couscous. Our technical genius selected a red Zinfandel as an accompaniment and completed the meal with a mouth-watering baklava and a very sweet tea served from a silver teapot in tiny glasses, all of which he brought from home for the single occasion.

To give you an idea of our pace, it was 1138 by the time we weighed anchor the next morning. It was a beautiful day with a clear blue sky. Our destination was the most popular anchorage in the area, the Benjamins, a group of islands forming a circle. There are two ways into Fox Harbour, an easy one and a tricky one known as "The back door". It consists of a long, narrow opening between weather smoothened rocky shores that slope steeply into the water. I placed Gaëtan at the bow and asked him to "point the way for me". I turned the engine to idle speed, moving at barely one knot. I thought I was too close to the starboard side, but immediately Gaëtan pointed to the right. So I steered the boat closer to the shore and as my guide spun around to tell me something, the boat lurched upwards, heeled over to the port and a loud, scraping sound confirmed that the keel was passing over a smooth rock. After the event, I realized that Gaëtan thought I wanted him to show me the position of underwater obstacles whereas I thought he was telling me which direction to steer. Another lesson here. Fortunately, there was no damage, as the keel was made of bare solid steel and our speed was next to nil.

Instead of displaying the white granite seen elsewhere in the North Channel, the Benjamin islands are made from huge, water-smoothened pink granite rock. On the south island one of these rocks rises gradually from the water forming a smooth hill nearly 200 feet high. We climbed to the top of a smaller hill about 50 feet in height and looking down a cliff on the other side, almost directly below us we saw four kayaks paddling into a little bay, with their paddlers waving at us. The sun shone on them, casting their shadows onto the sandy bottom. The water beneath them was so transparent and so calm that they appeared to be floating in mid air.

On a typical day we would weigh anchor after a leisurely breakfast, stop for lunch and a swim in a shallow bay, sail for 20 or 30 miles and drop the hook in a sheltered bay between 1700 and 1900. Gaëtan, a hulky man with hands the size of hockey gloves, wearing a full head of greying hair and the rugged looks of his farming origins, loved to steer and would take any occasion to steal the helm from Denise and Georges. Denis, a quiet, focused man of medium stature, kept tabs of the boat's position and direction on the navigation charts. Charles would steal any occasion to open a book. I found it quite amazing, the speed at which he flipped the pages. He could easily devour a 500-page novel in a day, an extraordinarily useful ability that I had always envied and tried to emulate in vain.

Every second or third day we had to attend to the delicate matter of disposing of digested material in the sceptic holding tank. It is quite surprising how six people can generate so much poop and pee. It is no doubt testament to the quality and quantity of the meals we shared! Pollution control laws regulating inland waters in Canada are very strict. Upon entering Canadian inland waterways, all foreign boats must seal the outlet valve that allows dumping their "black water" overboard. So any boat navigating inland waters must have a holding tank connected to a fitting on the deck and the only way to empty the tank is by mechanically pumping it out at a purpose-built pumping station. A PortaPotty is only allowed if it's built into the boat and adapted to a deck fitting for shore pump-out. As you can imagine these places are few and far between in the grand wilderness of Georgian Bay. Because of this restriction, planning of a journey must be based upon the whereabouts of pumping stations. For instance when we passed by the town of Killarney, we docked to have a meal at a restaurant, followed by a thorough pump-out. Thankfully, these rules don't apply to the "grey" water from the sinks and shower bilge. As for the legality of spraying "golden showers" overboard, there is controversy as to how to interpret the law.

On the sixth day of our trip we woke up to a nauseating smell of you-know-what. Either I had miscalculated the amount of our contributions, or one crew donated more than his share, but the result was the same: *sewage overflow*. I had planned on pumping out the tank later in the day but didn't quite make it. We were face to face with the prospect of cleaning smelly sewage from the bottom of the bilge. We weren't far from the town of Little Current, so we stopped there for our pump-out and a bilge cleaning. First, I paid a visit to the local grocery store for a bottle of ammonia cleaning solution. After having pumped out the tank and rinsed it out thoroughly I poured most of the bottle of ammonia over the smelly holding tank that had oozed from the top, splashing the excess cleaner into the bilge. The automatic bilge pump kicked in and with plenty of water from a garden hose, we gave everything that had come in contact with our malodorous wastes a copious rinse, and voilà! A sweet-smelling boat.

Having now eliminated the need to hold our noses for the rest of the trip, we set upon heading back in the direction of Gore Bay. George had a couple of friends, Paul and Lynda, who spent the summer at their cottage in Sounding Cove, on our route. We decided that since we were driving the ideal transportation vehicle, we would stop by and pay them a surprise visit. It's not every day that you have friends drop in to see you with their sailing yacht. The beach in front of the cottage was a gradual slope providing a bed of coarse, pebbly sand. I dropped the anchor in about eight feet of water and we used the dinghy to take us ashore. We were cordially greeted and fed beer and smoked salmon on crackers. When we headed back to the boat, the dinghy ride seemed very short compared to the ride from boat to shore. The light wind had overcome the poor holding power of my anchor and the boat had migrated towards shore until her keel rested on the sandy bottom. I was thankful that the wind had not been blowing the other way!

For our last night we anchored at Crocker Island, just a 15-mile hop from Gore Bay. Even if there had been no wind, we could have covered the distance in three hours using the Iron Genny, the motor. By mid-afternoon we brought *Citadel II* back to her home berth and set off for the nine-hour drive back home.

On the return trip I relished scenes of pine forest, a rich country of lakes, green pastures, well-tended farms, quaint villages and the rolling hills of the Gatineau.

After the sixth monthly course of chemo, I underwent another CT scan, which showed no enlarged lymph nodes. I was declared in remission! Dr. Tsai explained that Non-Hodgkin's lymphoma is like an ant's nest. You can kill most of its occupants, but if you leave just one little critter alive, eventually the infestation will recur.

&&&&&&&

And here, enjoying the calm of Bahía la Mar, Margarita, I counted my lucky stars for having survived a pirate attack three days earlier, thanks to incredible strokes of luck. Still waiting for Jacqui and Anthony to return from Porlamar, I retraced the events that led me, a wanna-be sailor, to meet Anthony, a lifelong Trinidadian expert in the world of sailing…

CrewSeekers
International

+44 (0) 238 115 9207

SAILING OPPORTUNITIES DIRECT SAILING ABOUT US NEWS FAQ's HELP

LATEST Sole Stewardes-

MEMBERS LOG IN   JOIN NOW

AMATEUR & PROFESSIONAL
YACHT CREW WANTED
FREE TO BROWSE AND POST

The website that worked for me!

JOIN NOW & GO SAILING

...ng Skippers and Crew together
...e variety of exciting yacht crew opportunities available worldwide.
from daysailing to transocean – for all experience levels

1990

A fine place
to jump ship from

Chapter 6

Searching for an OPY

January 3, 2002

"After that experience with des Aventures last fall, are you sure you still want to sail offshore? " asked Micheline, "You almost lost your life on that trip."

"Aw, come on, now. I'm still here and kicking."

I was on the Internet looking for my next adventure. My list of prerequisites for sailing around the world was almost complete. I had learned with certainty that I enjoyed all aspects of sailing. I had gained an adequate level of knowledge to be a competent crew. My recent experience confirmed that I could get along in a confined space with people I'd never met before. I had determined that I would gain my sea legs after a bout with seasickness. Finally, I had ascertained that just being on a boat out of sight of land was an experience I enjoyed. I felt nevertheless, that I wasn't quite ready to commit to sailing around the world yet. What I needed next was to sail a whole ocean. The Atlantic would be perfect – not too wide, not too narrow.

Ever since the days of the Vikings, sailors have crossed the Atlantic Ocean between Europe and the American continent. Before the invention of keeled boats or motorized boats they had no way to sail against the wind. The spinning of the Earth on its axis causes wind on its surface, known as the prevailing winds or trade winds. On the north side of the Equator, the trade winds blow from the northeast and in the southern hemisphere they blow from southeast. Remember that wind is named according to the direction that it blows *from*. So the northeast wind found north of the Equator will blow your boat westward. What has been helpful for sailors, ancient and modern, who want to cross the Atlantic both ways is that north of the 35th parallel the wind blows from the west. This means that you can cross the ocean from Canada to Europe in the northern latitudes with the west trade winds and come back home via the Caribbean with the northeast trade winds found further south. Since it takes at least three times longer to sail against the wind than with the wind in a modern sailboat, almost all long distance sailors follow the major air currents.

Another factor that sailors must take into consideration when planning a route is the direction and force of water currents. Generally these follow the trade winds, but not always. If your boat's speed through the water is seven knots and you're making way against a current of two knots, then your real speed, the speed over the bottom, is only five knots – a 28% difference!

By far the most important factor to consider when choosing a route is to take into account the weather. Storms and hurricanes follow seasonal patterns. For this reason, you would avoid the winter storms of the Northern Atlantic and the hurricane season of June to November in the Caribbean. The wise sailor wishing to sail across the Atlantic will arrange to be in the right place at the right time.

There are boat owners planning a long passage who need crew to share the watches and the various day-to-day chores. Correspondingly, there are people like me who are captivated by the call of the sea and hanker to fill that need. I call this sailing on an OPY. There are many organizations that cater to filling those complimentary needs. I've listed a number of those that have been in existence for some time at the back of this book. The most popular such organization in Québec is Voile Abordable, or Affordable Sailing. Here you can join groups that organize trips, usually one to three weeks, with charter companies. The cost in 2011 would be about $900 per week, plus your food, drink and airfare. Advantage Boating organizes trips to the Caribbean, the Mediterranean or Thailand as a winter get-away.

The organization that resonated most with me at the time was an outfit called Crewseekers, a British-based Internet passage-making matchmaker. The captain who needs crew posts a notice on the web site. He typically mentions the route, the make and size of boat, the timeframe. Then he will specify the conditions. Many skippers expect the crew to pay a daily stipend of ten or fifteen dollars (US) a day as a contribution towards food and incidental boat expenses. Depending on the level of expertise the

Searching for an OPY

captain is demanding of the crew, he might forego the stipend and in some cases he will pay the airfare back home. Anybody can see the posted trips on the web site without registering. But a potential crew who wishes to know the coordinates of the captain for a particular trip must buy a six-month membership for sixty pounds sterling. When a paid-up crew finds a suitable trip, he emails Crewseekers who will in turn send the contact information for the captain. (If you're interested please look at Annex 3 for information on crewing).

The first trip that struck my fancy was with Peter Savage, a man from Seattle Washington who was buying a boat. He was looking for crew to deliver a fifty-seven foot Mikado ketch from Malta to Vancouver. He had bought the boat sight unseen, which apparently is not an unusual practice, from a German who moored her in the Mediterranean. I'll save you the trouble of looking up Malta. It is a country composed of several islands totalling 316 square kilometres in surface, located in the Mediterranean, 50 miles south of Sicily, Italy. Numerous bays along the indented coastline of the islands provide good harbours for sailboats. The capital is Valletta. Great Britain took possession of Malta in 1814. The island faithfully supported Britain through both World Wars and remained part of the Commonwealth when it declared independence in 1964. Since about the mid-1980s, the island has transformed itself into a freight transhipment point, a financial centre, and a tourist destination. The country became a European Union member in 2004.

Peter had made the offer conditional to a survey, that all deficiencies be corrected, and to a sea trial. Very few people have the expertise to properly evaluate the condition of a used boat. There are so many components in a modern sailboat and so many things that can go wrong, that if you are buying a boat your insurance company will require that you have it inspected by a professional surveyor even if you are an experienced sailor yourself. Peter was waiting for the surveyor to complete his job and for the owner to correct the deficiencies before flying to Malta for the sea trials, mid-January. The survey that was scheduled for the second week of January ended up being completed by the fourth week. There were several minor faults to be fixed, but the owner couldn't go down to Malta before the first week of February to undertake the repairs. Then he couldn't get a mechanic to look at the engine before the third week of February, which turned out to be the last week. This is when I decided to look for something else.

The add read:

South Carolina to Azores to Weymouth, England
Reference: CS-477*-AD

Boat details: Endurance 37
Location: Charleston, South Carolina
Destination: Weymouth, England
Availability: March 15, 2002 for two months
Crew requirements: Two experienced crew required to assist captain in delivering boat to England.
Financial arrangements: No contribution by crew
Travel expenses: One-way airfare paid upon completion.

This was right up my alley, so to speak. After obtaining his phone number from Crewseekers, I called the captain. Over the phone David Rankin sounded jovial, enthusiastic and knowledgeable. He had just bought the 20-year-old boat, had had her surveyed and still had two weeks of work to get the boat ship shape. He wanted to replace all the rigging, including the stays and shrouds. The boat featured a recently overhauled engine, the usual comfort and safety equipment for offshore travel and especially, a working auto helm – which meant we wouldn't have to contend with steering 24 hours a day.

I emailed him my sailing CV, which included my recent experience with offshore sailing. I felt confident and up to the task. He emailed me back that he liked my qualifications and would be happy to have me aboard. I had told him that I was somewhat of a cook, especially when there are volunteers to take care of the dishes. Furthermore, I had recently read about offshore provisioning and could relieve him of this chore if he wished. He responded that we would get along very well since he likes to eat and doesn't like to cook. We agreed to meet the seventh of March at the boat, finish some of the repairs and maintenance over the next week and cast off on the Ides of March. Our first landfall would be the Azores, we would spend at least a week visiting, resting and preparing the boat for the last 1200 miles to Weymouth. Another crew member had joined and would arrive in Charleston a day after me. He was a 32 year-old Brit, a commercial shipping deck hand who was working toward his rank as captain of large commercial vessels and needed to accumulate sea miles in order to qualify. Everything was perfect.

On the appointed date I flew to Charleston. My flight came in late and by the time I arrived at the dock, it was 2330. David was to wait for me at the entrance of the marina, as the dockage was very complex and he was afraid I wouldn't be able to find the boat at night. When I arrived at the entrance with my baggage, I saw a man slumped in a chair, snoring profoundly. He displayed a receding, greying hairline and a plump, wrinkled face and was my age, which was right. I dared to wake him up and as it turned out, I had the right man. It was considerate of him to have waited up for me and this was a good omen, I thought.

The rattling of a kettle shook me out of my early morning half-sleep. I got dressed and made my way to the galley, stepping over boxes of cables, huge coils of rope, pieces of construction material, sailbags, and rolled up stay wire. David was pouring boiling water into two mugs. There was a container of Coffee Mate, a jar of sugar and a jar of instant coffee on the counter next to the mugs. I made a mental note to check into the coffee making equipment when the time came to plan the provisioning.

After breakfast I asked the captain whether there were any parts of the boat that were off limits to the crew, and I added that it would be important for me to know where everything was located. It is understood that the owner of the boat has personal effects he wouldn't want everybody to have access to. On the other hand, the captain and the crew of a sailboat at sea must always be ready for the worst manifestations of Murphy's Law, which states:

"If anything can go wrong, it will, and at the worst possible moment."

Imagine, for instance, being in a raging storm, with the boat thrown about like a cork and the captain suffering from a stroke or a heart attack or even just a broken leg. In such circumstances one of the crew would have to take over command. If an emergency repair were called for the crew would have to know exactly where to find the emergency supplies, the tools and the spare parts. There are dozens of nooks and crannies on a boat where essential supplies can be tucked. If you need to jury-rig a broken boom, you have to know where the pieces of wood, pipe, rod, wire, etc. are hidden. If you have to plug a leak, you have to find the cache of fibreglass, resin, epoxy hardener, putty knives, squeegee and disposable gloves.

The captain was quite taken aback by my question about off limits places. He turned stiff as a statue, eyes staring in the void, and after a long pause, we heard a knock knock on the hull. It was Chris, a stocky, freckled-face, red-haired, balding, round-faced man in his early thirties, who spoke with a thick, Cockney accent. After Chris had unpacked, David told us he had to make a trip to the chandlery to buy boat parts and that if we wanted, the crew could take the morning off to visit the town. I never got an answer about "off limits" places.

Charleston is a small city of 120,000 inhabitants located near the mid-point of south Carolina's coastline, at the confluence of two rivers. The city is well-known for its streets lined with majestic oak trees draped with Spanish moss, and the Cabbage Palmetto, the state tree of South Carolina. Along the waterfront in an area known as Rainbow Row are many beautiful and historic pastel-colored homes. The city has known at least two reconstruction efforts, after the 1861 Civil War and after the 1886 earthquake that destroyed 2000 houses. The architecture is typical colonial. We walked along the sea wall, watching the comings and goings of the commercial shipping in the port. The city is an important seaport, boasting of having the second largest container shipping volume on the east coast. We then turned away from the water and ambled leisurely through the downtown streets admiring the beautifully maintained period houses. Every house had well-tended flowerbeds, flowerpots on the balconies, and window flower boxes. I could just picture 18th century couples walking down the quiet streets, the lady wearing a crinoline dress, white cotton elbow gloves, a voluminous hat and parasol, and the gentleman with his walking cane, spats and top hat.

Chris had left his fiancée behind in England and kissed her goodbye for at least two months of absence. This trip would add another badly-needed 4000 sea miles to his CV. Linda would work as much overtime as possible in her nursing job to compensate for the income Chris was foregoing by engaging in this trip.

A light drizzle took us out of our tour and forced us to return to the marina. Chris stopped at a store to buy himself a pair of sneakers and I continued to the boat. I slipped on my deck shoes, climbed aboard by grabbing onto one of the shrouds and stepped into the cockpit. The companionway was closed to keep the rain out, so I knocked out of politeness and slid the companionway hatch cover a crack open and called out: "May I come in?"

Upon climbing down the stairs I was greeted by a sour faced David who said dryly, "Your shoes are wet. Take them off."

I was taken aback by both the statement and the order. The cabin floor of any boat will inevitably get wet when it rains. The small amount of fresh water involved can only do the woodwork good, especially if wiped dry once crew have finished coming in. I also found his reproachful stance disturbing. It begged the questions, "How will he react under pressure? Is this the way he will treat his crew once at sea?"

By the time Chris arrived, the cockpit was dry, so he didn't have the chance to learn his lesson about taking wet shoes off. David didn't have any particular task he wanted us to start on as it was getting late in the afternoon. We decided to go out for supper, so in the meantime, we talked about food. I asked David how he wanted me to go about planning the provisioning. I proffered the lists I had printed off my computer at home, but he brushed them aside without looking at them. He declared, with a big smile that the provisioning was done.

"You did the provisioning?" I asked.

I could see no sign of produce anywhere. Fruit and vegetables are usually stored in a mesh hammock suspended in the cabin, or in baskets on the floor under the salon table, and there was no such evidence. Before I asked, David proudly opened the lockers under the settees and showed us what we would be eating for the next two months. One locker was chock full with cans of baked beans, canned spaghetti and Spam, and another locker was packed full with giant bags of potato chips.

I asked him, "Are you planning on buying fresh produce next Monday before we leave?"

"Nothing stays fresh at sea, old chap, and besides, when underway it's impossible to prepare a full meal."

I decided he wouldn't be impressed if I tried to tell him that carrots last two weeks, cabbage, yellow onions and potatoes keep for two months, squash for four months, apples keep for two weeks and oranges three weeks and watermelon four weeks. However, since we were on the contentious subject of food, I asked him if he minded if I purchased ground coffee and the necessary equipment, at my expense. He answered, "I hate seeing coffee grounds messing up everything. Not on my boat."

Upon returning from the restaurant, I tightened some loose screws holding the door hinges of the head. Fortunately, and you will understand why I say it was fortunate, I made the mistake of not returning the screwdriver to its toolbox. When David found the offending tool sticking out like a sore thumb on the chart table, he took Chris and me aside for a little talk. Holding the screwdriver by its metal shank and repeatedly slapping the handle part into the palm of his other hand, he started lecturing us about the importance of having a place for everything and putting everything back into its place. Up to here, I silently agreed with him. But he continued:

"...For example, suppose we're out at sea at night and I need the torch (British for flashlight). I know exactly where to find it. In fact, I could just reach up in the dark and put my hand on it without looking. But, if ever a crewmember had used it and not put it back in its place, then there'd be hell to pay!"

That was the proverbial last straw that drove me to putting into effect Plan B. Life is too short to take abuse, especially when you're supposed to be having fun. There are situations in life when you may be victim of a dictator who uses his power to exercise control. It might be a boss who is full of his own importance and acts as the absolute ruler, leaving his subordinates no place for their own advancement, or worse still, a boss who will inflict verbal abuse upon his employees, because he knows he can get away with it. It might be a husband who uses his physical strength to terrorise his submissive spouse and control her every movement.

When faced with such a situation, a person must take action to escape the power of the maltreater. It was late in the evening and I decided to break the news to David the next morning.

By the time the morning kettle rattled, my bag was packed. As David was guzzling his instant coffee, I broke the news to him.

"David, I have to tell you something. I've decided that you and I aren't compatible and it would be better for me to let you find a replacement."

And to my surprise, he responded, "Yes, I was thinking the same thing."

Before leaving for home I had the chance to speak to Chris privately. I asked him how he felt about my unexpected mutinous act. He responded that he would do the same if he could afford the airfare back home. The understanding with David was that his airfare to South Carolina would only be reimbursed after arrival in England. I was thankful that I didn't have similar financial constraints.

My next search on the Crewseekers web site would turn out to be more fruitful. In fact, it would turn out to be the source of a lifetime friendship.

The add read as follows:

Curacao to Cuba to Jamaica to Curacao
Reference: CS-6666-AD
Boat details: Finnsailer 34 ketch
Location: Spanish Water, Curacao
Destination: Cuba, Jamaica, back to Curacao
Availability: April 3, 2002 till June 15
Crew requirements: Crew with offshore and navigation experience required as first mate to captain
Financial arrangements: No contribution by crew. Food and drink supplied while on board
Travel expenses: Crew pays travel.

It wasn't the Atlantic, but I rationalized that it wouldn't be too much of a sacrifice to spend two and a half months sailing in the Caribbean and in visiting new places as part of the deal.

Almost sank in the middle of the Caribbean

Enjoy a fresh muffin at sea

Music and dance: the soul of Cuba

Chapter 7

A Small Ocean for Starters

Wednesday, April 3, 2002. The taxi dropped me off just behind the bar at Sarifundy's Marina in Spanish Water. A man of about 65 with curly, greying hair and light brown skin approached me and asked,

"You must be Robert."

"So you're Anthony Johnson."

After showing me to my berth on *Mikky*, he suggested with a straight face, "Now, Robert, there is a tradition of great importance that we must carry out. It's a question of a captain's duty towards new crew. This has to be accomplished at the bar." Anthony's treating me to a beer was his humorous way of extending his offer of friendship.

As we enjoyed our suds, Anthony explained that he had left Trinidad in February with two friends who accompanied him to Curaçao (pronounced Cur a sow). It was understood that they were to fly back home and leave him for a crew change. His friend Wilfrid, an experienced sailor, was to join him at this marina in Curaçao for the rest of the trip. The crossing to their first landfall, Santiago de Cuba, was 655 miles, and they'd be out of sight of land for six days. From the point of view of safety it was important to have a second mate capable of taking over command should the captain become incapacitated. A third person, Sandrine, was waiting in Trinidad until a day or two before *Mikky* was ready to cast off before flying to Curaçao to meet them. However, Anthony explained, Wilfrid couldn't get his visa.

"Why wouldn't Cuba grant him a visa?"

"No, not Cuba. His wife's visa."

"Oh, his wife was to sail with you?"

"Heavens, no. She doesn't sail. But she doesn't want Wilfrid to sail either. So she wouldn't give him his visa to leave home. Consequently, I've been stuck here on this little island for the past month, trying to find crew."

It is interesting how some marriages persist in spite of major differences like this one. Some people think it is necessary that husband and wife share all of the same interests and that if there is a hobby or a sport they aren't equally passionate about there is something fundamentally wrong with their relationship. In some marriages, one spouse will not accept that the other partake in a particular activity – a manner of exercising control, I think. The important thing is to allow for such differences. It is essential, in my view, that each spouse allow breathing space for the other and that likes and dislikes be respected. In my case, Micheline wouldn't entertain for a moment the idea of spending two and half months on a small boat with two other people, let alone two people she's never met. Fortunately, she appreciates that sailing, even if it entails living situations that would be unpleasant for her, is important for me. When I leave for a trip, she kisses me goodbye and wishes me the best. She doesn't worry, as she has adopted a fatalistic approach to life: You do what you're driven to do and things tend to sort themselves out. When I return home, she lives my experiences vicariously through my stories and photographs.

Anthony's plan was to take six days to sail to Cuba, then navigate along the whole of the south coast, then cross over to Jamaica, where we would drop off Sandrine and pick up Pauline, another friend of Anthony's. We would spend a couple of weeks in and around the country of Bob Marley before returning to Curaçao.

Thursday, April 4. As previously arranged, I was to meet the third person of our group. The tiny taxi pulled up to the bar and a tall, elegant woman in her early sixties, extracted herself from its confines. Her flimsy silk dress let show much of her ultra-tanned Caucasian skin and plenty of cleavage. She had long red hair tied in a bun with flowing bits in her face. She showed fine facial features and was generously lipsticked and eyeshadowed. She walked with the exaggerated femininity and the "watch me" body language typical of Parisian women. As Anthony was approaching her she opened her arms with effusiveness, embraced him, and with a very French accent, "I ham so appy to resee you, my Antoine."

Anthony introduced me to his friend and she gave me a double double cheek kiss and exclaimed, "*Mon petit frère du Canada!* I'm soooo appy to met you."

After Sandrine finished unpacking Anthony treated us to the obligatory Captain's duty towards new crew along with a light lunch. In the afternoon we took a taxi to Willemstad, the capital of Curaçao. Willemstad is a beautiful coastal city divided down the middle by a navigable water channel that leads to St. Anna Bay, a large bay filled with commercial ships and lined with very pretty and busy streets. A 600-foot long, narrow floating pontoon bridge called the Queen Emma, links the two sides of the bay at its entrance. When a ship needs to sail in or out, one end of the bridge disconnects from the sea wall and a motorized propeller noisily pushes away the free end of the bridge, still attached to the opposite shore, and swings out of the way of naval traffic, in a long arc. Dozens of people remain on the bridge during its travel. It is said that this is the only one of its kind in the world that is used on a daily basis. It was built in 1888 and used to be a toll bridge. Only the poor who did not have shoes were allowed to ride without paying. Today it is toll-free for everybody.

The architecture of the town is of a Dutch style and the buildings are painted with contrasting pastel colours, as if to add life to an otherwise desert-dry island. The downtown consists mainly of shops, shops, shops, restaurants, restaurants, restaurants and bars, bars, bars. Sandrine accepted the offer of an iguana owner who "rented out" his pet to tourists at $5 a shot for having their picture taken. The green iguana draped around her neck contrasted beautifully with her orange halter-top. There were fishermen selling their catches directly from the starboard bow of their boats moored to the sea wall, that were ingeniously converted into retail sales stores, complete with street-level counters and shutters. We stopped at a supermarket to pick up some dry goods, beer, canned drinks and meat. We then made a foray into the farmer's market to stock up on fresh fruit and vegetables for our week on the sea. Anthony expertly squeezed, prodded, smelled, tasted and set the price of a variety of fruit, roots and vegetables.

Back aboard *Mikky*, we started putting away our last purchases, when I recognized a very unwelcome stowaway. A package of rice contained the telltale holes and bits of sticky powder, typical of the saw-toothed beetle, which Micheline and I had learned to contend with and destroy when we had just moved into our first house, a week before the birth of our son Philippe. Upon closer scrutiny, the little bugs were visible, travelling between the rice and the polyethylene packaging. I passed the package over to Anthony and he immediately recognized the gravity of the situation.

"Oh, my Lord, these are weevils", he pronounced, "We have to take action."

We put aside everything else and closely examined each package of dry goods such as beans, pasta, flour, nuts, cereal, crackers and cookies for the presence of the little critters and placed each offending package into a large garbage bag, which we regrettably dumped ashore. Then Anthony sprayed every surface of the cupboards and storage lockers with a residual insecticide to discourage any curious individual that might have left the safety of its package to explore its neighbourhood. About a quarter of the dry goods were contaminated, leaving us with sufficient food to make the passage. The main drawback was that we would have to do without a few luxuries in Cuba, where we didn't expect to find much variety.

Friday, April 5. Anthony discovered that one of the fire extinguishers wasn't operational, so we would have to delay our departure until after he went into town to find a replacement. Finally at 1545 we weighed anchor and waved goodbye to the island of Curaçao. We contoured the southeastern end of the island and headed north into the Caribbean Sea.

A few miles offshore the waves were 1½ to 2 metres deep and much closer together than any I had experienced in the Atlantic. Before I had the chance to give them much thought, my middle ear, eyes and stomach engaged in the now familiar and unwelcome tug of war. I precipitated myself head first to the toerail and with very thunderous vocalizations my stomach heaved one powerful spray, enriching the clear blue water of the Caribbean with what had been my lunch. I then repeated the same movements, but without the contribution to the sea, and performed the spectacle every three minutes to the consternation and exasperation of my audience. Unlike Henri on my Atlantic passage, Anthony and Sandrine offered no miracle cure like soda crackers and water as a solution to end the ordeal. Thankfully, after a solid hour and a half of uncontrollable contractions, my stomach decided it had created enough disturbances and desisted from any further mischief. When I returned to the cockpit after an hour of rest, Anthony and Sandrine looked at me as if I had resuscitated from the dead, as I had regained my composure and colours. The next day, Anthony confided that when I was vomiting non-stop, he thought I might collapse of heart failure right in front of him. Sandrine couldn't understand how someone who is so sick at sea would ever want to approach within a mile of the sea again. Fortunately, I was never to be seasick in any of my future passages.

Saturday, April 6. Ate a bit of rice and plantain and my stomach decided to accept it. The only notable event was the sighting of half a dozen large ships: Container ships, cruise ships, fishing trawlers. In the first 24 hours we covered 159 miles! This comes to an average of 6.6 knots, which is just about the boat's maximum theoretical speed. Excellent!

Sunday, April 7. A sticky substance was leaking out of the joint at the bottom of the starboard settee, oozing onto the floor. In the confusion generated by the battle of the weevils, we had forgotten to take the nice, ripe sapodillas out of their plastic bag and the bag had accidentally been left on top of the dry goods. The wonderful, sweet fruit had undergone anaerobic decomposition, resulting in a very smelly, sticky, gooey liquid that had soiled every package of goods that it came in touch with. Worse things can happen…and of course, they always do.

There was still a foul smell permeating the main cabin, even after we had thoroughly cleaned, scrubbed and disinfected the nauseating locker and floor. It turned out that something had decomposed in the bottom of the refrigerator. On most sailboats, the refrigerator is a large, heavily insulated box that opens from the top. The reason why the traditional vertical door found in household refrigerators is shunned by boat builders is that a top opening is supposedly much more energy efficient. Each time you open the refrigerator in your kitchen all of the cold air is dumped onto the floor. Not so with a top-loading arrangement, as you can appreciate. Sometimes a boat fridge has shelves at different heights along one side to accommodate small items. In all cases, getting to the bottom of a fridge to clean it requires removing the shelves as one progressively leans further and further down, head first through the opening, with arms stretched full length holding the rag and with feet and legs flailing in the air, trying to hold the body in balance to prevent falling in completely. You don't have to hold your nose, because the blood pressure building up in your head reduces your breathing and dulls the olfactory sense. You might want to take a small empty container to the bottom with you, in which you can wring out the slimy water, thus preventing you from having to work your way back up too often.

I have doubts about the common wisdom of a top-loading refrigerator. For one thing, air is 800 times less dense than water, so it should take very little energy to cool any warm air lost from a vertical door fridge. And if you consider that every time you have to reach the bottom of a top-loading fridge you have to take everything out and place it on the counters to warm up in the hot tropical air, doesn't a standard vertical door fridge which allows you to reach in quickly make more sense?

Later in the day, sitting topless in the cockpit, Sandrine noticed an unpleasant smell, "Antoine dear, your boat smells like an old gas station!"

Since the only apparatus that uses gasoline is the outboard engine, the guilty party had to be related to the little devil. We checked the two spare carboys of gasoline lashed to the deck and they were free of leaks. We checked over the outboard engine, and gave it a clean bill of health.

"Aha! – Remembered Anthony. Let's check the outboard gas tank."

Small outboard engines usually have two tanks. The main one is a tiny inboard reservoir, built into the engine casing, that's called into action only in cases of emergency. The outboard tank is a much larger, stubby, portable, non-tipping red metal or plastic container with a handle, a screw cap with a vent in the top to allow air in as gasoline gets burned up. The tank is connected to the engine, when needed, by way of a quick-disconnect rubber fuel line. Upon inspection, the entire outside of the tank was wet with freshly spilled gasoline. The guilty party was simply the vent, which had not been closed the last time it was used. A small amount of gasoline can generate a lot of smell. Unlike diesel fuel that has to be coaxed to burn, gasoline is highly flammable. And if Murphy's Law provides the right ratio of air and gasoline vapour along with a spark, it can generate inconvenient fireworks.

<u>Monday, April 8</u>, one o'clock in the morning. I had just started my three-hour watch, but hadn't slept a wink since going to bed. At 2200 when I tried to go to sleep the boat began being thrown around like the ball on a bolo bat. I had to wedge myself between the mattress and the leeward wall of the cabin to prevent being projected like a bug onto the floor. And now that I was in the cockpit I could see the reason why it was so rough: we were dealing with 12-foot waves on the beam and the wind meter read 30 to 35 knots! As a consolation, *Mikky* was barrelling along at seven knots. Perhaps it was uncomfortable, but at least we were moving!

By mid-morning though, the wind had died down and we had to run the engine to keep us moving. Around 1700 the wind picked up a bit and turned behind the transom, allowing us to set the sails wing and wing with a whisker pole. This way the sails were set on both sides of the vessel so that a jib filled on one side of the boat and the main filled on the other.

It was 2100 and Sandrine was ready to serve supper. Just then I heard an accented voice over the VHF radio, "North seventeen degrees, forty minutes, west seventy-four degrees, thirty four minutes."

The odd sounding message was read over a few times before it dawned upon me that the voice was calling our boat's latitude and longitude position.

A Small Ocean for Starters

I called the captain who was doing his watch in the cockpit, "Anthony, there's something very strange on the radio, you better come down and listen."

There is an internationally adopted protocol for hailing someone on a VHF radio. Most boaters will be monitoring channel 16, the internationally recognized emergency channel. It is also used for initiating a call, and once the two boats have established contact, they continue their conversation on a working channel (other than the emergency channel). First you call out the name of the boat you are addressing, and you may repeat the name twice if your transmission is of doubtful quality. Then you say, "This is" and the name of your own boat. Then you say the word "Over", which means, "I'm waiting for a response from you." Here's an example:

"Starmist, Starmist, this is *Mikky*. Over."

"*Mikky*, this is Starmist. Switch to six seven, over."

"Six seven, over."

The two boats switch to channel 67 and continue speaking. When the communication is finished each party concludes with the word "Out", which means that no further response is expected. One should never ever say "Over and out" like in the movies!

The call we just heard was highly unusual in its lack of protocol. I explained to Anthony what I had just heard and he took the mike and pressed the transmit button,

"Vessel calling coordinates north seventeen degrees, forty minutes, west seventy-four degrees, thirty four minutes, this is sailing vessel *Mikky*, over."

There was a silence, then, "We have no lights. North seventeen degrees, forty minutes, west seventy-four degrees, thirty four minutes, *you are in danger*."

I rushed to the cockpit to scan the horizon for a boat without lights, but it was so dark that I couldn't see a thing.

Anthony then replied, "Vessel without lights, this is sailing vessel *Mikky*, identify yourself please, over."

No reply.

"Vessel without lights, this is sailing vessel *Mikky*, provide your exact coordinates please, over."

"*You are in danger*", repeated the voice, faintly.

Anthony then contacted the US coast guard with his satellite phone and asked for advice. The advice that came back was, "Get the hell out of there!"

Upon which we motor sailed as fast as we could – a mere seven knots, of course, as we were limited by the laws of physics, which dictate a displacement hull's maximum speed. We never heard anything more from the mysterious caller and never heard of anybody having a similar experience.

An hour and a half later we had covered ten miles since the frightening call. We finally had supper at 2330.

Tuesday, April 9. It was a beautiful day, the wind fifteen knots, the waves one and half metres. Just before noon, Sandrine went down the companionway for a visit to the head. Anthony and I were playing around with the autohelm. Its electrical plug had broken and we were in the throes of repairing it. Sandrine bolted to the companionway, her face pale with fright, "Merde! There is water in your boat, Antoine!"

Anthony rushed down the companionway, leaving me to steer. There was no water in the main cabin, but the front stateroom and head were separated from the main cabin by a bulkhead, a small wall, about a foot high, and that entire area was full of water a foot deep.

Since we hadn't struck anything and we were floating in 3000 metres of water, Anthony suspected one of the three thruhulls under the floorboards in that area. A thruhull is a hole in the bottom of the boat, under the waterline, that either allows seawater into the boat for washing, cooling or flushing, or waste water to go out to the sea. Each thruhull has a valve called a seacock attached to it for cutting off the flow of liquid.

The floorboards had already floated up, so Anthony, lying down on his stomach, keeping his head out of the water, submerged his arm, to find the position of each of the seacocks. He felt a gush of incoming water near one of them. He closed the seacock, stemming the flow of water. He could hear the bilge pump working, but it didn't seem to be getting any of the water out. So he started bailing. While I kept steering, our captain and his French assistant formed a chain. Anthony would fill a bucket, pass it to Sandrine, who dumped it onto the self draining cockpit sole (floor). After a few bucketfuls I saw, swirling around with the water, peanut-shaped paper things that resembled very much what women use during their periods. As it turned out, one of these was blocking the inlet of the bilge pump. Anthony concluded that in previous years one of the crew must have discarded her sanitary pads in the bilge rather than putting them in a bag or whatever.

More troubling than an unknown woman's unsanitary habits, was the question of what caused the ingression of water, a potentially lethal situation. It was very fortunate that Sandrine felt the call of nature when she did. Had her bladder produced its signal half an hour later, the entire main cabin floor would have been flooded and Anthony would have had no idea where to start looking for the leak since the Finnsailor 34 had 11 thruhulls, many of which were located in very difficult to reach places. We were about sixty miles from Haiti, out of radio range, so if we had had to abandon ship we might have drifted for weeks before being rescued.

After we had all the water mopped up and had the bilge pump running again, Anthony examined the guilty thruhull. The stopcock was working OK, but attached to the stopcock there was a short piece of tubing joined to a 90-degree metal elbow fitting. Anthony removed the fitting and took it into the cockpit in the light of day to examine it. It was red in colour, and a third of it was eaten away.

Seawater with its high salt content is very corrosive. Anything that comes in contact with it must be resistant to its chemically destructive effect. That's why on the deck you will see all fittings are either made of plastic or stainless steel. On the ancient boats, before the invention of inexpensive stainless steel and plastic, fittings were made either of wood or bronze, a very resistant alloy. Even stainless steel can't resist the corrosive effect of sea salt for underwater use. The propeller shaft is made of stainless steel, you might say, but to prevent it from disintegrating, it has to be equipped with a sacrificial anode made of zinc. Consequently, all salt-water plumbing has to be either bronze or plastic. The defective 90-degree elbow, Anthony deduced, was made of brass instead of bronze. Bronze is an alloy of copper and tin, whereas brass is made of copper and zinc. Guess what? Zinc is very soluble in sea water, so a brass fitting that is continuously exposed to sea water will leach away its zinc content to the sea, leaving behind the copper lattice, which is porous and much weakened.

Anthony had purchased eighteen-year-old *Mikky* only four years earlier. He had no way of knowing what other "improvements" the previous owner might have inflicted upon his otherwise excellent yacht. How many other thruhull pipes might also have been replaced with brass? The only way to know for sure was to have the boat taken out of the water then each fitting removed and checked. Could this be done in Cuba? We were to discover that this incident would dictate a major change of plans and impinge on the rest of the trip.

As in any other sea-going sailboat, every nook and cranny serves for storage. In the case of the flooded front bilge which is usually perfectly dry, this is where Anthony kept his small spare parts, such as screws, washers, springs, pins, shackles, clamps, nuts and bolts, etc., all of which became thoroughly soaked. If they had been left in their plastic bags or containers in contact with salt water, after a few months they would have been corroded beyond use even though they were all made of stainless steel. For the next three days whenever I had free time, I spent it rinsing in fresh water, then drying these hundreds of little parts.

A Small Ocean for Starters

Wednesday, April 10, 10 o'clock in the morning. "Land ahoy!" cried out Anthony. What a joy to see, peeking above the horizon a row of tiny peaks in the far distance. Once we were within five miles of the coast, Anthony hailed the Coast Guard to announce our imminent arrival. The Spanish speaking man on the radio told us that once we arrived in the Santiago de Cuba bay we must drop the anchor and wait for instructions. At 1330 we cleared the entrance to the bay leaving the impressive fort Castillo del Morro to our starboard. Anthony apprised the Coast Guard of our arrival and this time he told us to dock at Marina Santiago off a peninsula inside the bay called Punta Gorda.

The bay was surrounded by mountains and the city's low skyline was tucked in between the hills and the water. In the distance we could see the giant smoke stacks of the coal-fired power plant that supplied electricity to the entire Santiago de Cuba province. We made fast to the dock and waited, as we were not allowed to leave the boat until we were cleared in.

At 1600 two officials approached our boat, each one wearing a white, freshly starched and ironed shirt bearing an official looking insignia and a blue cap decorated with a metal badge. They were with the Department of Health. We invited them aboard (not that we had any choice). They were all smiles and gave us a warm welcome. They explained that Cuba, being an island with ecosystems different from any in North America had to protect its indigenous species against invasion by foreign animals, insects and plants and therefore each boat that entered had to be examined. They told us that any meat, fruit and vegetables we had on the boat had to be eaten on board and wastes had to be carefully packaged and disposed of in the garbage bins provided at the marina. All conversations were held in Spanish, so we were lucky to have Sandrine as our interpreter, who spoke the language fluently. While the superior was talking, his assistant, with me in tow, was opening the cupboards in which he peeked, without disturbing any of the contents. His attention was drawn not to any elephant tusk, offending fruit or illegal insect, but to a collection of about fifteen baseball caps that Anthony reserved as gifts. He pointed to the caps and gestured requesting permission to try one. I nodded. He picked the yellow and black San Diego Padres cap and tried it on. I showed him to the mirror in the head, and he beamed with joy. I called to Anthony to ask him if we could give the gentleman the cap and he assented wholeheartedly. The captain had to sign a form in triplicate, swearing that he was not carrying any illegal animal or plant material and pay a $5 US fee.

No sooner had we said adiós to our health inspectors than we had the visit of two more officials, decked out in impeccable kaki-beige costumes bearing rows of brass buttons, and shiny badges. Again, a warm welcome to Cuba. One of the officials was the Harbour Master and the other from Immigration. Out with our passports, crew list and boat papers. They accepted a beer with slight hesitation, which helped lubricate the relationship and facilitate communication. The Port Captain, a young man in his early thirties, beamed with joyous surprise when he opened Anthony's passport. As it turned out he and Anthony had the same birth date and were to celebrate their birthdays in two days, April 12. In Cuba two people who share a common birthday date have something very important in common and upon discovery of this coincidence, any fear, suspicion or resentment evaporates, to be replaced by warm friendship. Immediately the two were best friends.

A third round of visits then followed. Two more clean-cut men boarded the boat with the same display of polite formality. The two officers were from Customs. The offer of a cold beer was accepted with the requisite feigned hesitation. The first question was whether or not we carried any arms or drugs, which was answered in the negative.

Then, "Do you have any flare guns and flares? Could we see them please?"

Anthony had a single shot flare gun and a six-shooter, along with a dozen hand held flares, which were placed on the salon table.

Then, "Do you have any portable VHF or short wave radios?" Anthony placed his portable VHF radio on the table.

Then, "Do you have any hand-held GPS units?" Anthony placed his GPS on the table with the other requested material.

The interrogator then listed the material on an official government form in triplicate, saving the ragged pieces of carbon paper for the next investigation, gave one copy to Anthony and signalled to his assistant, who proffered a plastic garbage bag. All of the declared equipment was then placed into the bag, the top carefully folded closed and taped shut. The official apposed his signature on the tape and instructed Anthony not to open the bag until we had cleared out of Cuba on our final day of visit.

After supper aboard *Mikky* we needed to celebrate our safe landing in Cuba. We picked the easiest target for a drink, the marina bar. The music, which was rendered by a group of four musicians, had already begun in earnest. Music, and by music I mean Latin American songs and instrumentals, is in the heart and soul of every Cuban. For the next seven weeks we would be inundated and transported by music everywhere we went. The manager of the bar recognized us as new visitors and offered us each a complimentary *mojito* and *Cuba libre*, an auspicious beginning for our stay on this lively and colourful island.

Thursday, April 11. I'll begin by telling you about *Mikky*. The make of boat is a Finnsailer 34, and you will have correctly deduced from the name that she was built in Finland and that she's 34 feet long. This boat is different in several aspects from the sloops that I had sailed before. First, she is not a sloop, but a ketch. *Mikky* has one tall mast about a quarter of the way from the bow and a shorter mast about a quarter of the way from the stern. The tall mast flies a large mainsail and the small mast bears a much smaller sail called the mizzen. In addition, *Mikky* has a furling jib like on a sloop and a smaller staysail at the front like on a cutter. With a total of four sails, this arrangement allows the boat to sail comfortably and efficiently in any wind condition. Because she has more sail front-to back, the total height is lower, so *Mikky* heels less than a sloop does, which makes her more comfortable. Another really neat feature is that the Finnsaler 34 has a centre cockpit, which, as the term implies, is not at the back of the boat but near the middle, providing better protection from pooping seas. Furthermore, the cockpit is equipped with a large, strong Lexan dodger, protecting the crew from rain, wind and breaking waves. A special attribute of this boat is that she has a separate aft cabin that has its own entrance. The small cabin can accommodate two people and has a small sink and mirror, allowing the aft crew an element of privacy.

On my first day aboard, Anthony had given me the aft cabin, thinking that I would appreciate having the privacy of my own space on the boat. However, I discovered that I was always the first one up. I then had to wait until Sandrine who slept on one of the salon settees woke up before I could start moving around and brewing my coffee. With that in mind, on this first day in Cuba, I offered my room to Sandrine in exchange for the salon, an offer she accepted with delight. As the only woman aboard, she would appreciate the privacy of her own separate room and she could sleep in as late as she wanted without interfering with others' activities. I slept better in the more airy salon and could go about my business whenever I wanted. This is what we call a win-win situation, isn't it?

"Knock knock!"

Then, "Buenos dias!"

A gentleman dressed as an official, bearing an insignia labelled "Departamento de la cartografía de Cuba" and carrying a large document holder was asking permission to come aboard. The official asked us where we planned to sail and which charts we had of the area. Anthony had only a few charts of the wrong scale and was counting on purchasing the missing ones in Cuba. The man unfolded a large map that was actually an index of all the navigation charts for the whole of Cuba and made a list of the ones we needed. His office was just a couple of blocks from the marina. If we would accompany him there he'd sell us the needed charts. Anthony wanted detailed charts of the Gardens of the Queen, which I will tell you about later, plus all those required for getting us to Cienfuegos. The three of us accompanied the man to his office, as we wanted to get to see a bit of the city.

On our way back, just a block from the marina, a man seated in a rocking chair on the front porch of his tiny house called out to us.

"Buenos dias, senores y senora" and he signalled us to approach. He introduced himself as Pedro and invited us to come in. He introduced us to his wife Rosita, a thin, 42 year-old woman with hunched shoulders, bearing a tired look on her face. He informed us that Rosita ran a laundering service for tourists from the marina. We could leave her our laundry one day and pick it up 24 hours later, washed, dried and folded. The house was a square of rough cinder blocks with a tin roof. It consisted of a single room divided down the middle by a wardrobe and a dresser. In the sleeping area there was a sagging, double bed for the parents, 2 year-old Lazaro and 3 year-old Roxane and a timeworn crib for 1½ year-old Clarita. We were standing in the living section, which acted as living room, dining room and kitchen all rolled into one. On the far wall of the living area was a 45-gallon barrel, the source of water for all family uses, a sink without faucets, but with a pipe draining into a bucket, a two burner kerosene stove, a homemade stove for cooking with charcoal and a tiny work table. In the place of a refrigerator there was an icebox. The centre of the room was dominated by a large kitchen table covered with a plastic tablecloth and surrounded by six rickety, rusty chrome and plastic chairs of Fifties vintage. Above the table, suspended from the ceiling, glared a single naked light bulb, the only source of lighting in the house. A crucifix depicting a very bloodied Jesus adorned the section of wall above the entrance door and on the wall above the water barrel hung a large picture of a Virgin Mary with a brilliant golden halo, cuddling a chubby, curly, rosy-cheeked, baby who also bore a golden halo like his mother's.

Spread out on the kitchen table were the casing and the guts of an antique vacuum tube radio undergoing major surgery. The only instrument in sight was, lying next to the excised parts, a homemade screwdriver unlike any I had ever seen. It was a jury-rigged tool Pedro had fashioned from a piece of hanger wire that he had shaped as a handle at one end and had flattened and filed down to the shape of a flat screw driver tip at the other. I congratulated him on his skills and he showed me his proudest possession, a working 12-inch black and white television set attached to rabbit ears made of…hanger wire. Rosita chimed in, informing us that it was a gift from a couple of tourists in appreciation for her laundry service.

Pedro also informed us that Rosita was an excellent cook and invited us for dinner Friday night.

"What would you like, chicken?" he asked, expecting nothing else but an affirmative answer. If we would give him ten dollars he would look after buying a bottle of rum. Although the bottle of rum cost a Cuban 80 cents I wasn't sure that would leave him enough money for the chicken and whatever else they would be serving. Ten dollars US is equivalent to two weeks salary for a Cuban blue-collar worker but meat is a luxury the average family can only afford occasionally. We felt somewhat uncomfortable accepting the hospitality of such poor people but didn't want to risk insulting them by turning them down.

This evening, we had a visitor come to our boat. Estevan, the official whose birthday coincided with Anthony's, had come to pay his respects. He very sadly confided that effective next week he was promoted to a higher position in Havana, but was very despondent because he did not have the choice of refusal. He would have to leave behind his wife and two children for at least six months, with no guarantee that he would be allowed to bring them with him. He blamed his raw deal on the fact that he had worked too hard and done too good a job. Anthony congratulated him and told him he had done the right thing to give his best in his job, and that in the end he will be rewarded for it and that he should continue giving his best.

By then the four of us had begun on a bottle of rum.

Anthony added, "I've been blessed with five lovely daughters, Estevan. But if I'd had the chance to have a son I would have wanted him to be exactly like you."

Estevan was so touched by Anthony's fatherly advice that he gave him a big hug, declaring in his best English, "Mee Fawdaw!"

I asked Sandrine to prod Estevan for information about Cuba.

I poured some more rum and asked how had the fall of the Soviet Empire affected life for Cubans.

He explained that they are undergoing the "Special Period", a euphemism for the post Soviet period. When the Soviet Union operated its military bases in Cuba, it paid the Cuban government generously for the privilege in the way of oil subsidies and sugar purchases. After the fall of the Soviet empire in 1991, Cuba entered the "Special Period", a period of severe financial difficulty that affected the lives of Cubans of all walks of life. The US did not lift its embargo and Cubans point this out each time the Special Period is brought into the conversation. Many Cubans survive thanks to cash donations from exiled parents in Miami. Those who don't have this source of funds must find other ways to supplement their meagre income.

"What about rationing, how does that work?"

More rum.

Estevan explained that the state issues a ration book known as *Libreta de Abastecimiento* ("Supplies booklet") to each citizen or family unit. The rationed supplies are only available in small amounts. He took his own booklet out of his pocket and gave us some examples, on the basis of per person per month: 3 lbs white sugar, 3 lbs dark sugar, 6 lbs rice, 20 oz beans, 12 eggs, 15 lbs potatoes, 15 lbs bananas. These goods are distributed in a local bodega where the items are purchased at a very highly subsidized price. Meat, poultry and fish, are purchased at the local *carnicería,* when they are available. Other supplies such as cigarettes, cigars, cooking fuels, and light bulbs are also listed in the libreta. Special consideration is given according to age and health status. For example, children of six or less are allowed one litre of milk per day. Supplies to the bodegas are very haphazard, and when a delayed item does arrive, people line up in long queues to obtain their ration. The rations only cover about a third of a family's needs, so the rest has to be purchased at free market prices from the mercado libre, or free market, or in a number of supermarkets and stores that sell items in convertible pesos or in US dollars. One convertible peso was worth one US dollar and for one US dollar you could buy 27 Cuban pesos (in 2002).

Another little shot of rum.

"We noticed some teenagers were wearing Nikes, where do they buy imported goods like that?"

Estevan rolled his eyes, and explained that those who wear such expensive clothes receive them or the money to buy them from expatriate relatives, or with US dollars they earn from tourism. Cubans who have access to American dollars can buy anything they want from tourist stores.

Another little shot of rum.

"What about salaries? How much does a worker earn here in Cuba?"

Our Harbour Master gave us some startling examples. A blue-collar worker or a store clerk earns the equivalent of five dollars per week. A doctor about $25 a month. A government upper management employee might earn as much as a doctor. The best paid state employees are the police and army personnel, who earn $70 to $80 a month. Fidel isn't crazy.

The bottle was now empty. Time to open another.

"What do you think of Fidel Castro?" I asked.

"Fidel is my God. There is no better leader in the world."

Upon which, Anthony's new son suddenly had a flash. He asked for a sheet of paper and a felt marker and made a poster, reading in big letters HAPPY BIRTHDAY! YOU & ME...12-04-2002. He and Anthony then posed for pictures with the sign. More pictures and more hugs and more rum. Another poster reading: "REMEMBER ME FATHER...Harbour Master" and more pictures and more hugs and more rum.

To seal the newly found parental and filial relationship, Sandrine and I sang in unison a loud and heartfelt Happy Birthday to father and son.

Estevan excused himself because he had to go home. To ensure that he didn't fall off the dock before reaching terra firma, we all decided to accompany him as far as the Marina Club House. After multiple goodbyes, hugs, hand shakes and kisses, Estevan tottered through the door.

The call of the Latin American music lured us into the Bar, where we decided to crown the celebration with a nightcap. As we were enjoying our *mojito*, Sandrine smiled at a young man in his thirties at a nearby table, and before we knew it the two of them were dancing. After each dance Sandrine ordered another *mojito* and soon, her dancing became more elastic and imaginative. At one point one leg refused to pace in the same direction as the other and Sandrine came crashing down on a knee, sending a shot of pain through it. Her young companion was at a loss to explain how the lovely French woman might have gotten hurt while in his charge. This declared the end of dancing and *mojitos* for the evening. Anthony and I helped support Sandrine on the walk back to the boat, while she was cursing the crumbling Cuban public infrastructure maintenance.

Friday, April 12. Sandrine found it difficult to extricate herself from the aft cabin this morning, with her knee swollen to twice normal. After having applied ice to her aching joint, Sandrine and I headed for a little boutique at the Clubhouse. There, before us, was the perfect birthday gift for a man facing three months of celibacy. It was a sculpture of a very shapely naked woman minus the head, arms and legs, showing just the main parts, the bust and buttocks. We asked where we could buy a birthday cake. The boutique lady answered that the marina was very far from downtown but that she could get one for us. We asked what choices of cake were available, to which she was dumbfounded.

"Choice???"

Later we would come to understand that in Cuba a birthday cake referred to a layered vanilla cake with pink icing regardless of whether the recipient was a respected official or a labourer, male or female, young or old.

Pedro had summoned us for dinner at 2130, so Rosita could put the children to sleep before we started eating. We arrived bearing a twelve-pack of beer for Señor, and a bouquet of flowers for Señora.

The table was already set with five places and all the mismatching dishes tastefully laid out, a tomato and cucumber salad (actually this is what is meant in Cuba when you ask for a salad), white rice, black beans, fried plantain, deep-fried chicken pieces, a large plastic bottle of cola, bottled water, a pink birthday cake and the bottle of rum without a label.

Pedro hurt his back at his job as labourer with a road repair crew and was now unemployed and convalescing. He received a pension equivalent to $9 per month. Rosita worked part-time at the marina, cleaning rooms, earning $3 per week. It was essential that they find other sources of income, because their meagre revenues were barely enough to buy their quota of *Libreta* rations. We noticed that Rosita was not eating any of the chicken. I asked her if she was vegetarian, but she said she would save the left-over chicken for the children. They only had access to meat once a month and that is not enough for growing children she added. There were no candles for the cake, as this little luxury was not available at the *tiendas*. Anthony affirmed that he already had all the luck he needed and couldn't handle any more wishes, so he would serve the cake *sin velas* (without candles). We sang *Feliz cumpleaños* with a mishmash of Spanish and English.

<u>Saturday, April 13</u>. While Sandrine and Anthony went to the marina to phone Astor, the nationally owned company that might take the boat out of the water to inspect its thruhulls, I stayed behind to continue rinsing and drying seawater-contaminated parts. The Astor representative said he would be at the boat by lunchtime. We waited all morning, then all afternoon, then just as we had given him up for dead, the man sporting a dark suit, white shirt and tie, armed with a clipboard, arrived in time for our 1700 sundowner. He spent more time drinking rum than inspecting the boat and left two hours later with the assurance not to worry and the promise of an estimate within a few days.

Anthony's lower back had been increasingly giving him pain. Tonight was the celebration of the Santiago de Cuba's 487th anniversary. Sandrine and I had arranged to partake in the fiesta with Elan, a tall, handsome man of perhaps 36 who had tripped her fancy, and his much shorter, mustachioed uncle Umberto. The pair made me think of an hispanic Mutt and Jeff duo.

The delapidated bus that we shared with dozens of revelling Cubans of all ages dropped us off on what was a wide multi-lane street that was closed to traffic for the occasion. On either side there were vendor stalls selling a variety of snack foods, souvenirs, Santiago de Cuba T-shirts, National flags, memorabilia of Fidel and the Revolution, Che Guevarra statues.

Interspersed amongst the vendors there were amusements for children, such as a battered Merry-go-round with several of its horses broken with missing ears or hooves. Further along, little children were screaming with delight on a ride consisting of half a dozen rusty, banged up metal cars going around in a circle, with most of their paint peeled off and with missing steering wheels. There was also a rusty swing ride for smiling toddlers, teeter-totters and pony rides. Every hundred yards there was a stage with an orchestra belting out ever louder Cuban music. Hundreds of fans were encouraging the artists with hand clapping, swinging hips and plaudits.

Everybody was wearing a huge smile, cheering *Viva Cuba*! Many brandished a Cuban flag or wore a *Revolución* or a Che T-shirt. Toddlers rode the shoulders of their fathers, older children led their younger siblings by the hand. The crowd was so dense that it was difficult for the four of us to keep together.

Umberto was leading us along, as if he had an objective in mind. After having walked for half an hour, he pointed to a column of smoke in the middle of a park. As we approached, the delectable odour of Bar-B-Q tantalized our nostrils. We were drawn towards an improvised outdoor restaurant on the other side of a fence to discover four whole pigs and four whole goats on spits being turned by hand cranks over charcoal fires. Dozens of tables were lined up in neat rows and a couple of off duty policemen were collecting tickets at the entrance. Umberto asked us to stay put while he inquired as to the timeframe.

"*Una hora solamente*", he was told.

He explained that the meal was not available to tourists, but that if he bought the tickets for us, he could get us in. He went on to ask me for $20, assuring me that he could get a better exchange rate than I could myself. He disappeared with the money and came back a few minutes later with a thick stash of pesos. He said that no Cuban worth his salt would exchange dollars at the official rate of 27 pesos to the dollar. Umberto then paid our entry fee and led us to a table for six that was already occupied by a young couple who gratiously welcomed us to join them. They were both medical technicians working at the Santiago de Cuba General Hospital. Umberto took it upon himself to order beer all around. An hour later, we were told the meat wasn't quite done but to be patient for another half hour. Every time the level of beer in a bottle reached a quarter full Umberto would wave his hand and a replenishment materialized. He asked if anyone would like rum. Sandrine and Elan were takers, so our trusty guide disappeared and reappeared within a few minutes brandishing a labelless bottle of pale yellow rum. He was splurging with the flair and éclat of a lottery winner who had just collected his prize. I was intrigued that there were so many pesos bills left in his stash. Finally, at 2200, after another half-hour, the moment of truth came. A large slice of juicy porc and a smaller one of goat were layered upon a bed of rice on our plates, decorated with an accent of tomato and carrots. The barbecued victuals were heavenly and so tender they could be cut with a fork – a handsome reward for our patience.

After the meal, we ambled among the crowd, observing Santiagonians, young and old, dancing in the streets. Even a stiff-jointed French Canadian like myself couldn't resist swaying to the rhythm of cha cha cha, samba and salsa. When somebody would cry out "Viva Cuba" or "Viva la revolución" a chorus of voices would emerge from the crowd, echoing the exclamation with patriotic fervor.

By the time we weaved our way through the multitude to reach the bus stop and completed the hour-long ride back to the marina it was 0300. Anthony had waited up till 0200, worried that something might have happened to us. Yes, something did happen to us, but not in the sense that he feared. Sandrine and I had been entranced by the festive atmosphere and realized that in a country where people have nothing in the way of material comfort, they can still be rich in joie de vivre.

Sunday, April 14. As I ambled by the entrance, the lady at the marina's boutique beckoned me to approach. With a mixture of English and Spanish she asked me if my friends and I would like to attend an afternoon concert of folkloric music by a very popular Cuban group.

The *Centro de Cultura Folclórica* was a corner property in a very affluent part of the city. The neighbourhood, as with almost every built-up area in Cuba, predated the revolution. The large, old mansions were richly adorned with intricate woodwork. The houses were set back a long distance from the sidewalk and their very large lawns were fenced with fancy wrought iron and stone or concrete posts. Mature trees ornamented the streets and their shade brought welcome solace from the penetrating rays of the tropical sun.

Inside the imposing gates of the Centro two hundred people dressed in their Sunday best stood in small groups, holding glasses and chatting. Ortensia, our hostess from the marina boutique introduced us to her husband Guillermo who insisted on being called William, to her mother and to her cousin, a 20-year old black dancer of generous proportions, named Ursula.

The director of the Centro took the microphone and adressed the gathering. After introducing the artists she invited the group to begin the show. The music was typical rhythmic Latin American and the songs were lyrical at first, then becoming increasingly rhythmic. The audience observed with polite attention, fingers snapping, feet tapping, hips swaying, while not neglecting their glasses. The director came back to the microphone to introduce a Dance Group from the National Ballet Association. The men wore black, tightly-fitting suits with frilly shirts and the women colorful, puffy dresses reminiscent of Flamenco dancers. They swung and swirled and twirled expertly, accentuating their moves with lots of foot stomping and hand clapping to the rhythm of castanets.

Then, as if cued to do so, the entire audience joined in. The orchestra then changed its repertoire to a more plebeian selection of cha cha chas, tangos and mambos to which the crowd responded with applause and with exhortations for more. It had never been given to me to see a hundred couples performing the swoops and turns and heel stomping of the tango on a grass lawn. I was standing under a tree, watching in amazement the collective frenzy that was being wipped up by the enlivened orchestra. Unbeknownst to me, I was swinging my hips and clapping my hands to the beat of the bongos, the maracas, the guiro and the cencerros. This sight didn't go unnoticed, as I caught the attention of Ursula the dancer. She grabbed me and dragged me into the action. As my partner was bumping and grinding along with the music, I looked around self-consciously as my inept attempts at keeping the rhythm just didn't measure up to her expert expression of the beat. It was only when the orchestra stopped for a little swig of rum that I was able to disentangle myself from Ursula's strong arms with the excuse that I needed to answer the call of nature. I was thankful for having learned the word *baño*, for toilet.

When the music stopped after three hours of breaking only for a few tipples of rum, the tired and dishevelled members of the audience retired from the grounds of the Centro.

It was early, so with Ursula tagging along, William and Ortensia invited us to their apartment for supper. It was too early, so why not stop for a little beer so we can plan supper? We were walking along, two by two. As it turned out, William was next to Sandrine, Anthony next to Ortensia and I next to Ursula. To my surprise and bewilderment, the young girl grabbed my hand in hers and nonchalantly kept on walking as though she had just gained a new boyfriend. Her hold was strong, so I couldn't wriggle out of her grasp without having to exert some force and thereby draw even more attention to my embarassing plight. Nothing looks more ridiculous than an aging man walking hand in hand with a very young girl friend in public. I was saved, a block further by the ice cream store where we all broke ranks. This hankering for love had to be cut short. Since I could not find the words in Spanish I asked Sandrine to tell my admirer that I was married and could not take on a girlfriend. My Spanish interpreter, ever creative when it comes to matters of the heart, spoke to Ursula, referring to Roberto. She related to me that she told Ursula that Robert had a girlfriend at the marina who would be very jealous if she found out he was cheating on her, so he could not take on a second one while in Santiago. I'll never know if that's *really* what Sandrine said, but whatever it was, I ceased being the object of unwanted attention.

William was a tall, milk-chocolate-colored man in his early thirties. A high forehead overhung a pair of large, bulging, transfixing eyes, which dominated his oval face. A straight nose, a well tended moustache and generous lips completed the picture. He explained that he was lead guitarist in a local band, and not unexpectedly, he recounted how difficult it was to find steady work. His group would be invited to play for the occasional wedding or private party and often would fail to get paid for their services. They had auditioned for several potential gigs and were vying for a contract with a nearby resort.

Ortensia, in contrast, was much shorter than her husband, of almost black complexion and slightly rotund. Her long, curly hair, tied tightly in a pony tail accentuated the roundness of her face, which assumed an engaging smile. She was one of those people you would find pleasant at first sight.

William asked if we would mind stopping at a dollar fast food joint (one that sells in US dollars) to buy a couple of chicken dinners.

"And what would my sailor friends want for supper? – Calamari?"

We agreed that that would be fine. On the way to the apartment we stopped at a *carnicería* for the calamari and at the chicken place for the take-out for which Anthony picked up the tab at US prices.

The cobblestone street where they lived was lined with crumbling stone buildings abutting onto the narrow sidewalks. From the sidewalk William opened a wide door that was suspended from a crooked, weathered door frame, leading to a long, narrow courtyard, which was more like a dead end lane than a courtyard. On either side of the courtyard were the entrances to a number of apartments. Over time, since the Revolution, most apartment blocks in the nation have been subdivided to create additional living spaces. Second floor balconies overlooked the courtyard and outside stairways connected the balconies to ground level. Several children were tossing a ball to and fro and others were playing a game of hide and seek between the half dozen water barrels bordering the walls of the apartments. Ortensia unlocked the second door to the right and beckoned us to enter. The main floor was one room lit with a single 18-inch fluorescent bulb suspended above the window, fed by bare wires connecting to an electric cord plugged into a wall outlet. On the wall facing the window was a large couch with visibly sagging cushions and with springs protruding. The fabric of the arms and back was torn, exposing tufts of grey padding material. Along the window wall were two mismatching sofa chairs, also of pre-revolution vintage and condition. On the left wall a perilously steep and narrow open stairway led to what I assumed was an upstairs bedroom. Beneath the miniature stairs was a makeshift shelving unit holding a modern sound system with CD player. On the right hand wall, as you came into the apartment was a wooden shelf not much bigger than a cafeteria tray attached to the wall by a set of hinges and propped to a horizontal position by a stick at a 45 degree angle underneath. This was the kitchen table. In the far right corner was a two-burner kerosene stove on a metal stand with a little flowery curtain concealing the contents of its shelves and an old porcelain sink with a piece of unpainted plywood covering it, acting as a removable counter top. Next to the sink was a 45-gallon drum of water, with the cut-out lid acting as a removable cover. A few saucepans were suspended on the wall. Nearer the entrance was a curtained doorway hiding the *baño*. The bathroom was about two and a half feet wide by four feet deep. The toilet was on the far wall opposite the curtain and a shower head was suspended directly above the missing toilet seat. A tiny hand sink on the right hand wall overhung the edge of the toilet. None of the plumbing was functional, save for the toilet sewer drain. To flush the toilet, one used the water from a bucket refilled from the barrel. As would become sadly obvious, much of the plumbing in Cuba had become non-functional. All the walls of the apartment had once been painted white, but had accumulated fifty years of wear and dirt. I vowed never again to complain about the size of the tub in my bathroom back at home.

No sooner had we sat down than the music blared and hips moved. Ortensia put a pan of oil on the stove and began preparing the calamari, swaying to the rhythm of the bongos. William began preparing the "salad", which, of course, consisted of slices of tomato and cucumber. A pot of rice and beans went on the other burner and the guests' supper was underway.

Our hosts asked if we would mind if they started on their chicken. "Of course not", we answered. The hosts devoured their fried chicken, French fries and cole slaw with appetite, plates on their laps. When the guests' meal was ready, Ortensia sat Sandrine and Anthony on shaky, homemade wooden stools, facing each other on either end of the tiny wall shelf and served them their plates, which barely fit on the limited surface. She gave me my plate and signalled me to be seated on the couch and to eat with the plate in my lap. After everybody had eaten, Ortensia moistened a facecloth and in turn, swabbed everbody's hands clean, like our mothers used to do to us when we were toddlers.

William embraced his role as disk jockey with earnest, ensuring that we wouldn't have to suffer one nanosecond without rhythm. No sooner had the remains of the meal been done away with, than a cousin of Ortensia's and his wife appeared, bringing with them a stack of CDs. A pent-up longing for dance needed to be fulfilled. The ladies appeared totally unconcerned and unfeeling about my ineptness at the art of the salsa or mambo and were quite content to swing and sway, whoever the partner, even if a woman. Stomping a naked toe would elicit the same smile as would the execution of a competent twirl. Ursula had understood and accepted Sandrine's story and respected my wish to be left unmolested. Eight people completely filled the floorspace of the diminutive living room.

It was a miracle that no jutting elbow or twitching head met an unsuspecting eye or nose. I sat down every chance I got, with the pretense of needing another guzzle of rum, but was immediately collared by the nearest woman. After everybody was drenched with perspiration and showing signs of terminal exhaustion William lowered the volume and prepared us a Cuba Libre nightcap. I sat down next to Ortensia's cousin Ramón, a quiet man who didn't talk much. I asked him if he had ever visited Canada. He responded that he would love to, but had never been outside Cuba. He added that he would not be allowed to leave for a holiday and that Cubans have no freedom. This turned out to be the only reference to freedom that I was to hear during my two-month stay in this communist country.

<u>Monday, April 15</u>. The man in the dark suit from Astor still hadn't arrived, so we decided to have lunch. Just as the plates were served, he arrived with his apprentice behind him. With great fanfare, he announced, reading from a document on his clipboard,

"*Señor Ionson*, here's what we can do for you. We will take the boat out of the water, place it on blocks, locate and remove each thruhull, inspect each thruhull and plumbing fitting to ensure they are bronze and not brass, reassemble everything. We will replace any defective fitting. We will check for leaks and put the boat back in the water."

"Very good. How much will it cost?"

"We have to talk to the ground engineers to determine what preparations are needed before we can take the boat out of the water."

"How long will that take and when can you start?"

"As soon as possible."

"I need an answer within 48 hours. We have a limited time to stay in Santiago de Cuba."

"*No problema, señor Ionson, no problema.*"

The man in the dark suit from Astor promised to have the answers and disappeared with his assistant in pursuit.

<u>Tuesday, April 16</u>. Ortensia signalled us from the stairway of the marina. The only Cubans who are allowed on the docks are those who have business there. All others have to keep away at the risk of jail or fine. This was our day as tourists, and the Cuban couple would be our guides.

It is evident from the quality of the architecture that the old city of Santiago de Cuba must have been very beautiful in her heyday, prior to the Revolution. The Spanish influence is very prominent, as evidenced by the Mission style houses with their stucco walls and arches, inspired by the Spanish churches of colonial America.

Our kindly guides took us into the Casa de Diego Velazquez on the Parque Cespedes. The conquistador and governor, Diego Velazquez lived in the upstairs portion of the house, while the lower level was used as a gold foundry, and a furnace for melting gold can still be seen. Built in 1522, the Casa is thought to be the oldest residence in Cuba. The house changed hands numerous times before becoming offices during the Revolution. Beginning in 1965 the house underwent restoration work and is now the *Museo de Ambiente Historico Cubano*. The museum displays a large furniture collection dating from the 16th to 19th Centuries. Each room represents a different time period, displaying impressive collections of china, dinnerware, varied household items and period furniture.

The couple then took us to the Cathedral Nuestra Señora de la Asunción, an interesting building featuring a pair of twin towers surmounted by cupolas and a central archangel with deployed wings on the roof between the towers. It is said that the church has survived attacks by French Corsairs, plunder by pirates, arson, earthquakes and hurricanes. It has undergone four reconstructions and found its final function as an ecclesiastic museum in 1963. This historic monument is in my view, symbolic of the dignity, the stoicism, the persistence and the viability of the Cuban people.

Transportation in Cuba is very problematic, with its aging bus fleet, quasi-absence of rail travel, its poor road system and scarcity of automobiles. To supplement the transportation means just mentioned, Cuba relies on 10-person horse-drawn wagons, three wheeled motorized doorless taxis and the *taxi particular*, the private taxi that the government had recently authorized in addition to state-run taxis.

The *taxis particulars* are particularly interesting, as these large American cars are owned by individuals who are most of the time much younger than their cars, which date back to the 1950s. There is a smaller number of old Russian Ladas on the road, which have miraculously survived for decades. Private cars are prized possessions that are often handed down from father to mechanically inclined son. The half-century old cars are held together with wire or have been patched with pieces of roofing tin or plywood. Mechanically, they have been repaired over and over again, often with the introduction of much ingenuity. The switches for the electrical get replaced with parts from radios or discarded appliances or with household switches. Broken door locks get replaced with latches and padlocks, the upholstery replaced with fabric from old curtains, the panes of glass with plastic bags or pieces of plywood, the buttons with coke bottle caps, the rusted out floorboards with wood from pallets, the horns with bells. Nothing cannot be fixed or jury-rigged in some way. In contrast, the state run taxi fleet consists of new Toyotas or other eastern cars that are driven by state employees and that are just as subject to cheating as anything else owned by the government, as I will have you discover later.

The next destination on our hosts' list was out of town. We hailed a *taxi particular*, a 1951 Chevrolet coupe, a very sleek car for its day. The driver agreed to drive us to El Cobre, then to Castillo del Morro, then to our marina, all for $10. We drove through hilly pasture and farmland, which, because we were approaching the end of the dry season, had converted their lush green colours to tones of yellow and brown. Half an hour later we arrived at the point of interest, *La Virgen de la Caridad del Cobre*. It is a small cathedral at the summit of a hill, situated in a stunning setting, surrounded by copper mountains in the old mining town, "The Town of Copper". The altar is dominated by a 16-inch high statue of the Virgin Mary of dusky complexion dressed in an elaborate golden gown, a richly jewelled crown and dangling earrings. She has been named Patron Saint of Cuba and hers has become the most important religious site on the entire island of Cuba. She has been honoured by Ernest Hemingway who gave her his Nobel prize for literature, by Pope John Paul II who crowned her upon his visit and by the mother of Fidel and Raul Castro who gave her a small golden guerrilla fighter while her sons were battling Batista and the Goliath of the planet. Believers of many religious stripes attribute impressive miracles to this quaint statue. And, college students take notice – she is even credited for having helped a student write his thesis and succeed in earning his degree!

Our driver then headed for *El Morro*, but stopped at our request at a sandwich stand for a light lunch, then at a farmer's market as we needed to refill our produce hammock. We finally arrived at El Morro, a massive fortress built atop a rocky promontory guarding the entrance of *Bahia de Santiago*. The sun was descending towards the horizon, bathing the sky, sea and land with a warm, soft glow. We entered the medieval Renaissance-style structure through an impressive drawbridge and paid the entry fee of a mere $4 US for tourists and five pesos for Cuban nationals (approximately 20 times less than for tourists). The fort is a warren of platforms, passageways and cells spread across five levels and protected by two-metre thick walls, built in 1638 to protect the city against pirate attacks. The site offers breathtaking views of the bay and the Caribbean coastline stretching as far as the eye can see. The fort featured a small museum about piracy, the history of El Morro and of the City of Santiago de Cuba.

What impressed me most was the action outside in the main courtyard atop the fort. We had the opportunity of witnessing the beautiful daily ceremony, called *La Puesta del Sol*, which takes place at sunset, recalling the 19th-century importance of the fortress. Adolescent boys and girls dressed as members of the Cuban rebel army solemnly march in unison to the commands of their drill leader, lower the flag from the flagstaff, fold it ceremoniously and shoot off the ancient 1805 Spanish cannon to cries of "¡*Viva Cuba Libre!*"

<u>Wednesday, April 17</u>. I awoke with the rising sun and all was quiet aboard *Mikky*. I silently dressed and stepped off the boat without making a sound. I began walking along the roads bordering the shoreline. There were white cloud puffs trapped in the depressions between the mountains. A light fog added a touch of mystery to the magnificent view over the bay and the sea. There were seabirds that dove underwater and surfaced with breakfast in their beaks. The homes in the foggy hills appeared as if I saw them through a ground glass lens, dissimulating the defects resulting from fifty years of neglect and giving them the appearance of pretty dollhouses. Roosters announced the onset of the day with their cock-a-doodle-doo and dogs responded to my passing in front of their houses with agitated barking to protect their sovereignty. Sounds of human activity started emanating from windows. A small group of men and women, flawlessly dressed in clean, freshly pressed clothes, stood at a corner waiting for a ride into town. As I approached *Mikky* at the dock, I was drawn further by the tantalizing odour of fresh coffee. A new day was underway.

Given the family's difficult financial situation, and the fact that we had approached the end of our supply of clean clothes, we felt compelled to give Rosita our laundry to do. I kept a few of my better T-shirts and Sandrine had kept a few "ladies' things" to do by hand at dockside. Our self-professed laundress would do the wash for the three of us for ten dollars, a little less than it would have cost at home, but far more than what a Cuban would gain in a day's work. Nevertheless, she had been so nice to us that we were not going to wheel and deal with her. She said that she was out of laundry detergent, and asked if we could supply her with some.

"Of course", I said, and went to the boat to fetch half a box of soap, a necessity she could ill afford.

Back at the boat I spent another session of headfirst in the refrigerator, to clean up another smelly mess. An hour after I reactivated the "ON" switch, there was no evidence of cooling. Anthony diagnosed the problem in short time. The clutch cover had come loose, fallen and allowed the drive belt to come off. It was just a matter of finding a screw of the right size to set everything cooling again.

The man in the dark suit from Astor never showed up, but Anthony had discovered a private Dutch company that could do the work. Within a few hours of having spoken to the owner over the telephone, we received a visit from one of the company's engineers. It would cost $500 to have the hydro lines taken down and reconnected to allow the boat to be brought into the yard from the boat ramp. The parts would have to be ordered from Holland and would only arrive next Wednesday, a week hence. They would have to go through Customs, a process that can take several days at best. It would entail *mucho mucho dinero* (lotsa moola). Anthony decided to postpone the inspection until we reached Cienfuegos, as a neighboring sailor assured him that there he would find a reliable private company.

<u>Thursday, April 18</u>. This morning, as Sandrine and I did our hand laundry the boat's fresh water pump gave out. Anthony to the rescue, with tools spread out and headlamp in place on his forehead, soon discovered the culprit; a jammed microswitch. It is a generally recognised fact that Mother Nature is constantly busy destroying the handiworks of its only intelligent mammal. In the warm, humid, salty atmosphere of the Caribbean, everything manmade corrodes, oxidizes, rusts, cracks, peels, bleaches, rots, erodes, abrades, wears down or disintegrates. As is the way with Anthony, out of the confines of the bilge, voilà! – He pulled out a spanking new spare microswitch that was waiting to be given a purpose in life.

This evening we had distinguished guests for supper. We had obtained special permission to have Ortensia and William come to the boat. Since the Revolution hundreds of thousands of Cuban citizens have escaped the restrictions of the communist regime to find a better life abroad, particularly in Florida. The government officials know very well that it is generally the more affluent, more educated and more intelligent of its citizens who succeed in leaving, thus ever impoverishing its remaining workforce. The officials who run the country know that when it comes to escape methods, Cubans have shown much ingenuity and creativity. That is why Cuban citizens are not allowed to have access to objects that the Customs man had us put away: VHF communication radios, GPS units or emergency flares, items that could be very useful for planning a getaway. Cubans are not allowed to leave the country for a pleasure trip. For a Cuban National to be granted permission to leave the country for a business or professional visit, he must have a record that is beyond reproach and must have strong ties in Cuba, such as a spouse and children, otherwise he would be considered a poor risk. Defection is very common amongst artists and athletes who go on tours outside the country. Just to make sure yachties don't take Cubans as stowaways, the government places severe restrictions on who amongst Cubans can come close to a marina. The onus is on the Port Captain to grant or refuse permission and to impose time limits on visits by ordinary Cubans at the risk of receiving a severe fine.

For our visitors, boarding a modern yacht for the first time in their lives, with its polished woodwork, its gleaming stainless steel fittings, its operational plumbing, its intact upholstery, its shiny white fibreglass, its pretty working portholes and hatches, its abundant electric lighting and mysterious instruments, was like stepping into a spaceship! They relished the chicken dish and accompaniments that our French chef Sandrine had prepared with her artistic flair. To our surprise, what drew their attention and interest most were the nautical charts of the south coast of Cuba that Anthony had bought from the cartography official. They had never seen such detailed maps of their coasts before and had never heard of the Gardens of the Queen.

Friday, April 19. An attendant from the marina informed us that our laundry was ready for pickup at our "personal laundry service". Pedro was in his rocking chair on the porch, waiting for time to go by, or perhaps for a new sailor from the marina. He yelled for his wife to come out,"The sailors are here for their laundry."

Rosita came out, looking as tired and dejected as usual and let the three bundles of laundry fall to the floor. Receiving her payment didn't elicit any upturn of the corners of the lips, as she would undoubtedly have to hand it over to her manager in the rocking chair.

Upon unpacking our freshly done laundry the three of us discovered that garments that had been white were now markedly grey in colour. Upon closer examination, we found that each piece of clothing had torn and pulled threads, some of which were inches long. New clothing was ruined and older clothing had now become suitable for working in the engine compartment or cleaning out the bilge.

Later in the day, Anthony and I speculated about what might have ruined our clothes. Rosita's washing machine was one of those small, twin tub washers on castors, which can be rolled around and connected to a kitchen faucet. This design allows for washing in one tub and spin wringing in the other. It now dawned upon us that since she didn't have running water, she would fill her machine from her 45-gallon barrel and process as many loads as possible with the same water. Each subsequent load would acquire a darker shade of grey. As for the damage to the clothing, we deduced that there was probably a sharp edge or a burr either on the agitator or inside the tub, which her well-intentioned husband might have put off repairing till "mañana".

After the laundry debacle, I had an errand in town. I had bought a beautiful little stuffed frog for my five-year old granddaughter Gabrielle. Today I would mail it to her. When I arrived at the post office I had to get in line. Cubans must be the most patient people in the world. Everywhere they have to deal with government employees they have to form a queue. When you consider that 70% of the workforce is government, that means waiting in line for almost everything. Mine was to be an uncomplicated order. I was simply walking into the post office with a parcel ready to receive stamps. I had placed the toy in an empty cardboard cylinder wrapped with thick brown paper, well sealed with scotch tape. I had addressed the package adequately with the marina as the return address. Finally when I reached a teller window, the lady looked at my package with a suspicious glance and sent me to another window. After another long wait in line, the employee took my package, consulted a colleague in the office next to her window. The two of them came to me and said something in Spanish that I didn't quite understand, but that sounded like *inspection*. I said "*Si*", which I felt I had no choice about. Now the ladies faced a new problem. They scoured about and one of them produced an old pair of scissors. Several minutes later the package was breached and destroyed and the little frog closely scrutinized. Another employee, perhaps one of the managers was consulted. Heads nodded and rapid Spanish was spoken. A new problem was yet to be resolved. The two ladies took off in different directions and after several minutes returned to the counter. One had a very well recycled cardboard box and the other a rumpled brown paper bag. Between the two of them they finally had the frog contained and the wrapping complete. I was then handed the package and told to address it anew. The final task was to apply the correct postage. The package was accordingly handed to another clerk who weighed it and wrote down the cost in the upper right hand corner. Then I was given the box and told to present myself at another window and wait in line to buy the stamps. And finally I was shown where to place the package for mailing. Two hours later I was out of the post office, looking forward to Gabrielle's reaction to the little stuffed frog, a representation of her favourite animal. You might not be able to guess the end of the story unless you've had a similar experience. I only heard what happened after I returned home in June. Three weeks after I mailed the little frog, the postman delivered a very lightweight mailing from Cuba. When Gabrielle opened the package she was a little confused as to why her Grand Papa would send her an empty box!

    I was to meet Sandrine at *Parque Cespedes*, a city park a couple of blocks up from the Farmers' Market. I was concerned that she might have given up on me in view of the inordinate amount of time I had been held up at the post office. But, no, there she was, in the shade of a cypress tree, gesticulating, obviously engaged in a gripping conversation with a young man.

    I was to get a haircut before catching up with my shipmate, but she offered to accompany me to the barbershop before resuming our exploration of the town. The tonsorial experience turned out to be completely uneventful, save for the extraordinary price of $1 US for a professionally done job.

The manufacturing sector of Cuba's economy is dismal to say the least. It is widely reported, for example that a Cuban made pair of shoes will wear out within a couple of months. Nevertheless, there is one export, where Cuba excels, and that is the manufacturing of the cigar.

Sandrine and I were passing by an open door when we noticed that it was the entrance to a cigar factory. Our curious approach merited an invitation from a man at the door. The man at the door gave us a royal tour, starting where the bales of dried tobacco are stored, then proceeding to the tables where the leaves are separated and sorted and to the desks where the *torcederos* (cigar rollers) made the finished product. What I found remarkable was the vintage of the desks, the grooved molds, the presses, the cutting boards and trimmers which could have come straight out of the 1920s. The reason why the Cuban cigar is so highly prized is that it is totally hand-made. Human hands have the ability of grasping, aligning and placing the long filler leaves that provide a smooth, cool and flavourful burn, whereas cigar making machines have to be fed short filler, which is of inferior quality, burns unevenly and too hot. The hands of the *torcederos* moved deftly and expeditiously like those of a magician. Within a few seconds the cigar roller could produce a perfect tobacco cylinder with a tapered end out of a fistful of leaves. The man at the door told us that they periodically hold productivity contests, where the best contestants roll in excess of 80 average sized cigars per hour. We could, if we wished, buy the product of the factory, so I bought a single cigar, as I am known to enjoy a good smoke on rare occasions. Sandrine wanted to buy a box to bring back to her husband, but William had already made arrangements for her to obtain a box from a friend who deals freelance. Tourists are constantly accosted by street vendors who sell boxes of 25 Montecristo cigars worth $450 for $25. Caveat emptor!

Every day since our arrival in Cuba the marina dockhand, Ariel, a man of about thirty, came for a visit to offer help with the boat. Today Ariel approached the boat's port side, pedaling a paddleboat. He was delivering four carboys of diesel fuel he had filled at a nearby gas station. The diesel pump at the marina had broken down some months previously, and would remain out of order for some time yet – the reason for hand delivery. Anthony was suspicious of the quality of the fuel, so he used the water separator filter for transferring the fuel to the boat's tank, a slow, backbreaking chore. Thanks for that precaution, because in the bottom of each carboy there was a thick layer of filthy sludge and water.

It would be Sandrine's birthday tomorrow. We had arranged to celebrate the event with our Cuban friends at their apartment. We had given William money to buy a bottle of rum and a birthday cake. It was understood that we would come to their apartment equipped with take-out fried chicken for our hosts and that our hosts would supply us with an entrée of fish.

Ortensia wore a very tight, semi-transparent white dress that revealed every curve and love handle of her black body and of course, her permanent warm smile drew my eyes away from her superfluous folds. As we were eating our fried fish in a batter, I noticed that Anthony and Sandrine seemed to have the same difficulty as I – locating morsels of flesh amongst the batter and bone. I was intrigued as to what kind of fish this was, as it seemed to consist of far more bone than flesh. The next morning over coffee we were talking about the previous evening's supper. Anthony too had been baffled as to the species of fish we had been served. Upon waking up in the morning, he figured out what Ortensia had served us: the discarded bone from filleted fish, which is sold for making soup stock!

<u>Saturday, April 20</u>. When Ariel came to the boat, he would invariably end up chatting with Sandrine who had the knack of treating a younger man as if he were the only male on earth. He would stand on the dock and she would sit on the deck of the boat and they would lose themselves in conversation. After ten days, the young man had developed an obvious attachment to his friendly Parisian friend. On our second day in Bahía Santiago de Cuba we had made a very unpleasant discovery. Overnight a chemical deposit covered every fibreglass surface with yellow spots of rust-like appearance. Ariel explained that its source was air pollution from the cement plant ten kilometres away. Every boat that moors in the bay is thus affected. He assured us that he had a chemical compound that removes the stain and that on our last day we could hire him to clean it up for us.

As Ariel attended to the fibreglass stains we took care of the last preparations: Filled the water tanks; Stowed the dinghy on the deck; Attached the outboard engine to the pushpit; Removed the sunshade; Scrubbed the fenders clean; Secured everything that might become a projectile during a storm; A last beer with Ortensia and William; Hugs, handshakes and adiós.

At 1645 we cast off the docklines and waved goodbye to a teary-eyed Ariel.

A sailboat is meant to float, it's true, and having spent ten days afloat tied to a dock fulfilled one of the vessel's purposes. More important than just floating, a sailboat is meant to sail. Attaching a boat to a dock is like tying a horse to a rail. Both are meant to be free and to express their purpose in life through their motion. After ten days of restraint *Mikky* was at last unleashed and with all sails flying, she broke through the water with unrestrained vigour, leaving a wake in her path. She was alive again.

After a couple of hours of sailing the wind died down, leaving us becalmed several miles from shore. It was Sandrine's birthday, an event worth celebrating even if she didn't want to reveal her age. After enjoying our first supper at sea, we stuck an emergency lighting candle on a cake and sang Happy Birthday again.

Sunday, April 21. 1349. Having covered 88 miles, we dropped anchor in 24 feet of water in *Bahía de Pilón*, off *Cayo Blanco*, a stunning white sand beach. After a swim, we extracted a bottle of Champagne from the bottom of the refrigerator to put a finishing touch on the celebration of Sandrine's birthday. As much as a French woman is reticent about revealing her age, she relishes being the centre of attention. Anthony carried out the old tradition of sharing the Champagne with the sea and the boat. He poured a trickle overboard to satisfy Neptune, the Roman god of the sea, dribbled a wee drop onto the deck to honour our trusty vessel, and then filled our three glasses. After the bubbly was consumed, we enjoyed an entrée of ham and *ratatouille*, washed down with liberal quantities of Pinot Noir. Finally, before spending our first night in the wilderness of the south coast, we facilitated sleep with a Cuban chocolate liqueur.

Monday, April 22. This morning I was up bright and early and baked my mother's banana bread recipe for breakfast. An easy morning, unhurriedly going about doing nothing. After a swim we weighed anchor and set off for another overnight passage of 85 miles. At 1500 a pasta and egg salad was supplemented with a well-savoured cold beer.

The days when each member of the crew was allotted his daily dollop of rum have long ago elapsed. Nowadays we place more importance on safety than on tradition. It is a generally prescribed rule that when a boat is underway there be strictly no alcohol consumed – a rule that Anthony has adopted in principle. It is essential that all members of the crew be sober and in condition to face an emergency at all times. Mother Nature will not discriminate when she decides to unleash her wrath upon a vessel at sea. She wouldn't be more conciliatory towards a boat whose captain and crew were drunk out of their minds. Because of this it is necessary to adopt an across-the-board dry sailing rule because, you never know when you will come across a crewmember who either can't hold his liquor or will drink to excess. The more numerous is the crew, the greater the chance of such a person being on board and endangering everybody. But the world we live in isn't black and white. As with any human endeavour or social circumstance, there is a wide range of shades of grey. When Anthony is with a small crew and he knows there will be no abuse, he will bend the no alcohol rule to foster a more sociable and pleasurable cruise. Ergo, salad with a cold beer.

<u>Tuesday, April 23</u>. During the past night we had variable and light winds mixed in with a squall, forcing us to spend the night making sail changes. I'd been fighting a cold for the past days and was at my worst this morning. At 1030 we ran the engine to cool the fridge, but it wasn't cooling. The culprit was some seaweed blocking the cooling water inlet pipe. How many days was it since we'd had nothing to repair on the boat? A record!

We were still underway when a sport fisherman in a powerboat waved at us and came alongside. We brought *Mikky* to a stop by turning her into the wind. The fisherman, a man with a northern European accent, was brandishing a large fish and offering it to us. He had hired a nearby purveyor company to provide him with a morning of fishing. He was flying back home and had no use for his catch. We jumped at the occasion and didn't have the chance to offer anything in exchange before he disappeared in the mangrove, leaving a heavy wake behind him. I filleted the beast and put the head in a pot of water on the stove for a soup stock.

At 1230 we anchored in Cayo Cachiboca. Since dawn we had been navigating *Los Jardines de la Reina*, the Gardens of the Queen, a ninety-mile long archipelago of small white sand islands in rows, like white pearls strung on a giant necklace. They were thus named by Christopher Columbus in honour of the Queen of Spain who had financed his expedition. Since the islands are 40 or more miles from shore, they are out of reach of ordinary Cubans and tourists. The shoreline itself is fenced by a very dense forest of mangrove, rendering access to the shore almost impossible for a Cuban entertaining the idea of planning an escape. It also assured our privacy and isolation.

A Cuban fishing boat approached us. The fishermen wanted to know if we had cigarettes. This is a lesson: always carry cigarettes when travelling in Cuba. You never know when they might come in handy. No, we didn't have cigarettes, but we had US dollars.

"¿Quieren ustedes langostinas?" Would you like lobster?

For ten dollars they sold us three giant lobsters weighing a total of 15 pounds.

<u>Wednesday, April 24</u>. It was 0400 and we all sprang out of bed at once upon hearing the noise! It was the amplified sound of the anchor chain rubbing against the hull. During the night the tide had turned. Since current has a greater effect on the direction the boat is pointing than does a light

wind, *Mikky* had turned and run up against the anchor chain. Anthony spun the wheel hard over and managed to get the boat away from the chain and within a few minutes *Mikky* had reversed to the end of the rode, the chain was taut and the boat stable. We looked at the speed indicator to discover that the tidal current was flowing at a powerful three knots.

Sleep doesn't come easily when there is a problem with your anchoring system, yet Anthony and I slept some and were up by 0830. At 1150 we weighed anchor and without raising the sails (even though the wind was a good 8 knots) we transited a tricky pass between reefs known as *Canal de Caballones*, Canal of Ridges, which was more safely done under the control of the engine. After a successful pass, we anchored at 1540 alongside a beautiful little island at Cayo Anclitas.

The tropical sun was beating down at its best, so we put up the sunshade and jumped into the water.

Thursday, April 25. We were having coffee and the mango muffins I had just taken out of the oven when the three of us looked at each other in disbelief. Were we hearing things? Out here in the wilderness, a hundred miles from the nearest village, we heard the unmistakable sound of…bagpipes playing! We sprang into the cockpit, looked around, and saw a huge motor yacht, probably 85 feet long, anchored just near us. On the deck at the bow a most unexpected vision was before us. A man in full Highland kilt dress was belching out tunes on a bagpipe. On the opposite side of the island *Hotel Tortuga*, Turtle Hotel, an ugly, floating building propped on top of a barge, was moored in the labyrinthine mangrove. Owned by Avalon, an Italian company that has formed a joint venture with the Cuban government, its purpose was to entice rich white men to bring in much needed foreign currency. As we were to find out when we were turned away from its bar, it was dedicated strictly to those who were ready to pay $1000 per day plus their transportation for the chance of fishing on a catch and release basis.

After the bagpiper finished his repertoire, a smaller motorboat came to fetch him and scooted off towards the concealed hotel. A few minutes later a helicopter rose from the mangrove and flew away northward.

At 1900 the three fishermen who had sold us the lobsters the day before came aboard *Mikky* for supper. In the afternoon they told us not to make supper because they would prepare something for us. They brought aboard a huge pot of lobster tails in a sauce of tomato, onion and garlic, accompanied by a large pot of cooked rice. We shared our rum with them, which was all they wanted. When they parted company with us at midnight, they insisted that we keep the left over food and Anthony gave them a bottle of Gold Magic Trinidadian rum. They each in turn held up the bottle to the light to scrutinize and admire the label, gestured their approval and thanked our captain profusely for the present.

<u>Friday, April 26</u>. This morning I baked bread for the first time on a boat. What a pleasure to inhale the heavenly odour of the staff of life straight out of the oven! What delight to break a piece of still hot bread, to spread butter on it and to savour it one morsel at a time! To bake on a boat is far more demanding than on land, as the ingredients are tucked away in hard to reach places, the countertop space is very limited, the refrigerator is hard to reach into, washing up is complicated, the oven is tricky to light, the baking temperature adjustment temperamental, and when we're underway, the movement of the boat makes it difficult to stand still. Thankfully, the rewards far outweigh the difficulties of the operation.

Weighed anchor at 1145. After covering only 14 miles, we anchored in Cayo Cuervo, a beautiful bay populated by seven fishing boats and for the first time since leaving Santiago de Cuba, sailboats – three of them.

<u>Saturday, April 27</u>. The usual swim, walk along the beaches, breaking into a new loaf of fresh bread anointed with butter and maple syrup.

Hi Cs, a 36-foot yacht, dropped the anchor near our boat. Cyril and Jacquie were from South Africa on a world tour. We invited the couple for supper to share with us a baked dish of the fish the sports fisherman had given us a few days before.

As we were chatting, unbeknownst to us, the oven had turned cold. We only discovered this when the cook checked the fish and found out it wasn't done. An inspection of the oven revealed what is the most common cause for a fuel burning apparatus to quit working – lack of fuel. The propane tank was empty! By the time we had discovered there was a problem, made the correct diagnosis, carried out the appropriate corrective, set the oven heating again and finished baking the fish, it was past 2200. In the meantime, we heard the story of our South African visitors. They were in their early fifties and had paid off their house and sent their kids to university abroad. The end of apartheid had made the country unstable and increasingly unsafe. As whites they no longer felt at home in the country of their birth. They had a taste for adventure, so they sold their house and used the money to buy a boat and the world had become their new home.

<u>Sunday, April 28</u>. When I poked my head outside this morning, there were eight fishing boats in Cayo Cuervo. Fishing in Cuba is strictly controlled by the state. The government owns the boats, dictates the rules, sets the quotas, decides who gets the spoils and puts the fishermen on its

payroll, just like all other state employees. Typically the fishermen work for three weeks during which they live aboard the fishing boat, then have two weeks off during which they go back to their families. After their day's work, they anchor the boat and while away the time whichever way they can. It is no wonder that they seek the company of a bottle of rum and of strangers who have a bottle of rum.

What I found disheartening is the shameful condition of their boats. Built of steel before the Revolution, the fishing fleet hasn't been renewed nor does it appear to have been maintained in fifty years. As a result, the vessels are hulks of rust, with not a spec of paint showing, held together by a prayer, threatening to fall apart and founder with the next passing wave.

The crumbling infrastructures of the nation are an indicator of the failure of the communist regime. It stands to reason that if you were in the shoes of Ortensia and William, who live in a house owned by someone else (the state), and whose roof leaks and you barely have enough money to feed yourself on a diet of rice and beans, that you won't be able to accept responsibility for the repairs. Likewise with fishing boats. The fishermen don't own the boats, they earn very little money and they are obviously not in a position to do anything about costly maintenance items. Presumably, the bureaucrat who is in charge of the fishing fleet, the one who is in charge of the sewers, the one who is in charge of the housing, have no budget for maintenance or if they do, they have "better" uses for it. Whenever I bring up the subject with a Cuban, the answer revolves around the Special Period and the US embargo. It is very convenient for the government to have named a scapegoat on which to pin the blame for its incompetence and for perpetuating a political system that just doesn't seem to work.

Anthony and I have plotted the rest of the trip on his computer using Nobeltec software. This would enable us to "see" the location of the boat in relation to the bottom, reefs, rocks and other underwater obstructions in real time.

Monday, April 29. Anthony and I went snorkelling off a nearby reef. Under a coral head in about ten feet of water we could see big, beautiful lobsters staring at us in mocking silence. Anthony went back to the boat and assembled a makeshift harpoon from a straightened out king-sized fishing hook and a broomstick. He swam back to the coral head for the assault. It is quite remarkable that at the age of 67 Anthony could still dive to a depth of 40 feet and hold his breath for 3 minutes! Our intrepid diver-hunter dove to the bottom, approaching the coral head circumspectly. He located his first victim, took aim and thrust his weapon adroitly at a juicy lobster lodged in a crevice under the ledge. Missed. A cloud of dregs formed and obscured his view. When the water cleared after a few minutes he repeated the cycle of attacks several times, but to no avail.

One lesson you could draw from this is that when you're surrounded by expert lobster fishermen, to let them do what they're good at.

Cyril and Jacquie came up to our boat in their dinghy with a bucketful of giant shrimp. In exchange for two packs of cigarettes, the fishermen gave them a huge pail of the crustaceans, more than our friends could eat and more than they could fit in their refrigerator. I had never seen such large shrimp. Six to nine inches long, it took only a few to make a meal for one person. We had shrimp every meal for the next three days.

<u>Tuesday, April 30</u>. Hey, this morning we were ready to raise the anchor at 1010, a speed record so far! In the total absence of wind, we had to motor. As the sun approached its noon position, it was becoming unbearably hot. We set up the sunshade, thereby reducing the temperature by almost ten degrees.

At 1445 we dropped the hook in *Cayos La Doce Leguas* in 6.5 feet of water. The water was murky here, a phenomenon related to the tides. When the tide came in, a flood tide, the current brought in crystal clear water from the ocean. But when the tide was going out, an ebb tide, the water from the mangroves carried with it large quantities of matter in suspension, rendering it unappetizing.

We explored the area by dinghy, looking for the twelve lagoons suggested by the name of the place. The beach here was desolate, with just a few thin palm trees, seaweed and driftwood littering the white sand. Beyond the beach there was a swamp, then very large trees. Beyond this the forest became impenetrable so we turned back without having found all those lagoons.

We now had to leave the Gardens of the Queen and proceed to Cienfuegos, 109 miles from our anchorage. Since it was important to make landfall during daytime we weighed anchor at 1745 and set our course for an overnight sail to the city of One Hundred Fires.

<u>Wednesday, May 1</u>. The coastline to our starboard had gradually changed from low mangrove to hilly to mountainous.

We entered the long, narrow channel to the Cienfuegos Bay and an hour later we were tied to a dock at the Marina Jagua. Unlike clearing into the country for the first time, we were only given the honour of two officials, the Customs man who checked all our papers and the Port Captain who made arrangements for the dockage fees. The moment the officials left Anthony was fast asleep. The overnight passage had been uneventful; yet,

Anthony had slept very little, worrying about finding a suitable firm to carry out the thruhull inspection.

Sandrine and I were not going to vegetate and listen to the good captain's snoring when there was so much to discover. My French sister, ever the extrovert Parisian wrapped a light silk scarf around her waist to cover the bottom part of her bikini and we moseyed on to the main avenue. There were bars, restaurants and inexpensive hotels meant for Cuban tourists. Children in neat school uniforms were sauntering back home. Tall, slim, Sandrine with her dark tanned skin, flowing red hair and wispy attire, strolling with the sway and assurance of a catwalk queen, attracted stares from passers-by while I, the conservative Canadian was fighting off pangs of self-consciousness.

We stopped to peek into a bar where hundreds of Cuban youths wearing up-to-date clothes and shoes were dancing to the beat of disco music, drinking *Cuba libre* and *mojitos* at North American prices. Some Cubans had access to many US dollars somehow.

We were drawn towards a very ornate castle, the Palacio de Valle. The dazzling structure with its turrets and scalloped arches is reminiscent of Spain's famous Alhambra, displaying a mixture of Venetian and Moorish styles. It was built by a rich plantation owner for his daughter in 1917 and was abandoned by the family in the throes of the Great Depression.

In the boutique I bought a T-shirt featuring drawings of cute, playful frogs for Gabrielle. Fortuitously, I decided to forego the rigmarole of the Cuban postal system in favour of giving it to her *de mano a mano* upon my return.

<u>Thursday, May 2</u>. The marina was owned and run by a private company that was making its first incursions into the socialist state. We might have expected better maintenance and service, but that didn't seem to be the case. We moved the boat to the end of the dock providing us with privacy and an extraordinary view of the Bay.

In the evening Sandrine and I took Anthony to see the impressive Palacio de Valle that we had discovered on our scouting expedition while he was sleeping. In the main hall an ageing Gypsy singer with two-inch long eyelashes and a good layer of wrinkled foundation makeup was at the Grand piano. When she spotted us at the door she stopped playing and invited us to sit, pointing to the chairs in front of her in the large foyer adorned by a high, ornate ceiling. If we would buy her a Cuba Libre, she would sing and play for us. With a faltering voice she belted out serenades, lullabies, and World War II melodies. Like the peeling paint and crumbling concrete of the castle our lady singer's better days were behind her. However, I think that her resolve in plying her trade in spite of her advanced age was typical of the Cuban resiliency and courage.

When the Gypsy informed us there was a band playing upstairs we went up the wide, richly carved stone staircase to the penthouse, which was actually the roof area. Ricardo the bartender was like the Maytag man, visibly lonely for lack of work. When Sandrine and he met, it was like a reunion of long lost friends, even though they had never laid eyes on each other before. Ricardo took her hand and kissed it with an elegant bow and the French lady relished the attention.

The band, till our arrival had been silent for lack of an audience, but no sooner had we sat down than they played one piece of lively Latin American music after another. Out of nowhere a very *bonita* young lady of no more than 25 appeared on the dance floor as if by magic and swayed sensuously to the rhythm generated by the five musicians. Her tight-fitting white dress contrasted with her dark Latino skin and revealed much of her pleasantly plump physique. She approached our table and asked if she could join us. We offered her a drink and she asked for a *coca* (Pepsi without alcohol). She called herself Lazara and characterized herself as a professional dancer. She had been on tour in Spain and other European countries with her dance school. She spoke of the increasing difficulties the school had endured obtaining exit visas for its students. She herself had been refused permission to leave the country once and had to appeal the decision. After much negotiation she won her appeal based on her loyalty to her family and the fact that she had a daughter who still needed her.

The musicians were finished playing, but were staying close to our table. I gave the leader $5 and he and his group graciously bid us *buenas noches*. Ricardo the bar tender came to join us at our table and served us a final round of *mojitos* on the house. He sat very close to Sandrine and put his hand on hers. He then very jovially told jokes. Each one was very vulgar and fell flat, without a punch line. Sandrine pulled her hand away and he continued with his stories. After each "joke" he would break out into uncontrollable laughter, inciting us to laugh even though his jokes were simply not funny.

Lazara invited the three of us for supper tomorrow night. It will be her birthday.

<u>Friday, May 3</u>. It was 1100. A mechanic from *Los Artilleros*, a privately owned boat repair company came to see what had to be done in the way of inspection of *Mikky*'s thruhulls. After a cursory look at the boat he informed us that an engineer would come later.

In the marina parking lot the driver of a horse drawn wagon waived at Sandrine and me, beckoning us to approach. Anthony was staying behind to receive the engineer from Artilleros. The driver was sitting at the reins of a homemade wagon drawn by a single, tired-looking horse. The carriage, made of wrought iron and wood, held two lengthwise rows of facing benches capable of seating five people each and bore a canvas roof and plastic curtains that could be drawn shut on either side in case of rain. He would take us right downtown, a four-kilometre ride for the modest sum of $1 each. We climbed aboard the ten-passenger wagon. Our *caballero* directed his old mare across the main boulevard and turned left onto a side street. Row upon row of houses lined the two sides of the street, with no space between them. A few kilometres further, the driver made another left and dropped us off a few hundred metres short of the main street.

Cienfuegos is host to many lovely buildings of a variety of styles. In the square José Martí there is an ancient theatre, *Teatro Tomás Terry*, an exquisite Italian style construction dating back to 1886. The majestic lobby displays a statue of the Venezuelan business magnate in whose name the theatre was dedicated. As with every other jewel of architecture built before the Revolution, the theatre has suffered a half-century of neglect as exemplified by the discoloured wooden seats, some of which were hanging from broken hinges. It struck me as emblematic of the Cuban spirit of endurance to stoically sit through an entire opera in agonizing discomfort.

We picked up a couple of loaves of bread at the bakery. Perhaps we were there at the right time of day because there was still bread on the shelves and there was no line-up. It's usually the other way around: no bread and a line-up of people waiting for the next batch to come out of the oven or waiting for the order of flour to arrive so the baker can start his work. What's particular about a Cuban bakery is that it's state run and therefore carries only one type of loaf – a small white wheat bread with a soft crust, a slightly crumbly crumb and with little flavour. When in Cuba, forget about miche, baguette, whole wheat, brown, rye, multigrain, pumpernickel, flat breads, sourdough, Focaccia, Vienna, bagels, croissants or breads filled with fruit or spices unless you decide to isolate yourself in an all-inclusive resort.

There were three ways we could go back to the marina – walking, taxi particular or horse drawn wagon. Having decided on the horse-drawn wagon we stood on a corner with other people, Cubans, waiting for the next ride. When the first wagon came to a halt, we let the Cubans board before us and when we embarked, the driver unceremoniously kicked us off and told us that this means of transportation was restricted to Cuban Nationals. Since our first experience had been so pleasant, we tried our luck with the next wagon. There were several unoccupied places. A woman and man each climbed aboard and paid their one peso fare. Before we could step aboard this driver waved us away and yelled that the carriages were off limits to tourists. Sandrine is not one to be shunned. She was so angry she yelled back, "Let me tell you, Mister, that we French can teach you Cubans one or two things about Revolution!"

As we were walking back towards the marina, we concluded that it was illegal for tourists to use this means of transportation, but that for a quick profit, some of the drivers would wait at the marina, pick up a few tourists at 27 times the going rate, and take them downtown through the side streets, hoping not to get caught by the authorities.

As we ambled down the main boulevard, El Paseo del Prado, we appreciated that in spite of its run-down state, Cienfuegos was a beautiful city. The buildings are of neoclassical style and of no more than three stories in height, which makes sense when you don't have elevators. In the city centre the Paseo del Prado was tree-lined and flanked by wide slate sidewalks. It marked the main division of the city and on either side were narrow streets with row house style buildings abutting the sidewalks. For the last kilometre it followed the shore to the marina.

We walked over to Lazara's apartment for dinner. I brought with me a maple syrup birthday cake I had baked in the morning. Our hostess introduced us to her 13-year-old daughter Heidi, a very small, shy, polite girl. It was remarkable that Lazara, a child herself when she gave birth, had managed so well in bringing up her daughter. The father, a 58-year-old drunkard had abandoned her before the birth of the baby. Heidi was diabetic and needed insulin daily. It was quite inconvenient because in the tropical heat the medication has to be kept refrigerated. Since she didn't have a refrigerator, she had to keep it in a neighbour's fridge, which was not easily accessible.

There was no request for rum or American style fried chicken on the part of our hostess. We were served what amounted to be a luxurious meal for a Cuban: Chicken, rice and beans, the ubiquitous tomato-cucumber salad as well as a hefty serving of homemade French fries. I ate with the guilty feeling that we might be depriving mother and daughter of their month's meat ration. Fortunately, we would have the chance to make it up to her some other way.

<u>Saturday, May 4</u>. At 0700 two men from Artillero were at the dock to take stock of the work to be done. They promised an estimate by Monday.

We spent the afternoon with Lazara, Heidi and a cute three-year-old girl, daughter of Lazara's neighbour, at Playa Rancho Luna, a crescent shaped sand beach for Cubans and their families. I rented a paddleboat and to the delight of the girls, rode the swell like a surfboard. Next to the beach there was a tourist resort that was off limits to all Cubans except registered employees. Lazara accepted such apartheid as a fact of life. I felt that generally there is amongst Cubans a sense of resignation vis-à-vis the restrictions placed on their liberties. Perhaps it's because the majority of Cubans are too young to have ever known freedom and that they can't appreciate what they're missing. In the same vein, today's young Canadians will think that the invasive airport security measures our government imposes on us are an unavoidable consequence of living in an industrialized society. Perhaps it is a collective wisdom found in the prayer:

> "Lord, grant me the courage to change the things that I can,
> The serenity to accept the things I cannot change,
> And the wisdom to know the difference."

We took Lazara out for dinner at a restaurant that boasted having served Fidel Castro during his incursions into the south during the Revolution. I wondered if *El Comandante* chose the standard fare of rice and black beans.

Sunday, May 5. Sandrine had reserved a *taxi particular* for the day to drive us to the town of Trinidad about 85 km from Cienfuegos, in the beautiful *Valle de los Ingenios*. Founded by Diego Velázquez de Cuéllar in 1514, the city was touted as a must-see, because of its colonial architecture. It is unlike others we had seen, as this one was inland, out of sight of the sea. The streets were extremely rough cobblestone, suitable only for four-wheel drive vehicles and for walkers with strong ankles and good shoes. We had to make abstraction of the disintegrating stucco, roof tiles and rusting wrought iron to imagine how beautiful the city must have been in its days of glory. A few vendor stalls lined the sidewalks, selling the same trinkets we saw elsewhere. Almost everything of interest in town is clustered around the Plaza Mayor in the historic centre, including two closed churches. The city is small and therefore can be visited on foot in little time. We went to a bar in the shade of tall cypress trees to ward off the oppressive heat. We sat down to each a large frosted glass of fruit cocktail. A flute player launched into a beautiful repertoire of classical tunes, carrying us into a temporary heaven, making up for the less than exciting attraction that was this "must-see" town.

Monday, May 6. Today the Artillero representative came as promised. He would take the boat out of the water and do what needed to be done, all for $500. It would be less if some parts didn't need to be changed.
"Agreed!"
It was just a matter of defining a time slot.

Tuesday, May 7. This morning the Artillero people were at the boat bright and early with a scuba diver to take measurements of the hull in order to build a cradle to hold it up while out of the water. In Cuba boatyards have no travel lifts to take boats out of the water and scoot them over to a storage or work area. They use instead, an ancient system of railway tracks that lead down a ramp into the water. The boat is floated onto a car that rolls on the tracks and is winched onto land.

Anthony had arranged for Lazara and Heidi to have supper aboard *Mikky*. When our guests arrived they were held up for half an hour at the gate, as the guard had not received clearance from the Port Captain to allow them entry. We served mother and daughter meat loaf with potatoes and vegetables and for dessert, a baked apple with brown sugar. They ate with little appetite, since they were unfamiliar with the strange foods before them. They just picked at the meatloaf and baked apple, and left most of the dinner and dessert in their plates. We barely had time to take a few pictures of our guests, when an hour after they stepped aboard, the marina guard came to the boat to announce that their time was up.

<u>Wednesday, May 8</u>. This was the day *Mikky* was migrating onto dry land. Anthony was to stay on the boat during the three days it would take to accomplish the inspection, but Sandrine and I would have to find another place to stay. We decided to take advantage of the opportunity to visit Havana. We hired a *taxi particular* operated by Sergio. Since his wife China (pronounced Chee-nah) had relatives in Havana, they would drive Sandrine and me to the Capital, we would stay over two nights and return to Cienfuegos. The total fee was $60 US for the return trip (2 ½ hours one way).

Sergio had reserved us two rooms at a bed and breakfast operated by an old couple, Aurelio and Maria Hernandez about three kilometres from the heart of Havana. We dropped off our baggage and broke company with our driver and co-pilot.

We took a little yellow three-wheeled fibreglass Vespa taxi into the town centre. There was a row of horse-drawn carriages waiting for us. We boarded one and our driver took us through some of the prettiest streets of old Havana. Our caballero brought his charge to a halt in front of a bar. The bartender came out and asked to take our order. What an original idea! We each ordered a mojito, served the Cuban way with a squeeze of lime, a jigger of rum, a sprig of fresh mint, a dollop of sugar, ice and soda water. It was the best mojito I'd enjoyed in Cuba. As our carriage plied the streets of Old Havana, I nursed my drink and felt like a member of royalty touring the streets of his kingdom. I was totally relaxed and happy. Not to take anything away from my French friend, the only thing that could have made the experience more enjoyable would have been if Micheline could have been here with me.

Here in the capital we also sadly observed signs of decrepitude, with a few exceptions where UNESCO sites had been restored. The buildings themselves could not look clean, since they lacked paint and suffered from a common tropical ailment, black mould. One thing that was remarkable, though, and this we had seen in the other cities we had visited, was the cleanliness of the streets. There wasn't a single piece of paper, rubble or vegetation littering the ground. We often observed ladies or young girls sweeping the sidewalk and the street in front of their houses and were impressed with the pride Cubans place in tidiness.

At the end of the day we retired to our B&B. The rooms were in the couple's large second floor apartment. Whenever they had guests Aurelio and Maria and Maria's sister Flores and her son Julio would all congregate in one room to sleep, leaving the other two bedrooms for the tourists. I was shown to the shared bathroom. Apologies were made for the lack of running water. The tap water gets interrupted once in a while, I was told, and sometimes remains off for several hours. Tonight I had to "shower" by ladling water over myself from a bucket I took into the bathtub with me.

Thursday, May 9. A basket of unbuttered toast accompanied our single fried egg served in a tiny plate no bigger than the egg itself. Maria apologized for the absence of jam to go with the toast, but she would have some tomorrow.

Once downtown we met by accident or by design a very prim and proper white woman who introduced herself as Judy, a professional guide and proved her claim by flashing her *Guía de turista* card. For $5 she would spend the day with us and show us all the main points of interest. She spoke English to boot.

Havana, with its population of 2.2 million is Cuba's largest city. Although Cuba is in a semitropical zone, I think there is something that Canadians can learn from studying its urban planning, in view of the coming worldwide energy crunch. When gasoline reaches $2 per litre, we will have to rely much more on walking to get from point A to point B. In Havana most of the territory consists of row housing, two to three stories high, with the buildings abutting the sidewalks, thus eliminating unnecessary front lawns. Furthermore, zoning bylaws allow a mix of residential, small business and retail, which eliminates the need to drive to a distant shopping centre of Big Box stores.

Much of the Capital city is badly run down, but for the delight of the tourist, many of its historical buildings have been faithfully restored. Our guide took us to the house where Cuba's national hero, José Martí, was born in 1853. He was the leader of Cuba's independence movement as well as an important figure in Latin American literature. The modest stucco house with a tin roof, has been converted into a little museum displaying Martí's modest personal possessions.

Judy then took us to the Museum of Colonial Art, an interesting building with a beautiful central courtyard decorated with a multitude of tropical plants. What struck me were the stained glass panels crowning the windows and doorways and the high, cathedral ceilings of carved wood painted sky blue. The exhibits consisted of fine antique furniture and dinnerware used by aristocrat families during the latter years of Spanish rule.

Next, we walked through the *Plaza San Francisco de Asiz*, a spacious square dominated by a convent of the same name, whose main feature is a high tower made from multiple stories piled one upon the other. Near the cruise ship terminal at the other end is the Fountain of the Lions, a remarkable sculpture showing four resting lions ejecting streams of water from their mouths. A couple of newlyweds in full wedding dress and tuxedo posed for pictures on the edge of the fountain while children played tag, screaming with delight. A little farther, an old woman feeding pigeons was being swarmed by her protégés. Tourists with big bellies, wearing designer sunglasses, skin-tight T-shirts, short pants and fanny packs were snapping pictures of each other.

Judy then took us through *Plaza Vieja* (Old Square), which, when it was designed in mid 16th century, surprise-surprise, was called *Plaza Nueva* (New Square)! It was surrounded by recently restored two to three story buildings of varying styles and stages of restoration. They consisted of private residences equipped with covered balconies, internal courtyards and wrought iron gates. Salsa music was bellowing from the *cerveceria* (pub) in a corner of the square. A man and woman were dancing the cha cha cha next to the tables and a little girl wearing a ponytail in front of the adjacent house was dancing by herself, swinging her arms and her head to the contagious rhythm, oblivious of anybody watching.

We stopped to treat our guide to supper. As usual, there was music, this time produced by a duo of singers. Our table was right next to the sidewalk and we were seated next to a large, open window. An old man was sweeping the sidewalk adjacent to us. When he became aware of the music emanating from our eating place, he flipped his broom brush-side-up, held the handle in his right hand and propped his left hand up and away as if holding the hand of an imaginary dancing partner, and carried through the steps of a tango. Then, leaning towards our window, he flashed Sandrine a blissful smile and a wink.

The drawback with a B&B located in bedrooms of the owners is that you have to be in by their bedtime, which wasn't a terrible sacrifice, as we were pooped after a day of walking and listening to our tour guide. Shower consisted of ladling from a bucket once again.

Friday, May 10. Slept in till 0900. Maria apologized for the lack of running water for our second night and for the lack of jam for our second morning. We spent an easy day, stopping frequently to sit on a bench and watch the comings and goings.

We passed by *El Capitolio*, a splendid building that used to be the seat of government but is now home to the Cuban Academy of Sciences. Regrettably, it was closed to visitors that day. Just a few blocks farther we made an incursion into one of Ernest Hemingway's favourite watering holes, *El Floridita*. In a corner of the restaurant there is a statue of the great novelist and journalist, which provides credence to the restaurant's claim that "Papa Hemingway" spent much of his time drinking there. Although the man's staple drink was the daiquiri, Sandrine and I opted for our trusty mojito, which, we should have predicted, turned out to be anaemic and overpriced.

Aurelio and Maria weren't the only ones in Havana who had water troubles. A few times we came across a water tank on a trailer. People took their empty carboys to the tank and filled them up and then carried them home. In one case a trailer was parked on the street in front of a five-story apartment building. Out of a window of the fifth floor a pulley with a long rope was attached to the end of a pole. There was a man in the window and another at the sidewalk. They worked as a team to hoist carboys of water with rope and pulley from street level up to the apartment.

We met Sergio and China and treated them to supper. Sergio was excited. He announced he'd heard through the grapevine that a famous Cuban orchestra, Sol al Sol, would be playing tonight at a bar known as the *Casa de los Intiernos*. The group was the most popular in Cuba and was known for creating a style that Cuban bands have been imitating ever since. They apparently made their mark in a film entitled Buena Vista Social Club.

We were greeted at the entrance of the club by a heart-thumpingly beautiful girl in her early twenties. She had a dark complexion accented by a moulding, white décolleté dress and introduced herself as the granddaughter of Bartolo, the 84-year-old leader of the group. Every chair and every square foot of standing room was occupied and everybody had been served at least one drink, when there was a stir in the audience. Out trotted a group of eight very aged men wearing white shirts and caps. The audience applauded exuberantly, postponing the start of the show for at least five minutes. Finally, the first bars of *Solamente Una Vez* were sounded, prompting the crowd to rise in standing ovation with a frenzy of hand clapping and hurrahs. The first notes of every piece elicited the same enthusiastic reaction. Sometimes the members of the audience joined in the singing, seemingly familiar with every word of the songs, or they would engage in energetic hand clapping to the beat of the maracas.

The beautiful girl made the round of the tables, selling CDs for her grandfather's group. When she arrived at my table, she bent down, displaying a distracting amount of cleavage. She looked at me in the eye and smiled as though I were the only man stranded on a desert island with her. With a wee wiggle of her generous hips and a smile that would melt the heart of an ogre she whispered, "*¿Y para usted señor?*" Inasmuch as I inherited no natural defence against such a merciless sales pitch, I capitulated without a soupçon of resistance and bought the latest CD.

We left before the show was over because it was a long way to Cienfuegos and our driver was tired. Sergio and China drove us back to our marina on the south coast. Before parting company with our drivers in the wee hours of the morning, Sandrine embraced and kissed them both as though she were bidding farewell to a brother and sister leaving for long tour of duty in a faraway land.

Anthony and the Artilleros had completed the inspection of the boat and everything was back to normal with *Mikky* waiting for us at her berth with all her thruhulls certified safe. As Murphy would have it though, that wasn't the end of our troubles.

<u>Saturday May 11</u>. We were invited for coffee and muffins on Hi Cs with Cyril and Jacquie. A Cuban woman, Anita Ricardero was with them. The couple had met the lady at an art exhibition and struck up a friendship. Anita, in her mid thirties, was an art professor at the *Universidad de Cienfuegos* and had exhibited her works in a gallery in Toronto the previous year. She invited us all for dinner at her home tomorrow night to have a look at her paintings and to celebrate Mother's Day.

In the afternoon the three of us left the marina and went off in our own directions. I very much enjoyed an afternoon without any company once in a while. If you want to be successful in living on a boat with other people it's essential to elaborate coping strategies. Cienfuegos is an attractive town to spend time in. There is virtually a complete lack of automobile traffic in this, as well as other Cuban cities. Its absence makes you appreciate how simply delightful it is to walk along a sidewalk without the noise and the smell. It is very useful to keep this in mind when one tries to imagine what it will be like in Canada after the oil peak. We will suffer much deprivation, but the collapse of our rapacious consumer society will afford some interesting silver linings.

When I indulged in my solitary excursions I would sometimes sit in a café in one of the several charming courtyards in the shade of tropical trees and vines or I would sit in a park and read a book. Often I would not remain alone for long.

In one instance a young man of 18, a high school student, approached me as I was in concentration and all he wanted of me was the chance to practice his English. We spoke for a good hour in a mixture of English, Spanish and hand gestures and before parting company he took down my address, promising to write, a vow that didn't materialize.

In another case I was waiting for Anthony in the town square. I'd had a previous experience where a woman approached me offering her friendship, but this one was special. She was a very pretty 23 year-old Latino girl who came and sat next to me. I kept on reading, watching her with my peripheral vision. She sidled up to me and struck up a conversation. After asking me where I was from, what I was doing in Cuba, how I liked her country, she came to the point.

"Do you have a girl friend in Cuba?"

"No, but I have a wife in Canada."

"That doesn't matter. I could be your girlfriend while you are in Cuba."

"I'm too old for you, dear."

"But love has no age" she replied.

I had to be blunt and tell her that I thought she was very charming but that I wasn't interested in starting a relationship. Then she REALLY came to the point.

"I have a three-year old daughter who is epileptic. I don't have money to buy her medication. Can you give me fifty dollars?"

I politely turned down her request, after which she readily lost interest in pursuing the love affair. To this day I am unsure of whether it was true that a Cuban could be faced with such a huge medical expense since their socialized medical system highly subsidized the cost of pharmaceuticals.

There is one case that will stay burned in my mind. He was a very old man, walking down the street with the help of a cane. He said hello and asked how I was. Then he asked me if I had a pencil or a ballpoint pen I could give him. Unfortunately, that day I had neither. Just before he turned away I offered him a dollar and that evoked an ear-to-ear smile and seemed to have energized his faltering gait.

Cubans don't always want something from you when they approach you with their friendly smile, but there is frequently some kind of expectation. Often the friendship that is struck between a Cuban and a tourist becomes a symbiotic relationship. The Cuban benefits from economic fallout in the way of a restaurant meal, or a beer or gifts. The tourist, on the other hand, might benefit from the lower cost of pesos restaurants or bars when he has a Cuban tagging along and what better way to get to know the people?

One case in point occurred when I met a 62 year-old man who started telling me about the difficulties of living in the Special Period. It was lunchtime and I asked him if he wanted to join me for a meal at a restaurant. He led me to a pesos restaurant where we both enjoyed a very satisfactory dish of pork stew, rice and beans, and put down a couple of beers each for a grand total of $2.60. You do have to keep in mind that when you eat in a pesos restaurant there may not be any running water, so the dishes may not have been washed adequately. Also, luxuries that we take for granted, like toilet seats, are a thing of the past in those establishments.

I was enjoying a few hours on my own seated on a bench in the public square. A soldier in full official dress walked by me holding a Cuban pink birthday cake, unwrapped, balanced in one hand. Then two men walking abreast came by me, they too each carrying a pink Cuban birthday cake (not in a box either). When I saw two others doing the same it dawned upon me that the next day was to be Mothers' Day. I was to learn that Mother's Day is a very important event in Cuba.

When I returned to the boat Anthony informed me that tomorrow would be a busy day. Lazara invited the *Mikky* crew for lunch at her parents' place to celebrate Mother's Day and this was in addition to supper at Anita's.

Sunday, May 12. Mother's Day. Since Lazara's parents lived in a nearby village we hired Sergio and China to chauffeur us. Music blared from the large windows of the second floor apartment. Kitchen, dining room and living room were a single wide-open space where the furniture had been pushed against the walls to create a dance floor. Lazara introduced us to her mother and father and all the cousins, uncles and aunts. Sergio and China were called in and treated as special guests. Mrs Dueñas was in her late-forties, Latino looking like her daughter, but with long, dangling curls and dark, sparkling eyes. After the introductions were over, she took my hand and gestured to the dance floor with the inquisitive look that said, "Want to dance?" It would have been rude to decline making at least a token effort at satisfying my hostess. Since the floor was already full of swinging bodies, my shyness evaporated and I managed a reasonable imitation of the cha cha cha. When the piece was over, she thanked me graciously and headed for Anthony who was waiting on the sidelines. I have to remind you that my friend lived all his life in places where dance music dominated the streets and airwaves, so these expressive dances were second nature to him.

The dining room table, which had been moved into the kitchen area, held a dozen dishes filled with not only the standard fare I was getting to expect, but also with pork, deep-fried breaded fish, onion rings and calamari. Of course, in the middle of the table there was the ubiquitous pink birthday cake waiting to be partitioned. We were served a delicacy that is common in the Latin American world, called *chicharrón*: slices of pork fat with the rind, deep-fried until crisp. In a distant part of the world, this specialty is popular during sugar bush time in French Canada, when the sugary sap is collected from the maple trees. Known as *Oreilles de Christ*, or Christ's Ears, we like to serve them with a generous anointment of maple syrup.

In addition to pre-teen Heidi, mid-twenties Lazarra and middle age mother, there was a fourth generation present, Mrs Dueñas' own mother, an octogenarian with much curvature in her back. Arthritis confined the old lady to her rocking chair, but didn't prevent her from keeping the beat by tapping the floor with her cane.

After the celebration at Lazara's parents we headed directly to Anita's to join our South African friends Cyril and Jacquie for supper and art appreciation.

Our hostess lived with her parents in an interesting building. The street itself was lined with block-long row housing. The attached buildings were two stories high and were faced with beautiful, intricate wooden window frames and doors (at least they were certainly beautiful when built at the beginning of the 20th century). Upon entering I was faced with a makeshift arrangement of plywood walls with a door leading into a main floor apartment and another leading to a long stairway. The floors were of beautiful ceramic tile and the walls decorated with fine Italian tile. It was obvious that this had originally been a large single family dwelling for a family of means. The upstairs was further divided but vertically instead of horizontally. The living room ceiling was the original height, about fifteen feet, and showed beautiful, intricate mouldings and medallions. The rest of the apartment was subdivided in such a way as to create a second story within the second story, each one with a low ceiling of about seven feet.

We met Anita's parents, a couple a little older than I, who were retired and living off a government pension. They owned the building, as Cuba is now open to private ownership, and rented the first floor to Mr. Ricardero's nephew and family of four children. Outside the kitchen door Anita had set the table on the very pleasant terrace built above a section of the first story roof.

The main dish was *tamales*, a mixture of pork, corn, flour, garlic, onions and tomato wrapped in corn husks. It was followed by a delicious dish of *calamares*, squid, and yellow wax beans. For dessert we had the choice between a potato pudding or birthday cake.

After supper Anita led us to the living room to treat us to an art display. Bowls of fruit, vases of flowers and pieces of furniture were reproduced as if seen reflected from a funhouse mirror. Abstract still life painting has never excited me. If you see a beautiful vase filled with nice fresh flowers, why make it look like a crooked vase holding wilted flowers? As they say, beauty is in the eye of the beholder, because Sandrine loved the art professor's work and purchased three paintings of vases to hang in her New York home. For my part, I couldn't bring myself to buying any of the pieces, but felt slightly guilty to have accepted such a nice meal with nothing to give in return. So I resolved to offer her a day of travel outside the city.

<u>Thursday, May 16</u>. So far what I had seen of Cuba was either flat countryside, seacoast or cities. The two greatest gifts Mother Nature has provided me with are the sea and the mountains. I am never more contented than when I'm surrounded by either. I knew there were mountains in Cuba and devised a way to kill two birds with one stone – that is, get to see some natural spaces and give something back to my hostess. I queried Anita about Cuba's mountain ranges and how to get there. She told me there was a national park in the *Sierra del Escambray* mountain range, which she had visited as a student and that the only way to reach it would be by private car or by taxi. The cost of travel in Cuba prevents many Cubans from getting to know their own country, even if by Canadian standards the territory is very small. I thus asked Anita to be my tour guide and to invite a friend to come along for a day of exploration of the area. She said that her friend Salvadora, a radio announcer who loves the outdoors had never visited the park and that she would love to go. I told her that I knew a reliable *taxi particular* owner who had provided me with excellent service to Havana. She winced and responded that we would be much safer with a state taxi. The government cars were newer, in excellent working order and she knew a driver who would charge no more than $45 for a day trip.

On the designated day Anita introduced me to Salvadora, a small, attractive white woman of 27, who enunciated Spanish with a clear diction, as opposed to the rapid-fire dialect most Cubans speak. Our taxi driver Ramiro arrived at the wheel of a new subcompact car. He drove us through to the outskirts of the city and gradually we entered hilly, then mountainous terrain. After an hour, as the car was climbing a steep hill, I glanced at the meter and realized that it had reached $40 and we still had half an hour to go before arriving at our destination. Anita was in the back seat next to me and I drew her attention to the meter. She saw the concern on my face and gave me a knowing smile that said not to worry. A little while later, when the meter clocked $45, Ramiro pulled over to the side of the road, opened his door, lay down on the floor on his back, head under the dashboard. He fiddled a bit, then pulled himself up, took his seat and drove on. He had disconnected the speedometer and left it that way for the rest of the trip. The final part of the road was extremely steep and rough, worthy of a four-wheel drive vehicle. I had to admire Ramiro's skill in contouring large rocks, steering around huge holes and in avoiding bashing the oil pan. He would be a perfect driver on the Canadian logging roads that lead to my favourite canoeing rivers.

We arrived at the entrance to *Gran Parque Natural Topes de Collantes*, whose protected slopes are swathed in Caribbean pines and an abundance of ancient tree ferns, bamboo, and eucalyptus. We continued to *El Nicho*, a series of beautiful waterfalls and clear blue pools. We walked along the creek above the waterfalls. Anita and Salvadora understood that I enjoyed walking for the pleasure of walking, a concept that Cubans find bizarre. When the locals saw tourists panting and dripping with sweat, jogging for pleasure, they would scratch their heads in bafflement.

We picked natural growing *mamey* (also known as *sapote*), a delightful fruit with a large black shiny stone and a very sweet, orange-coloured flesh and *poma rosa*, a small, yellow fruit whose stone is loose inside and tastes a little like a sour pear. We arrived at a lookout where we stopped to admire the view. The scene was a panorama of tropical forest vale and mountains. At the bottom of the valley a river meandered like a blue ribbon dividing a green carpet.

Salvadora exclaimed in Spanish, "This is the most beautiful place on Earth!"

Anita begged to differ, asserting that there are other places, like the Alps that are much more stunning, and many Canadian rivers that offer much more spectacular falls. But our young friend who is a staunch nationalist would hear none of that. In her position as a radio announcer she might influence public opinion. In order to merit the government's confidence, she had to have gone through a selection process that ensured that she would not only fail to criticize but would defend the interests of the Regime.

"No Anita, this is the most beautiful in the world."

She was probably being true to herself, since, having never been outside Cuba, this was her world.

We stopped at a little restaurant for lunch. I bought lunch for everybody including Ramiro. Our driver took his plate and made his way to another table. In spite of my insistence on joining us, he kept his distance, and Salvadora explained that it "wouldn't be correct" for the driver to mingle with the customers.

Later I asked Anita what was the advantage for Ramiro to cheat with the odometer, as he would still have to give his boss $45 at the end of the day. Apparently the driver appreciated the chance to get out of town for the day, he was guaranteed a good day's fare and he expected a tip in precious US dollars. Anita was appalled when she saw me hand him a $5 tip – a week's salary!

"You gave him too much." she said. "One dollar would have been more than enough."

Thursday, May 23. The previous few days had been partly dedicated to preparing *Mikky* for the return trip. This time has been difficult for Sandrine. To start with, the entire trip had been delayed a month because Wilfrid couldn't get a "visa" from his wife. The original plan was that after leaving Cuba Sandrine would sail to Jamaica with Anthony and me and fly home from there. The all-important inspection of the thruhhulls completely dominated the itinerary. Furthermore, as bad things sometimes happen, Pauline, the lady who was to replace Sandrine was victim of an unexpected personal tragedy and could not join Anthony and me. Our Parisian friend agreed to complete the trip to Curaçao with us, although she would have much preferred to be home in Trinidad as planned. Since we were too far behind in the schedule, Anthony had to cancel the Jamaican leg of the trip. This was a further disappointment for Sandrine, as she had counted on visiting an old friend who lives there. Furthermore, she had run out of medication, which resulted in making her irritable.

The stress of knowing she should be home looking after her property, her Bed and Breakfast and her personal affairs was taking its toll on her. And on her shipmates.

To add to her stress, we were supposed to leave three days earlier, but according to the weather forecasts a stationary low above Cuba was holding back several storms. As cautious sailors we decided to postpone our departure for a few days.

At last, at 1042 we cast off for the windward trip. At 1600 we experienced our first mechanical breakage! The autopilot motor decided to work in inverse direction. We put a twist in the rubber belt and resolved the problem for a while – until the belt broke after three hours of twisting. We'd have to steer by hand until we reached our first anchorage the next day.

At 2100, our second breakage. This time it was the jib halyard that gave away. Here I'm going to have to burden you with more information about halyards than you might care to learn, because, as you will see, it is significant in this story. Unlike with *Tulip One*, whose halyard ran through the inside of the mast, *Mikky*'s jib halyard was attached to the head of the sail, slid up one side of the foil, then through a pulley near the top of the mast, and back down parallel to the foil. The crew stands at the base of the forestay and raises the sail by pulling on the halyard as though raising a flag on a flagpole. It is important that when the sail is raised it be good and tight, otherwise it will be baggy and the boat will sail inefficiently. To achieve a good tight sail you need a non-stretch halyard. To this end, *Mikky*'s halyard was made from a combination of rope spliced onto a multi strand 4-millimetre wire. The end made of wire is attached to the head of the sail and the end made of rope is the end that the crew pulls on. With the mainsail the halyard is used every time we need to raise or lower the sail, but with the furling foresail, we raise it once, we cleat it so it doesn't drop and then we never have to touch the halyard again for the rest of the season.

Now with a broken halyard our sail should have fallen onto the deck, but since it was partially furled, the tightly rolled up part prevented the whole sail from disengaging from the foil. We rolled up the rest of the sail to get it out of the way and continued sailing without it, benefiting from the redundancy provided by the multiple sails of our ketch. We then examined the broken halyard. Strangely, it was the wire portion, about six inches above the head of the sail that was broken. The wire had become frayed to the point of breakage.

Friday, May 24. We sailed all day, without autopilot or jib and after 149 miles, anchored at 1805 in Cayo Manuel Gomez. Once in the stability of an anchorage, we could deal with the faulty auto helm. Anthony had a complete spare autopilot still in its box, so it was just a matter of swapping the old for the new. Went to bed early. To heck with the broken halyard. That could wait till tomorrow!

Saturday, May 25. We decided to re-anchor at *Cayo Algedon Grande*, 6 miles further, in a better-protected bay. That would make it easier to climb the mast to replace the halyard.

Then it started to rain. The sky was very heavy and a deluge poured on us. We went onto the deck in our bathing suits and lathered ourselves with soap and rinsed with the wonderfully clean distilled water from the sky. Anthony decided to take advantage of the downpour to fill the boat's tanks with nice, clean, fresh, pathogen-free water. By then the deck was thoroughly free of sea salt, so we opened the filler pipe. On *Mikky*, the filler cap is located on the aft deck near the toe rail. It was just a matter of letting the water run into the tank. On some boats it would not be as easy. Some sailors rig up a system of collecting rainwater in a bucket from the raised mainsail, which is sometimes easier done underway than at anchor. The quality of the water we obtained at Cienfuegos was doubtful, so we would not drink it without boiling it first. Would it be that we could always have access to such pure water as that provided by the heavens!

<u>Sunday, May 26</u>. The stove had quit on us in the middle of making our morning coffee, disaster of disasters! On a sailboat, the propane tank is located in a special locker accessible from outside the cabin. Because propane is heavier than air, the locker is vented from the bottom to allow any unwelcome leaking gas to escape to the outside. A solenoid open-close valve is attached to the tank and wired to a switch in the galley. That way, as soon as you're finished cooking you can shut off the gas at the tank with a flick of a finger without having to go outside on the deck, open the locker and twist the valve shut and vice versa when you want to cook. A cursory examination of the gas system by our trusty captain *et* repairman revealed that the solenoid was jammed in the closed position due to corrosion. As expected, Anthony had some spares, so in no time we had the coffee going again.

One of the great qualities of Anthony as captain was his policy of keeping spare parts. He confided that a year ago the jib halyard had broken and this prompted him to buy three spares. In the calm of our anchorage, it was a straightforward task for Anthony to climb the mast with me cranking him up using the winch on the mast and replace the broken halyard with a new one.

The day before we had noticed a small tear in the mizzen sail, which was very old and tender. I spent a couple of hours repairing the damage with a stick-on patch that I then secured with a couple of rows of zigzag stitching all around and across.

<u>Wednesday, May 29</u>. The past couple of days were pretty tough. We faced a 30 to 35 knot east wind, accompanied by lots of rain. The wind was smack in our faces, which forced us to beat, day in, day out. Finally today the wind veered to southeast, which meant that we could sail without tacking, and at last gain some headway.

<u>Thursday, May 30</u>, 0330. If we hadn't been in Santiago de Cuba before, we would have hove to and stayed outside the bay until daylight. But we felt confident that we could find our way into the bay in safety under the cover of darkness. What we hadn't predicted was the difficulties of anchoring. After dropping the hook we decided to have a cup of tea before going to bed. Immediately we had our first sip that we felt the familiar tugging of a dragging anchor. As I was raising the anchor the electric windlass gave up completely in the middle of its job due to a burnt fuse. I let the chain out again. Anthony decided to put out a second anchor to add

holding power to the first one. However the wind picked up, blowing towards shore. The silt bottom was just simply too mushy for our two anchors to hold. We had to run the engine at idle in forward gear to prevent the boat from being blown against shore. Finally at 0500 the wind died down and we dared go to sleep. At 0600 Anthony woke me up.

"Robert, the sun's up. We'll go and tie up alongside the dock."

Once securely tied, we went back to sleep till 0900. We had much sleep to catch up with, so the day was spent sleeping, relaxing and reading. Since we had severely neglected our intake of mojitos, we had to make up for the deficiency. We went to a local bar with Ortensia and William to catch up on news of our friends. If Canadian musicians have trouble finding work it is infinitely more difficult for members of a small band to make a living at music in Cuba. William was ecstatic to announce that his band had been awarded a contract with a resort to play three nights a week for the tourists.

After our friends had left, we brought up the subject of supper. Sandrine didn't feel like cooking, understandably. Neither did Anthony, nor I. The marina restaurant was closed, so we went walking around Punta Gorda peninsula in search of an eating-place. For some unfathomable reason, none of the three restaurants was open. When we banged our noses on the door of the last closed establishment, Sandrine was very unhappy and cursed Cuba's inept socialist system.

Back at the boat I offered to prepare a spaghetti with salmon sauce, but nobody wanted to wait that long. Sandrine started reheating leftover rice soup, but she got angry because Anthony and I were sitting watching her and not helping. In a fit of anger, she threw the ladle in the soup pot and stormed out to her cabin. Anthony and I finished off the soup and also went to bed, having not yet caught up on our much-needed sleep.

Friday, May 31. While Sandrine went into town to buy provisions and propane, Anthony and I had preparations to make:
    1) Changed the engine oil
    2) Adjusted the alternator belt
    3) Changed a burnt out navigation light bulb
    4) Cleaned the refrigerator water pump filter
    5) Cleaned out and dried the starboard cockpit locker
    6) Repaired the head seat
    7) Washed the cabin floors
    8) Cleaned out the engine bilge
    9) Reorganized provisions storage
    10) Went up the mast to grease the sheaves
    11) Checked the aft cabin portlight for water leaks
    12) Repaired another rip in the mizzen sail

In the evening Anthony and Sandrine went dancing with Ortensia and William, but I needed some quality time for myself so I stayed aboard *Mikky*, listening to an eclectic variety of music, from Bach to Polo Montañez, Cuba's rising star, with his CD *Guajiro Natural*. When my shipmates came aboard late, I could hear Sandrine bitching about this and that, in a very sour humour. This wasn't the cheerful, enthusiastic person that I had known.

<u>Saturday, June 1</u>. Since the marina's diesel pump was still not working, Anthony arranged for a local gas station to deliver 150 litres of diesel fuel to the marina for us. They left the six big carboys at the top of the stairs near the street. Since Anthony's back was killing him, it was up to me to carry the fuel down the long stairway and along the docks to the boat. Thankfully my back survived.

Sandrine again got up on the wrong side of the bed and was in a killer spirit this morning. I found these changes of mood increasingly difficult to cope with. For the past couple of days I had been thinking of putting in effect Plan B and jumping ship. I couldn't do that to Anthony. He had been very generous and respectful towards me. He had provided me with a beautiful experience and I felt I owed him to assist in the return trip to Curaçao. On the other hand, I couldn't imagine having to cope with Sandrine's increasingly venomous tantrums. I decided I had nothing to lose in trying.

So I took her aside, and said, "Sandrine, we have to talk."

She saw from my expression that I was up to something serious. She listened.

"I don't know if you realize it Sandrine, but since the past couple of weeks you've not been yourself. Up until recently you've been an excellent travel companion and we shared lots of good times. But in the past week particularly you've been critical of everything and everybody. I realize that the delays at getting home are a major cause of stress for you. All this stress has had a negative bearing on your behaviour. Anthony appreciates that you've agreed to stay on till we get to Curaçao, and I do too. But I find these mood swings impossible to live with. I can't envisage the long passage to Curaçao if you continue like this."

As I was speaking her expression changed from one of listening to one of grave concern, to one of contrition. She took me by the neck and gave me a hug.

"I know that I've been in a bad mood. I'm sorry I've caused you grief. I just didn't realize how it might affect you and Anthony. Don't worry, it won't happen again."

And incredibly, that was all that was needed to change her back to her old self.

Sunday, June 2. Last minute preparations, goodbyes to our Cuban friends, Sandrine cooked up a large pot of pea soup for the trip, and finally at 1400 we cast off!

It was with mixed feelings that I viewed the beautiful bay of Santiago de Cuba receding into the distance. I had been away from home for two months – the longest I'd ever been away. I missed my family, my home with my lifelong companion Micheline in it, the stimulating conversations with my son Philippe, the joviality of my daughter Natalie and especially seeing my grand daughter Gabrielle who was growing up so fast. On the other hand, I was leaving my Cuban friends and would probably never see them again. There are many other parts of the world to be visited and it's unlikely that I'll be coming back to Cuba.

We were no sooner outside the bay than we discovered two problems. First, the brand new autopilot that Anthony installed a few days ago conked out. It was impossible to figure out what was the problem with it. It was still under warranty, so he could put it back into its box and send it for repairs.

Now, if only we could figure out what was wrong with the old one to cause it to steer in reverse, we could put it back in duty.

"What could cause this?" we wondered. *When all else fails, read the instructions!* Upon studying the user manual, Anthony understood what had happened to the old auto helm. While the boat was underway, someone accidentally knocked out the power plug, causing a short or a surge of electricity. This disrupted the steering software of the unit. It was simply a matter of doing a "reset", the equivalent of rebooting a computer, and Presto! The patient was cured of its inversion disease!

The second problem occurred when we raised the mainsail: The boltrope that is sewn into the luff of the sail had squeezed out of the slot in the top half of the mast. We had to lower the sail with great difficulty, as it was badly jammed, and had to start over. All this time we had been motoring, and finally at 1830 we were underway with all four sails flying.

Tuesday, June 4. At midday yesterday we had Cap Tiburon of Haiti to our port beam. It seemed like an appropriate opportunity to celebrate, so we made ourselves real Cuban mojitos with fresh mint and ice.

At 1300 we tied up alongside the tiny dock at *Marina Port Morgan*, in *Caye Coque* of *Ile à Vache*, Haiti. A veritable corner of paradise, Hotel Didier with its beautifully manicured landscaping and flagstone paths was built into the side of a hill. In the background, from the dock we could see gently sloping hills of green, topped with palm trees. Cows and goats were grazing peacefully amidst the sounds of tropical birds. There were no cars on the island of 10,000 souls. We paid ourselves the luxury of sundowners at the bar (even though we had plenty of alcohol on the boat) followed by an elegant supper. For a long time Anthony had been dying for lambi, so here he realized his culinary craving – conch bathed in a delectable sauce prepared with just the right proportion of spices under the supervision of the hotel's owners, Didier and Françoise Boulard. We topped off the dinner with delicious Cognac flambéed crêpes stuffed with fresh fruit.

<u>Wednesday, June 5</u>. We were awakened by the sound of knocking on the hull. Two young men in a dugout canoe were alongside to sell us bananas, papaya, melon and mangoes. Later, a sweet little black boy of no more than six, wearing nothing but greyish boxer shorts came to the dock to see the lovely red haired lady on the boat. He offered Sandrine four tiny chicken eggs cradled in his hands and insisted that she take them as a gift.

A fisherman came to our boat with his catch – three very small lobsters of less than half a pound each. Anthony remonstrated with him about the lack of wisdom in taking such immature creatures out of the sea. We could not as a matter of principle buy the fisherman's catch, as this would just encourage the behaviour we were preaching against. This is going on because Haiti is extremely overpopulated and her people are hungry. They have reached the point where their stomachs hurt, so they have to nourish themselves today at the expense of tomorrow. This unsustainable plunder of the sea (and that of all other resources) is happening in all parts of the world and will continue until the formidable human population collapses and starts rebuilding again. It is the first time in the history of mankind that ecosystems are destroyed on a global scale, causing the extinction of a large number of species and the exhaustion of the resources required for a technical civilization. What is unfortunate is that the survivors will have a much-impoverished planet on which to rebuild.

At 1125 we cast off. Our plan was to sail eastward along the coast of Hispaniola to its extreme eastern end by tacking back and forth, then we would sail directly south to Curaçao. This would be making the best of an unfavourable wind direction.

<u>Friday, June 7</u>. Last night at 1045 when Anthony turned off the engine we heard a strange noise from the engine compartment. For the previous hours we could hear the bilge pump run more frequently than normal. Anthony, thanks to his lifetime of experience with sailboats, suspected something wrong with the exhaust system.

A Small Ocean for Starters

Most sailboats are equipped with an inboard diesel engine like the one in *Mikky*. Remember that the engine is cooled with seawater. After going through the cooling system the water is not evacuated directly to the outside but into the exhaust pipe. This serves to cool and silence the exhaust fumes. Water and exhaust gasses are then expelled from the boat by way of a thruhull just above the water line. The fitting where the evacuated cooling water joins the exhaust pipe was located below a false floor in the bottom of the port cockpit locker. It was a very deep locker, chock full of stuff. We had to remove a couple of hundred pounds of things before Anthony could have access to the false floor to reach the engine compartment and exhaust system. The joint where the exhausted cooling water pipe coupled onto the exhaust pipe was loose, allowing cooling water to pour into the bilge. It was a simple matter of tightening a few clamps to set everything right again. By the time we replaced the false floor and all the equipment into the locker, it was three o'clock in the morning, time for Anthony to go to bed. I volunteered to do the 0300 to 0600 watch.

After three solid hours of sleep I was perky and hungry for something sweet and satisfying, so I baked two banana loaves. We had an enormous papaya that was too ripe to keep another day so I made a big recipe of papaya jam, which unintentionally complimented the banana bread.

<u>Saturday, June 8, 0600</u>: An unpleasant finding! Anthony discovered that the starboard settee cushions were soaking wet. It would appear that the portlight above the couch hadn't been closed tightly. During the entire night, as we sailed on a port tack, the southeast wind drove large breaking waves. The starboard side of the boat was underwater most of the night, allowing seawater to leak around the window's seal. This may not sound like much of a big deal, but keep in mind that sea salt is hydrophilic, that is, it likes to drink water. If you let a seawater-soaked cushion dry out without removing the salt, it will always remain moist, thus attracting smelly, unhealthy mould. Sandrine was contrite and apologetic for this lapse of precaution, but what the heck? As they say, "Shit happens!"

1345: Anthony and I were in the cabin, doing some navigation when we heard Sandrine's excited voice from the cockpit:

"Mon Dieu Antoine, come to see, your sail eez again broken!"

Unquestionably, the jib halyard had broken again! This time three quarters of the luff had slipped down the foil and we had to work hard to gather up the loose sail and secure it to the lifelines. We were navigating in two-meter waves 50 miles from shore. Rather than going back to shore and looking for an anchorage, Anthony decided to carry out the replacement of the halyard out at sea. I winched Anthony up while he helped by pulling himself upwards with his hands around the mast. The boat was pitching, rolling and yawing wildly and Anthony had to use all his strength just to hang onto the mast. As he was trying to let go of a hand to pass the end of line into the pulley, he was being thrown from side to side onto the shrouds, risking the loss of his manhood on the thin, tight wires. After 45 minutes he finally managed to put the halyard in its place. I let him down gently and when he reached the deck, he was so exhausted that he lost consciousness for a few minutes.

As it had been a while since Murphy hadn't given us a serious challenge, we discovered that the halyard had been passed into the wrong side of the pulley, meaning that all that we had done was for naught. We had to start over and Anthony had to risk sex life and limb at the top of the mast once more.

After four hours of arduous work had elapsed since the breakage, we finally had the halyard in place and the headsail raised and unfurled the way it was meant to be. We decided to make as much progress as possible eastwards parallel to the Hispanola coast so as to have a more southern heading once we turned towards Curaçao.

Sunday, June 9. What a tough night it was! The wind constantly changed from 6 knots to 28 knots. It would blow from the east, then from the south. It rained cats and dogs. Anthony slept like a log, as he was totally exhausted. I had to awaken him a few times to help take or shake a reef, since the way *Mikky* is configured, one crew had to go on the deck to handle the halyard and the reefing cringles while the other eased and hardened the mainsheet. After the manoeuvre was over, he would fall asleep again as if a switch was turned off in his brain. Within two seconds he was snoring as though nothing had happened.

0630: When my turn came to doze off, I was sleepless. I kept on thinking about the return airline ticket that I had bought in advance two months previously and worried that I might miss my flight. Maybe I haven't told you, but in spite of my advocacy for logic and coherent thought, I am sometimes, in the middle of the night, given to irrationality. As I lay awake, listening to the slopping of the waves on the fibreglass hull, I forced myself to rationalize that worrying would accomplish absolutely nothing and would even be counterproductive, as I too needed my sleep. In spite of my best efforts at fighting off senseless pangs of anxiety, I turned and tossed and counted sheep and only managed to muster a couple of hours of fitful shuteye.

1902: Our bearing on Curaçao was 190 degrees (almost due south) and our distance 361 miles. With the wind direction 130 degrees, we could sail straight for our destination on a close haul on one tack. So this is when we came about and set our heading and our sails for Curaçao!

2330: Disaster! Incredible! We couldn't believe our senses! Another broken jib halyard! We rolled up the jib and sat down to think about our options. We had only one spare halyard left. Since the previous replacement had lasted only 31 hours, we had to make sure this time we elucidated the cause of the breakages before installing the last new one. We had no choice but to turn around, anchor near shore, analyse the cause of the breakages and carry out a permanent fix. We'd have to backtrack and sail all night to reach an anchorage in the Dominican Republic.

Monday, June 10, 0735. We were now half a mile from the west coast of *Isla Saona*. We contoured a large reef on the tip of the island and then sailed into the large bay. We dropped the anchor in front of a luxurious-looking resort on a magnificent white sand beach that formed a carpet leading to thatch roofed houses shaded by palm trees.

This time we had only one spare halyard left. We had to determine what was causing the multi-strand, 4-millimetre stainless steel wire to break. Once again, I winched Anthony up the mast. Upon close examination of the top of the forestay, Anthony realized that the headfoil was six inches shorter than the steel wire of the forestay, and that the top of the foil was worn sharp as a razor blade. It became evident what was cutting our halyards. The repairs consisted of cutting away the sharp part of the foil and filing the edge smooth, which required that Anthony climb the mast again with a hacksaw and file on his tool belt. As a form of protection, we cut a piece of small diameter pipe through which we passed the wire part of the halyard. This would insure that the open end of the foil would rub on the protective pipe and not on the wire of the halyard. After everything was ready for installation Anthony went up the mast for a third time to carry out the final touches. The job was made ever more difficult because powerboats ferrying tourists around were speeding back and forth between *Mikky* and the beach, creating large waves and unwittingly putting at risk Anthony's private parts (once again!).

After we finished cleaning up and putting the tools away we went for a well-deserved swim followed by a very welcome rum punch.

1950: We weighed anchor and for a last time, set our course directly for Curaçao. Anthony went straight to sleep while Sandrine prepared Teriyaki chicken and rice. I was at the helm, holding *Mikky* on course through a very rough chop that was bouncing us about, making it very treacherous to move around on the boat.

Sailors have established a safety procedure for passing hot food or drink from the cabin to the cockpit. The method is simply to deposit the plate or cup on the cockpit sole on the lee side, the side that the boat is leaning towards. Then the crewmate it is destined for picks it up off the floor without risk of spills. Sandrine passed me my plate according to protocol. Then she proceeded to come and join me in the cockpit with her plate and her little bottle of spicy sauce. It's probably the little bottle of spicy sauce that put her off the traditional procedure. Instead of depositing her things on the sole, then climbing into the cockpit and picking them up once safely seated, she climbed the stairs with plate in one hand and little bottle of sauce in the other. She was doing OK until she arrived at the top step and stretched a leg over the bulkhead. But as soon as her foot touched the sole the boat gave a big jerk, projecting my French friend onto the starboard cockpit wall, smashing her cheek. Immediately the boat gave a big thrust the other way, sending poor Sandrine backward, causing her to hit her head on the opposite seat. Although there was no open wound, she suffered from a good case of whiplash and was totally incapacitated for the rest of the night.

Tuesday, June 11. A southeast wind continued blowing at 20 knots, a blessing from the Gods of the wind and sea. We were sailing on a close reach on a port tack, in other words with the wind on our left cheek. Sandrine awoke with a sore neck, but in good spirits. I was really happy that I hadn't decided to exercise Plan B but rather chose to talk things out with Sandrine when her mood swings became too much to take. I never anticipated that she could change back to her (good) old self so radically.

Wednesday, June 12. The wind had veered a bit, putting us now on a beam reach, enabling us to go faster, without crashing down on waves. Our through the water speed was 6.5 knots and comfortable, since *Mikky* was well balanced. However, according to the GPS our speed over the ground was 4.5 knots, telling us that we were fighting a current of 2 knots. Nevertheless, we were doing an excellent average mileage.

This morning I baked a batch of date muffins, which were awarded a very high rating by my appreciative captain.

Sandrine's neck pain had transferred to her shoulder blade. After the accident with the little bottle of spicy sauce I was afraid that she might have been seriously hurt, but today she didn't look too badly out of kilter.

Friday, June 14. Yesterday was a terrific sailing day, allowing us to cover 134 miles. At 1950 we had the eastern point of Curaçao to our starboard beam. In a few hours we would come to the end of our journey.

Finally, at 0030, we anchored in Spanish Water after covering 2600 nautical miles and after being away for 70 days. Sandrine cautioned me that nobody would give any credence to a round number like 2600. Therefore I fudged the record and wrote 2601 nautical miles in my official logbook.

<u>Saturday, June 15</u>. I felt light hearted as I was packing my suitcase. I had just completed the longest sailing adventure of my life. I had made two good friends. Already, Anthony was inviting me for sailing with him next fall and Sandrine was offering me shelter at her bed and breakfast in Trinidad and her summer home in New York City. Later that evening, I arrived at the Ottawa International Airport and my family was there waiting for me. Life couldn't get better than this.

&&&&&&&

That trip to Cuba and my ensuing friendship with Anthony were what eventually led to my being here, sitting on the deck of *Ventus*, in Bahía la Mar, mulling over the troubling events of the past few days: our terrifying experience of being boarded by pirates and our frustrating dealings with the hapless Margarita law enforcement authorities. I cast my mind to pondering about my experiences that unfolded following my memorable Curacao-Cuba trip.

Advanced cruising course

My turn to teach

Learning through practice

Chapter 8

Teaching and Learning

Summer 2002

It was still early in the sailing season when I returned home from my Cuba trip. The previous winter I had prepared my teaching material in view of putting in practice my newly acquired instructor qualification. It consisted of handouts to supplement the CYA-issued book and a series of flashcards illustrating various concepts such as "rules of the road", aids to navigation, safety equipment, anchoring technique, tides and currents, etc. While away in Cuba I had reviewed the curriculum several times.

As a qualified Canadian Yachting Association instructor, I could either teach for a recognized sailing school or on my own as an independent. My relationship with Advantage Boating was that of a contractor. Its teaching fleet consists of Tanzer 22s and Sonar 23s, both ideal teaching keelboats, as they have large cockpits that accommodate five people comfortably and are pretty forgiving for beginners.

The typical course is taught over four seven-hour days and consists of 8 hours of classroom and 20 hours of on-water, hands-on experience. There are normally four students at a time. Any more bodies in the boat and each individual would not get enough kicks at the can, so to speak.

I start the course in the marina's clubhouse with a briefing. I explain that this is purely a hands-on course, in other words, they will be performing

Teaching and Learning

all the manoeuvres and I will be mainly giving instructions. I explain the basics of sailing theory, i.e. what makes a boat move through the water. I assure them through diagrams that a keelboat can't capsize in the conditions we are likely to encounter on Lake Deschênes.

Before our first sail I spend about an hour on the dock explaining the safety equipment, procedures, the pre-departure preparations and the use of the outboard engine. Following my hair-raising experience with the Hobie Cat in Florida, the first thing I teach my students, once we're out on the water, is how to stop the boat. I haven't yet needed to be rescued, but I came close to falling off my perch at the transom one day and the scare got me thinking about what my students should be told if I were the one to fall overboard.

Although I take great pains to teach safety practices once in a while a mishap takes place unpredictably. One of the skills a sailor must learn is to undock and to dock the boat. One nice May day, when the water was still quite cold, I was teaching a full crew of students aboard No Luffing Matter, a 23-foot Sonar. It's relevant to mention that the Sonar is a racing keelboat, built without lifelines. The boat was approaching the main dock on the port side, with a rather nervous Mary at the helm. I was sitting on the seat next to her, and two students were standing near the shrouds on the port side. Margaret was gripping onto a shroud with the stern dockline in her hand and Gerry was likewise positioned with the port bow dockline in his hand. The instruction I had given them was to wait until they heard the command "Step off" from the helm before disembarking with their respective dockline, then turn their line around a cleat on the dock.

"Remember," I told Mary, "to give the command to step off when the boat reaches about a foot from the dock."

Mary was following my instructions for the approach perfectly. She headed towards the dock at 90 degrees. She slowed the boat down, turned it to about 30 degrees to the dock.

"Now get ready, when the bow is about three feet from the dock, to push the tiller hard over to bring the boat parallel to the dock," I reminded her.

She understood what to do, then I heard a distinct SPLASH!

I looked towards the shroud and Gerry was missing! He had somehow let go of the shroud and fallen overboard.

I put the boarding ladder in place and pulled up a very wet man. After he had changed into dry clothes and was comfortable I asked him what happened, as my attention at the critical moment was on the helm. Gerry explained that as the boat was approaching, he noticed that there was another dock line lying on the foredeck, the starboard one. Without thinking, he decided to pick it up, letting go of the shroud. He lost his balance and then the splash.

On this boat the two bow docklines were actually one single line knotted in the middle and attached to a centre cleat in the middle of the deck. So the unused starboard one had to remain coiled on the deck. It seemed so patently obvious that it never crossed my mind to point it out.

Another little incident happened when Chris, a very competent powerboat owner was at the helm motoring the boat out of the Nepean Marina. I was sitting just behind him on the transom, not concerned about his ability to take us out of the harbour. He had to turn to starboard after the second green buoy. For some unfathomable reason that Chris didn't know himself, after the first buoy he pushed the tiller hard over to turn starboard and within a few feet the boat came to a springy stop in the mud.

Chris apologized for his error, as he was familiar with the marina and had simply been absent-minded. I decided to take advantage of the situation to teach how to free a boat that has run aground. First, I had the students sit on one side to make the boat heel. This way it is sometimes possible to get the keel to ease off the bottom. However, the bottom here was pure clay, which is very sticky. I then had Chris add power in reverse gear, but still to no avail. If you have a very heavily loaded boat, sometimes it can be freed by making it lighter by removing weight, but that wasn't possible without the use of a dinghy. There was another trick up my sleeve. I would put in effect a method that had been drilled into my mind, but which I had never had the misfortune of needing to apply.

"Now," I explained, "we will carry out the technique of kedging the boat off the bottom. I need a volunteer to strip down to his shorts and go in the water," I said.

Since he felt a little guilty for putting us in this situation Chris volunteered (the captain is nevertheless ultimately responsible for what happens on his boat).

I had a student take the anchor out of its box and wrap it up snugly in a life jacket to make it float while Chris stripped down to his shorts and lifejacket. The anchor was passed down to Chris in the water. I instructed our swimmer to take the anchor out behind the boat as far as the rode permitted, then to unwrap it and let it fall to the bottom. I then instructed another student to give the rode a few light tugs, and then to pull lightly on it to set the anchor into the bottom. Once I was sure the anchor was well set, I had another student put four wraps of the rode around a winch and take up the slack on the rode by pulling on it. Once the rode was taut, I had him crank the winch with the winch handle. And seemingly by magic, our boat was pulled out of its muddy trap. As an instructor, you don't often have the opportunity to do a live demonstration of this sort.

There are two emergency situations I've had the good fortune not to have experienced and they are dismasting and loss of steering. Losing a mast is normally due to the standing rigging breaking, or one of the turnbuckles used to tighten the shrouds and the stays coming loose. In the basic course we teach the student what to do if a shroud, or a stay breaks, or if the steering fails, or if the engine fails in a narrow channel or a traffic lane. My friend Anthony once told me that he had all three mishaps occur in the same trip! I remembered that he had just bought *Mikky* in the British Virgin Islands and had it surveyed. The surveyor wasn't able to examine the chain plates to which the shrouds are attached because they were hidden behind all the woodwork, called "furniture" on a boat. It would have taken a team of experts a full day to take the furniture apart and put it back together, a job Anthony preferred deferring until his return home in Trinidad. He decided that the risk of these pieces of stainless steel letting go after 18 years during a single 600-mile trip was very slim. I had forgotten the details of the events, so I emailed him asking if the mast had actually fallen down and to remind me about the details. This was his response:

No, the mast did not come down for the following reasons:
*There was redundancy in the rig. Two forestays, and two separate backstays run to each side of the boat so as to contribute some lateral stability as well.
*The mainsail was reefed.
*I spun the wheel to bring the boat about within no more than 2 seconds of the break. In fact I spun it so hard that the steering cable broke!! However the boat did come about. I could then only steer to starboard.

"ALL HANDS ON DECK!!!"

We got the sails down and set up the emergency tiller. This meant steering from inside the aft cabin and this was not convenient because I could not see the compass properly. With the sails down, we made a jury rig for the port cap shroud by connecting it to the port aft lower shroud chain plate. This put the spreader out of alignment but we pulled that back with a Spanish twist to the port forward lower shroud. Thus we could have gone back to port tack with further reduced sail, but since we were about 100 miles west from nearest land, I opted to stay on starboard tack and head for Martinique.

So I rigged up an extension to the emergency tiller using a piece of pipe, and put some sail back up. The wind was blowing a rather fresh breeze of 35 knots and seas were in the vicinity of 12 feet so we did not put a lot of sail up. I was able to pack some cushions behind the extension to the emergency tiller such that the sails could be set to hold the boat on a windward course. We then could compensate for slight changes in wind direction by moving the main boom a little in or out. This got us to within 15 miles of Martinique, for which we were duly thankful. The wind dropped and we started to use the engine but that soon stopped as well. So we hove to and spent the night in violent motion but we were tired enough to catch a little sleep. When it was light, we fixed the engine and the steering. My son in law John is a first class mechanic and played the major role in fixing things. My daughter Trudi stoically supported us from the galley and in every other way possible. We had some cable clamps and by taking a spare halyard down, (I think it had 5mm wire) we were able to splice new cables in place of the parts that were worn and get wheel steering going again. The house battery was dying and that was another problem.

At Martinique we had to tack south again and the jury rig on the port side took us to St. Lucia where we got a new chain plate made and installed. (a whole day taking out the furniture to get at it). Here we also discovered that the jib halyard was about to break so we bought the wire and made up a new one.

And the story goes on and on.................

It took us 6 days to get to Trinidad from Tortola, BVI, and that was all that John and Trudy had. We had other breakdowns along the way and John took care of them. However they both said that they thought it was a wonderful adventure.

Although Anthony had never taken formal sailing courses, his lifetime of experience had taught him much more than I've learned in all the courses I've ever taken. He had the right reaction when he heard the explosive sound of the breaking chain plate. He immediately tacked, putting the wind on the opposite side of the mainsail, which took the tension off the side of the broken shroud. He was simply unlucky that his steering let go at the same time. Turning the wheel vigorously doesn't break a healthy steering cable. The cable was weak in the first place. It is surprising that the surveyor had not spotted this deficiency. As for the engine quitting before they could get to terra firma, well, that was Murphy at work enforcing his law.

One of the most serious emergencies one must be prepared for on open water is a man overboard. This usually follows Murphy's Law, as a person is most likely to fall overboard in rough weather. The swell is big and the waves crested by whitecaps, making the victim very difficult if not impossible to see. The noise of the wind and waves might muffle the sound of his voice yelling for help or the sound of his emergency whistle. Moving around on the boat is tricky and hazardous to boot, opening the possibility of a second person overboard.

There are some basic precautions one can exercise to avoid falling overboard, as I mentioned before, such as wearing a harness and clipping it onto the boat. It is a widely circulated fact or myth, but it is said that many a sailor's body retrieved from the water was found with his fly zipper open.

Whereas sailing schools worldwide preach the use of the harness, there are still some captains who ignore such a common sense precaution. The most shocking example I can think of was the drowning death of Laura, the daughter of Bob Gainey, the former manager of the Montreal Canadiens hockey team. She was crewing on the *Picton Castle* tall ship and had been sent on the deck at night, where she was washed overboard by a rogue wave, about 700 kilometres from Cape Cod. According to one of her crewmates, she had requested a harness, but was refused one and sent onto the aft deck without even a life jacket.

The basic cruising course places a lot of importance on the student being able to master a crew overboard (COB) recovery technique. We don't actually put a person in the water for this exercise but instead, we use a floating fender with a looped line attached to it. I position myself in my teaching spot at the transom and at the appropriate moment, I throw the fender in the water with the cry, "MAN OVERBOARD!"

The student at the helm is in charge of manoeuvring the boat and directing his crew. The procedure entails turning the boat to sail downwind from the floating rubber victim, then turning upwind towards the fender, bringing the boat to a stop, head into wind and pick it up on the windward side of the boat with a boathook.

Now, if it were a real person in the water, then we could have him grab the end of a rope and lead him to the boarding ladder so he can come up on his own. However, if the victim were unconscious or unable to help himself due to hypothermia, then the boathook just wouldn't do. Sailing textbooks describe different tricks that can be used, such as using a halyard to winch the person up or attaching a block and tackle at the end of the boom and using the boom as a crane. Another method described in textbooks is the use of a storm sail. You would attach the foot of the sail to the toerail, lower the head of the sail into the water, float the victim onto the sail and hoist him up with the halyard. All of those tricks would be difficult and dangerous to apply in heavy seas. To lift the person out of the water with a halyard or the boom would require putting a harness of some kind on the person – not a simple job if your boat is thrashing about in five metre waves!

Before I give you a real life example of how to pull a victim out of the water, I will mention the Collision Regulations, known officially as Regulations for the Prevention of Collisions, or colloquially as the Colregs. The purpose of these regulations is to prevent collisions with other boats or with natural objects like easy to see islands or difficult to see submerged reefs.

Teaching and Learning

I attended a seminar by a Canadian sailor who spoke of his experience in life saving. In September 2000 he was in the vicinity when the ferry *Express Samina* hit a rocky islet and sank, 2 km off the coast of the Greek island of Paros in the Aegean Sea. She was carrying 473 passengers and 61 crewmembers. As incredible as it may sound, her captain and mate had left the bridge to watch the replay on television of a goal in an important soccer match. The autopilot was entirely in charge of the ship until moments before the collision, at which time it was too late for human intervention to alter course. As you might guess, the Colregs stipulate what would be obvious to a child, that *"every vessel shall at all times maintain proper look-out..."* and this regulation and many others were breached by the captain, the crew, the owner of the boatline, the Greek safety inspectors and others. Google *Express Samina* if you want to read some interesting accounts and view some revealing videos of this senseless accident.

Our Canadian sailor carried a portable VHF radio whenever he was away from his sailboat. He was having coffee in a restaurant within radio range when he heard the ship's mayday call. He gathered his most competent crew and immediately cast off for the islets that had claimed the ferry. When he got to the area it was dark and the seas were very rough. Many fishing boats had already started plucking victims out of the water. A large number of passengers never had the chance to board a lifeboat since only four of the eight lifeboats could be launched. Some of the *Express Samina*'s crew had already abandoned ship, leaving passengers on their own. Many passengers couldn't find life jackets before the ferry sank.

Without sails up, the Canadian vessel was rolling too much to allow picking up a victim from the side. It was unthinkable for the sailboat's captain to put one of his crew in the water to tie a rope around a victim or slip a harness on him. He found that the only way to lift a person aboard was to reverse the vessel until he was close to the stern and have two strong crewmembers lean over at the transom, grab him by his clothing, and physically yank him up onto the aft deck. They were able to rescue three of Samina's passengers this way. Unfortunately, that was all they were able to do under the circumstances and 82 persons were lost. The moral of this story is that a textbook might describe a procedure that appears straight forward when carried out in calm conditions, but if you have to put it in practice in heavy seas, it might prove to be impossible, meaning that you will have to improvise.

It has been said that a mid-ocean collision with another vessel can ruin your whole day. And running aground can be anywhere from a minor nuisance to a major catastrophe, like the fate of the Greek ferry.

These are emergencies that are best to be avoided. That is why the CYA sailing courses place so much importance on teaching the Collision

Teaching and Learning

Regulations. I've already told you about the powerboat that capsized when it crossed over the towline of a tugboat in English Bay, and that was because the skipper didn't know the part of the Colregs that deals with navigation lights.

An important part of the regulations is the section that deals with who has the right of way and these are commonly known as the *rules of the road*. The boat that has the right of way is called the *stand on boat* and the one that must give way is called, as you'd never guess, the *give way boat*. The folks who invented the regulations must have gotten together over a beer one day and made some logical decisions and other rules that had to be, by their nature, arbitrary.

An example of a purely *arbitrary* regulation is the rule that dictates which of two powerboats on a crossing situation must give way. The rule states that the one that has the other vessel on its starboard side (or sees the other vessel's red running light) must give way.

A *logical* regulation, for example, is the one that dictates that boats that are more manoeuvrable give way to those that are less so. According to this logic, a powerboat must give way to a sailboat, and there is a whole pecking order that deals with every vessel from dredging boats to floatplanes. I've got a good question for you: Who has to give way to whom, the powerboat in the middle of the lake or the floatplane coming in for a landing?

If you said floatplane, you guessed right or already knew the answer! In fact the floatplane is the lowest on the "right of way" totem pole.

Another logical regulation is the one that deals with the behaviours of the stand on and give way boats. In the basic CYA course we teach that if the other boat's bearing or position relative to yours doesn't change over time, then you're on a collision course – it's simple geometry. And we teach the rule that states that if two boats are on a collision course, the stand on boat must maintain constant speed and direction and the give way boat must take evasive action. What's more, the rule says that the evasive action must be done as early as possible and the change of course must be large enough to be readily apparent to the other vessel. For example, if you made a tiny course change, say 5 degrees, it might be enough to clear, if you're far enough away to avoid collision, but the other skipper wouldn't recognize that you made a change of course. I've taken the habit of making a decisive 20-degree course change when mine is the give way boat so that the other boater knows that I've seen him and that I've taken evasive action.

Before I talk about the collision of the Italian ocean liner *Andrea Doria* with the Swedish MS *Stockholm* near Nantucket Island, I'll mention two other Colregs that applied to this story. One is that in reduced visibility a boat must reduce speed – makes sense, huh? The regulation, however,

180

doesn't specify *how much* to slow down, so it's a matter of judgement on the part of the captain. The *Andrea Doria* had suddenly run into fog. The captain, in his wisdom, decided to reduce speed from 23 knots to 21.8 knots. That's still 40 km an hour, which is a pretty good clip if you need to stop a 26,400-ton ship.

The two boats had seen each other on radar in sufficient time before the collision. However, instead of making large course corrections, both made tiny corrections – *towards each other*, narrowing, rather than widening, the passing distance!

The other Colreg is that when two vessels meet head on, they should both turn to starboard, in other words pass each other port to port – like cars on an American or Canadian highway. In this case the *Andrea Doria* turned port (left) and the other ship, the MS *Stockholm*, turned starboard, smashing the Italian boat broadside at a full 18 knots!

The *Andrea Doria* sank 11 hours after the collision, all passengers and crew were saved except for 51 who died as a result of the impact of the strike and the MS *Stockholm* was towed to a shipyard to be repaired.

There were several other factors involved, mistakes made by the captains and crew of both ships, culminating in the disaster. It was 1956, and this turned out to be the last large ocean liner shipwreck before the airplane took over trans-oceanic travel.

September, 2003

What I found most attractive about the Advanced Cruising Course being offered by Cooper Boating School was not as much the content of the course, but the venue where the course was to be offered. I had never sailed in the Straight of Georgia, but everybody who had ever done so came back enthralled. The area between Vancouver Island and the mainland of Canada's west coast is known for its beauty, its mix of wilderness and quaint villages, its scenery of snow capped mountains overlying large expanses of cedar forests and its numerous, well protected and uncrowded anchorages. The Advanced Cruising Standard was a course that would teach me to act safely as skipper on a sailing vessel of up to 15 metres in length, operating by day and night, in coastal or inland waters, in any weather, taking into account tides and currents and dealing with marine traffic. It would be a perfect way to finish the 2003 Canadian sailing season.

Constantia was the name on the stern. This was the boat I'd be sailing for the next 7 days, a German-made Dehler 37. She was a sleek, low profile sloop, a boat with the looks of a racer. The instructor, a middle-aged man with a Santa Clause complexion and a long, white beard, extended his hand, "I'm Jim, welcome aboard." Also welcomed aboard were three other men, the youngest at 35 was Duncan the computer geek, then Steve in his early forties, the airline pilot and James the dentist, who was in his mid-forties. I was the only totally free man, i.e., retired, and I felt much too young to be 61 (this bizarre state of mind is very common in people my age).

The passage plan was a circular route from Vancouver, Silva Bay, Nanaimo to Port Graves, circumnavigating Texada Island and over Comox Bar, Chrome Island Light, Ballenas Island, Thrasher Rock, Sands Head, Port Graves and back to Vancouver. It was designed to provide us students with as many and as varied situations as possible within Georgia Straight, such as narrow passes between islands, harbour entrances, transit over a shallow bar and sail for 48 consecutive hours on a non-stop passage. The course was also planned to teach us a variety of anchoring techniques, docking techniques, advanced sail trimming, the use of the big, colourful spinnaker, how to interpret weather forecasts and how to identify a variety of lights and buoys not found on Lake Deschênes. Much of this was not new to me, but it's always good to know the formal way to accomplish certain tasks.

Jim was laid back enough to make the course enjoyable and rigid enough to take back control of the conversation when the chitchat became too boisterous or when James wouldn't stop telling jokes. The most lasting impression for me was the discovery of a spectacular area for sailing. I promised myself that I would return.

As soon as I got home I phoned my sailing friend Don Bedier (pronounced Bid Dear, à l'Anglaise). Don, who is a few years my senior and sports a headful of grey hair is of average stature and fit as a fiddle. He had retired from his career as air travel policy maker several years previously and had thereafter taken a job as travel agent for a few years. He now volunteers for Meals on Wheels and other social services. Combine that experience with excellent organizational skills and why should I have been surprised that while I was away on my course in the Straight of Georgia, my friend was reading and searching the Internet for the different sailing options for that body of water! He already had compiled a list of the various boat rental agencies, had made phone calls to obtain quotations and had ordered a set of sailing guidebooks and charts for the area. If travel is involved, Don will organize it.

The boats on Lake Deschênes had been hauled out and placed on their supporting cradles, the fall leaves had displayed their dazzling colours and then tumbled to the ground, the Halloween decorations had showed up on people's lawns and then absconded, and presently we were seated on the floor in Don's apartment, almost oblivious to the November rain dribbling down the fogged up living room window. Charts, pamphlets and books were spread out over the floor and we were poring over the various anchorages described in the guidebooks. Plans were taking shape.

We already had firm commitments from all our crew. We had Raymond and Carole, both of whom had belonged to NCSS and now had their own little boat on Lake Deschênes. Raymond was a competent sailor who would be a valuable addition to Don and me. Rachel, the same chef extraordinaire who had accompanied me on previous trips I told you about was part of our crew. Finally, Lana, who had been member of NCSS the previous two years, had just confirmed her participation by putting up a cheque for her share of the deposit. This was not to be the first time she would sail on a live-aboard cruise, as she had crewed for a week on Georgian Bay with our sailing club. We had no reason to suspect that she would have difficulties on this trip.

June, 2004

Don, Lana, Rachel and I flew from Ottawa to Vancouver together while Carole and Raymond would meet us at the boat on the day of departure. We embarked on a four-day ground tour of Vancouver Island before our two-week sailboat trip. Don had organized the rental of a van, the itinerary and all our accommodation for the tour. With its 32,134 square km, we would only see a small sample of what the island had to offer.

Our tour started with crossing the Straight of Georgia over to Sidney. After disembarking from the ferry, we drove southwards to British Columbia's capital. Many people are surprised to find out that BC's capital is not Vancouver, but Victoria. It is a beautiful city with the most hospitable climate of any other in Canada. I guess what is special about this city is the clean streets, manicured lawns, well kept houses and buildings, shade trees and there is the same unhurried atmosphere you find only in the Maritime provinces in Eastern Canada.

Our first stop after Victoria was the resuscitated town of Chemainus with its stunning murals. About 40 commercial buildings downtown are decorated with large mural paintings, up to 100 feet long, depicting life as it was in the 19th century as well as reproductions by Emily Carr and the Group of Seven. What is special about this town of 3000 inhabitants is not just the presence of its outdoor art works but also the events that led to their creation.

The town was founded in the early 19th century as a centre for the area's mining, forestry and fishing industries. In the 1980s when the land's natural resources dried up the creative people of Chemainus developed a new vision for the future to revitalize the town. That plan was to encourage the creation of giant outdoor murals to provide work for its artists and to attract tourists. This vision has transformed Chemainus from a dying mining and logging town to worldwide fame as a remarkable tourist destination. The town's official web site boasts of the "...incredible story of *The Little Town That Did* © and the *magic* it has created for all who come here."

The lesson I draw from this story and the fate of numerous similar towns that have been abandoned once their mines and forests were exhausted, is that our industrial civilization can't exist without resources to extract. When the underground resources are gone we will have no metals for making our machines, no plastics for making consumer goods, no coal for heating and electricity production, no oil for all of the hundreds of services it renders our society, especially with regard to transportation and agriculture. So far when a mine was no longer economical to exploit, we've always been successful in finding slightly more difficult to extract resources further afield and in founding new towns in those places. One day there won't be any more places to mine or wells to drill or trees to cut. What will happen to our extraction-dependent consumer society then?

I usually don't dwell on those uncomfortable thoughts too long before thinking about the next natural wonder to see or where I will go hiking, canoeing or sailing next – which brings me to our next point of interest.

We usually think of rainforest as the Amazon, or Costa Rica or the windward coast of some Pacific islands. Few realize that Canada has some of the most extraordinary rain forest on Earth on the west coast and on Vancouver Island. Our little group was headed for a forest that features giant trees, in the way of the Douglas Fir, the Western Red Cedar, the Western Hemlock, the Sitka Spruce and the Grand Fir. Cathedral Grove in MacMillan Provincial Park is home to old-growth trees that reach heights of 60 metres (196 feet) and diameters of up to 4.4 m (14 feet).

I'll let you in on an anecdote about how this forest was transformed into a public protected area. Around the turn of the 20th century new roads and a railroad were built linking the south of the island to the north. British Columbia's first Chief Forester, H.R. MacMillan, a shrewd opportunist, staked his claim on the coastal old growth forest by obtaining logging rights to large numbers of virgin river valleys. Further improvements to the road encouraged increases in population northward and the area known today as

Cathedral Grove became a popular picnic area. For a long time the Vancouver Island Tourist Association and the local chambers of commerce petitioned MacMillan to donate Cathedral Grove as a public park. The gentleman steadfastly refused, citing the high values of the old-growth timber as necessary to his company's bottom line. Finally, in 1944, at a memorable meeting of the Vancouver Island Tourist Association in Port Alberni the millionaire forester was pressured by all present to donate the grove to the public. After much ranting, raving, verbal battling and clamouring, Mr. MacMillan stormed out of the hall, shouting, "All right! You can have the God-damned grove," slamming the door as he left. This public victory resulted in Cathedral Grove being granted provincial park protective status with its 136 hectares of old-growth forest in 1947.

For me, walking amongst those ancient giants was an emotional journey, a chance to see a living slice of my world before the destructive intervention of Mankind consumes it entirely.

"Life is too short to stay in cheap hotels", or such was the comment of a movie star whose name I can't recall. Don had booked us rooms at the Middle Beach Lodge in Tofino on the island's Pacific coast. We arrived just in time for dining room service, which was friendly, informal and professional and its food perfect in every way. The main lounge featured a wall of windows displaying the waterfront in all its magnificence and providing us with a spectacular sunset over the Pacific Ocean. In the morning we went down to the lounge to enjoy the smell and the taste of fresh bread and giant, steaming hot cinnamon buns.

Another highlight was Long Beach, a 10 km long expanse of sandy seashore with breaking ocean swells. To access the beach from the parking lot we walked two kilometres along a meandering boardwalk through awe-inspiring old growth rainforest. The workings of the tides are never as evident as along mud flats. Here is where the intertidal area can be hundreds of meters wide. Three young teenage boys were skimboarding on the shallow water left by the breakers as they spread thinly on the flat, compacted shore sand. Although the sun was with us, the water was yet too chilly to entice a single brave soul to swim. In the near distance we could see a whale-watching tour boat in search of big, black shiny curved emerging forms. For their money the passengers were rewarded with a furtive whale back and the occasional eruption of mist emanating from an emerging blowhole. Even though we rarely see any more of the behemoths than the middle of their backs, it is nevertheless inspiring and exciting to see and hear them when they come nearby.

We ended our tour in the little city of Nanaimo with its intricate downtown streets and its beautiful waterfront and marina. We took the ferry back to the mainland to make an attempt at climbing Grouse Mountain, which would have afforded us a view of Vancouver City, but since the summit was in the clouds we decided to visit Stanley Park, the refuge of Vancouverites from the hustle and bustle of city life.

A sailboat seems out of place when moored right next to high-rises and heavy automobile traffic. A sailboat is a noble creation that is meant to navigate freely on the open water, explore coastlines, roam between islands, and rest at anchor in wilderness bays. That was the impression I had when I approached the Sunsail Yacht Charters' dock and laid my eyes on our 40-foot Beneteau sloop tied to the dock. As we had previously convened, Carol and Raymond caught up with us and now we were dropping off our bags onto the boat at the Bayshore West Marina.

First priority was provisioning. Rachel had prepared the grocery list and we all tagged along with her to the supermarket. She had each of us take a cart and a section of the master list. By having everybody participate, she was certain that nobody would have reason to complain if they didn't have their favourite snacks.

Now back at the boat. We had to decide how to share the three double berth cabins. It wasn't complicated for Carole and Raymond; as the only couple, they shared one of the cabins. Then Lana and Rachel decided to share a double berth. Don and I flipped a coin to decide between the remaining cabin and the salon settee. I ended up with the cabin, and Don the settee.

While Rachel and helpers stowed the provisions Don, Raymond and I attended the traditional boat and chart briefing by Ian, the boat rental manager. Our vessel was named *Tyee* from the native Canadian word for Chief. Ian apprised us of the must-see anchorages, the weather forecast, the tides and currents, the precautions to take, the places to reprovision and buy souvenirs, where to get rid of garbage, etc.

With regard to waste, this is what he reminded us of: Less than three miles from shore the only things we are allowed to put into the water are fish parts and grey water from the sinks and shower. Unlike Georgian Bay, the Straight of Georgia is the ocean, so once we're three miles from shore the law allows us to dump our decomposable food scraps cut up in pieces of less than an inch long and the contents of our holding tanks. Since no part of the Straight can be more than twelve miles from shore we are not allowed to dispose of cans and glass, and nowhere in all the oceans is it allowable to discard plastic of any kind. In the Straight of Georgia we have to store any solid non-biodegradable garbage until we dock near a garbage disposal facility where we pay $2 to $5 a bag for someone to dispose of it in a municipal landfill for us. In many marinas in the Straight, cans and bottles can be recycled as long as they are separated from the garbage. This way we can save a bit of money on waste disposal and have the satisfaction of knowing that we are causing less harm to the environment. If you want to learn more about ocean waste, see www.greenhorsesociety.com.

The atmosphere aboard *Tyee* was quite different from what it had been the previous autumn on *Constantia*. It's always nicer to be with friends than with a boatload of people you don't know. Besides, this was a pleasure trip and would present no element of stress like writing an exam at the end. What we hadn't counted on was that one of our crew would be very unhappy living aboard a boat at anchor.

Since it was 1615 when we cast off the dock at Vancouver, we opted for tying up at the Snug Cove Marina on neighbouring Bowen Island. An advantage of this place was that Lana could arrange to have her friend Irene, a resident of Bowen Island, join us for lunch aboard *Tyee*. The next morning while the others slept in Raymond and I went for a hike to Killarney Lake. The morning air was fresh and the moisture from the night's dew accentuated the smell of the cedar trees and wildflowers. We found our way to the lake after passing through a meadow, across a wooden bridge and a few forks in the road. After having walked the length of the boardwalk at the north end of the lake we continued around the opposite side. We ambled through groves of cedar and hemlock, across more boardwalks, enjoying the morning sun when the occasional ray bathed us in its warmth. Hundreds of dead tree trunks were strewn around the periphery of the lake like so many giant pick up sticks. When we regained the boat after our 9-kilometer walk lunch was ready for the taking.

While Raymond and I were away Lana's friend came to the boat for a visit and after lunch Don and the ladies wandered in the vicinity of Snug Cove, enjoying the very attractive Union Steamship Company store and the many little boutiques.

Again, it was late by the time we cast off, 1645, so we picked a destination just twelve miles away, Plumper Cove. The provincial park installed mooring buoys in the bay, which precluded the choice of using our anchor. However, once tied to a government buoy, you're pretty sure your boat won't drift and run aground in the middle of the night. In the Caribbean there are several places where the entire anchorage is filled with privately owned mooring balls. Anthony doesn't trust these improvised arrangements, as there is no way of knowing how securely they will hold your boat in a strong wind. In some of the islands anybody can take an old engine block, a piece of rope and a float and make himself a mooring he can rent out for $10 or $15 a night.

Lana remarked that she couldn't go ashore. I indicated to her that she was free to take the dinghy and she had two choices. She could either motor about one hundred metres to the park dock and go for a walk in the park trails, or she could drive the dinghy a mile across to Gibsons Landing where there were stores and facilities. Her decision was to stay with us, which I thought was wise, since she would need to return before dusk and it was getting late.

The following day we crossed the Straight over to Nanaimo on Vancouver Island. There is no option to anchor here, since it is a busy harbour and it has an excellent marina and waterfront. What is particular about this marina as well as others in the Straight is its very high tidal range, where the difference between high tide and low tide can be as much as fourteen feet. The dockage system is composed of floating docks attached to tall piles planted in the bottom, but which protrude vertically to an impressive height at low tide. The Nanaimo Port Authority should be congratulated on the wonderful job they did in planning this exceptionally beautiful and practical waterfront.

We left late – again. This time it was mainly because Whiskey Golf (WG) was closed most of the day. The name Whiskey Golf refers to a very large rectangular area in the Strait that is used for military exercises. It is closed to civilian traffic much of the time on weekdays to allow the Navy to test different armaments. Monday to Friday boaters who want to navigate that area must listen to the VHF radio to find out if the military is going to be *active* in that large zone. The times of activity are announced over the radio every day. If a civilian boat should wander within the limits of that virtual rectangle, a military escort boat will immediately be on her tail and order her to get out.

Since a good part of our proposed route was through WG this morning, we waited till 1545 before casting off. After having covered 20 miles it was getting late so we decided to anchor in Nanoose Bay even if it was not listed in our guide. We found out why. It is a large bay, used for mooring large commercial and military ships and submarines. On the northern side of the bay there is an extensive array of salmon farming cages. Its water is deep, which is good for large ships and submarines but not so for sailboats. According to our chart there was a small area near the end of the bay of 9 metres depth that would allow us to anchor, but it took us 20 minutes of searching to locate it. Finally we had the hook well in place and we could proceed to the sundowners. As we were enjoying our drinks, Lana alluded to the search for the anchorage as an unpleasant chore. To the rest of us it was just a normal part of the sailing experience.

Bright and early the next day, at 0929, we weighed anchor and set sail for a splendid little bay that Ian, the boat rental manager had strongly advised us to visit. It was partially across the Straight towards the mainland,

Jedediah Island, home of the Jedediah Island Marine Provincial Park. It was in fact just as beautiful and peaceful as Ian had described it. However, when we put the anchor to the bottom, it wouldn't hold. It just slid over the smooth, rocky bottom. We moved a little further and tried again, with the same result. We repeated the procedure a little further and still the anchor would slide over the bottom. Finally, after an hour of trying, we gave up and headed for the mainland, 10 miles further and anchored in Pender Harbour, a very well protected bay, home to a dozen marinas. It is in fact a major boating centre featuring marine stores, hotels and repair facilities.

"There are docks here. Why are we anchoring?" Lana whispered to Don.

Don explained that it was the preference of the crew. It started to become apparent that Lana preferred to avoid anchorages in favour of marinas or public docks. She appeared uncomfortable when she wasn't able to step off the boat at will.

Whenever we have the choice we will anchor rather than moor to a dock. First, anchoring is free. Lying alongside a dock costs upward of $30. Our second choice, tying to a mooring ball usually involves a cost of $10 to $15, but presents the same advantages as anchoring. When a boat is on a mooring ball or anchored it will usually point into the wind. The hatches on a sailboat usually open forward, towards the wind, forming big scoops that direct the breeze inside the boat, acting like a large air conditioner on a hot summer day. In addition to this, at anchor we are a lot farther from our next neighbour, his smells and his noise.

Pender Harbour had so much to offer that we decided to stay a second night. In deference to Lana's discomfort with being at anchor, we decided to move the boat to the Madeira Bay public dock for the second night.

For lunch we discovered the local Legion Hall in Madeira Park, a rather unassuming building past a row of magnificent flowering fruit trees cloaked with white blooms. When the waitress at the cash register turned her concentration away from the TV set to address us she asked where we were from, and then informed us that since we were not members we could not eat or drink at the Legion hall unless we were sponsored by a member.

"But wait a minute," she said, as she turned around and yelled at four men seated at a table covered with beer bottles, "Would one of youse fellers cum'n sponsor these good folks from Down East fer me?"

One of the foursome, without getting up from his chair yelled in reply, "Welcome to our town, folks," then to the lady at the cash register, "You kin sign them folks under my name, Honey."

The menu offered the type of fare you would find in a Mom and Pop diner, which threatened to be unexciting and possibly indigestible.

"Honey" recommended the fish and chips, claiming that they were the best in the world. We very wisely and fortuitously followed her recommendation, and I can affirm that the Madeira Legion's fish and chips were in fact the very best in the world, or at least in my world.

The 90-mile stretch of coast from Vancouver to Desolation Sound is known as the Sunshine Coast. A brisk, following wind accompanied us northward to our next stop, Lund, a picturesque fishing village of 800 permanent residents. Once a port for isolated coastal logging operations, Lund is nestled around a secluded harbour backed by the magnificent peaks of the Coast Mountains. Not relevant to boaters, is the following fact: Lund is at the top of Highway 101, also known as the Pan American Highway, a very very long road that leads to the South American town of Quellon, Porto Monte, Chile 15,020 km away! During the summer months vacationers use Lund as a staging point for trips to nearby Savary Island, Desolation Sound and points further north up the rugged BC coast. Furthermore, it's a practical stop for sailors, as all the facilities are available, like showers, Laundromat, bakery, garbage disposal, etc. When we arrived the docks were full, so we rafted onto an old boat that appeared to have been moored there since WW2. It is customary in busy marinas to tie up to another boat this way. But then, when you have to get to the dock you have to step across the deck of the other boat.

We were stopping here merely to get rid of garbage and take on more water, then we were to anchor in Finn Bay, half a mile north of the village. Lana raised the possibility of staying here overnight. This got Raymond's dander up and he riposted that those who dislike being on a boat should take the train. Others opined that they preferred to get away from the noise of the marina. As captain, Don had to settle the issue. In the end, it was getting late and he decided that we would stay at the dock overnight.

Nothing was lost in having to moor in Lund. Don's decision enabled us to discover a little arts and crafts shop where Carole and I were transfixed by the beauty, variety and quality of its merchandise. Located in the Historic Lund Hotel it is called the Tug Ghum Gallery operated by wildlife artist and gallery owner, Debra Bevaart. She is a soapstone carver who works at her craft all winter and runs her store in the summer. Her shop displays, in addition to her own carvings, high quality works from 40 local artists and artisans. You would usually have to drag me screaming and kicking into a shop, but this one had such beautiful and original pieces that perusing the displays was more like visiting an interesting museum. I ended up splurging. I bought Micheline a carving of the head of a seal emerging from the water. When I gave it to her I told her that I am like this seal. I'm relentlessly drawn to the water, but always come back up. It was going to be my daughter Natalie's birthday at the end of the month, so I bought her a very original jewel box in the shape of a beaver head. Carole bought herself a large candy jar made of pottery, with an incredibly accurately made, tight fitting lid whose handle mimicked the form of three birds seated on a branch.

The previous day, while I was spending my children's inheritance at the crafts shop, a discussion was taking place between Don and Lana on the boat. Our reluctant sailor didn't want to continue any further. It had been understood that we were to sail for two weeks and that we would sail the Sunshine Coast at least as far as Desolation Sound before turning back. Lana couldn't stand the thought of more nights at anchor, so she decided to jump ship for the next two nights, find lodging in Lund and sail back to Vancouver with us when we would stop to pick her up on the way back.

After bidding Lana a good stay in Lund, we untied our lines from the old boat that had served as our dock and headed northward. A brisk southwest wind propelled us along the coast that dominated the view on our starboard. We kept on the outside of Copeland Islands Marine Park and a few miles further we reached the end of Malaspina Peninsula. We turned starboard past Sarah Point and Bravo! Ahead of us was Desolation Sound and the heart stirring view of the snow-capped mountains. We proceeded to West Redonda Island on our port and stopped at the entrance of Roscoe Bay.

Here we double-checked our calculations before engaging in the narrow inlet that leads to the bay. The reason is that halfway into the inlet there is a rocky bar which, when the tide is at its lowest, protrudes slightly *above water*, restricting access to the inner portion of the bay. Sailboats transit this little pass regularly, but they do so at high tide. According to our tide tables, the next high tide was to be 14 feet above chart datum and was expected at 1640. Since we were two hours early, we performed a little calculation based on the tidal range, which revealed that the actual depth over the bar would be 11.5 feet at the time of our transit. *Tyee* had a draft of 5.5 feet. We knew that the 11.5 foot calculation wasn't accurate, since the values given in the tide and current tables were for a reference station **several miles from our location. Even though we would appear to have had** six feet of play, as a precaution, we crawled through the pass with just enough speed to allow steerageway. When we reached the shallowest part, the depth sounder read 8.5 feet, three feet short of our theoretical calculation.

I breathed a sigh of relief after we successfully passed over the bar, but no sooner had we made it through than something else took my breath away: The splendour of this little bay surrounded by high, pine-covered mountains was astounding! Once we put down the anchor and killed the engine, the only sound to be heard was a trickling of water from the stream at the far end of the bay, originating from nearby Black Lake.

I thought of poor Lana and what she was missing. Perhaps the mountains enveloping this little bay would have made her claustrophobic, so she might have been just as well wherever she was.

All thoughts of going for a swim were quickly dispelled: The water in this restricted bay was filled with thousands upon thousands of white jellyfish about 4 to 5 inches in diameter, eagerly and indefatigably pumping away, moving incessantly on their quest to getting nowhere.

Black Lake stood at 10 feet above sea level, about 100 metres from the terminus of the bay. Since the guidebook said the lake's water was warm, we wore our swimsuits for the short walk. We all jumped into the water like a bunch of Polar Bear Club ice swimmers. I stayed just long enough to prevent emasculation by freezing, but once I towelled myself dry I felt refreshed and invigorated. Walking back to the bay, we found remnants of an old timber flume and a salmon ladder built in the olden days of logging, witnesses of the days of yore.

By the time we returned from our fresh water lake excursion, we were locked into the bay, as the tide had gone down. If ever we got the notion to skedaddle, we'd have to simply forget it until the next high tide. In parts of the world where the tide is diurnal, that is, twice a day, each subsequent high tide is about 12 hours and 25 minutes after the previous one. The next high tide would be around 0415 next morning, so that wouldn't fit in with our lackadaisical cruising lifestyle. Our plan, accordingly, was to leave the next day around 1530, two hours before the afternoon high tide.

During the night I was in a semi-sleep for a while, thinking about our depth sounder and imagining myself running aground on the way out of Roscoe Bay because of an error in a depth reading. A depth sounder is an electronic instrument that measures the time lag when a transmitted sound echoes off the bottom and is received by the instrument's receiver, then converts that reading into a distance, the depth. The first such instrument was a huge contraption, invented by Dr. Harvey Hayes and was installed on U.S. Navy ships in 1922. Technological advancements and mass production have rendered the depth sounder cheap enough to be considered indispensable on today's sailboats.

The instrument can be calibrated in several different ways. The display screen is located in a prominent position in the cockpit, and the send-receive probe is placed in the bottom of the hull near the bow. In its default mode it reads the distance from the bottom of the boat to the bottom of the water, which is fine for a rowboat. However, a cruising keelboat has a deep keel to take into account. The keel can be anywhere from two feet to six feet lower than the probe, so some sailors calibrate their machine to give them the depth under the keel. Others prefer to add a couple of feet more than actual to give them a greater margin of safety. The draft of each boat is a known factor, so other sailors, like myself, prefer simply to be told how deep the water is for real and figure out for themselves whether or not a particular depth is safe for their boat. At the Vancouver Marina Ian had told us the depth sounder on *Tyee* read the actual depth of the water from the surface, my preference.

The next morning I had to confirm or refute what Ian had said for my own peace of mind. We made a simple depth gauge with a wrench and a length of string. We lowered the wrench until it touched bottom, marked the string at water level and measured the length with a tape measure. To our surprise the boat's electronic depth sounder read one foot more than the real depth. So when the instrument read 8.5 feet over the bar at the entrance, we actually had only 7.5 feet, which was cutting it a little close. The moral of the story is that when you rent a boat, check out the calibration of the depth sounder yourself before you get into a critical situation. If you will be bareboating in the future you might want to use the checklist in Annex 5.

It was with a twinge of regret that we weighed anchor at 1530 to leave our enchanting bay, but we had only one night left before meeting Lana in Lund. We thus headed westward, motoring most of the way for lack of wind. After a brief twelve miles we anchored in Cortez Bay, surrounded by low-lying land, in contrast with our previous night's alpine scenery.

The next morning we went for a walk along Manzanita Road where we discovered a most unique attraction, Wolf Bluff Castle. This site is known locally as "Karl's Castle", after the owner who was building his life project with his own hands. Admission to visit the castle was by voluntary donation. The five-storied structure boasted a dungeon, dining hall, eight bedrooms and three turrets, two of which had cannons and the third, the tallest of the three, flew the Canadian flag. Karl, who was 64, told us that as a child growing up in Hungary, he would draw pictures of castles and dream of owning one. When he moved to Cortes Island, he decided to fulfill his dream and build his own. To date it had taken him 10 years and 12,000 cement blocks to complete what was there. He designed the castle and did most of the work himself, hauling buckets of cement up to the top floors with a makeshift crane. It was an ongoing project, as he still had to put a finish on the outside and the inside of the cement blocks and fix some leakage problems from the roofs.

Standing at the top of the highest tower, I was eyeing the ground below and felt a little insecure. The gaps in the battlements showed clearly that the entire structure of the walls consisted of a single layer of 8-inch thick cement blocks. Relative to the precipitous 40-foot drop to the ground below, the walls just felt too flimsy.

Nevertheless, because from this vantage point the view of the hills was very pretty and the designer-builder had put so much effort into realizing his dream, I felt a donation was de rigueur.

Our next stop was Lund, a further 11 miles south, to pick up Lana. She reported having had a pleasant two-day stay in Lund, but I felt sorry for her for having missed the best part of the whole trip. We spent the night at the dock and the next day we left for a re-visit of charming Pender Harbour. At 1725, out of concern for our "anchorphobic" crewmember, we again tied up to a dock. Carole asked if anybody needed the dinghy and no, nobody needed it, so she went off on her own for a quiet little tour of the convoluted bay, using only the oars for propulsion.

The rest of us attended to a few maintenance jobs, like filling an empty water tank, getting rid of garbage and preparing supper – the usual stuff. Just as supper was ready to be served, Raymond came down into the cabin and asked, "Have you seen Carole?"

We were all dumbfounded, as we realized that it was 2115 and our wayward Carole had still not returned from her dinghy ride. I should mention that some years ago Carole had had brain surgery for a life threatening condition. Ever since, part of her brain affected her reflexes and her ability to concentrate. Often, she would fall asleep when others were still carrying out a conversation. What we feared was that she might have somehow been carried out to sea with the ebb tide. We didn't have a second dinghy with which to go search for her, so we undocked *Tyee* and started circling around the bay. It was difficult because Pender Harbour is large, very convoluted and has several bays within the bay. There was no sign of her in our section of Madeira bay, so we motored around the first peninsula, into the next section. The sun had already gone down and darkness was rapidly closing in on us. In the distance we could see what appeared to be a dinghy, but it was hard to tell if it was on the shore or away from the shore. As we got closer it appeared as though there was nobody in the boat, but it became clear that it was in effect an inflatable dinghy. After another three quarters of a mile we could detect something that looked like a foot over one of the sides. Raymond declared, "It's Carole, I'm sure of it."

A problem though, was that the depth gauge indicated 11 feet, which was really only 10 feet. So Don stopped the boat and we called out, "Carole, Carole!"

No response.

Raymond blew hard in a whistle, and still no response.

Don shifted into forward gear again and nudged closer to a (true) depth of 8 feet. We were still about 100 feet from the dinghy, but we could see part of Carole's form, supine and asleep in the bottom.

"I can't go any closer," he said.

Then Rachel retrieved the foghorn and gave it a good, long blast. Thereupon, we detected some stirring in the dinghy. A very sleepy Carole drew herself sitting up and stared bleary eyed in the direction of the noise, puzzled and confused. She looked around, noticed it was getting dark and understood that she had been gone a long time and that her shipmates had come to fetch her. All is well that ends well... The prodigal child was unhurt and glad that her personal search and rescue team had found her.

After a good night's sleep and with everybody on board, we bade goodbye to Pender Harbour, with the resolve that on a future trip we would spend more time there to discover its numerous trails, its ample coastline and its restaurants.

As a result of popular vote, we returned to Plumper Cove to tie up to a mooring. I could see that Lana, the only dissenter, was uncomfortable with the idea. I realized then that she wasn't being selfish or obstinate, but that she felt a strong discomfort bordering on phobia of being disconnected from shore. I remembered that when she was speaking with Micheline at the previous NCSS annual barbecue she had expressed incredulity at my wife's dislike of being in the restrictive confines of a sailboat. Perhaps Lana was just rationalizing her own fear and discomfort.

The next morning Rachel began the day with *crêpes bretonnes* filled with sections of fresh pear and a delectable chocolate sauce. A dollop of whipped cream crowned the work of art.

Not a breath of wind this morning. Keats Island, in the lee of which we were moored, was quite scenic and merited more exploration. Lana decided to go ashore for a hike while the rest of the crew stayed aboard for a slow circumnavigation of the island under motor, which took a leisurely hour. When we returned to the mooring to pick up Lana at the prescribed time, she wasn't at the government dock as expected. We waited on the boat of course, since she had taken the dinghy ashore. She appeared an hour later, explaining that the trail was longer than she had anticipated, which didn't endear her to the crew whose patience was already threadbare.

Once all hands were on deck, we crossed over to Gibsons Landing Harbour on the mainland. Lana would have her wish for our last night aboard *Tyee*. The consolation for the rest of the crew was that the harbour is poster card pretty, had an interesting museum, a fine bakery and afforded us a pleasant walking trail.

The government docks were chock full so we rafted up to a large wooden boat whose owner wasn't to be seen or heard. When Raymond stepped onto the vacant boat to secure our mooring lines, he found the deck somewhat sticky. We then noticed that the owner had transferred all of the things that were on his boat onto the dock in order to varnish his deck. So we furtively untied the lines and motored away to Gibsons Marina on the other side of the harbour. As we guiltily stole away from his boat, we saw the owner on his knees on the dock, bent over his painting supplies, cleaning his brushes. Someone quipped that he should have put up "Fresh Paint" signs, which elicited chuckles. We all laughed uncharitably when Raymond pondered, "He'll be wondering how those footprints appeared on the deck when he never saw anybody boarding his boat!"

&&&&&&&

From my vantage point on *Ventus* in Bahía la Mar, I could still feel the anticipation and excitement that filled me in the month before the trip at the prospect of a marvellous trip to Margarita, Venezuela with Anthony, oblivious of the terrifying ordeal that was awaiting us in Boca del Rio.

Porlamar, Margarita: once rich, now poor

Three not-so-young sailors about to face horror

BOCA DEL RÍO

Second night anchored in here

First night anchored out here

BAHÍA MANGLE

10° 57.0'N
64° 10.0'W

Chapter 9

Margarita, Here We Come!

Thursday, July 8, 2004.

Deplaning (as goes the expression in the airline industry) in a Caribbean island is always a bit of a shock to the senses even when it's summer at home in Canada. If you did so blindfolded the telltale heat, humidity, smells and sounds would leave you no doubt that you've landed on a tropical island. Anthony was waiting for me at the Port of Spain airport and gave me a warm welcome.

It was my first time in Trinidad, the most southern of the entire chain of Caribbean islands. Amongst the larger of the Caribbean islands, it measures about the same in area as Canada's smallest province, Prince Edward Island (PEI). I would have the chance to visit more extensively at a future date, but I had read that its topography consists of a combination of mountains in the north and plains in the south.

It features a rich forest that provides shelter and food for over 100 species of mammals and 468 species of birds. The land is also very rich in reptiles and invertebrates such as butterflies of which 617 species have been identified. Trinidad is known for its Carnival, calypso, soca (a form of dance music) and steel-pan music. It has more of everything than PEI in the way of fauna and flora. It also has more people – nearly ten times the population of PEI and 190 times the number of murders per year!

We proceeded for the circuitous drive Anthony had described in an email he had sent me before I left. In a very long paragraph, he describes in minute detail how to get from the airport to his street, Ragbir Street. In the next paragraph he goes on to explain how to find his house on his street:

> Turn left into Ragbir Street and go up a slightly steeper incline and winding road without turning off while there is still an incline. About a quarter mile up, the incline will change to a decline as you round a corner. About 20 metres from the corner, you will immediately be faced with what will look like a fork. Take the left fork and proceed downhill for about 30 metres when you will be faced with a trifurcation. The left side continues down the hill – do not go there. Take the middle path which goes up a short steep hill over a ridge and my gate is at the bottom of the other side of the ridge. The number "13" is on the right hand gate pillar and you are headed back south again. Ring the doorbell and smile, as your face will appear on a TV screen inside the house. Of course, none of this will be necessary because I will be at the airport to meet you.

This sounds complicated because it is indeed. To begin with, in Trinidad driving is on the left as with all former British colonies. I find that even though I've driven hundreds of kilometres on such roads, it still takes me a while to realign my brain to accepting that everybody *should be* on the wrong side of the road. The road to Anthony's street was an hour of a mishmash of four lane highways merging into two lanes, roads under construction, two lanes merging into a narrow street bordered by stores and houses abutting narrow sidewalks or no sidewalks at all. The traffic was bumper to bumper and drivers were impatient, passing each other on the right or on the left, horns blaring. The smell emanating from the thousands of vehicles lacking pollution control mechanisms was suffocating. One could *taste* the clouds of black exhaust belching from the diesel engines of the trucks and busses.

The high prices of natural gas have spurred new drilling within its legal boundaries, which has been a boon for the country's economy. Trinidad is a very large producer of natural gas and has signed long-term agreements with American companies for their precious resource at absurdly low prices. It presently supplies the US with 70% of its imported LNG. A large drill rig manufacturer has set up shop in Trinidad and many chemical companies have opened new processing plants to convert the gas into easily exportable liquids in the form of methanol and urea. More Liquefaction plants have been built to feed the numerous LNG ships that are thirstily drinking Trinidad dry. As a consequence of this economic activity, much new wealth has been created, thus many more people have disposable income. The American dream of having a car in front of every house is very much alive here, and Trinidadians have been relentlessly chasing this dream with their newfound money. However, road construction hasn't kept up with the increase in car ownership, with the result that roads and streets have become proverbial parking lots of slow moving vehicles. Gridlock begins at five o'clock in the morning and ends after supper.

Anthony tells me that instead of spending money on improving its water and sewer infrastructure the government has been concentrating on making this third world country resemble a first world country, by promoting the construction of massive high-rise office buildings, shopping centres and convention centres.

Anthony's neighbourhood has been built on the side of a mountain overseeing the district of Saint Augustine, near Port of Spain, the capital. There are numerous individual hills, or humps on the mountainside, with narrow streets winding between them, bifurcating and trifurcating here and there, going up and down very steep inclines, branching out to ever more little streets, each one of which leads to elegant houses. Anthony's house is built atop a one-acre mound alongside another house. Enough tropical trees have been planted to hide the neighbours, yet in front of the house there is an unobstructed panoramic view of the sprawling suburb. There is a large yard and enough fruit trees to supply the household year-round. At the entrance to the driveway by the street there is an ornate electric gate remotely operated from the car or from the house to allow visitors in. Once clear of the gate, the car goes up a steep incline of paved laneway to end up facing a twin carport.

Anthony and his wife designed and built the house themselves 30 years ago when their five girls were tots. There is an ample living and dining room with unglazed windows on each side. The house is cool, given that it was designed for convection cooling with the addition of generous roof overhangs to keep the beating sun out. The bathrooms are aerated with four-foot by four-foot ventilation towers above the shower stalls, open to the sky. It is not unusual to find a bird or other creature looking for a way out of the shower. Each of the five bedrooms has windows overlooking the garden, the yard or the city. Now that the children are gone, aside from the master bedroom, one room is used as an office, one as a sewing room and the others as guest rooms, which the Johnsons generously fill at every occasion. The one drawback of a lovely house in Trinidad is the matter of security. All the windows are protected with steel bars and the front door has a steel gate that is locked with two high security, bolt cutter-proof locks. His wife

Krimhilde has told me that in Trinidad the innocent live behind bars and the criminals run loose.

Anthony once recounted that one night upon arriving home he had a terrifying experience. As he stepped out of his car in the carport he was accosted by two young men, one of whom pointed a gun at his chest. My friend's reaction was unhesitating. He brushed aside the weapon with his hand and berated the two assailants:

"You guys are on the wrong track and you will end up getting your necks stretched!" – and pointing towards the bottom of the hill, where the young men lived.

He added, *"Go home where you've come from."*

To Anthony's relief, the young men were intimidated by the older man's unexpected and aggressive response and perhaps influenced by his authoritative stance and simply left the premises.

Krimhilde is a lovely woman in her sixties who has not lost the German accent of her youth. She and Anthony met in Glasgow, Scotland when they were at university, she in arts, and he in engineering. He graduated in mechanical engineering, settled in Trinidad and worked in power plants, tool and die, and he spent a major part of his career in procurement and construction management in heavy industry. He and Krimhilde were also heavily involved in the manufacture of a wide range of cleaning chemicals.

Krimhilde was waiting for us with a hot supper in the oven, which I appreciated like a salvation, because although American Airlines had me in their care for 11 hours, they only chose to feed me two tiny pouches containing 13½ peanuts each.

In the morning we headed for the Trinidad and Tobago Sailing Association (TTSA) marina in Chaguaramas, an area on the south side of the northwest peninsula. The expanse of water in view was the Gulf of Paria, protected from the Caribbean to the north by the Charaguamas peninsula projecting westwards like a stubby, pointed finger. Anthony showed me around *Ventus* and explained the arrangement he and the owner Ian had concluded.

Ian is a British businessman who had married a Trinidadian woman. He and Anthony became friends 20 years previously through a common interest in sailing. Ian took his holidays in Trinidad to spend time with his in-laws and to crew for Anthony on his 30-foot sailing sloop, a Farr 30, named *Les Remous*. They sailed together many years and in so doing became close friends. When in recent years Anthony sold *Les Remous* and bought *Mikky*, Ian became a convert to the comforts of a larger boat and later decided to start looking to buy one of his own.

In the previous winter (2004) he found this 2002 Hallberg Rassy 39 in impeccable condition for sale in the Caribbean, and jumped at the occasion. He arranged to moor her in Trinidad in the off-season. Hurricane season extends from the beginning of June till the end of November. Since tropical storms don't usually travel below the 12th parallel, Trinidad is a popular place for yachties to put up their boats during the hurricane season. Another popular place for storing boats in the off-season is the island of Margarita, our destination on this trip.

The arrangement Ian proposed was that Anthony become the boat's manager. This would entail seeing to the maintenance of the boat, the installation of any new equipment and improvements, hiring the expert help necessary for the work, delivering the boat to wherever in the Caribbean the owner would like to sail her and deliver her back to Trinidad in June to escape hurricanes. Ian would use the boat in the winter for a maximum of two months and Anthony would have use of her the rest of the year. Another advantage for Anthony is that Ian would pay all the maintenance and repair costs.

This sounded like an ideal arrangement, but Anthony confided that as a matter of "excessive precaution", as he put it, he was to keep *Mikky* for a while to test out the agreement. To make things easier, Ian and he signed a formal contract stipulating the rights and responsibilities of each party. This was a wise move in my view, because it does not rely on memory, which can, even with much younger people, colour an agreement differently from its intended form. The written word eliminates the danger of the two parties having a different recollection of what had been said.

Aside from the problem of memory, this arrangement would place the two friends who had always been equals in every way on a different power sharing footing, akin to that of an employer and employee. The two of them know each other as if they had been brothers. Yet, this was new territory for both of them. Would the newly created hierarchy show up later as a cause of tension between the two pals? Not at all likely, since Ian and Anthony are sensitive and respectful of each other's feelings and concerns.

And there was the matter of the almighty dollar. Sometimes two good friends can tragically become enemies as a result of a quarrel over money. Is it possible that in the future a difference in opinion about who should pay for what cause a rift between the two friends? Ian is financially comfortable, but also a very generous person, so the chances of a money problem creating an intractable dispute are very slim, especially since these matters are probably covered in the written agreement. For Anthony, this is certainly the ultimate in OPY sailing!

We cleared customs in the morning, then did some provisioning. We could buy fresh fruit and vegetables pretty well anywhere in the Caribbean, but dry goods were cheaper in Trinidad than elsewhere. Anthony didn't pick up any more beer than what we would consume before arriving in Margarita, as in Venezuela it would be available for the derisory price of 20 cents a can. Fuel is cheap in Trinidad because of a government subsidy, but that is expensive compared to the price in Venezuela, the country with the cheapest diesel and gasoline in the world. Mr. Chavez keeps the peace with his constituents by having his government foot the bill for most of the cost of their fuel. As an example, in 2004 diesel fuel went for 9 cents *per gallon* – *not per litre* and gasoline 12 cents! One can question the wisdom, or lack thereof, of subsidizing a finite resource instead of taxing it.

Anthony, ever the master in balancing work and pleasure suggested we go to the Club's bar to decompress. After all, we were to cast off at 0200 in the middle of the night in order to arrive in Grenada during daylight hours. We still had several items of maintenance to attend to before leaving and we couldn't attempt all that work without first replenishing our energy.

As is common in the Caribbean, the bar was a central square surrounded by tables under a roof supported by pillars, without walls. There is a difference, however, between the bar in a private club and one in a tourist area. The private club bar is populated mostly by its members. Consequently, there is a core of regulars, whom you can count on to be there anytime you go for a meal or refreshments. They may be chatting away in groups and each group tends to stay by itself.

In a tourist area the bar is populated by yachties who make a career of island hopping. They will stay several weeks or even months in the same place before moving on to the next island. You can spot the yachtie versus the club member by his or her dress. The club member dresses casually but neatly, but the yachtie will display an excess of casualness bordering on sloppiness.

Both groups share one trait that is common to all sailors, and that is their sense of humour, their friendliness and their sense of camaraderie.

We had barely sat down with our beer, when we heard a cry from a duo of female voices,

"Awn-to-neee!"

Anthony invited the ladies to sit down with us and introduced me to two of his very dear sailing friends who had crewed on *Les Remous*, Nadine and Brenda. They had come to TTSA especially to see their friend off.

"Jacqui eez so lawkeee to go weez you Ontonee. I have so sorry I add to con cell," exclaimed Nadine in a very French accent.

I learned that we were to have had two women aboard but that Nadine's replacement in her little cheese factory had a serious health issue that forced her to take leave, so out of necessity, she had to stay behind to mind the fort. Brenda expressed regret that she couldn't take time off work to join Anthony since she would so much have wanted to return to Margarita and its beautiful, peaceful anchorages. She asked me if it was my first time, to which I replied in the affirmative. She then assured me that Margarita is the most scenic island in the Caribbean. None of us at the table had any sense of the irony of our conversation. This was the trip that culminated in our surviving an unprecedented pirate attack in what had always been considered safe cruising ground for sailors. I'm sure that when Nadine and Brenda heard about our ordeal after our return they must have thanked their lucky stars for the "misfortune" that had prevented them from joining Anthony on this fateful journey. And, of course, if we had had the wisdom of hindsight that we now possess, we might very well have chosen a different destination.

After we returned to the boat, Jacqui joined us, bright eyed and jubilant. She immediately got busy preparing supper while Anthony and I planned the route for our first landfall, Grenada. Anthony didn't need to plan, of course, because he had made the 85-mile overnight passage many many times before. He was doing this navigation on the chart for my benefit.

Now, if you've looked at a map of the area, you could be forgiven for thinking that there is something wrong with Anthony's navigation because, after all, Margarita is practically due west of Trinidad and Grenada is directly north. Why make such a long detour? The reason is that the alternative would take us close to the coast of Venezuela, an area known for pirate attacks. Some years ago cruisers would choose this coast as prime sailing grounds, as it was reputed to be the most beautiful in the Caribbean. Unfortunately, the security aspect of the country has deteriorated to the point where now it is advisable to keep at least 50 miles from the coast to avoid boarding by pirates.

After supper we carried out several maintenance jobs then made the usual preparations for an offshore passage and at 2300 we were asleep.

It was 0200 when the alarm clock shook me out of a profound sleep. Within seconds I was fully alert, my three hours of sleep having fully revived me. We cast off the docklines and headed west towards the tip of the Chaguaramas peninsula. When the chunk of land that was to become Trinidad separated from the South American continent eons ago, this peninsula broke up into little pieces, creating the islands of Monos, Huevos and Chacachacare. We were sailing on calm water, headed for the quarter-mile wide opening between Trinidad and Monos, known as the First Boca, under the silvery light of a full moon. As we came closer to the opening, I could behold the Caribbean Sea, beckoning us on the other side of the Boca. What struck me as remarkable as we were navigating in the calm, protected waters of the Gulf of Paria, was that past the Boca, row upon row of large,

Margarita Here We Come!

white, fluorescent waves were streaming towards us, dissipating themselves before reaching the opening. The difference in wave size between protected waters and those of a sea was never so obvious as from this vantage point in the Boca.

Half an hour past the Boca, the wind died down and our boat speed fell below 4 knots. As is customary with Anthony, this called for putting on some engine power to supplement the lagging wind power, to bring our speed up to a more respectable six knots. At 0935 we saw our first boat, directly ahead of us on a collision course, a fishing boat that was immobile in the middle of nowhere. There were no nets deployed and there was no fisherman in sight. We had to change course to avoid running into her.

At 1540 land came into view. About a mile from shore we left the Porpoises to our starboard. They are a group of dangerous rocks awash and visible only when the waves are large enough to break over them. Finally, we dropped the hook in the turquoise water of Prickly Bay, one of the numerous pretty bays Mother Nature has created for the pleasure of sailors seeking safe anchorages on the south coast of Grenada.

"Come back tomorrow" was the terse message scrawled on a piece of cardboard at the door of Customs and Immigration. A perfect occasion for cleaning the hull. We donned masks and fins and scraped the barnacles off the propeller and scrubbed the green growth along the waterline and the underwater portion of the hull. Otherwise we obeyed the rule for Sundays and made the latter part of the day one of rest.

We cleared customs, then moved to anchor at Hog Island, in the neighbouring bay. Lunch was the first time I'd ever tasted, or ever heard about for that matter, *turkey steaks*!

"How can you cut a steak from a bird?" you ask.

It consists of the turkey leg cut across into three-quarter inch thick slices with the bone. They look like disk-shaped steaks of varying sizes, each one with a little bone in the middle and are only available in the frozen meat section. We sauté them with butter in a frying pan. What is most unbelievable is that they taste like…steak! It is only in the Caribbean that I've found them. Back at home I asked for them at several meat counters and every time the butcher responded with an incredulous look, as if he were dealing with someone who had lost his marbles.

The next morning Jacqui served us "bakes", an unleavened bread cooked by frying in a pan, about an inch thick. They resemble the bannock that Canadian aboriginals and trappers cook over a fire. They make a reasonable substitute for bread in a pinch.

We left our Hog Island anchorage to visit Saint Georges. Under a moderate following wind, we sailed for a relaxing hour and a half with the genoa fully unfurled and without bothering to raise the mainsail. Once we were clear of the southwest point, we raised the mainsail and tacked several times to reach our anchorage in Saint Georges harbour.

We rode the dinghy to the Grenada Yacht Club bar to celebrate our safe arrival in Saint Georges after what we jokingly referred to as our gruelling sail. There we met friends of Anthony's, residents of Grenada. One of them, Justin, had just started an Internet provider company, figuring there was a burgeoning market for this technology and no competition. It's an advantage to be the first to offer a new service.

For lunch Anthony took us to The Nutmeg, a typical Grenadian restaurant by the seawall, overseeing the bay known as the Carenage. One of the pleasures of travel is to discover the local cuisine. Those who aren't fussy eaters and have a sense of adventure have access to a whole world of gastronomy. Anthony pointed out a typical Caribbean fast food item on the menu, the roti, pronounced roh-tee. It consists of a flat flour dough folded over itself a few times to form a thick envelope, filled with a potato based stuffing with the addition of either fish, meat, or whatever. It sounded good, so I decided to go for the calamari version. I began by chewing into one of the ends. I had to take several bites of the white dough before I reached any of the stuffing. As it turned out, amongst the massive quantity of potato I was able to discern just a few microscopic fragments of squid. My experience with Anthony and his roti reminded me of an experience in a greasy spoon in St-Hyacinthe, Quebec. I was treating a visiting scientist from Australia to a quick lunch between two stages of an experiment. I had convinced him that if he had flown halfway around the world to work on a research project in rural Quebec, he couldn't return home without having sampled the National fast food specialty of French Canada, the Poutine. The waitress placed before my guest a huge dish of the famous (or infamous) mixture of French Fries, curd cheese and brown gravy.

When he was done, I asked him his impression and he replied, "Well, Robert, it was quite nice at first, halfway through it got a wee bit repetitive, and by the time I reached the end, it actually got a little boring."

I could have said the same of roti, but I always keep in mind what my mother used to say, "Never say something bad if you can say something good."

So I will say one good thing about roti: It is filling.

Anthony and Jacqui had seen everything there was to see of the first landfall island to the north of Trinidad, so they weren't interested in sightseeing. Ergo, I decided to take a day by myself and play the tourist. I started with a visit to the Office of Tourism to inquire about the must-see places in the Island and to pick up a good road map. Next, I went to the car hire place to reserve a vehicle for the next day.

Back at the Yacht Club, we met Mary Ellen, a lady of 70 whom we had noticed the day before when she arrived in the bay aboard her tiny, rather time worn 22-foot sailboat. She had been travelling around the world solo with her cat for the past fourteen years. She was so enthralled with Thailand that she spent six years there before continuing to other destinations. I asked her if she ever suffered from solitude. She responded that she prefers to avoid the company of others. I was curious to know how she had dealt with strong katabatic winds, squalls and storms in such a tiny boat. What I found incredible was her statement that in all those thousands of sea miles she had never encountered winds of more than 30 knots! I wondered how she did it. Maybe it's the cat.

Whenever I rent a vehicle I choose the smallest possible, in other words, a subcompact. In Grenada however, rental agencies only carry SUVs in the expectation that all their customers will demand a rugged four-wheel drive machine with big tires to negotiate the rough roads. On the very narrow roads of a Caribbean island, there is a big advantage in driving the narrowest possible car, preferably with folding side mirrors, so I'm somewhat at a loss to understand the SUV only practice.

I thought the map I had purchased was a good one, as it was so detailed that it even showed groups of houses and buildings. The towns and villages were named, but unlike maps elsewhere, there were no circles indicating their position. Furthermore, there were no names or highway numbers on any of the roads on the map, which didn't bode too well for my chances of finding my way around.

My first destination was Grand Étang National Park. First priority was finding my way out of Saint Georges. I picked what was the most likely street leading to the unnumbered highway. I navigated through intersections, Ys and Ts in the road, not knowing which way to turn, as there were no street names, highway numbers or signs indicating directions. I drove and drove, stopping to ask directions once in a while. Finally, after having gone several miles over half an hour, I came to a town. I proceeded to follow what seemed to be a major street. It twisted and winded, then started downhill and then I could see the sea! Something was wrong. I shouldn't have been near the water at all if I had been where I thought I was. And then it dawned on me. I had driven full circle and come back to Saint Georges!

The roads that appeared like highways on the map were windy two-lane roads with no shoulder, and the secondary roads were often just the width of one car. Often there was a square, concrete ditch with vertical sides, within centimetres of my tires and when I met another vehicle, I had to either stop to let it by, or crawl, with my left wheels dangerously close to the ditch, which, if they fell into it, would wreak considerable damage to the undercarriage. Sometimes there was so little space for the meeting vehicles that we had to fold our driver's side mirrors so they wouldn't hit each other. After much turning and twisting, dodging potholes, stopping to ask directions, I found my way to the entrance of Grand Étang Forest Reserve. I drove on to Grand Étang Lake, a pretty 15-acre body of water that lies in the bottom of the crater of a long-extinct volcano, about 1800 feet above sea level. Thick rain clouds obscured the rim of the volcano and drizzled a heavy downpour of rain, which, I understand is par for the course in this lush tropical forest. I donned my raingear and walked along the Lake Circle Trail admiring the diverse vegetation, while peeking at the lake from time to time in search of the mythical seductress from the depths. Legend has it that the mermaid-like goddess Orisha seduces men who walk along the trail and drags them down to the bottom to drown them. It is said that these victims then resuscitate and reappear in distant islands, such as Trinidad, St. Vincent and even Margarita.

    I then made my way to Annandale Falls, stopping by stunning Beauséjour Lookout for picture taking. When I arrived at the Annandale Falls visitor Centre, I was offered a guide, which I turned down since there were only a couple of hundred metres to walk along a wide, smooth path before arriving at the falls. The cascade was about 30 feet high and plunged into a deep pool of water where it is possible to swim. There were four young men in bathing suits at the top of the falls and another at the bottom, who approached me. He explained that they were part of the Grenada Dive Club, and that they were there for the pleasure of the tourists. For ten dollars (US) they would provide me with the thrill of seeing them dive all the way from the top of the falls into the water below! Since that didn't sound like an earth shatteringly exciting spectator sport, I politely declined.

    I headed back in the direction of Saint Georges, but detoured southward to take a peek at one of Grenada's finest beaches, Grand Anse Beach, a popular golden sand shore for sun worshipers – when it's not raining, that is. I'm really not a beach person, as even the grandest of beaches doesn't stir any passion in me. For one thing, I feel very uncomfortable with skin exposed to the sun for any length of time, so when I accompany somebody to the beach, I take refuge under a tree or better even, a roof if there is one around. Another reason is that I dislike crowds and the most popular beaches tend to be carpeted with baking bodies. Still, early in the morning or after sunset, I sometimes enjoy going for a stroll along a secluded beach.

Micheline once made a joke at my expense when we were driving along the Côte d'Azur in France. Access to the beaches in that part of the Mediterranean is severely controlled because of an extraordinary demand. Every little parcel of beach offers lounging chairs placed abreast of each other in neat, orderly rows. The number of rows depends on the width of that particular section of beach. For a sum of money, you can rent a chair for the day. Micheline kidded with me that as a wedding anniversary gift she would rent me a chair–in the third row, because that's all she could afford. She knew very well that finding myself in that situation would be the subject of an unimaginable nightmare.

Finally, through a great deal of uneducated guessing plus a good dose of trial and error, I found the rental agency and returned the vehicle without a scratch. That was in spite of having deviated to the right of the road every once in a while and having come within a hair's breath of being totalled by an oncoming car that was overtaking in a blind curve.

Back to the chart table to plot the course to Margarita. The plan now was to sail southwest with a little jog in the otherwise straight line above Los Testigos islands about halfway along the course. I thought that the word testigos was Spanish for testicles, but Anthony corrected me and no, it has nothing to do with male gonads. It means witnesses, "The Witnesses", which makes sense, as the word shares the same root as testify. It is a group of a dozen small rocky islands inhabited by about 200 persons who live off fishing and tourism. We calculated the entire passage at 143 miles.

After Anthony had cleared us out of Grenadian customs, we completed our offshore preparations and weighed anchor at 1351 on Saturday.

A 24-knot wind and a 2-knot west setting current propelled us on a broad reach, bringing us abeam the islands that are not parts of the male anatomy at 0345. As you will see from reading Annex 7, Musings About Piracy, Anthony was wise not to make this a layover point. After a slight change of course southward we continued and anchored in Bahía la Mar, Margarita at 1142 on Sunday.

The next two days were spent at odds and ends. Anthony hired the manager of Marina Juan to take care of clearing us and the boat in this country of red tape. The $50 fee would save us two full days of running around between Customs, port authorities and Immigration on clearing in and on clearing out. We took a taxi downtown to exchange dollars for Bolivars (Bs). We entered the currency exchange house as common sailors and came out millionaires. For each US dollar we were given the princely sum of 2300 Bolivars! However, any impression of having joined the *nouveaux riches* was quickly dispelled when we had to pony up 303,000 Bs to settle our grocery bill.

We spent happy hour at Jack's Bar, as it is customary for sailors to meet for sundowners. There we met a very interesting couple, Horst and Eva, owners of a 43-foot sloop they named *Nele*. They had retired from their jobs in Germany to become permanent cruisers and lived a little bit like rich vagabonds, hopping from island to island. They had equipped their boat to make it practical for two people to live on. One of the berths was converted into a full workshop with workbench, drill press, vice and just about any tool you can shake a stick at. Eva had made another berth into a library or study. The largest was used as the master bedroom and if they received any guests they would have to put them up in the salon. They had splurged and installed a watermaker.

"You can MAKE water?" you might ask.

Well, the word is a bit of a misnomer, as you aren't *making* water as you would if you were combining the two constituent elements (O_2 and H_2) chemically to form water molecules (H_2O). The "watermaker" starts with seawater, which contains 3.5% dissolved salts and metals and filters it to produce pure water of drinking quality. It accomplishes this feat through the principle of reverse osmosis, using semipermeable membranes.

I can explain it this way. Let's say you're soaking beans in a pot to make a baked bean dish. And lets say there is suddenly a severe drought in your country and now the water is worth more than the beans. The beans represent the salt molecules in seawater. In the kitchen to separate the water from the beans (salt) you would pour the contents of the pot through a sieve and collect the water in a container. The semipermeable membrane is similar to the sieve, in that the minuscule holes prevent salts and minerals from going through, yet they are just big enough to let the water molecules through. Be aware though, that nothing is free in this world. If you want good water, you have to work for it. Thus it won't pour through the membrane by gravity. The resistance through the holes is so great that you have to force the water through with pressure from a powerful pump. The holes can easily plug up with dirt, so you need a series of prefilters to clean up the seawater that is fed into the system.

The product is water you can use for drinking, cooking and washing. The unit works automatically on demand and pumps its product water into the boat's water tank, providing an infinite supply of this most precious resource.

As the expression goes, there is no such thing as a free lunch – which is the same as saying that you can't go against the second law of thermodynamics.

The first drawback is that the system places a demand on your boat's electric supply, which in turn, requires energy either from additional solar panels which you probably don't have room for, or from a generator, which most boats don't have or more commonly, from running your engine more frequently to charge up the batteries. Secondly, you have to dish out several thousand dollars for the purchase and installation of the apparatus. Thirdly, the system requires some maintenance with regards to changing filters. Fourthly, the system takes up a fair amount of space, which is always at a premium on a sailboat. Fifthly, it's something that Murphy and his Law just *loves* to tinker with.

As a result, whenever you plan a long passage you have to assume the unit will break down on the second day out when it's too late to turn back. This means you must carry enough water in your tanks for the entire voyage, just as if you didn't have such a unit on your boat in the first place.

On the positive side, in the middle of the Pacific, fifteen days out at sea, it would be the height of luxury to be able to take a fresh water shower or wash one's laundry. For cruisers who putter around the Caribbean and rarely sail on long passages, a watermaker is an ideal alternative to searching for sources of clean, safe water and sometimes can prevent leaving a comfortable anchorage for the only purpose of filling up with water.

Horst and Eva had been sailing *Nele* around Margarita for the previous month and were enchanted with what they saw and experienced. They were able to provide us with useful information about the anchorages they had been to.

At a table next to us were three German men in their sixties, exhibiting the typical appearance and dress of hardened cruisers. I learned that each of them owns a 40-foot sailboat and has been sailing it single-handedly for years. It is much more common to find a man choosing the solitary life of a singlehander than a woman, for the reason that more men than women take up sailing as a sport or hobby. There is a dearth of women in the sailing community, so if you are a single woman looking for love, you know what to do now!

Anthony and I were impressed with Horst's eternal source of pure water. We got talking about different ways of producing potable water from seawater and the subject of an emergency came up. I remembered reading *The Seaworthy Offshore Sailboat* in which the author describes how to rig up a simple homemade water still. It was so elementary it just couldn't go wrong. It consisted of a large black bucket in the bottom of which you place a couple of inches of seawater. You then place an empty glass in the centre on the bottom. Then you stretch a piece of transparent polyethylene film over the top of the bucket and secure it hermetically by wrapping a bungee around the top of the pail, or by taping it. Finally, you push your finger downwards in the middle of the film, thus forming the film into the shape of an inverted cone, which has the effect of directing the condensation down and towards the middle, so the droplets of water fall into the glass. We placed our still on the deck near the bow, in full sunlight.

It was 1100 and we now had an important matter to attend to. In one of the lockers there was a collection of flags of every country in the Caribbean except Venezuela. So before a bureaucrat with time on his hands decided to give us trouble on that account, Anthony decided we should go into town to buy a flag of our host country. We had to inquire from five different shops and walked the equivalent of a marathon before locating an inconspicuous bookstore that carried what we were looking for. It wasn't really urgent to return to the boat, so we stopped at a snack bar for a very late lunch. We then made arrangements with a taxi driver named Umberto to take us on a tour of the island of Margarita the next day. By then the afternoon was over. It never ceases to amaze me how little you can get done in a day in the tropics.

We were anxious to see how our still was working, but being rational and patient scientists, we knew we would obtain better results if we allowed our apparatus the necessary time. So, out of a sense of duty to the advancement of science, we decided to make a foray to the bar to allow our water making apparatus to complete its task. There we met our German friends again, and this time Anthony practiced his German with them. I perceived the words *plastik, glas* and *wasser,* accompanied with much miming and could deduce he was telling them about our work in progress.

Finally, enough time had elapsed, that now we could reap the fruit of our labour, which was beckoning us on the deck of *Ventus*. Anthony motioned me to board first and to be the first to peer into our distilling apparatus to evaluate the results of our work. I couldn't quite see the glass in the bottom on account of the condensation on the film. So I carefully removed the sealing tape from the circumference of the pail and lifted the plastic...Imagine our disappointment when we measured the product of a whole day's work: two measly ounces of foul tasting water!

Umberto was at the door of Marina Juan right on time and greeted us with a big smile. He had told us he would take us wherever we wanted for the whole day for the sum of Bs 50,000 which worked out to $29.34 Canadian. We didn't haggle over the price!

Shortly after we began our tour, a sudden squall came over us, generating a powerful wind and pelting rain. Anthony's first thought was for *Ventus*. Had he known this would have happened he would have stayed on the boat. A powerful wind such as this one can easily result in a dragging anchor. And this you can't do anything about when you're touring around the countryside in a taxi. Beyond the danger of your own boat dragging, there is a much greater chance of another boat's anchor not holding. This can result in a ten-ton boat drifting uncontrolled in the anchorage, menacing every vessel in its path. If your boat happens to be in the path of the loose cannon, then again, you're better off being aboard your boat. If you have reason to think the owner is on board then you might try sounding your foghorn to alert him. If the boat is certain to collide with yours you can take measures such as fending off with a boat hook or by placing fenders between your boat and the oncoming aggressor. If it's of a really menacing size, you might start your engine and get out of the way. In one case I saw a boat adrift and three sailors went to its rescue with their dinghies and managed to reset the anchor for its absent owner.

We were too far from the marina to get back to the boat in time. The rain pelted down torrentially for ten minutes, filling the streets with water to the level of the wheel rims. Then it stopped as suddenly as it began and the sun reappeared in all its glory. We were in the picturesque village of Pampatar when the rain stopped. Fishing boats filled to the gunwales with sardines were coming into the port, accompanied by hordes of hungry pelicans that were following with great interest.

Umberto took us along the beautiful mountainous east coast to see the pretty beaches of Playa Cardon and Playa Zaragoza where small fishing boats are either beached or at anchor. Parallel to the beach there is a pleasant red brick boulevard lined with beautiful colonial houses. We continued northward to the town of Manzanillo. Our driver then took us to Juan Griego a little fishing village towards the drier western end where we sat down in a restaurant and had lunch. On the way back he made us visit the capital of the state, Asunción, an industrial and manufacturing centre lying in a fertile inland valley.

After filling up with bargain basement diesel we raised the anchor and set off for Isla de Coche (Island of the Car), which is also part of the Nueva Esparta state, located south of Margarita. The origin of its name is a mystery, as it measures only about 11 by 6 km and is sparsely populated. We anchored in Samphire Bay in the northwest portion of the island. The water was pristine, the typical light blue-green colour found when the bottom is white coral sand.

We went for a stroll to visit the town. From the top of a barren hill on the edge of the town we could see that the land was very arid, almost desert-like, with only an odd tree in sight. The buildings were concrete-bloc construction with peeling paint. Only a few cacti broke the monotony of the drab, rust coloured backdrop of rocky hills. The streets were deserted, save for two boys playing at rolling an old bicycle wheel. There were no *coches* in sight, not even a beaten up pickup truck. We witnessed a spectacular sunset, as the sun sank to the horizon right behind *Ventus*, colouring the sky with streaks of orange, pink, white and blue.

After a breakfast of raisin muffins we raised the sails and made our way to El Saco bay by executing a couple of tacks. We anchored in view of an abandoned fish plant, on a very muddy bottom, a relic of decades of biological waste being transformed into silt. We took the dinghy to shore and started out for a walk along the shore. No sooner had we turned our backs on the dinghy, than three boys appeared out of nowhere to examine our strange rubber craft. This beach was unattractive, so it became evident that the fish plant buildings would remain unsold and unused for a long time.

Once back to *Ventus*, four more boys approached the boat on a sailboard board, propelling themselves with their hands. They jabbered non-stop in an unintelligible Spanish or a language we assumed must have been Spanish. They gesticulated profusely, and from their body language, we assumed they were asking questions to which they expected answers. We understood that they wanted to come aboard and were sorry that we had to turn them down.

The decaying carcass of the defunct fish plant was a grim reminder of the way the human animal is using up the natural capital that he needs to sustain his own life. If we wanted to fish sustainably we would only take from the sea the surplus that can be easily replaced by the reproductive stock. But that is not the way we operate. Fish are a commodity that belongs to everybody. The prevalent philosophy dictates, "If I don't take it, somebody else will". That is what Garrett Hardin has termed "The Tragedy of the Commons" in an article he published in the journal *Science* in 1968. We are not just living from the natural surplus, which some thinkers have compared to the "interest" but we are using up the basic stock, the "capital". If you take only the interest out of your bank account, your capital will remain untouched. However, if every year you take some of the capital out as well as the interest, eventually your bank account will be empty. This is what we are doing with the bounty of the sea.

After a few hours in this uninteresting bay, we sailed back to Samphire Bay, but this time we anchored in front of the hotel. There were hundreds of lounging chairs lined up on the beach, but only half a dozen were occupied. This, we presumed, could be explained by the time of the year, when tourists stay home to enjoy their swimming pools in the city or their cottages in the country.

I awoke in the middle of the night with the sound of voices on the VHF radio. Anthony likes to monitor Channel 16 continuously, in case someone puts out a distress call. At 0400 two fishermen began chatting away, engaged in a conversation that they delivered at ultrasonic speed, in a dialect that sounded nothing like the Spanish I learned at school. I put a pillow over my head in an attempt to muffle the sound, but only managed to reduce the volume reaching my brain by one decibel. I was just too sleepy to get up and turn the radio off. The illegal use of the emergency radio channel lasted a whole half hour. Such flagrant disregard of radio etiquette is very common in this part of the world.

We weighed anchor and set the sails for Margarita. After having covered 16 miles we entered the wide entrance to a bay called Boca del Rio. We noticed that there was a very considerable swell coming into the bay, which would have made staying at anchor very uncomfortable. We lowered the sails and attempted to enter Marina Del Caribe, a boatyard on the eastern side of the bay near the town of Chacachacare, where boats are left for repair or for drydock during the hurricane season. We had not reached the entrance when two men waved us away. We nudged closer just enough to be able to speak to them. One of the men spoke with a French accent and explained that they were carrying out dredging operations in the harbour and could not accommodate us for berthing overnight. We asked him if we could come in just long enough to fill our fresh water tanks.

"I'm sorry, it's too dangerous for you to come in with your sailboat, but we can let you have water if you want to come in to get it with your dinghy", answered Mr. Philippe Philippart, the owner. He told us we could anchor just outside the boatyard.

After we determined that our anchor was holding securely, we set upon the job of filling the tanks. Our dinghy could only carry two 30-litre carboys of water at a time in addition to two men, because the swell was so large. We then puttered over 500 metres from *Ventus* to the water dock, filled the carboys, returned to our anchorage, hoisted the carboys onto the deck, poured the contents into the boat's tanks through its deck fitting. We repeated the procedure four times. On the last visit, we saw Mr. Philippart again and asked him what are the points of interest to visit in the area. He told us that many tourists join an ecotour of the mangroves. However, he warned us that although there hadn't been any aggression towards tourists, not to leave the boat unattended, as petty theft had become pervasive.

&&&&&&&

This is when I snapped out of my reverie. It had been 48 hours since we made our deposition to the police chief in Boca del Rio, and as of this morning we still had no news of whether or not they had any bandits in custody. I didn't think Anthony would want to wait here in Porlamar forever. My ear caught the sound of an outboard. It was Anthony and Jacqui returning from their errands.

"I just called the police chief in Boca del Rio, and guess what", said Anthony as he was passing the groceries up to me from the dinghy.

"What – they found the culprits?"

"Heavens, no. He told me they just got a hot lead and they know exactly who is the leader of the group. He said to call back Monday or Tuesday. Good Lord, it's *Friday* now!"

"Do you believe what he said?"

"Not a word, Robert. Know what? I'll get Juan to process our clearance papers and we'll leave for Grenada."

Tobago Quays, Grenadines

English Harbour, Antigua

Chapter 10

Life After Margarita

I came out of the shower and wrapped my towel around my waist and pulled on a T-shirt to circumvent the Grenada Yacht Club "*No swimsuits at the bar*" rule and joined Anthony at his table. A new person had joined him and Jacqui, a small framed, serious-looking woman he introduced me to as Daisy. She was reclined in her chair, cradling a bottle of beer in one hand and holding a cigarette between yellowed fingers of the other. She wore her brown, straight hair very short, her lips were thin and rather Caucasian looking and her skin was like smooth, brown leather stretched over her visible features.

Anthony was in the throes of detailing our brush with death in Boca del Rio, and Daisy was listening, seemingly with nonchalance, flicking ashes from her cigarette and nodding perfunctorily.

"There's a party on the beach tonight," she said in her deep voice, "I'll take the three of you. It'll help you forget that crap in Margarita," she offered.

She drained her bottle in a couple of swigs and a replacement materialized in front of her automatically. She explained that this was

Emancipation Day, an important fete in Grenada, which is always celebrated on the first Monday in August and takes place at Grand Anse beach.

We all boarded her SUV. As she drove she talked with a cigarette dangling from her lips while holding her unfinished beer in her right hand.

"The beach party is an annual affair," she said, lighting a new cigarette with the butt of the previous one, steadying the wheel with the pinkie of her beer hand, "You're going to enjoy it," as she blew a big puff of smoke.

The public beach parking lot was full to capacity so the principle, she explained, was to squeeze the car anywhere you could find a spot. The grassy area between the beach and the road was fair game, as well as anywhere on either side of the maze of sandy beach roads. Just past a split in the dirt road, our resolute driver eyed a spot barely a few feet wide. She enjoined the three of us to get out of the car, and she squeezed the SUV into the space, an inch from the neighbouring car on her left. With only a few inches on the driver's side for her door to open, she extricated herself with the ease of a contortionist, as if she practiced this Houdini feat on a daily basis.

Rap music was blaring from a temporary stage set up on the sand. Thousands of people were standing, watching the show and moving to the beat of the drums. In the distance, I noticed a white form. It dawned upon me that what I saw was the only other white person aside from myself on the entire beach, amongst these thousands of black people celebrating their freedom from white slave owners. I suddenly became self-conscious of my colour and wondered why I wasn't attracting any dirty looks from the people surrounding me or why I wasn't being lynched to hang from the nearest tree. To the contrary, nobody seemed to be aware of my existence, even though I'm sure I must have stood out like a sore thumb.

The experience did make me ponder the phenomenon of slavery and the ending of the practice. I asked myself what change could have taken place to turn bad slave owners into good abolition supporters. My friend David Delaney had recently made me aware of peak oil and I had just read Richard Heinberg's *The Party's Over*. My understanding of the role of energy in the development of a civilization had since undergone a great transformation. I now understood that the end of the slave trade had not come about because people had suddenly become good, but because slaves were simply no longer necessary for ploughing fields and separating cotton seeds from its fibre. The invention of the steam engine and concurrent efficiencies in coal mining reduced dependence on human muscle energy for carrying out work. The subsequent discovery of oil spurred further technological innovation, reducing dependence on human power ever more.

In a way, I mused, tonight on the beach we should be celebrating Nature's gift of fossil fuels.

As I mentioned earlier, Rap is not a combination of sounds that is pleasant to my ear, so I didn't join the throngs that had packed themselves like standing sardines in front of the stage. Nevertheless, away from the show and the thousands of the audience, the evening was pleasant. Children played on the beach, doing what children always have done over the eons, building castles and moats filled with water. Teams of young men had set up nets and played volleyball without respite. Barefoot lovers ambled hand in hand leaving their footprints on the hard-packed sand shaped by the receding waves. Groups of friends seated on lawn chairs were gathered around coolers filled with beer, chatting and laughing. The sun was gradually working its way down toward its resting place below the horizon.

After dark, Anthony and Daisy were ready to call it quits. Our driver backed the SUV out of its space, we climbed aboard, she swung the vehicle around, and then came to a stop. Two cars were parked right in the middle of the road, completely blocking off the only exit. Two other drivers had been waiting in their cars for a while for one of the offending vehicles to move. Daisy waved her cigarette and said, "Its like this every year."

Anthony asked a police officer to get the owners to move their cars out of the way or to have them towed away. Our inept upholder of the law simply claimed, "It's like this every year."

We then went to the bar to plead with the manager to call a tow truck to move the blocking vehicles away. He appeared fearful of getting the police involved, and in the way of excuse he explained, "It's like this every year."

Finally, Anthony forced his way through the crowd of cheering fans and after fifteen long minutes of pushing and shoving, he reached the stage. He asked the MC to make an announcement over the PA system calling for the owners of the cars which bore the licence numbers Anthony had written down to please remove their vehicles from the road. He came back to the car after half an hour and by then one of the delinquent cars had departed, allowing us free and clear passage.

In preparation for our crossing to Trinidad, I baked two apple pies while Anthony and Jacqui were still asleep. I then whipped up a recipe of raisin pancakes, Anthony's favourite.

While the captain and crew were away to the store to pick up last minute items of groceries, I began preparing the boat for our offshore transit to Trinidad. By lunchtime Anthony and Jacqui were back and had brought with them a litre of ice cream. Since we didn't have a freezer, there was only one way to deal with the emergency: We devoured the entire soft, creamy creamy contents ferociously.

We left Saint Georges at 1422 to anchor in Prickly Bay in order to be more in line with our destination when came the time to depart. At 2230 we weighed anchor and set our course for the First Boca. We couldn't turn off the engine, as there was no wind. In fact, the wind didn't freshen except for an hour in the middle of the night. Thank you, Iron Genny! The TTSA saw us enter the Chaguaramas Bay at 1430.

For the next two days Krimhilde and Anthony housed me and fed me, treating me like royalty. Anthony took me for a sail around the islands south of the Chaguaramas peninsula. The following day he and Krimhilde took me on a tour of the entire country. We started with the Point Lisa Estate Industrial Park in the south where I saw heavy equipment factories, methanol and urea plants as well as other petrochemical plants. For me this was a way to fill in some of the blanks in my learning about the world energy supply. Having lived in Ottawa most of my life, I had not had the chance to see much in the way of heavy industry, since Canada's Capital is mostly dependent on government bureaucracy and high tech for employment.

We then drove to the northern end of the island, through the rich, dense rainforest, all the way to the north shore. We stopped at Hotel Laguna Mar by a river of that name for a swim at Blanchisseuse Beach followed by lunch. This is one of the rare places where you can swim in salt water and the next minute soak in fresh water, as the river accumulates in a pool, just inches above sea level before streaming into the ocean. Anthony attempted to teach me how to belly surf. He had practiced this sport as a child when he grew up within minutes of the beach in Barbados. I didn't do too well, for the surf breaking on the beach invariably sent me scraping the bottom with my chest, filling my mouth and nostrils with water and sand. It must be the old dog thing.

The northern part of the road on the west side of the island runs along a beautiful shoreline of cliffs. The setting sun bathed the coast with its golden hue, transforming the whole canvas into an exquisite work of art.

January, 2005.

Anthony invited me to join him to sail for three weeks in the Grenadines. I enjoy winter in Canada, as there is so much to do. Even now that I'm retired I don't have enough time to do all the skating, cross country skiing, downhill skiing and snowshoeing that I'd like. Nonetheless, it's nice to put aside all of these activities and switch from the dead of the winter to tropical summer within a few hours of flight.

The Grenadines, a group of islands north of Grenada, belonging to the nation of *Saint Vincent and the Grenadines*, are reputed for their beauty, their clear aquamarine water for snorkeling, their bird sanctuaries, their tranquility and secure anchorages.

This time I arrived a week early in Trinidad to help out with preparing the boat. Anthony had spent the summer working on a new project for *Ventus*. Ian wanted the boat to be equipped with a davit, a transom support for hoisting the dinghy. The davit was to be equipped with solar panels, a pair of wind chargers, the radio antenna and the TV dish antenna. With the new apparatus, we would no longer have the hassle of dealing with a halyard and winch for the nightly dinghy hoisting ritual. It would be simply a matter of clipping the dinghy onto the steel cables of the electric hoist and raising it with the push of a button.

This day the job was to find the right position for the pulleys attached to the overhanging structure. We hoisted the dinghy to the top, but Anthony wasn't satisfied with the position of one of the pulleys. He asked me to lower the dinghy a little bit so he could get in to adjust the faulty pulley. He climbed into the unsteady, dangling dinghy and proceeded to loosen a nut and bolt. Suddenly, in a flash, the dinghy flipped over and Anthony vanished in the sea below with a large splash, having been offhandedly dumped into the water like a big piece of expendable jetsam! He climbed out of the water, his clothes dripping wet, his glasses dangling from the string around his neck, a stream of water pouring out of his fanny bag.

"Oh no!" he exclaimed. "My cell phone! Oh, Lord, the remote for my garage door. Aaagh! My wallet!"

Ian and I had to make a concerted effort to withhold our laughter in view of Anthony's distress, but it wasn't long that he recovered his composure and joined us in laughing about the incident.

"They should make a waterproof cell phone. There would be a market for them with people like me. This is the fourth cell phone that I lose to salt water."

One thing that makes Anthony Anthony, is his self deprecating sense of humour that helps defuse any tense situation.

On this trip, exceptionally, Krimhilde would be joining us for two weeks. Marlise, an old German friend of hers, a sailing buff, was visiting her in Trinidad. In order to give her friend the chance to sail in one of the most beautiful spots in the world, Krimhilde offered to accompany her friend for the trip. The two of them would fly to Grenada to avoid the 14-hour passage by sailboat, and then would join *Ventus* in Saint Georges.

The day before our departure, Marlise received a phone call from Germany. It was her neighbour, a good friend of the family. She was breaking the news to Marlise that her husband had suffered a stroke and had been rushed to intensive care. So distraught Marlise took the first flight out of Port of Spain for Frankfurt. Since her return flight to Grenada was already paid for and all the provisions and clothes were ready for the trip, Krimhilde decided to stick with the sail plan but without her friend.

I think there's another factor that came into this decision to join us, but this is only conjecture. Anthony has been surrounded by females all of his married life, what with a wife, five daughters and even two female dogs, he was accustomed to having things done for him. On all of his sailing trips he's had at least one woman on board to prepare meals. On this trip Krimhilde and Marlise would have been the meal makers for the first two weeks. For the second two-week period, two American ladies were scheduled to join us. My assumption is that Krimhilde didn't want to leave Anthony and me shorthanded.

From Trinidad, we sailed to Prickly Bay, Grenada to pick up Krimhilde. Then we sailed northward along the west of Grenada and anchored off Petit Saint Vincent, a totally privately owned island, the first of the Grenadines from south to north. Its resort restaurant accepted visiting sailors and offered excellent cuisine.

We stopped at Union Island, a little further north, as it is one of the points of entry into the country, where clearing in is compulsory if one is to visit the islands. Anthony took us for supper at Lambi's, his favourite restaurant on that island. Mr. Lambi the owner, a huge, smiling black man, welcomed Anthony like a long lost friend, and led us to a table near the dance floor. A good buffet was followed by a Limbo dance show, to the tune of pan music. This is where lightly clad, beautiful girls barely escaped scorching the tips of their breasts on the flaming bar that Mr. Lambi himself lowered a notch at each round. The giant man, wearing a golden crown and a bright, wildly coloured African dress laughed heartily and applauded profusely with each bosom that passed unscathed under the bar. Then it was the guests' turn. After everybody had eaten Mr. Lambi had all of his patrons stand in line and he lit the bar afire, putting us in competition with one another. The Calypso music began and for the first round Mr. Lambi placed the fiery bar ridiculously high, allowing everybody, including me, to succeed the first passage. The purpose of the game is to pass under the bar without touching it or touching the ground with any part of the body except the feet, or losing one's balance and falling. Upon each subsequent passage the bar was lowered a notch, eliminating some of the participants at each turn. When the bar reached about four feet above ground I fell flat on my back and was ousted from the competition. Anthony had mastered proper technique, learned through his years as a mechanical engineer, which taught him the principles of centre of gravity and balance around a fulcrum. Furthermore in spite of his being five years my senior and suffering from a bad back, he had not lost the agility of his youth and claimed honourable mention.

Tobago Cays was next on the program. Boat rental agencies such as Sunsail or the Moorings place restrictions on who can bareboat in this particular area. There are tricky shoals and reefs to negotiate to get inside the protected area between the islands, which requires the captain to have some navigation experience. Before allowing a sailor to venture in this area they will insist that he have at least 20 days or 400 nautical miles of experience as captain of a similar size boat.

Telltale breakers reveal the position of some of the reefs, but the most treacherous ones are those you can't see. Anthony's been sailing these waters all his life and knows the area like the back of his hand. Thus he can weave his way around the Tobago Cays without even consulting his charts. For me this was an opportunity to practice my navigation. First, I had to positively identify each of the islands. This you can do by taking stock of their size, the heights of their peaks, their relative positions to each other and their compass bearings. Once I had identified the islands by sight, I located two elements that appear on the chart and took their compass bearings. Lastly, I drew lines on the chart reproducing these bearings. The point of intersection of the lines marked our position. From this known position I could trace the course to the entrance to one of the passages between the reefs.

All this work can be circumvented with the use of an electronic chart plotter. The danger with chart plotters is that the actual territory you're covering is enormously larger than the tiny image on the screen, and the icon that represents your boat is disproportionately large. In a small, tight entrance, you can be fooled by the delay in the instrument's positioning of the icon, so you have to remember that the icon indicates where the boat was fifteen seconds ago, a hard lesson I was to learn the following year on my trip to Desolation Sound.

The Tobago Cays are a group of five small, uninhabited islands with quaint names – Petit Rameau, Petit Bateau, Baradol, Petit Tabac and Jamesby - located east of Mayreau Island. The Saint Vincent and the Grenadines government has made the Tobago Cays into a marine park and a national park and wildlife preserve in which spear fishing is prohibited. With 50,000 visitors per year it will be difficult to maintain the pristine beauty of the cays. As a means of controlling access to the islands and generating revenue for enforcing the rules, the cruising fee has now been increased substantially regardless of the length of stay. Anthony believes that this high fee will discourage cruisers from visiting the other islands of the country, like Canouan and Bequia, and that they will simply bypass the entire Grenadines on their way to and from Grenada and Trinidad.

It is certainly a tragic paradox that by the very act of visiting the world's most beautiful and fragile ecosystems, we are contributing to their destruction. It is a moral dilemma that I can't seem to come to grips with. If I had the opportunity to visit the Galapagos Islands, for instance, should I turn it down for the sake of saving them? Are they worth saving if I can never see them? If I make the sacrifice of foregoing my desire, will the void simply be filled by somebody else? Before the Age of Oil this dilemma didn't exist, as it was not possible for such large numbers of people to travel long distances from home without access to (cheap) air travel. When oil runs out, tourism will come to an end and Mother Nature will reclaim her place.

"I can't find Beck-Way anywhere on the chart, Anthony," I said, out of desperation.

"It's right there, the last of the Grenadines, just south of Saint Vincent."

"What I see there is Beck ee ah."

"Well, it's there, Robert. B-e-q-u-i-a, Beck-Way."

We anchored in Admiralty Bay, Bequia, the most popular gathering place of the island with the funny spelling. Anthony's friend Arlene picked us up at the Port Elizabeth dock. She drove along a narrow, windy and hilly paved road, through lush vegetation. The houses along the road were built on large, treed lots, most of them not visible from their neighbours. Arlene's house had been built by her architect husband Michael, Anthony's cousin, as a home and small inn of three suites. It was a brilliant, multilevel architecture, designed to marry itself to the topography of the hillside upon which it clung. The entrance driveway led to the garage at the level of the top floor. The landscaping and building were one, with ornamental lighting, trees, bushes, flowerbeds and flowerpots strategically built into the sides of the house, the garage, the driveway, and the external stone stairways that led to the lower levels. The owners' section was on the top floor, completely apart from the guest suites, affording everybody privacy, yet ensuring that each apartment had a view of captivating Port Elizabeth Harbour.

I didn't get to meet Michael, but Arlene gave us a tour of the new complex. A thirty thousand-gallon cistern was built into the hillside to be filled with rainwater from the roofs during the rain season. There are no rivers on the island, and most of the wells have gone dry due to overpumping and overpopulation. Although the owners had placed signs in the guests' washrooms pleading for restrained use of water, the cistern only provides water half the year. For the other six months they have to buy their water from a dealer who ships it from Saint Vincent, 9 miles north of Bequia. Life's most essential resource is no longer in sufficient supply to meet the island's needs. The islanders depend on cheap oil to supply the energy for pumping and transporting the water. What will happen when oil runs out?

Talk of the end of oil is increasingly becoming mainstream as we've entered the second decade of the 2000s. The problem isn't as much a matter of running out of oil as of falling production. Once we reach peak oil, the point in time when the year's production reaches a historical high, every subsequent year will see production declining. Since our economy requires growth for its existence and oil is the fuel of the economy, the entire world economy might collapse. The combination of oil shortages and a collapsing world economy will converge, thus preventing the average person from flying to distant destinations. It is interesting to conjecture what the Bequians will do when tourism comes to an end in that case. Its 14 square kilometres of forest, mountain, built-up surfaces and beaches will only suffice to feed a small fraction of the 5,000 present mouths. They won't be able to get it from their neighbours, as almost every island in the Caribbean will suffer the same fate.

Our next stop was Saint Vincent, to drop Krimhilde off for her flight back home. The next day we left at 0310 for our next passage northward. We sailed along the west side of Saint Vincent and ended our cruise 75 miles further, in Rodney Bay, Saint Loo Shaw. I wasn't going to be fooled by a strange pronunciation a second time. This time around I surmised correctly that we were headed for Saint Lucia.

I met Michael Camps (another Michael) an old friend of Anthony's from Trinidad. Michael was a retired paediatrician working as a volunteer in the local hospital, carrying out very badly needed medical work for children whose parents could never hope to have the means to pay a doctor's fee. We had him come aboard for supper.

The two American ladies landed in Saint Lucia, starved. They had been prisoners of a modern airline for many hours, so we fed them too. Jane was a remedial teacher from South Salem, New York and her old school friend Jackaline was director of Fire Prevention and Control for the city of Albany. Anthony had met Jane briefly at a yacht club the previous year, instilled in her an interest in sailing and invited her to join him on a cruise. They subsequently communicated by email during which the invitation was reiterated. There was hesitation on the part of the lady. It's understandable that she was wary about going sailing with a man she hardly knew and his friends whom she had never met. We live in a dangerous world, which breeds bad apples. In addition, there are many ways a captain can be unpleasant. Nobody wants to be stuck with a Captain Bligh for two weeks. The impasse was finally breached when Anthony suggested she bring along a friend.

During the two weeks our American friends were with us we went back to Tobago Cays to spend a few days for the snorkelling. It's there that we bought a bag of ice from an itinerant salesman in a pirogue for $20 EC ($10 US); but what the heck, you can't have rum and soda without ice!

We arrived in Salt Whistle Bay in neighbouring Mayreau in time for happy hour and spent the night anchored in the pristine bay. Then the next evening we got a bite to eat at Lambi's on Union Island followed by another flaming Limbo dance competition.

It's important on a boat that the food be kept at a safe temperature to avoid spoilage, wouldn't you say? So then to achieve this you need to implement a system for checking the refrigerator temperature, right? Before I continue, I have to mention that Anthony was stricken with type 2 diabetes recently. Through experimentation he has been able to control the disease without medication by monitoring his sugar with his blood glucose meter and implementing a number of changes in his diet. This has led him to discover that every day around 1130 his blood sugar reaches a low. This means his body is in need of a source of carbohydrate with just the correct glycemic index. His engineering background has trained him to take an analytical approach to solving problems. Accordingly, he has found that a standard sized can of beer provides just the right amount of carbohydrates to tide him over till lunch. So now he kills two birds with one stone. At 1130, most mornings, when at anchor, Anthony retrieves a can of "temperature test material" from the refrigerator and through the effect on lips, mouth and throat, he can estimate the temperature of the refrigerator, all the while boosting his blood glucose level. Hence, his crewmembers understand what he means when he says,

"It's time to check the refrigerator."

Being the responsible captain that he is, he welcomes assistance in this important endeavour. He explains that this is a subjective test and that the margin of error can be reduced by averaging the estimations of several shipmates.

The next day, as Anthony and I were in the process of "checking the refrigerator", he revealed how he had come to adopt the policy of never sailing single-handedly. After sailing with Anthony for twenty years, Krimhilde had changed her focus towards other interests. The children were either away from the home or old enough to have their own social lives. She had followed her husband in his passion for sailing to provide the children a valuable experience and a healthy lifestyle. She was happy to provide the girls with the opportunity to be close to nature and to acquire the love of the sea. She took pleasure in seeing her children thoroughly enjoy living on tiny *Les Remous*, swimming, diving off the pulpit, snorkelling, discovering new shores, building sand castles, making friends wherever they decided to drop the anchor. However, for Mother, it was not always a picnic, as the expression goes. Before a trip she had to spend several days planning and preparing food, clothes and supplies. It was no mean feat then to pack all of that material into the car and then to transfer everything into the many nooks and crannies of the diminutive boat. Preparing meals for seven in the confines of a small vessel required a certain measure of magic. Nursing seasick children, manning the helm through storms, doing night watches, these were all challenges that she had graciously embraced. But now they were no longer necessary.

Krimhilde had a remarkable talent for impressionist art and needed to devote more time to discover the plethora of possibilities it presented. While she was raising her five daughters her interest in painting had been curtailed for the sake of the family; but now she wanted to explore this means of expression, unimpeded by family responsibilities.

With some couples a situation like this could result in an intractable dispute, but Anthony and Krimhilde had a profound respect for each other's needs and personal space. The newfound freedom retirement provided would allow Anthony to sail year round if he wanted. He decided to spend six months per year away from home sailing, starting in November and ending in the first week of June in Trinidad for the hurricane season. Krimhilde knew her husband was an accomplished navigator and sailor, but would be worried sick if he were sailing single-handedly. What would happen if ever he sustained an injury or incapacitating illness while sailing alone offshore? To assuage his wife's apprehensions Anthony promised that he would never sail solo. This would impose some limits on his freedom of movement, however. It meant that he would constantly have to search for crew, juggle schedules to fit the availability of shipmates and plan itineraries in view of being near an airport at crew changes. It was this promise that paved the way to my getting to know this great sailor and friend.

The two ladies and I were to fly back to our respective homes from Saint Vincent, so we set our course northward. On the way we anchored in Britannia Bay off Mustique, a tiny island that rises out of the blue and green water and is bordered by crescents of white, powdery sand. It is totally owned by the Mustique Company, created by an act of the British

Parliament. Only 3 miles long and one and half wide, the island nevertheless has its own little airport. This little jewel of the Caribbean is the winter getaway for many great celebrities. The entire island is a well-tended lawn and tropical garden with peaceful, winding, wooded footpaths and paved roads. For "as little as" $5000 per week you can rent a two-bedroom villa with maid service and a car, or if your tastes are more refined, you can open your wallet a little wider and fork out $55,000 for a week. However, if you are part of the truly sophisticated elite, you can partake in the "Estate Collection of villas" that do not appear on the Mustique web site due to the owners' request and they range in price from $100,000 to $150,000 per week.

In case you wonder what you could *do* on this little island, well, aside from the run-of-the-mill water sports, the gorgeous white sand beaches await the sun worshipers. The guests have access to an equestrian centre, a soccer field and cricket pitch, tennis courts, a fitness centre, a full spa, and for those who are all tensed up and in need of finding themselves, then they can enjoy the "Energy, Harmony and Balance" range of products. If that's not good enough, you can get treatments in the privacy of your own villa. For the travellers for whom shopping is their favourite sport, there are boutiques, of course.

We had supper at the very pretty and popular Basil's Bar a restaurant built on stilts extending from the beach over the water, where proper footwear was either opened sandals or bare feet. The view of the sea from our table was spectacular and the multi-coloured lanterns suspended overhead cast a pleasant glow onto the tables. A good band entertained us with old blues tunes. Unfortunately the restaurant's choice setting and high prices weren't testament of quality. I thought of the poor people in the "Estate villas" and hoped they were provided with a chef from a better school.

The ladies went for a long walk on the island. Since they had not had much chance of being by themselves, Anthony and I chose to stay on the boat to repair one of the hatches and service one of the winches.

We returned to Bequia, to be close to the international airport on the south end of Saint Vincent. On our final morning we sailed to an anchorage off Saint Vincent. Anthony ferried us to shore with the dinghy and we bade our farewells. He called a taxi to take the two American ladies and me to the airport. There we parted ways, they flying to their homes in the State of New York and I to Gatineau.

I had the impression that this time Anthony had failed to acquire a recruit for future trips. It's important for Anthony to have a supply of reliable persons he can pick from for crew for the six months he needs company and he was pinning his hopes on one or the other of them. There was never an off word exchanged during the ladies' stay aboard *Ventus*. To the contrary, the relationship between them and Anthony had been cordial. Cordial but not warm. Cordial but not fraternal. Cordial but not exuberant. You just can't win all hearts.

June, 2006.

I have to tell you about my last sailing trip in the Straight of Georgia. This time I didn't have the benefit of Don's organizational skills, as he was to spend the summer in Brazil. Raymond, Carole and Rachel who had crewed on my previous trip joined me on this one. I was glad to have Raymond, as he is probably more competent than I am, so he was going to be a great support. In addition to these three, Jennie, a fairly tall, but delicate woman in her late fifties was part of the group. Jennie was a nurse in the same nursing unit as Rachel had retired from and was just a year or two shy of retirement age herself. I had known her when she joined NCSS before buying a share in a small sailboat with Rachel. I knew her to be fun loving and easy going. I knew she preferred doing the dishes while enjoying a rum and soda than cook an elaborate meal. I knew that I could rely on her to steer or partake in other manoeuvres or undertake maintenance chores without complaining.

My two other crewmembers were a couple in their late forties, Christelle and Maxime, both members of NCSS. Of the two, Christelle was the sailor and Maxime the husband that follows. I had had them sail with me on the club's boats only a few times for day outings. They were friendly, cheerful and enjoyed sailing. They were very enthusiastic about the prospect of sailing to Desolation Sound.

We boarded Serina, a beautiful, 50-foot Beneteau Oceanis 500 at Sunsail Boat Charters in Vancouver. This ship had five cabins and five heads, affording the captain his own private quarters! She had a large galley with a generous expanse of counter space. She was double helmed, that is, having a steering wheel on each side of the large cockpit. Everything about her was big. The winches, the sails, the anchor.

She was in very good condition except for a tiny detail; when I did my walkaround I found a defect that could have caused us much grief. The connection of the boom to the mast is made through a universal joint-like attachment quaintly named the gooseneck. A large bolt connects the gooseneck to a fitting on the mast, but its nut was missing. When I pointed this out to Ian the manager, he thanked me profusely for having spotted the fault and sent an assistant to fetch a replacement, which delayed our departure by an hour. But, better to lose an hour at the start than a day or two once in an isolated location.

Our first day out taught me several lessons in one single error. I had brought the boat to the entrance of Secret Cove and it was high tide. The chartplotter showed that once inside the first bay there was a large rock protruding from the water that I had to leave to my starboard. When I got past the narrow entrance, the first bay was much larger than I had thought and I couldn't see the large rock. I slowed down and kept an eye on the chartplotter and the depthsounder. On the chartplotter the boat's icon filled half of the bay and there was a big rock ahead and to the port of the icon. I looked for the large rock in the bay, but all I could see in that general area was a small rock. I slowed down almost to a stop, just maintaining steerageway. Suddenly it dawned upon me that the small rock I saw in the distance to the port was actually the large rock on the chartplotter that I had to leave to starboard. Of course, at low tide, when the water level would be 12 feet lower, it would be much bigger! But it was too late – the depth was rapidly decreasing: 8 feet, 7 feet. I jammed the gear lever in reverse and gunned the engine full throttle. It takes more than a couple of feet to stop a 30,000-pound boat. The depthsounder now showed five feet and…we came to a smooth, if somewhat sudden halt. We had run aground on a muddy bottom! My heart sank below the level of the keel! I kept the engine in reverse, as that's the direction I wanted to go.

One fact I must tell you about propellers is that they are designed for one thing only, to push the boat forward. The engineers have shaped the blades so that they grab the water from the front and push it as directly as possible rearwards, thus producing the maximum possible thrust. Consequently, they are not efficient at all at pulling the boat backwards. In reverse mode the blades grab the water from the side and pitch it out forward, very inefficiently. This inefficiency results in a phenomenon referred to as prop walk. The propeller in reverse actually pulls the stern of the boat towards port.

The sailing books recommend several ways of freeing a boat run aground, and I've already told you about the wonderful lesson I taught my students on kedging off with an anchor. The books say that if you're aground in a tidal area, just wait for high tide, and voilà! You're free! But my predicament was that this *was* high tide. It couldn't get higher and within minutes it would start falling. Taking the large anchor and its 200 feet of heavy chain out of its locker, lowering it into the dinghy, motoring the dinghy out the length of the chain to drop the anchor, then winching the boat out of its quagmire would be a major undertaking, which would take much effort, and especially, what we didn't have – *time*! My heart raced at 3000 beats a minute. I was, as the saying goes, in deep sh-manure. I had visions of the bay at low tide with Serina lying on her side on the rocks like a dead horse. I could visualise myself and my crew sitting in the dinghy in the middle of the night waiting for the next high tide so we could kedge our vessel out of her muddy trap.

The engine was still hard in reverse. I noticed that Serina was no longer pointing straight ahead, but had turned somewhat to starboard. "Prop walk", I said to myself, "the propeller has pulled the stern over to the port."

Then I thought, "Hey, lets wait and see."

I gave the order for all the crew to stand on the port side in case it might make her heel a bit. But it would take more than six bodies to make a 30,000 pound boat heel. And lo and behold! She was still turning. In fact the powerful prop walk effect was making her pivot on her keel. I held her hard in reverse, and crossed my fingers.

"This just might work," I said to myself.

And just as if by magic, our grounded boat turned almost a full 180 degrees. Now we were pointing in the direction away from our muddy hold. I then put in effect the other half of my idea. I took power off, placed the gearshift in forward, then gave it full throttle in forward...

And, a miracle happened. Our revived horse slowly eased herself forward and before I knew it, we were free! This is my secret of Secret Cove.

Princess Louisa Inlet is known as the most majestic of the fiords of the BC mainland coast. As with any beauty worth courting, one has to be ready to hustle and make compromises to reach her heart. And this princess is one beauty that plays hard-to-get. The shores of these fiords are so steep that they prevent a steady wind from building up. To reach the Princess we must relinquish our sails and become, horrors! – a motor boat for many hours, because to reach her entrance we have to transit 45 miles of convoluted fiords. If you start out from the Straight of Georgia, you have to scoot behind Texada Island and travel east along Jervis Inlet for 12 miles before it trifurcates. At this point you're amongst royalty, and enter Prince of Wales Reach, which changes its name to Princess Royal Reach, which then changes again to Queen's Reach. Halfway into Queen's Reach we come to the Princess Louisa Inlet entrance.

All the time the tide is flooding or ebbing, there is a strong current in her entrance, either rushing in with the rising tide or rushing out with the falling tide. In order to transit the entrance safely you have to do so at high tide, just at the turn of the tide, (also referred to as slack water), that is, during those few minutes when the tide has stopped flooding or ebbing, when there is no longer any current going in or out. At any other time there is a tidal current, which at its peak velocity reaches 7 knots and forms a dangerous rapids known as Malibu Rapids.

We arrived at Malibu Rapids at 1300, an hour and two minutes before the calculated turn of the tide. A dozen or so boats joined us near the entrance, unable to anchor in the 800-foot deep water of Queen's Reach, thus circling slowly in wait of the time to proceed. At 1402 the boats began approaching the rapids, in single file. Because the inner side of the narrows is not visible from the outside, the head boat broadcast her intention over the VHF radio:

"Inside traffic at Malibu Rapids, this is Happy Camper. About fifteen boats preparing to transit Malibu Rapids from the outside. Any inside traffic please confirm you are waiting. Over."

A response followed,

"Outside traffic, this is Papillon. We are waiting for you before proceeding. Out."

From the outside of the channel I could still see a lot of white water, indicating that there was still a strong head current. But the boats ahead of me were all going in, one after the other. Finally, the last boat went through and I was last in the queue. I had to follow, even if the current was still very strong, because the boats on the inside would start going out as soon as the last boat in arrived. At the narrowest point the current was so strong that I had to apply full power to make headway. I had never imagined that I'd be barrelling up rapids in a 50-foot keelboat!

Once inside I could relax and enjoy the glory of this marvel of the BC coast. At the entrance we were greeted by 1400 metre mountains on either side. Navigating along the half-mile wide fiord we were flanked by magnificent black granite walls covered with rain forest on their lower half. The melting snow from the mountains created dozens of waterfalls that cascaded down the precipitous walls to mingle with the waters of the inlet below. We motored 4 miles to the end, where the spectacular Chatterbox Falls tumbled from a height of 45 metres into the fiord. Near the falls there was a public dock where we tied up for the night. We were asked not to stay another night as the following day a group of Albin 25 club members were scheduled to moor their diminutive motor cruisers for a couple of days.

So the next day we changed places and made fast to a mooring ball behind MacDonald Island. We had just barely settled down when a man and a woman in their dinghy came abreast our boat. She was brandishing a chilled bottle of white wine and he asked us if they could come aboard to share their bottle with us. Raymond answered that there were seven of us aboard, so if they accepted to leave empty-bottled they were welcome aboard.

He was a smiling man of about 30, with red hair and a round, freckled face and introduced himself as Greg, the best fisherman in the world. She, a petite, blue-eyed brunette introduced herself as Debbie, wife of the best fisherman in the world, and a fishing buff herself. They spent all their holidays and weekends fishing off their 32-foot power cruiser. Greg had introduced himself without overt signs of pretension, but I was never able to figure out if his self-characterization was tongue in cheek or boasting. Maxime had brought fishing tackle with him from home and had purchased a BC fishing license, but so far had had no luck in catching fish. Greg made it a personal mission to teach Maxime the basics of the sport.

For starters, he told us about a delicious fish that was in limited supply but easy to catch, the Rock Fish. This species delves in very deep water. The method for catching it is to attach a worm to the end of a lure, lower it to at least 200 feet of depth and troll slowly. Greg and Maxime left in the dinghy and came back half an hour later with four fish, each of the fishermen having fished his legal limit. Only about 10 to 12 inches long, this fish looks like a prehistoric monster, with its very spiky appearance, very large and spiky fins and large mouth. What is the most striking about it are its large, bulging eyes. Greg explained that when one of those unsuspecting bottom dwellers is brought to the surface it doesn't have time to decompress as it is reeled up and the tremendous pressure inside its body makes its lungs and eyes bulge, killing it instantly and giving it a surreal look. Once fried in butter, however, this ugly little specimen is tender, delicious and almost bone-free.

Our two fishermen became inseparable. When, a few days later, in another anchorage, we met our expert fisherman, Greg taught Maxime how to trap crab, what to use as bait, where to place the cage and what are the best times. As a parting gift he gave Maxime a cage, which allowed us to enjoy crab every day for the rest of the trip.

At the entrance to the Inlet we had noticed a large, luxurious-looking lodge just at the Malibu rapids, with a sign saying "Welcome to Malibu". Mr. Tom Hamilton, the inventor of the variable pitch propeller purchased the property from a homesteader in the 1930s. He built and operated the Malibu Club as an exclusive resort for the elite Hollywood set. It is reputed to have hosted John Wayne and John F. Kennedy, amongst others. He abandoned the business after a number of years, as it was not profitable to operate in such a short season. In 1951 he put the place up for sale for the asking price of $1,000,000. As there were no buyers for this most beautiful property, he eventually sold it to the Young Life Foundation for $300,000, happy that the property would be put to the service of Jesus.

We all got into the dinghy, dressed in our yellow rain gear, as it was raining. We motored the two miles from MacDonald Island to the Camp. A

Camp organizer hooked us up with one of the team leaders who became our guide. He showed us around the building and the grounds and we saw well-behaved youths at play at different sports and indoor activities. As we were the only visitors that day, and as our yellow raingear made us stand out like sore thumbs, we soon became known as The Yellow People. The building was of a rustic style and had large windows on all sides. Each side rewarded the eye with a view of unimaginable beauty. There was a huge lounge with a cathedral ceiling, a games room and a heated swimming pool. The cabins, we were told, would qualify for a five star rating.

The Lodge offers American Christian high school kids one-week stays for a life enhancing, spiritual experience in a place of extreme beauty. The adolescent comes to camp with his volunteer Young Life counsellor who has usually been relating to him on a one-to-one basis for over a year and spends a lot of time with the kid in various activities.

Places of such incredible beauty are not so terribly numerous. I wonder why one of the levels of government didn't buy the property in the first place, or doesn't expropriate it now to put it to the service of the whole of society.

Trips like this one are social occasions, especially from sundown till bedtime. Even preparation of supper and the ensuing washing of dishes are opportunities for conversation.

With seven guests around a table every night for two weeks, there is much opportunity for reminiscing over the day's events, engaging in boat talk, expressing opinions on politics and public events, telling of jokes and sometimes even exchanging of personal confidences.

One evening, Christelle brought to the table a book she wanted to show us. It had a beautifully designed cover with embossed golds, creams and blues, with the title *Secrets of the Millionaire Mind*. She explained that the author's main premise for success and happiness is to change the way we think. Not to think like losers, but to think like the rich think. Those who have become millionaires have become rich because of their outlook on life, and because they set their "financial thermostat" high. The theory is that if you can adopt the same way of thinking, the same outlook and the same attitude as those of millionaires, you will be happy and fortune will follow. Effectively, you could will yourself into fortune.

The book was replete with positive thinking, upbeat phrases, examples of real millionaires, real-life stories, testimonials, citations from the rich and famous and anecdotal evidence. At the end of each section the author gives a phrase that one must repeat like a mantra to reinforce the principles evoked throughout the text. Of course, there are many references to the three-day seminar that is guaranteed to change your life – the usual stuff you find in "Get Rich Quick" books. The basis of this particular one though, is that by simply *thinking* you were going to get rich, you were going to get rich. The most outrageous statement was that anybody can become a millionaire.

When Christelle broached the subject of will, happiness and fortune, it came to us seated at the table as a statement of fact. My feeling was that she wasn't presenting her newly found road to success as a subject for discussion. However, her presentation seemed open-ended and Raymond couldn't help interjecting that money doesn't bring happiness. I too, thought that her statement was an opening for comment, and I added that the rich either inherited their fortune, worked very hard and long to earn it, or simply got rich through a stroke of luck. Her face stiffened when she heard our comments. Rachel had read the book and explained her interpretation of the author's theory, in an attempt at taking pressure off Christelle. Suddenly Christelle left her unfinished plate on the table and rushed out of the cabin, into the cockpit, leaving all of us perplexed.

We continued our meal in awkward silence and muted conversation resumed as we finished off the wine. Then after about an hour of absence, she returned, her eyes red and cheeks moist, and took her place at the table. Nobody knew what to say. She took a deep breath, preparing to speak.

"I'm going to say something that may sound strange at first, but it's important that I tell somebody about my commitment."

She placed her right hand over her heart and declared, "I solemnly pronounce that within ten years from tonight, I will become a millionaire."

There was silence and hanging jaws in the boat. We were thrown off guard by this unexpected declaration. Raymond broke the silence.

"Why are you telling us this?"

She explained that what she needed to set her on the right path was to set herself a goal.

"But why do you have to tell everybody?

She answered that by making her intention known in a formal way, she was going to reinforce her resolve to adopt the way of thinking of the millionaire.

She went on to explain the principles expounded in Millionaire Mind.

The conversation then became more relaxed and the field was open for discussion. I asked her about the author, who he was and how he has made his fortune. It turns out that the man's main claim to fame was that before the age of 30 he had run 13 businesses. He made his fortune by borrowing $3000 on his Visa card and opening one of the first retail security systems stores in North America and with that store opening 11 more. Within two and a half years he sold half his company to a Fortune 500 company for 2 million dollars. He enjoyed all the favours of fortune, including a mansion on the French Riviera, an Alpha Romeo, a huge motor yacht. Now he felt it was time for him to give something back to society in thanks for all that the world has given him. In that vein he has made public his secret through his book and through a wide variety of courses he offers. As a sign of his sincerity at the back of the book there were two tickets worth $2599 for attending the Millionaire Mind Intensive seminar. Christelle had attended the course, which was simply a brainwash that convinced her to spend $3000 for the course that she *really* needed, where the "secrets" to success would be revealed. She had thus become a convinced apostle of the millionaire's way of thinking.

It seemed to me that somebody who has sold a million copies of a book and presents seminars at $3000 a head isn't giving very much back to society.

Speaking of money, I've made an interesting observation with regard to how money can be a powerful motivating force in driving human behaviour. My observation in a nutshell is that the value we attribute to something depends on how much it costs us.

Advantage Boating is a for profit, private enterprise that needs to generate enough revenue to pay for its publicity, the cost of berthing and storing the boats, the salaries of its management and its maintenance staff as well as the fees it pays its instructors. To make ends meet and generate a profit it has to charge $650 for the four-day course, the books, the written exam and certification costs. This works out to more than $150 per day for a student, doesn't it?

By contrast, the North Channel Sailing School has minimal publicity costs, since all the labour is offered free by its members. Likewise for the cost of management and maintenance. Contrary to Advantage Boating, NCSS charges its instructors a fee for sailing instead of paying them. Consequently, it was deemed reasonable not to charge the members for the course, except for the costs of the books and certifications, which amount to only $75, or less than $20 a day.

What I have observed is that with my non-profit club I might have four students the first day, three on the second day, and in some cases I'd finish the fourth day with only two students. They arrived late for the course, or claimed they had to leave early. Any excuse was good enough for missing a class and just about anything in their lives was more important than showing up for Robert's course. I had taught 15 NCSS students and experienced this kind of frustration with every group.

On the other hand, with Advantage Boating, where the students have dished out big bucks for each of the four days of their course, I find that nobody skips a course, arrives late or leaves early. Remarkably, so far I've taught 120 Advantage Boating students and in all those days, only one student missed half a day and that was because he had an absolutely impossible-to-miss business meeting, and he made sure to make it to the marina to catch the afternoon part of the course, apologizing profusely and swearing that he had no other option.

My conclusion was clear. In order to reduce absenteeism and frustration for the instructors, NCSS had to charge its members for the Basic Cruising Course. Last year I reported my findings to the skipper committee and recommended that a fee on top of the manuals and certification fees be charged. The Board of Directors approved charging an extra $200. That summer I was not able to teach because of my debilitating eye problem but the instructors reported that they've had no absenteeism since the introduction of the new fee.

Human nature is interesting, huh?

November, 2006.

There is no month in Ottawa that is duller, colder, darker, wetter and more downright unpleasant than November. So it was with much enthusiasm that I joined Anthony for another sail in the Grenadines. This time we were accompanied by Rachel, who was preparing to leave for a trip around the world the following July.

The dinghy was anchored on the sandy bottom a hundred metres or so from the nicest reef in the Tobago Cays. After an hour of snorkelling Anthony, Rachel and I climbed aboard and headed back to *Ventus* anchored half a mile from the reef, our need for exploration satiated. When Anthony reached in his swimsuit pocket for the key of the boat, to his horror, the key was no longer there. All the hatches were closed and locked, so there was no way to open the boat without the key!

It was obvious that the key, attached to a floater, had inconveniently floated away out of the pocket. We got back into the dinghy and motored towards the general area where we had been swimming. The wind was blowing from the reef, which was good, because we wouldn't have been able to use the dinghy beyond the reef. Anthony planned to comb the area systematically by making long passes back and forth from upwind to downwind. Immediately we started our search, the engine stalled. As Murphy would have it, the engine stubbornly refused to come back to life.

Two Frenchmen relaxing in the cockpit of their catamaran anchored nearby noticed our difficulty and offered to help us find the key. Only, they didn't have enough gas for their dinghy. Anthony led them to *Ventus* to fill their tank from a jerry can tied to the deck. We then all boarded the French dinghy again and began the difficult search. I translated Anthony's directions, for our saviours didn't speak English. The wind freshened; creating large wavelets that made locating the tiny floater very difficult. It was getting late, and remarkably, at that latitude darkness falls rapidly once the sun sets, as there is almost no twilight in the tropics.

We had been searching for half an hour when suddenly, pointing to the horizon past the reef, Anthony exclaimed, "Oh Lord, we're going to get it! There's a line squall coming. Better go!"

The Frenchman at the helm gunned the engine and drove at full speed towards *Ventus*. But the oncoming squall caught up with us, enveloped the entire cay with a heavy blanket of black cloud and dumped a drenching downpour. It felt like someone pouring bathtubs full of water over us.

We climbed into the cockpit, soaked and cold and waved the helpful Frenchmen goodbye. We sat in the cockpit, looking at each other and discussed what to do next. We came to the realization that the key had disappeared for good and that the only alternative left was to burglarize the boat.

As is customary on most sailboats, the companionway closure was made of two teakwood washboards that slid down a pair of wooden tracks. The larger, top board was built with louvered slats within a strong frame.

Teak trees grow mainly in Indonesia and are becoming increasingly rare due to an insatiable demand for its golden brown colour and beautiful grain. It is mostly used for manufacturing outdoor furniture, boat decks and constructions where resistance to rot and termites is wanted. It is a wood that withstands the rigors of weathering even if it's not coated with varnish or oil. Many boat manufacturers choose teak as the wood of choice for the inside finishes of their luxury boats as its rarity has made it a status symbol. There are simply too many sailors with too much money for the good of the planet. The world demand for teak has put a strain on supply, with the result that it now has become extremely expensive. Just to replace the broken slats would cost $50 in lumber.

It had stopped raining and the sky had cleared, but it was almost dark. We could have used the anchor to smash the washboard to smithereens, but we didn't want to ruin the entire closure and its slides. Any woodworking tool we would need was safely stowed inside the locked boat. Anthony hailed the owner of a yacht anchored a hundred metres from ours, using the foghorn. When he finally attracted the man's attention, he asked him to lend us a hammer and chisel. Anthony carefully broke each of the louvers one by one, taking care not to ruin the frame. The resultant opening was just barely large enough to allow him to squeeze through to the inside and unearth a spare key.

After we got out of our wet clothes, I fixed Anthony a much-needed white lady, a mixture of rum, milk, honey and Angostura bitters. After two or three of these Anthony had regained his calm and we laughed about the whole episode.

One night, I woke up after a few hours of sleep with the terrifying realization that I was going to be sick to my stomach. And assuredly, what I feared happened – my delicate stomach rebelled at something I ate at supper that it didn't appreciate. Rachel had heard the commotion and came to ask me if everything was OK. I answered not to be concerned, that it was probably food poisoning and that I'd be fine after a night's sleep. However, ten minutes later the same horrible experience repeated itself. After several minutes of incessant retching, I crawled back into my berth, lying on my back, drenched with sweat and trembling with cold. Then I felt a hand put something in my pyjama pocket, and Rachel apologizing, "Sorry I don't have the right medication, but this will do just the same."

I continued being sick in fifteen minute cycles for a couple of hours, then when my body was satisfied that it had rid itself of the unwanted toxin, I fell into a much needed sleep. The next morning when I awoke, I remembered my pyjama pocket, reached into it and read the note. It showed solely two words:

"Arsenicum Album."

I understood what this meant. Rachel was a registered nurse and practiced alongside medical doctors during all her career. After she had retired she had acquired an interest in homeopathy, one of a plethora of alternative medicines. Homeopathic treatment relies on the theory of like is cured by like. If an ailment is caused by a certain poison, you can treat the patient by giving him an extremely dilute potion made from the same substance. What is particularly interesting is that the poison is so highly diluted that there is not a single molecule of the substance left in the solution. The belief is that the water molecules have a memory of the toxin that had touched other water molecules. What homeopathic specialists hang their hat on is the placebo effect. Of course, scientists are aware of the power of the placebo effect, and that is why in any scientific study a control group is given a placebo, an inactive substance. It is only if the experimental drug shows a stronger effect than the placebo that it is deemed to possess the desired therapeutic effect. Rachel goes one step further than the standard treatment. Her homeopathy teacher discovered that by having the patient wear a piece of paper with the name of the remedy on his person, the same effect was obtained as if he had taken the actual remedy. Rachel has personally tested this method many times and has found that it works just as well as the actual homeopathic remedy, which is really not surprising.

Although I am not a believer in alternative medicines, I think their practice might be serving our society an unintended benefit: that is, relieving the congestion in hospital emergency wards and doctors' offices. Furthermore, patients who get discouraged with our modern medical system when their doctors can't find a cure for their ailment often find solace in one of the alternative medicines. In my case, what I appreciated of Rachel's treatment was her concern for my well-being and her display of friendship. What can be sweeter?

On this trip we stayed several days in Saint Lucia anchored in Rodney Bay. This time we met an old friend of Anthony's and colleague of Michael, the paediatrician. Her name was Brigetta, a forty-ish, very attractive, tall, blue-eyed, blonde German lady with Swedish facial traits.

She had been working as a volunteer in the paediatric department of the local hospital for ten years. She wasn't receiving any salary or stipend from the hospital, her patients or the department of health. In order to earn a living and finance her volunteer activities, she went home to work in Germany six months of the year.

She invited Rachel, Anthony and me to her place for dinner, along with two lovely young ladies, medical students from Australia whom she was mentoring and billeting during their two-month stint in St. Lucia.

I told Brigetta that Rachel and I intended to rent a car to visit the island and I asked her if she could recommend which were the "must-see" places. At the top of her list were the Pitons, a set of two very high and perfectly conical mountains on the west coast near the south end of the island. She advised that the best vantage point by far to view the natural monoliths was from the bar at the very posh Ladera resort. She also offered us the use of her car for the day. I tried to decline the offer, on the basis that I didn't want to deprive her but she pressed us to accept the offer, which, she insisted, was made from the heart. She assured us that she didn't need the car, as she commuted with a colleague.

The following morning we stopped by her place to pick up the vehicle. It was the smallest car I had ever driven, a Fiat 500 with a tiny engine and a four-speed transmission. We drove southward, up and down steep hills, shifting down to second gear, and sometimes the poor car couldn't quite manage a hill in second and had to be downshifted into first. We got thoroughly lost in the town of Castries with its absence of signage and the need to find the main highway at the other end of town. We drove along magnificent cliffside roads, which offered stunning views. A little before the Pitons we came to the top of a high hill providing us with a bird's eye view of the town of Souffrière. We descended the long hill of hairpin turns to the waterfront. There we had lunch in a restaurant of the evocative name The Pirate's Den. I find it interesting that people have no qualms about glamorizing the brutal world of piracy, yet would think it inappropriate to name a restaurant The Torturer's Den, or The Rapist's Refuge or The Beheader's Cove.

Finally we arrived at the Ladera and made a beeline for the bar. Wow! The view was so astonishingly beautiful that it made us literally speechless with awe. Beyond the edge of the open terrace stood the two towering natural monoliths resembling inverted cones enshrouded with green vegetation, revealing in their cleavage an expanse of turquoise water under a blue sky studded with white puffs of cloud. When I recovered from the initial state of wonder, I sat down with Rachel and we ordered drinks. At $10 US they were worth every cent, given the exceptional ambiance of the setting.

On the drive back we found our way through Castries a little more easily than on the outbound trip and arrived at Rodney Bay. Just before returning the car to its generous owner I decided to stop to buy her a bottle of wine as a gesture of appreciation. It was starting to get dark, so I decided to switch from sunglasses to clear glasses. This is when my heart sank! I had left my knapsack at the hotel bar. In it were my clear glasses, my passport, my wallet containing my money and my brand new Tilley hat. We were now three hours' drive from the Ladera. Returning would have entailed a 6-hour drive in the dark. Rachel paid for the wine and we proceeded to Brigetta's place.

Coincidentally, Anthony arrived at the same time as we did. There was no way around it. If I wanted to retrieve my possessions I would inescapably have to humiliate myself. I sheepishly announced my stupid forgetfulness. Recently, Anthony had had his share of embarrassing moments, so this was his chance. He approached me with the serious poker face he always puts on when he makes a joke, he embraced me, then held me by the shoulders at arms' length, staring at me in the eye, and said, "Robert, my brother! We understand each other!"

We all laughed and then I felt slightly less idiotic. There was an urgent need to get serious and retrieve that bag. I asked to use Brigetta's phone to call the hotel. Brigetta, having inherited the supreme German sense of organization, coached me in how to go about this:

"Make sure you talk to the manager, not just a waiter."

"Make sure he identifies the knapsack by checking your passport information."

"Ask him if he knows a reliable taxi driver personally and if the hotel uses his services regularly."

"Ask him to contact the driver himself and that he confirm with you that the driver will come tonight with your bag."

"Ask him to instruct the driver to phone you just before leaving the Ladera."

"Tell him to meet you at the entrance to the Rodney Bay Marina."

"Ask him the driver's name and cell phone number in case he doesn't show up at the appointed place and time."

Whew! It was a tense hour, waiting to talk to the manager, waiting for him to find the bag and confirm its identity and waiting while he made arrangements with his driver and waiting for the driver to phone me. But in the end, Brigetta's instructions proved invaluable. The driver phoned me before leaving, which was a great reassurance.

All is well that ends well. The driver showed up at the marina on time, with his girlfriend by his side. I paid him the $100 US fee we had agreed to; I invited the two of them for a well-deserved beer; I was the happy finder of my wayward bag and its valuable contents; and I could at last shed my dark sunglasses and replace them with the clear ones.

May, 2008.

On a return trip to Trinidad on *Ventus* we made a detour eastward into the Atlantic to visit Anthony's country of birth, Barbados. The most eastern island of the Caribbean, it is pear shaped and measures only 32 km long by 21 wide at its widest. It consists mostly of lowlands and rolling hills with no impressive mountains. It is the most prosperous island in the Caribbean as its 285,000 inhabitants enjoy a per capita GDP of $19,000. The main drivers of the economy are tourism, offshore banking and financial services. Whereas in Anthony's childhood sugar exports accounted for the greater part of the economy, they now provide less than 1% of the gross domestic product.

Our first landfall was the marina of Port St. Charles, which is part of a very posh resort on the west side of the island, not far from the north end. We spent a couple of relaxing days tied to the dock, enjoying full privileges of the restaurant and bar. During this time Anthony invited his daughter Trudy and her family for a sail. Although he was given the gift of five charming daughters, none of them have chosen to stay in Trinidad, the country of their birth. One lives in Canada, two in the United States and two in Anthony's country of birth, Barbados.

The next day Trudy, her husband John, their boys, nine-year-old Luke and six-year-old Jacques as well as their niece Rorie boarded *Ventus* for the 19-mile cruise to their home town Bridgetown further south, down the coast. If you recall *Mikky*'s maiden voyage, when she was almost dismasted, Trudy and John are the ones who had been on board with Anthony. This time their adventure on *Ventus* would be much more subdued. We sailed on a moderate beam wind all the way. Luke, who wasn't taller than the wheel took the helm and did a superb job of steering. John hadn't sailed for a couple of years and was eager to take the helm after a long abstinence. He had to tell his son to relinquish the helm, as he wanted to see how a Hallberg Rassy handles. Two minutes after John took over, Luke inquired, "Dad, can I steer now?"

And John answered, "No, Luke, you can't have the helm, it's my turn."

Luke, disappointed, waited, almost adhered to his father's side for 45 minutes before having the helm returned to him.

After having tied to a mooring by the Barbados Yacht Club, Anthony took the boys for a ride in the dinghy, barrelling at full speed over waves, generating splashes that delighted the grandchildren. This was the highlight of the day for them, as for the rest of the day they talked excitedly about the fun they had with Grandpapa.

The Barbados Yacht Club, ironically, doesn't have a dock, which meant that we had to get to shore by dinghy. When there's not much of a swell landing on a beach isn't much of a hassle. It's a matter of bringing the dinghy close to shore, then one person steps out into the water, pulls the bow onto shore and then the other passengers can step out over the bow without getting their feet wet. Once everybody is out, the boat is dragged onto higher ground. However, when there's a heavy swell – well, read this email Anthony wrote me on Christmas day:

> I am sitting on board "VENTUS" on a mooring outside the Barbados Yacht Club watching the ground swell continue to build up and wondering whether it will be still possible to get ashore tomorrow morning. I was just able to do it today by driving the dinghy to within 50 metres of the shore and anchoring to wait for a gap in the breakers that were rolling in. Then during the gap, reversing to shore with the engine while paying the anchor line out until we were in shallow water and the waves were breaking 2 metres behind the boat. [I sent one] crewmember into the water to carry the bags ashore while the anchor held the dinghy from being swept in and capsized. Then to haul the dinghy back out to the anchor before the next really big wave came in. I had to re-anchor quite far out (100 metres) from shore and then swim in through the surf to use the washroom to shower to change into street clothes in order to go out for the day driving all around Barbados.

We were fortunate, during our stay in Bridgetown, not to have to strip down to our bathing suits to go ashore.

Trudy took us to visit Sunnyside, the family home where she and her family now live, the same house Anthony was born in. It was an elegant single storied bungalow with a wide veranda on two sides on a large fenced lot covered with fruit trees and flowers.

That evening we were introduced to Christine, Anthony's other daughter who lives on the island, and her veterinarian husband Dereck and her 17-year old daughter Shayle.

Dereck confided that his 15-year-old daughter Rorie, although a very charming and well brought up young lady, has at times provided her parents with challenges that stressed their patience. There are occasions in rearing a child when it is difficult to contain one's frustration and anger. In Barbados, Dereck informed me, the majority of parents exercise corporal punishment and adhere to the belief, "Spare the rod and spoil the child." He and Christine believed that there was a better way, as beating a child does not eliminate the underlying causes of the unwanted behaviour, but generates fear and mistrust of the parents. They discovered a group of like-minded parents who have formed an association for the prevention of corporal punishment and ever since, they learn strategies for dealing with different disciplinary situations and they play an active role in the association in trying to change the old mindset.

In my job as manager of a biotechnology laboratory I supervised the farm hands who took care of our cows. One of their duties was to release the 40 animals from their tie stalls twice a day to observe and note their oestrus behaviour. After the prescribed time, they had to bring the cows back into their stalls and tie each one up again. They were alone to accomplish this job. The first man I hired, to my chagrin, turned out to be an animal beater. He would literally beat the animals into submission with a stick and it took him 45 minutes to coax the animals back to their stalls even with the attraction of nice, fresh feed grain. When he left, I hired a new animal keeper who was the opposite. He would talk to the animals gently, walk calmly behind them, pat them softly, touch them on the rump when necessary, never using a stick. He was able to corral all the animals and get them tied up in 15 minutes. There was an atmosphere of peace and quiet in the barn, as opposed to the air of tension that existed under the reign of the animal beater. I have since believed in the old adage, "you can attract more flies with honey than with vinegar."

I have for a long time believed that a civilized society should not condone the use of corporal punishment as a means of influencing children's behaviour. To me, it is an abdication of human intelligence to lower oneself to the needless act of hitting a person, even less a defenceless child that is your own flesh and blood. Children are much more intelligent than most adults make them out to be. A parent has to exercise intelligence and restraint to influence the child's behaviour through discussion and example. There are strategies to child-proof a house to keep toddlers safe from physical danger. It places much more demand on one's intellect and time to take the trouble to explain to a child that he can burn himself on a hot stove than to expeditiously whack him on the head.

I realized that the decision to renounce violence is not a subset of civilization. You just have to look at the world's most powerful nation, the one that claims to be a beacon of democracy, to realize that a country that thinks of itself as civilized is not necessarily one that refrains from violence. If the gentle treatment of children is a sign of civilization then some primitive societies would be amongst the most civilized. A case in point is illustrated by a comment by Captain Bob Bartlett after he had lived more than 30 years with the Stone Age Esquimo at the turn of the 20th century. Upon witnessing a mentally challenged Siberian mother strike her child, he commented that in all his years living with the Esquimo he had never seen an Esquimo father or a mother hit their child, and that these simple, primitive people made very gentle, loving parents. I once met a highly educated veterinarian from Eastern Ontario who meted out corporal punishment to his children on a regular basis, convinced that he was carrying out God's will. So I now conclude that the adoption of corporal punishment is not a matter of being or not being civilized, nor is it a matter of intelligence, nor is it a question of religion… I don't know what it is. Perhaps it is a learned behaviour.

When I returned home, I did a bit of research on institutionalized beating of children. I found out that in most Caribbean countries as well as in 20 states in the US corporal punishment is allowed in public schools and that in peace-loving Canada it has only been outlawed since 2004.

Trudy lent us her car for the week, which enabled us to come and go at will. The affluence of the little nation is evident through the quality of its roads, the large number of elegant houses and the low prevalence of substandard housing. Like Bermuda, Barbados is replete with well tended properties and flowers abound on the roadside. For nature and wildlife buffs, there is Welchman Hall Gully, a three-quarter mile long, very deep canyon formed by the collapse of the roofs of ancient caves. It is home to a number of trees, such as nutmeg, bamboo, clove and palms, as well as a large number of tropical plants. A guide takes us along the trail through the forest and explains the flora and fauna, some of which is found only on this island.

For those who love caves, there are the very beautiful Harrison Caves through which a train of open cars on pneumatic wheels takes about

70 tourists at a time on a ride along a paved, winding, underground road. The train stops at various points of interest where camera-toting visitors step off to photograph an incredible variety of stalactites, stalagmites and strange calcareous formations.

I won't go into nightlife, as we didn't have time for any of that, but I will mention that for the techno-savvy, there is a very interesting museum displaying one of the seven extant mothballed Concorde supersonic airplanes. The museum is situated at the Barbados International Airport, which is a major airline hub, serving as a connecting point for a large number of Caribbean flights. The tour of the museum starts with a documentary video that is projected onto the aircraft's fuselage, which explains the history of that extinct species of flying machines. Then you can climb inside the aircraft itself and sit in the pure leather seats that have received the hind ends of famous movie stars and rich tycoons. A guide dressed as a period airhostess describes how it was to cross the Atlantic in one and a half hours. You can see mock-ups of the refined menus that were offered as part of the $15,000 one-way trans-oceanic ticket. Upon exiting the plane, visitors can have a crack at driving one of these beasts at a realistic looking flight simulator. I put into practice my experience as a former Cessna pilot and amazed myself with what I could do: rolls, inverted flight with the Barbadian coastline upside down, and spins always ending with a death spiral and an explosive crash. The museum reminds the visitor of a slice of oil-age technology, the way our children and grandchildren will see it – as an extravagance of the good old days of ample energy, a reminder of how their ancestors lived it up while the oil lasted.

Give a man a fish and feed him for a day. Teach him how to fish and feed him for life. Having left Barbados, we stopped at the little island of Mayreau, in the south end of the Grenadines. Anthony wanted to touch base with one of his protégées.

Conscientious individuals in the developed world constantly struggle with the moral dilemma of the growing disparity between rich and poor. A Canadian or an American earning an average salary can afford luxuries while there are a billion of us who don't even have enough to eat. That's the system we're caught up in.

Foreign aid has been fraught with unintended consequences. Since the 1950s developed countries have donated hundreds of billions of dollars to provide food, medicine and sanitation knowledge to poor countries with the valiant intention of doing good. The unintended consequence is that the populations of the recipient countries have mushroomed beyond what their environment and their economy can sustain and they are less capable of taking care of themselves now than if they had never been offered "help".

The old saying, "The road to hell is paved with good intentions" never rang so true.

So how can we help? There are hundreds of organizations that provide assistance to poor countries, but we hear stories of charities that waste 90 percent of donors' money on supporting the excessive lifestyle of their fat cat executives in fancy downtown office building towers. Once the aid arrives in a destination country, the goods are frequently highjacked by rebel organizations or druglords.

Anthony was grateful to have been born into a good family that provided him with the tools to obtain a good education, which allowed him to lead a comfortable life, much better than the average Trinidadian's. He was looking for a way to repay society in some measure for his good fortune. He was no more capable of solving the problems of the world than you and I, but he found a way he could make a life-altering difference for at least a few individuals.

A few years ago, upon stopping over on the small island of Mayreau in the Grenadines he met Suzan on the beach selling clothing to the tourists. Barely thirty, she was the mother of seven children. Since the father had disappeared from her life, she was left with the burden of providing for her brood. One of her daughters, Nikisha, was exceptionally successful in primary school but when she graduated, her mother could not afford to send her to high school. Because there is no high school on the tiny island of Mayreau, children who graduate from primary school have to be expatriated to the island of Saint Vincent in order to pursue their education. This meant Suzan would have to pay for her child's transportation, boarding, books and uniform, which was impossible on her meagre income. This was an opportunity for Anthony to enact his resolve to make a difference in someone's life. He undertook to pay for Nikisha's boarding and school expenses. Since then he sends monthly cheques to the mother and keeps abreast of his protégée's progress. On this visit to Mayreau I had the chance to meet Suzan and her lovely, 15-year-old daughter who is being given the unique opportunity to learn "how to fish". Nikisha is actually the third girl Anthony has taken under his wing.

Becalmed

Chapter 11

A Whole Ocean at Last!

I remember the first time Sami spoke of his circumnavigation plans. He and I were in the cockpit of *Namaste*, heading upriver with a strong east wind on our stern. His tanned, olive skin gave him the aspect of a seasoned cruising sailor and his slight Arabic accent confirmed his Palestinian origin. He was Jack-of-all-trades and master of *many*. In the days of the first personal computers he built home computers from scratch and sold them for half the cost of a store-bought Commodore or Apple 2E. There was nothing he could not repair, from avionics to X-ray machines. He was very popular at the Aylmer Marina, since he would drop whatever he was doing to lend a hand to a boat owner with anything, be it resuscitating a dead engine, or replacing broken rigging, or revitalizing sun bleached wood trim.

He was standing at the wheel, steering carefully to prevent an accidental gibe, when out of the blue, "Hey Robert, I'm gonna sail around the world!"

He went on to explain that he, his wife Marielle and Rachel had bought a 42-foot Pearson cutter and that the three of them were going to be leaving for a trip around the world in a year's time. The couple decided to take Rachel on as an equal partner and one-third owner of the boat. They put their heads together to hatch a new name for the sailboat that would become their home for many years and they decided on the apt epithet *"Three's Company"*. My first thought was how a *ménage à trois* would work out, especially with a large financial amount involved. I knew Marielle as a strong-willed person. Rachel, on the other hand, is generous and conciliatory. So perhaps their differences would be complimentary and conducive to forming a strong team.

Sami's plans were yet very preliminary, but the circumnavigation would start with a stint in the Caribbean, then a transit of the Panama Canal, then a crossing of the Pacific.

"The Pacific," I thought, "that would be OK for a first long passage."

Sami knew of my interest in long passages and told me I could join them on any leg of the trip. I indicated that I'd like him to reserve a place for me when crossing the Pacific Ocean, whatever his planned landfall.

When came the NCSS annual méchoui (lamb roast) Sami and Marielle, the happy couple would-be round-the-worlders as well as their partner Rachel were the centre of attraction. The place was abuzz with talk of long passages, sailing adventures and future plans and aspirations.

Micheline who is not a sailor, but gets invited to the club's parties, was on the floor, mingling with the crowd. Even though it is something she would never consider doing herself, she had always found the idea of sailing around the world fascinating. At one point during the evening I noticed that she was engaged in a conversation with Marielle. Micheline had worked in sales most of her life and had learned that one can gain more from listening than from talking.

Sami was an electronics technician who had worked as a service engineer for a large helicopter manufacturer and had just taken early retirement at age 58. Marielle, his wife of 22 years, had started at the bottom of the ladder in a computer software company and now held a top management position, which paid more than she had ever dreamed of. What worried me about Sami was his approach to investment. The couple being childless and earning two large salaries, had accumulated a substantial sum that needed to be protected, making themselves an irresistible target for the bloodsucking investment managers. Sami had been talked into a Ponzi scheme in which he would benefit from leverage to increase the value of his investment by a factor of ten, thus doubling his capital every five months. He enjoyed seeing his monthly statements reporting immense gains, so my unsolicited advice to cash out was not received with enthusiasm.

The next morning at breakfast, Micheline was sitting at the other side of the table. She had been stirring her coffee for at least sixty seconds.

"Micheline, what are you doing with your coffee?"

"Oh!"

She was shaken out of her reflection.

"I was thinking about my conversation with Marielle last night. 'Know what she said?"

"Search me."

"She told me that Sami will never go around the world without her."

"Well, that's OK. She's going with him when they leave next year."

"She is? She told me she's not ready to retire before five years. What do you suppose that means?"

Indeed!

July 3, 2007.

It was a perfect day for a grand casting off for a trip around the world, sunny, and not too hot for the time of year.

Sami and Rachel were the stars being celebrated by a small group of friends who had made the trip from Ottawa to the Chaumont Yacht Club on Lake Ontario in the state of New York to see them off. Present was Rachel's new boyfriend, Jake, who kept a yacht in the Chaumont Marina. Absent was Marielle, Sami's ex wife. Yes, EX! I was to learn the details of the break-up five months later. The significance of this divorce was two-fold: primo, there were only two persons making the trip instead of three, and segundo, Rachel owned two-thirds of the boat, having bought out Marielle's share.

Sami and Rachel had spent the previous year making improvements to the boat, such as upgrading all the standing rigging and installing up-to-date navigation equipment. This is where Rachel met Jake. They spent many good moments together and discovered that they were on the same wavelength with regard to the important things in life. Jake, who was in his mid-sixties, couldn't commit to joining the adventurers on their trip because of knee problems. He was waiting for an operation, which might eventually prevent him from sailing forever. Rachel promised to come back occasionally so they could spend time together.

After having shared the traditional bottle of Champagne, I got into Jake's boat, which was designated as the official photography boat, with me as cameraman. Once *Three's Company* was underway, we followed her and I kept snapping pictures until she was out of the harbour. I had an odd, inexplicable feeling about this situation. Perhaps I just hadn't adjusted to the idea that Marielle was no longer in the picture. Something seemed amiss, but I couldn't quite put my finger on it.

I'm not one who enjoys dishing out gossip, but it is necessary that I provide you the reader with these personal details about the protagonists so that you can understand the unravelling of my Pacific Ocean tale.

A few months later, I phoned Marielle to see how she was recovering from the trauma of the divorce. I knew that Sami had taken it very hard and came close to sinking into a depression. What she revealed floored me. She said that they lost most of their fortune from their investments and that the nest egg they had built up was gone. There was so little left that if she were to go ahead with the cruise around the world, they would have to work along the way to scrape enough to get to the next port. There would never be enough money to maintain the boat properly and she didn't want to have to pinch pennies and live the life of a vagabond. Besides, she had just had a promotion, which reinforced her decision to stay with the company for several more years.

I asked her why not, since she was committed to working for a few years, spend her holidays with Sami in whatever part of the world he might be, and when she had enough saved up, she could join him for good. She responded that she didn't want Sami to be out on the boat having fun and living the easy life while she stayed behind labouring away.

I was kept abreast of *Three's Company*'s progress through periodic emails from Sami and Rachel. They started off in Lake Ontario, made their way through the Oswego and Erie canals, then down the Hudson River to the Big Apple. From there they swung northward for a bit to spend a few weeks in Newport, Rhode Island. An absolute must was the giant boat show in Annapolis, Maryland, where the circumnavigators had several sailing friends stay with them aboard *Three's Company* for the duration of the event. This was an ideal occasion to stock up on parts, as Sami was like Anthony; he insisted on keeping spares of everything.

After Annapolis, they sailed and motored along the coast as far as Beaufort, South Carolina. From this position, they sailed offshore for ten days, to make landfall in Saint Barts. Then they spent a couple of months in the vicinity of the British Virgin Islands, St. Martin and back to St. Barts before heading southwards. Rachel could have spent ten years moseying around the Caribbean, but Sami was always itching to be on the move, which might be the reason why they bypassed Bermuda, the huge Bahamas archipelago, Cuba, and many other islands.

They continued to Trinidad, stopping in Antigua, Guadeloupe, Les Saintes, Martinique, St. Lucia, Bequia, St. Vincent and the Grenadines and Grenada. They arrived at their summer destination in Trinidad on May 31st.

Rachel flew home for the summer, leaving her shipmate alone to carry out maintenance work on the boat. In October, they reconvened and had the pleasure of welcoming a new crewmember to join them on their adventure. It was Jennie, the lady who had joined me on my trip to Desolation Sound, the good friend and nursing colleague of Rachel. Jennie had just taken retirement, decided that she would vagabond about the oceans and sold all her possessions except for what she could carry in her numerous suitcases. There was no romantic relationship involved. Not yet.

They sailed across the Caribbean, staying 150 miles away from the shores of Venezuela and Columbia to avoid boarding by pirates. To Rachel's sorrow, Sami did not want to visit the famous San Blaas islands before transiting the Panama Canal. Once passed the canal, they sailed northward to El Salvador, stopping over in Costa Rica on the way.

March, 2009.

It was confirmed! Sami, Rachel and Jennie were expecting me in El Salvador March the 12th. The plan was to leave Bahía del Sol the following week and undertake the long passage across the Pacific Ocean and the transition between the northern and southern hemispheres. We were to make landfall on the island of Hiva Oa, the most eastern of the Marquesas group of islands, belonging to French Polynesia.

This prompted me to buy charts of the Pacific and travel books about this enchanting part of the world, reputed to be paradise on Earth. Since Sami had not obtained pre-authorization for entering the French Polynesian nation, there was no way of knowing if the boat would be allowed to stay longer than 30 days. I made different contingency plans, as I intended to spend three months in the area, since my costs of getting there and the flight back were the same regardless of how long I stayed there. Just as well get the most out of it.

Sami intended to spend two weeks in the Marquesas before moving on. Apparently, the Tuamotus, the most beautiful atolls on Earth are an absolute must for sailors, but there was no way of knowing if we would be allowed to spend time there. Nevertheless, we would eventually sail the 500 miles from the Marquesas to Tahiti, and from there I could continue my exploration on my own if Sami was compelled to leave French Polynesia with his boat. I looked up information on hiking trails on the different islands and made lists of inter-island flights and ferry schedules. The dream of a lifetime was coming true, so I wasn't going to miss out on anything because of lack of planning.

I'd never heard of Taca Airlines, but my friend Don, the ex-Transport Canada policy maker and travel agent assured me that not only did it have an excellent safety record, but that it operated modern airplanes and good old fashioned service. My experience confirmed that all of that was true of the Salvadorian company. In fact, it had been a long time since I'd enjoyed hot meals served on an airplane.

Sami was driving the dinghy and I was in the forward seat with my bag, admiring the tropical scenery surrounding the bay when *Three's Company* at anchor came into view. It was a feeling of excitement to think that this vessel would be housing me for the next three months and would be my transportation for crossing the planet's largest ocean.

Jennie was to arrive at Bahía del Sol early in the morning the next day, as she had gone to visit her mother in Montreal, to buy a special modem for the short wave radio and to write her ham radio exam. Rachel was in Nicaragua, and was due the following day late in the afternoon.

It was about 0930 the following day when Sami and I were in the cockpit, planning the installation of additional cockpit drains. Suddenly, a ponga pulled up alongside and a very angry-looking Jennie climbed aboard and announced, "I'm really pissed off with you", glowering at Sami.

"Oh, I thought you were arriving tonight."

The driver of the ponga passed up her baggage. She took her bags down below, and looking out from the companionway, she said with trembling lips, "You can't really care for me if you don't even listen to what I say. Last night on the phone I told you that it was an overnight flight arriving at five a.m. and that I'd be at the marina by seven. I've been waiting for you at the marina for two and a half hours."

She disappeared into the forepeak cabin, fuming. Sami and I carried on with our maintenance work in silence. Several hours later, after waking from a much-needed sleep, she apologized to me for her anger, even if it hadn't been directed at me.

It was happy hour and I was passing the beer up from the cabin into the cockpit, when I witnessed a surprising turn of events. Jenny and Sami were not just seated together, but seated *really* close; she was wedged between his legs, with her back against his chest, and they were holding hands, fingers intertwined, both of them beaming a broad smile. When I handed them their beers, we clinked our bottles together and I toasted, "Here's to love!"

I deduced not only that Sami was forgiven for his misdemeanour, but that there was more to their relationship than just being shipmates.

Later in the evening, Rachel arrived from her trip to Nicaragua. She insisted that I take her stateroom for the duration of my stay on *Three's Company* and that she preferred sleeping in the salon. It was then revealed that Sami and Jennie, who had been just friends the previous fall, now shared the same bed.

The following days we were occupied making an inventory of the hundreds of parts and tools on board, installing cockpit drains, trying in vain to get Jennie's new Pactor modem to work, checking equipment and provisioning.

What is the most important item you should have on the boat for a long passage that is absolutely indispensable? Water, of course. On the last day, we purchased 22 three-gallon containers of drinking water and tied them all down under the salon table to prevent them from shuffling around. *Three's Company* was equipped with two built-in water tanks, an 80-gallon tank located under the forepeak berth and a fifty-gallon one located under my bunk in the port quarter berth. The smaller tank was empty and Sami asked me to fill it. After it was filled, I asked, "Sami, do you want me to top up the forward tank, just to make sure it's full?"

"No, don't bother to fill it. I filled it last week and we haven't used any of it."

For some reason or other, I wasn't fully reassured.

Perhaps what made me uncomfortable revolved around his unconventional approach to water conservation. On all the boats I'd sailed, the galley sink has two distinct water supplies. One faucet supplies fresh water from the on-board tanks and one draws seawater from a thruhull. The seawater is used for washing dishes, washing hands, brushing of teeth and even boiling vegetables when mixed with fresh water. Sami had disconnected the seawater pump and used fresh water for washing dishes, which is a waste of precious water. On the short legs that he had navigated to date, this had not resulted in a problem. But on a passage that might take as long as fifty days, we could not use water in this way. Within the first days of this trip I instituted a method of fetching seawater with a bucket and storing it in a jerry can for washing the dishes. We also used this water for bathing and brushing our teeth. The two women, who had a lot of experience living on a boat, diligently joined me in this way of doing.

You might be wondering why we were installing new cockpit drains. The boat was built that way, so how can two simple sailors improve the design of a boat that was built by smart naval engineers? Smart engineers don't think of the safety of the potential buyer. They think of the safety of the builder's bank account. On her trip across the Caribbean *Three's Company* unexpectedly sailed across a powerful katabatic wind. The gust was so sudden that the boat suffered a knockdown, that is it was suddenly heeled over to the point that the mainsail was parallel to the water, causing the cockpit to completely fill up with water. This is when Sami discovered a serious fault with the Pearson 42 with regards to its suitability to sail offshore. The cockpit was equipped with two tiny drains that led to thruhulls in the cockpit lockers. Consequently, it took a good ten minutes for all the water to drain out to the sea. The danger with this design is that should the boat find herself in a raging storm with breaking stern waves pooping the boat every few minutes the extraordinary weight of water sloshing around high above the centre of gravity of the boat would make it unstable and would increase the boat's susceptibility to capsizing. A good sailboat for ocean passages has a small cockpit – a centre cockpit preferably, with very large drain holes, making it unlikely to be filled when pooped and making it drain rapidly should this happen. Another advantage of a small cockpit is that its smaller width makes it easier to brace yourself with your feet against the opposite seat when the boat is heeled. The Pearson 42 is an excellent boat for coastal or inter-island navigation, as its cockpit can accommodate a large group of guests for socializing.

Late in the evening, ten days after having arrived at Bahía del Sol, I sat down with my laptop at the hotel bar and I wrote an email to my family and friends. The following dispatches recount the story of my dashed dream:

FIRST DISPATCH FROM ROBERT – EL SALVADOR

20 March, 2009

It is late, but nevertheless, I will violate one of the rules of offshore sailing, and will go to bed late the night before casting off for a long passage. Thus I am writing you to share with you this exceptional event in my life.

Each has his reason for doing what I am about to do early tomorrow morning. Some as a quest for adventure, others because they love the sea, some because they have a passion for sailing and there are surely some who do it as a means of escaping the reality of their sedentary existence. In my case crossing the Pacific Ocean in a small sailboat to end up in French Polynesia is the realization of a dream of my youth. I'd often dreamt of accomplishing a circumnavigation by sailboat and to visit all the corners of the globe like the ancient explorers did – with the advantage that today we know how to prevent scurvy and we have accurate maps of the whole world...

Which explains why I'm here at the bar, connected to Wi Fi supplied by the marina run by Bahía del Sol hotel on la Costa del Sol in this tiny country in the isthmus that separates the two Americas. Our first landfall will be Hiva Oa in the Marquesas, 3,356 nautical miles from here, which at this time of the year should take from 26 to 30 days to cross, although it could take as much as 50 days in extreme conditions. We will be incommunicado all this time, which I hope will not be cause for worry for my immediate family...

Once in that paradise in the Pacific, I will write again and perhaps send you photos.

Before ending this, I must tell you that I am extremely grateful for having this opportunity – of having lived my whole life during the era of oil, this short period of human history that allows hundreds of millions of middle class people to live like kings. And thus, those who have the inclination can travel by aircraft to distant lands. I also recognize that at the age of 67 I am very lucky that the hundred trillion cells that constitute my body are still humming along in harmony, allowing my mind to take it on such a marvellous adventure. I'm also fortunate to have so many friends and a supportive family with whom I can share my pleasure of travelling.

I'll write again in about a month.

SECOND DISPATCH BY ROBERT – ACAPULCO, MEXICO

April 8, 2009

In life, as with sailing, one must sometimes face major changes in heading. In the last two weeks the crew and the boat have entertained both kinds of changes.

On the 21st of March we cast off from El Salvador and headed for Hiva Oa in the Marquesas islands. Then, six hours after having crossed the sand bar off Bahía del Sol, the God of the winds mercilessly took the power out of our sails, leaving us adrift.

The weather reports had predicted light winds for the first seven days, but somehow we didn't expect *this*.

Ever since our departure from El Salvador, we had been dealing with an over-the-ground speed of 0 to 5 knots. In addition to having to cope with unreliable, light or inexistent wind, we had to fight multidirectional currents of up to 2 knots. One night, with the boat keeping a constant heading we reversed by 11 nautical miles and according to the GPS, the currents made us complete two circles of 150 meters in diameter!!!

But that's not all. Even though there might be no wind, there were nevertheless waves of one to two metres in height. Hundreds of miles from our location there can be wind. The flow of air upon the surface of the water creates waves and these undulations can travel vast distances before losing their energy. Thus, a boat that finds itself in a windless zone can be rocked by substantial waves that have migrated from afar.

In these swells, when the boat is without forward motion and has its sails down, it rocks violently from side to side. When you have to walk around on or in the boat, you need to hold on with both hands. If the sails are up, they will go FLICSHT, FLACSHT, FLICSHT FLACSHT, and will gradually autodestruct. Everything inside the boat must be firmly secured; otherwise someone would risk getting knocked out by flying projectiles. If you try to sleep in a cockpit seat, good luck, as you risk being brutishly thrown off your seat. Those sleeping inside must endure the constant shaking and the noise of dishes crashing inside the cupboards.

At any moment, a breeze would materialize. We would then deploy the spinnaker or the duo of mainsail and jib. A few minutes later, FLIP FLOP, FLIP FLOP! And if we persisted in leaving the sails up, we would then be dealing with FLICSHT, FLACSHT, FLICSHT FLACSHT again. Often when this happened we would run the engine in forward gear. The forward motion thus produced, especially with a raised sail, resulted in a welcome stabilization of the boat, thereby relieving us temporarily from the rocking motion. Twice a day we had to run the engine to recharge the batteries

A Whole Ocean at Last!

and cool the refrigerator. So instead of leaving it in neutral to save fuel, we would run it in gear with more RPM, to stabilize the boat and make way.

At the end of a week we had covered 262 of the 3356 miles to the Marquesas. A new weather report revealed that over the great area we were sailing in, about 2000 miles by 1000 miles there would be light winds for the next seven days.

If we continued, we would be starting our trip after having used up half our fuel, a quarter of our water reserve and all of our fresh produce. If you look at a map, you will notice that our southwest course wasn't taking us very far from land. In fact, we were only 160 miles from Puerto Angel, a port of entry on the Mexican coast.

So we decided to make a radical change of course. We had enough fuel to take us to Puerto Angel, so we would clear in at that port of entry, fuel up and then motor another 150 miles to Acapulco. Once there we would rebuild our provisions, take care of a few repairs, and wait for a more suitable weather window. There were other advantages in choosing Acapulco as a departure point. Being further west, the distance to Hiva Oa would be shorter by 530 miles. And being further north, the wind speed and direction would be more favourable. Another advantage of the more northern location is that the angle of our course to the Equator would be more obtuse, which would shorten the time spent in the ICZ, the intertropical convergence zone (the doldrums, that windless zone near the Equator).

The day after making this decision, the wind picked up. A perfect wind on the beam, 15 to 18 knots! "At last, we have wind!!!" Another consultation. Another change of plan. It was unanimous – we'd change course and head directly for Acapulco, which was 240 miles away, beyond range of our fuel supply, but not presenting any problem in view of the favourable wind.

The following night... FLICSHT, FLACSHT, FLICSHT FLACSHT...And on with the engine.

You know that the modern sailing vessel is not restricted to sailing along the major wind corridors, but is able to sail upwind. The closest a sailboat can sail against the wind is about 45 degrees. Simple geometry would inform us that tacking, or beating across the wind would require twice the distance than going straight into it. However, when you're sailing on a boat loaded with several tons of water, fuel, tools, spare parts, a lifeboat, a dinghy, three anchors and their rodes, four people with their personal belongings, then theory parts with reality. Under these conditions we were sailing at best, 65 degrees to the wind. To add insult to injury, the combined effect of waves and wind cause the boat to drift sideways, away from its desired track.

We were in a quandary. Our nice wind gone, and we didn't have sufficient fuel to cover the 240 miles to Acapulco by motor. When the wind would subside we would run with the engine and when the wind picked up we would navigate under sail. We would frequently motor-sail, which allowed us to sail closer to the wind, at a smaller angle than 45 degrees. However, our profligate use of the engine ran our fuel supply dangerously low. Finally, seven days after changing our course away from the Marquesas, we arrived at the fuel dock in Acapulco with six litres of diesel sloshing around in the bottom of the tank.

Acapulco is a tourist town of 400,000 residents and I don't know how many hotel rooms. The old part of the city, the one visited by ordinary foreign and Mexican tourists is built upon the shore of Acapulco Bay, a beautiful round bay about five km in diameter. A wide boulevard borders the entire bay. On the other side of the boulevard there are restaurants, bars, night clubs, souvenir shops, hotels, American fast food joints and street vendors selling either jewellery, clothes, hand made art, or a variety of foods cooked under doubtful sanitary conditions.

Every business has a storefront sign that wants to be bigger than its competitor's. Some of these signs compare favourably in size and height to those found at service centres along Canadian expressways. Private cars, taxis (Volkswagen beetles), busses and trucks drive at breakneck speeds, only to come to a screeching halt at the next traffic light, with horn blaring. In Mexico a car horn doesn't rust. It dies of overuse. Hundreds of Mexican tourists soak up the sun on the blond sand beaches, packed together under rented umbrellas, and then walk along the sidewalk in T-shirts and flip flops, carrying lawn chairs, lunch coolers, water toys and wet children.

Here in Acapulco there was a lot to do:
Uno, clear in and then clear out - an extremely complex and time consuming task in Mexico, which took four days of our time.
Dos, Have several damaged areas of the jib repaired professionally.
Tres, Replenish our provisions, especially fruit and veggies
Cuatro, Wash and clean the boat
Cinco, Fill the tanks with fresh water
Séis, Laundry
Siete, Oil change

I had quite a shock when we checked the water tanks. We had been working uniquely off the 50-gallon aft tank and had been very frugal with it. I lifted the cover of the aft bunk to check the water level in that tank and was quite pleased to find that our water conservation efforts had paid off. We had used only one third of its contents, which showed that we had used only 15 to 20 gallons over the two weeks, plus the drinking water from the purchased containers. However, the front tank, the 80-gallon one, which we hadn't used at all, was completely empty. Sami was sure that he had filled it before leaving El Salvador. We checked the tank for leaks and ascertained that it was intact. Had the trip lasted more than 30 days, and it certainly would have if we had continued, we would have run out of fresh water for several days, which would have been disastrous.

I learned an important lesson here. Don't be afraid of insulting the captain by double-checking. He should welcome an extra verification of such a vital element of the trip. Furthermore, I think we should make it a habit on a long passage to visually check water levels daily and to record our findings. It would be a good idea that hard-to-reach tanks be fitted with water level gauges.

Sunday night, Jennie, who had been Sami's girl friend since October, dropped a bombshell. She announced that it's finished between her and Sami. He doesn't love her any more and therefore she can't continue the trip with us under those circumstances. She'd be flying back home on the first flight she could book. We were all shocked and dismayed, as you can well imagine.

We would thus have to share the watches with three people instead of four, but with an auto helm, the task wouldn't be particularly daunting.

The plot thickens. Monday night, after long reflection, Rachel, who is co-owner of the boat with Sami, thought it would be a good idea to remind him that she never planned on sailing year-round and still intends to limit her sailing with Sami to six months out of the year. Now that she has a new love, Jake in her life, she will want to go back to the US periodically to spend time with him.

The plot thickens even more and Sami drops his own bombshell. If Sami still had a life companion with him, it wouldn't matter that Rachel left the boat six months per year. However, under the new circumstances he would find himself alone in the middle of the Pacific or some distant anchorage and alone for much of his circumnavigation. He had spent four months alone on his boat in Trinidad last year and hated the solitude, even if he was in an environment where he could meet other cruisers. Our clearance papers out of Mexico having been arranged, Sami found himself in a jam. He had to make a quick decision. He felt he had no choice but to cancel the trip to the Marquesas. He could not envisage travelling around the world alone, so he abandoned that great project. I suggested we sail north to Vancouver so Sami might spend some time in that beautiful part of the world to think things over. However, he decided to sail *Three's Company* back to Lake Ontario via Panama and to put her up for sale.

During my travels I've met many men who sail single-handedly and live alone on their vessels. In many cases it would be a man of a certain age who loves travel and loves sailing. Most of these men would wish to have a life companion with whom to share their passion. But, in the sailing world there are just not enough women to go around. Women are perhaps less willing than men to embrace the inconveniences and discomforts of life aboard a small boat. I could talk at length about the trials and tribulations of preparing a meal at sea. Women are perhaps less inclined to face the challenges imposed by the whims of the weather or the woes of the sea. I could bend your ear describing the gymnastics required to work one's way from the companionway to the forepeak inside the boat in heavy seas. Another thing that might turn women away from life at sea is the possibility of being mistreated by a captain who thinks he's king and dictator and makes all the decisions without consultation. I've heard such stories!

Another factor that might have troubled Sami and that would influence his long term plans, was his financial situation. Since his revenues didn't cover his expenses, he couldn't avoid getting in debt.

That wasn't supposed to be part of the picture. Although Sami would be quite capable of handling the boat single-handedly, he is not the type who would enjoy sailing alone and would continually be on the lookout for crew with whom to share the joys of discovery. Thus he decided to sail *Three's Company* back to Lake Ontario and put her up for sale.

The long and the short of it is that we are no longer sailing to French Polynesia. Instead, we will sail to Panama, transit the canal, sail across the Caribbean north of Cuba, head for New York and motor to Lake Ontario through the inland waterways. So we will leave Mexico tomorrow and I will accompany Sami and Rachel for the trip.

Of course I'm disappointed, because I had spent a lot of time preparing for the South Pacific islands, but the Marquesas won't disappear from the face of the Earth just because I can't go this year. The trip to Lake Ontario will provide me with new experiences. So it's an opportunity I can't dismiss.

Life is full of surprises, eh?

A Whole Ocean at Last!

THIRD DISPATCH BY ROBERT – EL SALVADOR

Friday, April 24, 2009

I'm presently seated at a table near the pool at the Bahía del Sol Hotel Marina. If you look at your Atlas, you'll see that I'm back where I was a month ago, not even halfway between Acapulco and Panama. And you'll be asking, "What on Earth is going on with *Three's Company* and her crew? When Robert last wrote he said his next stop would be Panama."

Well, here's the story:

On April 9th, it was with a little disappointment that I watched Acapulco Bay recede in the distance as *Three's Company* motored her way towards the open ocean. For one thing, an important part of the crew was missing with the sudden and unexpected departure of Jennie, and for another thing, my chance of crossing over to the Marquesas was no more.

In spite of all this, it was with a measure of optimism that I envisaged the long passages ahead, totalling 3700 nautical miles on waters that would be new to me. The first leg would be from Acapulco to Panama under following seas, since the wind, waves and current would be behind us, pushing us along gently over the 1250 miles separating us from the famous canal. Transiting the canal with ships having a displacement thousands of times that of ours would have been a unique experience. The second leg of the trip would have taken us to the San Blaas islands, 50 miles to the east of the canal, renowned as the most beautiful of the Caribbean. For the third leg, we would have sailed 1300 miles to Key West, Florida, rounding the west tip of Cuba. The fourth part would have been from Florida to New York via the intercoastal waterway and the coast. Finally, we would have motored up the Hudson River and the Erie Canal to our final destination on Lake Ontario.

Once outside Acapulco Bay, we sailed with a northwest wind – a wonderful tail wind! And the current was in our favour this time! We raised our sails, headed offshore for a while then set our sails for Panama. Ah! The joy of sailing with 15 to 18 knot winds under a reefed main sail and full genoa!

Sometimes at sea, as in life, one must endure difficult conditions in order to deserve a moment of sheer pleasure. At last, we were enjoying pure bliss...the sensation of the breeze on one's neck; the gentle yawing motion of the vessel, whose movement is stabilized by the aerodynamic effect of the keel through the water and the sails through the air, the sensation of the power of the sails when they aspirate the air like a whale regaling itself on the abundant krill on its passage; the sound of the bow wave being thrust aside as our little ship ploughs through the water; the feeling of the vessel coming to life, like a race horse responding to the command of its rider. At last the sea and the wind had resumed their normal state, and now they were providing conditions propitious to the movement of a vessel equipped with sails. A quick calculation revealed that at this rate we would make landfall at Panama in ten days – or maybe less!

BUT...The God of the wind had something else in mind for us...at 2130 the wind dropped to 8 to 10 knots. Because we were experiencing a large residual swell caused by the good wind we had during the day the boat was now tossing from side to side. When she heeled to the windward side, the boom would swing towards the centreline then when it heeled to the leeward side, the boom would swing back into

A Whole Ocean at Last!

its position with a powerful whack. In no time this would tear the sail out of its slides. The solution was to affix a boom preventer. This consists of tying a long line to the aft end of the boom, passing the other end to the front of the boat and stretching it tight.

This worked to perfection...for half an hour...and the wind died down to nothing. But the swell was oblivious to the paucity of wind and continued rocking the boat. At this point the sails were simply flogging themselves to death, so we had no choice but to go bare poles. All night, we were shaken mercilessly. I had the graveyard shift, that is, the 0100 to 0400 watch, during which I was thrown around like in a Midway ride.

We lived a déjà vu of our El Salvador-Acapulco voyage. A bit of wind on the quarter, so we'd deploy the spinnaker. The wind would turn against us, forcing us to douse the spinnaker and sail close-hauled, tacking across our desired track. The wind would peter out and we'd motor for several hours until another breeze would entice us to raise the sails again...and so on.

"One thing for sure", I told my crew mates, "when we cross the Tehuantepec Gulf we will have wind".

This wide bay, a hundred miles from side to side, is the nemesis of every sailor who must sail across it. Upon navigating this body of water, one can expect winds of 25 to 50 knots. A "Tehuantepecker" is a powerful wind caused by a weather system in the Caribbean, which blows across the continent through a pass in the mountain range, and acts like a giant funnel. We didn't need to be concerned! *Three's Company* was not to be given the dubious gift of a Tehuantepecker. We ended up traversing the entire bay under motor upon calm seas.

Typically, on this trip we were sailing for 20 miles and motoring for 80. Our fuel reserve was drying up rapidly. We had used up two thirds of our diesel and still had 900 miles to go for Panama.

A wise sailor puts aside one third of his fuel for emergencies. So what next? Resign ourselves to waiting for wind and to trusting that Aeolus, the ruler of the winds, will care about us? Perhaps, but maybe not necessarily, since on our path lay El Salvador, a place we knew well, where clearing formalities are simple and inexpensive and where we could fuel up. So it was decided. We were heading for Bahía del Sol!

Thursday in the middle of the night, put put put. Out of fuel. We poured three of the four five-gallon carboys of diesel into the boat's tank, conserving the last carboy for transiting the sand bar at the entrance of Bahía. We fired up the engine. At sunrise we noticed that we were just a few miles from Acajutla, El Salvador, an enormous seaport. Why not stop here to fill up? We might be able to avoid the trouble of clearing in and out and then we could simply continue on to Panama.

Acajutla is in fact a gigantic seaport. Its main dock, a kilometre long, is an enormous loading pier where huge ships are tied for offloading bulk materials. No sign of any small dock where a boat like ours could tie up, nor any sign of a fuel dock. Sami hailed the port captain on the VHF radio. The English speaking man said that he could arrange for an agent to prepare the appropriate paper work and that the fuel dock was in another bay to our right. We couldn't figure out if he meant to our starboard or our port side, so we decided to forget this idea and to carry on to Bahía under sail. Tomorrow we would be there early even if the wind were light.

A Whole Ocean at Last!

The next day, Friday, April 17 at 0745, after eight days at sea, we reached the entrance of Bahía del Sol. Our captain hails the Marina on the VHF. A sailor whom Sami had met in previous ports, Alex, responds.

Before continuing, I have to explain about the topography of the entrance we are about to transit. The Costa del Sol is a beach on the Pacific side of a long peninsula 25 km long and 1 or 2 km wide, which runs parallel to the coast. Inside the peninsula is a very long bay, in which the Hotel is located. On the outside of the peninsula, the wind and the ocean swell carry the sand from the beach towards the entrance of the bay. The flood tide travels the length of the bay and then the ebb tide has to forge its way through the sand bar to reach the ocean, creating a meandering path. There would be no point in installing navigation buoys, since they would have to be repositioned every day.

Adding to the difficulty of recognising the path to take, there is the swell from offshore. As a wave barrels towards the shore, it must apply the brakes. The wave glides up the gradually sloping shore, forming a large hill of water in the shape of a roller, its crest breaking up and collapsing. When a boat comes in with the wave, it is transported as though it is surfing. Should a sailboat deviate from the deepest part of the path and run aground, the soft sand bottom wouldn't harm the hull, but the thousands of tons of water breaking up on the boat would smash it to smithereens in no time.

One would think, from what I just described, that no self-respecting boater would risk his life and boat to come into this bay. But that's not the case. The locals are accustomed to recognising the navigable path into the entrance. It is a matter of "reading" the breakers as they come up on shore. This is analogous to an art that I've had the chance of practicing when canoeing in rapids. The white water canoeist "reads" the water by observing the shape of the currents, waves and rollers, and thereby forms a good idea of where are the rocks and ledges at the bottom of the river. In the same way, through reading of the water, a Salvadorian guide can determine the path of the navigable route.

The Hotel marina provides the service of a guide to direct visiting boats into the bay in safety. Upon receiving a radio request for guidance from a boater on the outside, the Hotel reception sends a local guide in a ponga equipped with a 75 hp motor to meet the visiting boat. The passage must be timed with high tide and suitable wave conditions, which can sometimes necessitate a delay of days.

So Sami advises Alex that we are back in El Salvador and need to be guided into the bay. Alex assures us that he will alert the Hotel manager as soon as he arrives and arrange for a ponga to come to our aid. We're lucky. It is high tide and within an hour a ponga appears through the surf. The driver signals us to follow, then to accelerate. *Three's Company* barrels through at full throttle. A large wave lifts our boat and pushes us at 11 knots. And quite unexpectedly the rollers are behind us and we find ourselves in calm water. At 0855 we arrive at the marina dock.

After connecting hydro and water and installing the sunshade, we go to the bar to connect to our Internet umbilical chord. Rachel immediately "Skypes" Jennie (Skype is an application that allows one to use a computer as a telephone) to find out how things went after her tearful departure from Acapulco.

So Jennie, at the other end of the Skype connection in Ottawa, tells Rachel that she regretted the suddenness with which she broke up with Sami and left us in Acapulco. Rachel is astounded to hear Jennie say that she bought an airline ticket for Panama, as she wanted to meet us there to apologize for having left us the way she did. Then Rachel informed her,

"Jennie, we're not in Panama, we're in El Salvador."

"Oh, my God! A good thing you called me. My flight for Panama is scheduled for tomorrow morning."

Armed with this new information, Jennie changed her flight to come and join us at Bahía del Sol.

Instead of experiencing the greatest adventure of my life I found myself embroiled in a complex soap opera within which I had no role to play. It was a little like half-awaking from a dream and coming to the realization that the events one is witnessing are just that, a dream. Only, I wasn't dreaming; the drama that was taking place was for real. I'm one who never watches soap operas and here I am writing one. I'm not one to talk about the lives of others either. But we didn't total the vessel by running it aground, nor did we sink it by striking a whale, nor did we have to abandon ship due to damage in a storm. The reason we turned around was because of interpersonal events, and my story wouldn't be complete if I didn't explain the details of these relationships.

The day after her Skype conversation with Rachel, Jennie arrived in El Salvador. In the days that followed, she and Sami reconciled their differences and made up. Within hours of her return, they had become like young lovers who had just discovered each other.

Since I was unwittingly involved, I took it upon myself to offer Sami a little advice. I suggested that he take time to think things over before carrying out an irreversible decision like selling the boat and instead put the boat up on the hard in El Salvador for a few months. Sami did heed my counsel and chose to leave *Three's Company* in El Salvador until next October. Besides, after looking over the trip from here to Lake Ontario we calculated that there wouldn't be enough time to make it before hurricane season. A few days ago I accompanied Sami to make arrangements with a boatyard to reserve a space. We will be taking the boat out of the water next Monday April 27, after five days of preparation for haulout.

Afterwards, I will leave the boat and take some time to visit Central America for a few weeks. Now I'm surfing the Internet in order to plan some kind of itinerary.

What was supposed to be the voyage of a lifetime took an unexpected and undesired turn. However, there are many positive aspects to the experience. I learned about sailing on the Pacific and acquired many ideas on how to manage a boat for a long passage. For example, I've learned that on a long passage you should only use the engine for recharging the batteries and should only count on the sails to move the boat. I've known fascinating visits by marine wildlife, witnessed magnificent sunsets, and basked in glorious starry nights. I've gained practice at using the spinnaker, a sail that many sailors avoid using, because they don't want to make the effort to learn how to use it. I found myself in a situation where I was able to help friends overcome a difficult time of their lives by lending a sympathetic ear. And to top it off, the weeks to come will offer me the chance to discover natural and archaeological wonders in a fascinating part of the world I might not have visited otherwise.

I will keep good memories of this trip, even if at times Aeolus was uncooperative and a human drama caused the cancellation of the voyage to the ultimate destination. A wonderful summer, a loving wife, a daughter, a son and a lovely grand daughter are waiting for me at home.

A Whole Ocean at Last!

FOURTH DISPATCH BY ROBERT – GATINEAU, CANADA

Thursday, May 14, 2009

I basked in the breathtaking sight that unfolded before me on the beach of Belize. Beyond the white sand beach, transparent turquoise and grass-green shades of water intermingled, and near the horizon, under a perfect blue sky, white breakers were rolling off the second largest reef in the world. The sound of the breaking waves was enhanced by the enchanting music of Pachelbel on Itunes, creating a mood of absolute tranquility. This moment of bliss was sufficient to mitigate the suffering I endured last week and the sequels I'm dealing with today.

Having failed the extraordinary opportunity to sail across the Pacific to the paradise-like islands of French Polynesia, I was resolved to make the best of my stay in Central America before flying home.

The previous Wednesday *Three's Company* crewmembers and I had met Jorge Martinez, a Salvadorian tourist guide, at a fund-raising barbecue offered by a lady who runs a not-for-profit English language school for local children of Bahía del Sol. Jorge proposed an interesting itinerary to provide us with a brief glance at El Salvador, Honduras and Guatemala. If we could muster a group of six, he would provide transportation in his van, good hotel accommodation, entry fees to the attractions, services of a professional local guide for the archaeological sites, and would leave us in Flores in northern Guatemala at the end of the fourth day.

The previous week Sami and I accompanied the ponga driver to guide two sailboats through the sand bar into the bay. One of those boats, a beautiful Tayana, belonged to two American men, John and Shawn, of very disparate age and appearance. The former, tonsorially grey, about 60 years old, was a retired scientific equipment sales representative. Fair skinned, John seemed to have a permanently reddish face. Shawn, only 28, had dark olive skin and a permanent, black, two-day stubble. He could have easily been taken for a middle-east terrorist. In spite of his young age, Shawn had acquired a wealth of experience, having navigated from one job to another all his life. He had, amongst others, held a job as debt collector, psychic for a 900 phone line, multiple restaurant jobs, male nurse. He made us laugh every time the subject of conversation led to his declaring that he had held a job related to the topic of discussion.

So at the planned time on April 28, Jorge and his driver picked us up: Sami, Jennie, Rachel, the two Americans and myself. En route to our first point of interest, Jorge made a stop at a restaurant specializing in El Salvador cuisine so we could sample pupusas, a specialty of his country. It consists of a tortilla that is stuffed with either refried beans, cheese, ham, chicken, veggies or a combination thereof. Although I haven't taken a liking to Central American tortillas, I found pupusas quite edible.

Next, Jorge brought us to the public square in Santa Ana, a typical small Salvadorian town. The main square teemed with activity. People from 7 to 77 strolled amongst the numerous vendors who sold corn on a cob, deep fried plantain, homemade potato chips (not French fries), tacos, tortillas, pupusas, empanadas, fresh mango-on-a-stick, fried chicken and a variety of strange food items that I had not seen before. The theatre, the town hall and the bank were among the buildings of Spanish colonial style that ringed the square.

Our next point of interest was the village of Ceren, which Jorge characterized as the Pompeii of the Americas. This inappropriate term risked raising unreasonable expectations with those like myself who had seen the real Pompeii. The very rich roman city was buried under a heavy layer of hot ash when the Vesuvius erupted in the year 79 AD, leaving behind petrified bodies, which today can be seen lying in their beds. As with Pompeii, the town of Ceren was entirely buried with volcanic ash on the day of eruption in the year 595 AD. But instead of elaborate stone houses and beautifully paved streets, the houses of Ceren were modest adobe constructions. Whereas most of the city of Pompeii has been excavated, only a dozen structures have been the object of the same attention in Ceren. The site comprises foundations and walls of private houses of working class people, a common kitchen, a sauna and the shaman's house. What is interesting, though, is that unlike the Roman city, which was surprised in the middle of the night, consigning all of its inhabitants to an instantaneous death, residents of Ceren had time to escape. Because no bodies were found and all personal objects were left in place, it is assumed that Ceren's citizens just barely had time to skedaddle.

Next day we changed countries to visit the ancient Maya city known as Copán in Honduras. The common elements of Mayan societies was their advanced knowledge of mathematics, astronomy, stone sculpture, pottery, a hieroglyphic writing system, an advanced calendar based on 19 months and the elaboration of a complex mythology. Dating back from the 5th to the 9th centuries AD, Copán is an imposing archaeological site, which has been partially excavated and restored. Jorge describes Copán as the Paris of the Mayan world, due to its artistic wealth. Its history has been immortalized by hieroglyphic sculptures adorning temple steps, tombs, sacrificial tables and obelisks. The most striking feature of the Mayan world, and its most shocking one, was its barbaric human sacrifices. To ensure that the Gods were satisfied with the quality of the human sacrifice, the victim was straddled on his or her back onto a special altar equipped with canals to collect the blood. The shaman had to, in one fell swoop, cut open the chest and pull out the still warm, beating heart.

I'm really thankful to live in an era where science has dispelled (most) myths, superstition and bizarre religious beliefs. I am therefore completely liberated from irrational beliefs, whether it be faith in rabbits' feet, goblins, spirits, reincarnation, transubstantiation, or fear of a jealous, vengeful god that scrutinizes my every thought and action. Do I believe in a Creator? I can't commit myself to accepting or rejecting this hypothesis for lack of evidence. I therefore leave this question open. There are some grand questions that the puny human brain may never fathom. I observe human behaviour, and I've come to believe that all our actions are the product of our genes, whether the behaviour consists of buying a more expensive car than that of the neighbour, flirting with the opposite sex, or deciding to take a flight to a distant territory.

The following day was spent on the road, covering the 450 km that separated us from the island city of Flores in northern Guatemala. In the evening we strolled amongst the shop and restaurant-lined streets getting acquainted with the town. The day after, subsequent to a further hour on the road, we arrived in Tikal, the New York of the Mayan cities, according to Jorge's characterization. Here the religious leaders played a game of one-upmanship to see who would build the tallest temple. The highest one of all, Temple IV, topped 72 metres, including the large stone billboard-like structure stuck at the top of the prayer platform. Scaling the monument allowed us to see in the distance two other of these monuments, as well as mounds covered with vegetation, hiding more temples of the same kind, which might be unearthed by archaeologists in the future.

What I find most striking in the region of Northern Guatemala is the poverty and paucity of the soil cover. Everywhere fields are strewn with rock, weeds and burned vegetation. Steep slopes are denuded of forest cover for conversion into pastureland or for cultivation of a few miserable sticks of maize. It is most likely that what brought the Mayan civilization to its collapse, was a combination of overpopulation and depletion of the soil. Undoubtedly, these ancient people got trapped in the mortal game of the exponential function. You may find an example of such a disaster in this fantastic web site ☺, http://peakoilandhumanity.com (Select English, then Chapter 6). It is just a matter of one final doubling of the population to send the whole civilization down the tube. I think that Albert Bartlett makes an interesting point when he claims that: "The greatest shortcoming of the human race is our inability to understand the exponential function."

The day after our visit to Tikal, our group dissolved itself. John and Shawn returned to El Salvador with our guide and Sami, Jennie and Rachel left for Belize.

I was now free to embark upon my next adventure: a trek in the jungle in the heart of the Mayan Biosphere Reserve. In fact, all the travel agencies in Flores promoted the same tour, a six-day expedition to the largest Mayan city, El Mirador, still uncovered by archaeologists. Although the total distance was considerable, at 140 km, the trail would be easy, since it is well travelled and relatively flat. Furthermore, all our equipment, baggage and drinking water would be carried by pack horses. The price was reasonable and a new group (of 3 including myself) was leaving the day after tomorrow. The young Israeli couple with whom I would be travelling were friendly, and to top it off, they spoke English and Spanish.

There is something that I refrained from telling in this dispatch. As I was in the hotel room selecting what to take on my adventure, I realized that many of the safety related items I would need were at home in Canada. I felt increasingly anxious. This was the first time ever that I was to join a *guided* trek, as I'd always planned my own adventures either alone or with friends. I would have felt more at ease if I had been trusting the planning to a reputable organization like the Black Feather group in Canada, but I knew nothing about this organization in Northern Guatemala. When I left home it was to sail across an ocean on a boat with two nurses who had with them a substantial pharmacy and the basics for performing emergency surgery. For that reason, I had left my personal first aid kit at home. If I had planned this from home there are some essential items I would have taken with me: water sterilizing filter in case the *agua purificada* was not safe; freeze dried food rations, as I was certain that the guides wouldn't respect sanitary precautions; my own camping cookware and utensils, also for sanitary reasons.

That afternoon I visited six pharmacies to look for band-aids, Imodium and oral rehydration salts. I was able to locate Immodium in one of the pharmacies and the sixth one had one single yellowed box of band-aids in its display cabinet. Back in my hotel room when I opened the box, I found a bunch of dried up slivers of crumbling paper and plastic strips, as the adhesive had completely vanished.

The feeling of dread was mounting. I had reached the point where I questioned whether or not to abandon the project and just show up at the tour company office the next morning and tell the man that I was not able to go. The cost of the six-day tour was modest and the financial loss would be inconsequential.

Then I rationalized that I had no valid grounds for worrying; that dozens do this trip every year; that everything will be all right; that I just had to have confidence in myself. I reasoned that I was succumbing to irrational fear. And I asked myself, "How many times will I have an opportunity like this? I'm already here on the biosphere's doorstep. It would be silly to back out now."

The expedition started early Sunday May 3. We boarded the tour operator's minibus with our baggage and off we were, to the most northerly Guatemalan town, Carmelita, the starting point of the trek. After half an hour of paved road, we endured two hours of a tooth rattling ride on a rough dirt road. The further north we drove, the poorer the land, the houses and the people appeared. A common practice is to burn the vegetation before the next rainy season to adjust the pH of the soil. Everywhere the fields and roadside were blackened. Houses were made mostly of unpainted boards with thatch or tin roofs. Some of the houses were of unfinished cinder block or made of two-inch trees lashed together vertically to form the outside walls.

I suffered a shock upon arriving in Carmelita. The village was simply a group of these small, very poor houses with no evidence of any public structure that might resemble a church, a school, a government building. At 0915 the van dropped us off in front of an unpainted wooden house with a tin roof and with a front porch bearing two plastic tables and chairs. A woman greeted us and within minutes, our breakfast appeared on the table – three plates decorated with red bean purée, scrambled eggs and white rice accompanied by a basket of tortillas covered with a dirty cloth.

It's when I asked the way to the toilet that I realized the extent to which this household was poor. The lady pointed towards the back and signaled me to walk through the house to the backyard. The house had no floor, being built directly on the ground. However, it was tidy and the earth floor had been freshly swept. The house had no doors, only old bedsheets hanging on the doorframes. Getting across the yard to reach the outhouse entailed tiptoeing between the scampering chicks and piglets.

It then dawned upon me that the greatest danger menacing me on this expedition would not come from jaguars, crocodiles, snakes or scorpions, but from microorganisms invisible to the naked eye.

Contrary to myself, the Israeli woman, Nufar and her partner Giore (nicknamed Gigi), seemed to be enjoying their meal, and apparently during their four months in Central America they had cultivated a taste for the sticky beans and pasty tortillas.

Having completed their compulsory military service, the young couple, both of whom were aged 23, had planned this eight-month backpacking trip through America for a long time. The imposing young man, with a full head of long, black curls and a short, well trimmed beard had sparkling blue eyes and an engaging smile. His fair-skinned girlfriend was tall and slim, bore a perfect Greek nose, held her hair in a pony tail and had a smile like the Mona Lisa's. They made a handsome couple. Having been fascinated and disturbed by the never-ending Israeli-Palestinian conflicts, I was itching to ask them a question, but had to wait for an appropriate time when I got to know them better.

As soon as we finished eating, our guide Edi and his assistant Umberto were waiting for us with the loaded horses. We began walking at a moderate cadence. The terrain is very muddy during the rainy season, so it was opportune to be doing this in the dry season. In the lower regions the trail showed long stretches of dried, black mud where the horses' hooves had sunk 12 to 18 inches during the previous rainy season, leaving deep holes in the hardened mud.

The whole northern part of Guatemala belongs to the Biosphere, a supposedly protected zone. To enter or leave the area, one had to drive through two different guarded check points. The guard throws a cursory glance into the vehicle and lifts the gate with casual indifference. Thus, I suppose, he has satisfied the requirements for the area to qualify as a biosphere reserve, ascertaining that no species of fauna and no artifact of ancient art has been illegally removed.

My worries about my arthritic hip, my arthrosed big toe, my osteoarthritic knee, the bunion on my left big toe and my plantar fasciitis all evaporated when, after two hours of walking, nothing hurt. The worst discomfort was the extreme sweating, drenching my clothes making them feel as though I had walked from one end to the other of a car wash.

A troop of spider monkeys was waiting for us in ambush, high up in the treetops. Their piercing cries were proof that our intrusion into their territory was not welcome. One of them confirmed this observation; it went about breaking branches and pitching them at us with anger.

Five hours and 25 km after having left Carmelita, we arrived at our first camp, located in the Mayan town of Tintal. Immediately upon arriving, a lonely archeologist grabbed onto us to talk to us about his map of the village and to explain in great detail the history of this region of the Mayan world. All I could think of was that I wanted to sit down. I did retain some of what he had explained, however.

He mentioned the system of canals that surrounded the city, which were 8 metres deep and 15 metres wide. The map showed a long straight line joining the city of Tintal with that of our next objective, the largest of the basin's cities, El Mirador. A system of roads joined El Mirador to its satellite cities to favour trade. This road was 40 km long, straight as an arrow, built up to 2 metres high and six metres wide and was paved with limestone, whose white colour made night travel easier. They didn't have draw animals nor had they invented the wheel, so all transport was accomplished with human energy.

When this city was abandoned 2300 years ago, Mother Nature invaded the man-made structures with every weapon she had in store: ultraviolet rays, wind, lichens, mosses, root plants, water, hurricanes, earthquakes, animal droppings, microorganisms, insects, etc. The result was a gradual accumulation of new soil and plants which eventually blanketed the entire metropolis with jungle. Now even the largest temples are hidden. Our lonely archeologist explained that unlike Tikal, the Mayan cities in this northern part of the country have not yet been unearthed. He showed us an artist's impression of the city reconstructed from ground imaging radar scans, showing a beautiful, orderly city with an advanced architecture.

Umberto had already set up the tents and put a kettle on the fire. I asked him for a cup of tea. The purified water, being at ambiant temperature, was warm as peepee, so it was unpleasant to drink. If you can't drink it cold, just as well to drink it very hot. Umberto dug into a green garbage bag, rattled some dishes, pulled out a mug, examined the inside, threw it back into the bag, pulled out another, examined its interior, gave it a shake, looked again, wiped the inside carefully with his fingers, checked it out again, was satisfied, filled it with tea and handed it to me with a smile of satisfaction. He had probably not heard about microorganisms.

We climbed the north pyramid, 50 metres high. It was eerie. No sign of any man-made structure. You get the impression that you're climbing a very steep, natural mountain enshrouded with trees and vegetation. The only evidence that this was once a great temple is the presence of a few squared stones at the summit. From the top we admired a 360-degree panorama of forest as far as the eye could see. Toucans circled around us with their undulant wing movement. Their bright yellow color adds to the shape of their long, unwieldy beak, to make them look like flying bananas. Directly to the north-east, far in the distance, we could see a hill; this is the largest of the El Mirador temples, 40 km away, our destination for the next day. We waited for sunset, reflecting on the fact that in the Pre-Classic Mayan era, this time of the day was the object of a daily ceremony on the very spot we were occupying. The strange roaring of the howler monkey dominated the sound waves of the jungle and fills me with wonder every time I hear it.

It was still dark and I heard the clatter of pots and pans. I peered at my watch through half-closed eyes: it was 0400. I turned over and went back to sleep. I woke up again and heard Edi's voice: "Senior Roberto, son las cinco" – five o'clock, the dawn of our second day. We were to take advantage of the coolness of the morning. After breakfast we resumed our march. The cadence was easier than it was the first day. "If I can withstand this day, I thought, the longest of the trek with its 40 km, the rest should go well." We came across a couple of magnificient Ocellated turkeys that scampered into the bush. I heard bird songs from species whose Spanish names I didn't catch when pronounced by our unilingual guide.

We stoped for lunch at an abandoned Chicleros camp. Chicle (gum) collection is one of the commercial activities that provide value to the forest Reserve for the local people. In order to protect the resource, the camp is moved yearly over a seven year cycle. There is also an active industry of selective cutting of precious lumber that is allowed under the park rules. However, there is an even larger illegal black market for the valuable trees whose product is carried across the Mexican border a few kilometres to the north. The incentive for this activity is very great, as one mahogany tree can be worth three years of salary for a forest worker. The tragedy is that the demand for these products cannot have any other effect than to increase as the world population continues its relentless augmentation. It's as simple as that. My voice for population control is but a cry in the wilderness of world trade, industrialization, overexploitation of resources, overconsumption and instant selfgratification.

After lunch we continued our journey. Advancing was simply a matter of commanding my right foot to move ahead of the left one, then left ahead of right, alternately, and voilà! We arrived at our destination at 1410. Tents got erected without my input and the sandwiches appeared as per magic. It was too hot to lounge around doing nothing. Nufar, Gigi and I went for a little walk and met a Russian couple, Dmitri and Anna, who were part of another group. They spoke good English, so I had somebody else with whom to exchange conversation. The couple were medical doctors of Russian origin doing their fellowship in a New York hospital.

They were ardent outdoors people who enjoyed visiting places that are off the beaten path. They planned and reserved their jungle tour some time ago from home, but chose to do it on horseback instead of on foot. I had that option, but since I had never done much horseback riding, that would have been an unwise idea for my fanny.

The schedule showed that tomorrow we would spend the day exploring the El Mirador site. Then on the fourth, fifth and sixth days we would return via a different route, taking in another ancient Mayan site. It is in El Mirador that we find Danta, the largest pyramid in the world with its 2,800,000 cubic metres of rock fill, bigger yet (in volume) than the giant pyramids of Giza. However, with its 72 metres of height, it doesn't match its Egyptian cousins in this respect.

Plus ça change, plus c'est la même chose: The more it changes, the more it is the same. In the days of the Mayas, it was a contest to see who could build the biggest pyramid, the most impressive temple, the largest city. Today, it is a contest to determine who can build the largest high-rise, which city will build the largest convention centre, which country can host the olympics in the most ostentatious way. At the personal level, it is a contest to see who will live in the largest house, who can drive the most expensive car, who can watch the largest TV set. The striving for domination, the need for conquest, the search for ways of attracting admiration are firmly wired into our genes.

For the second supper of the expedition, we had spaghetti with tomato sauce and ...red liquefied beans. I declined to eat the beans but had a hearty dish of the pasta, accompanied with a cup of tea that tasted of swamp. Very early, I went to my tent and fell into a profound sleep.

At midnight I awoke suddenly with an indigestion. This was the beginning of a whole night of vomiting and diarrhea. Every half hour I had to rush out of the tent to evacuate both ends. By sunrise I was exhausted and completely washed out.

Since this was to be a day of rest, everybody arose late. Around nine o'clock, Dmitri approached me. He reminded me that he and his wife were doctors and he asked me to describe my symptoms. I answered in the negative to the questions of whether I felt abdominal pain, had fever or blood in my stools. He concluded that I must be suffering from some kind of food poisoning. My guide might have used swamp water to make the tea and omitted to let it boil long enough. He told me: "The danger, in your case, is that you might be severely dehydrated. People die of that, you know." There was nothing in the station's medical kit with which to administer intravenous electrolyte solution, but Dmitri was given a few envelopes of electrolyte powder to mix with water. He advised me to drink as much of it as possible, sipping it slowly. I forced myself to take in a few millilitres at a time of the foul tasting solution. No sooner that I'd consumed a cup of it, than I would expel it in a powerful jet. I persisted, little by little. It seemed to work. But at 1430 everything I had kept down since late morning came up with a vengeance.

Dmitri then told me he was worried, especially since I was stuck in the sweltering heat of the jungle so far from civilization. The organizers of these expeditions had not foreseen evacuating a victim of an accident or medical emergency, except than by helicopter. However, the radio was not working, so there was no way to call for help. The only way to get me out of here at this time would be on horseback. He advised me to leave as soon as possible. I pleaded with him that I had not ridden a horse in thirty years and that 12 hours of horseback would kill me. He assured me: "Getting out of here by horse won't kill you, but dehydration could". He conferred with Edi, Nufar and Gigi, and all agreed to leave immediately (they on foot) to accompany me on horseback.

An hour later, camp was taken down, the horses were loaded, I climbed onto my horse and we were en route. For the first fifteen minutes, I managed to support myself on the stirrups, but afterwards, I was so weak that all my weight rested on my butt, which made for a bumpy and painful ride. The saddle was hard and lumpy and uncomfortable. However, the alternative, to walk, would have been impossible. I would simply not have had the strength. Since I had no choice in the matter, I resolved to hang onto the horn of the western saddle and to hold out to the very end.

Darkness came and with it a new difficulty: avoiding overhead branches. Occasionally, when my eyes closed from fatigue, I would be awakened by a branch in the face. At one point an invisible branch robbed me of my hat and another struck my glasses and bent the frame out of shape. Another, more sturdy branch wacked me across the forehead and came close to catapulting me off my mount. At long last, seven hours later, at 2145, we arrived in Tintal, having covered a little more than half the distance to Carmelita.

The next day at five o'clock, Edi bent over my tent door: "Senior Roberto..." At 0550 we were en route again. My strength was coming back, as I was finished vomiting. I felt better. From the height of my perch I could even admire the warm morning light beaming through the branches and breathe deeply the fresh morning air. "I will survive!"

Once in Carmelita, a small, commercial bus took us to Flores and I survived that horribly rough road. I was then able to eat and drink. I still had diarrhea and was going to have it for two more days, but I was out of danger. In retrospect, we could have waited till the following day to leave and have avoided the hazards of travelling at night – and maybe I could have continued the hike.

I invited Nufar and Gigi out for supper to thank them for their comprehension and empathy, as they had showed an exceptional degree of compassion. They were both vegetarian out of principle. From the conversations we had along the trip, I observed that these two fine persons are sensitive, considerate, courteous and of high moral standard, which lead me to the question I wanted to ask them. Nufar, as a woman, served her two years of compulsory military service in a special nursery for children from problem families. Giore had to endure a strict military training programme and served as border guard. I asked him how he rationalizes having served a regime that is known for its brutality. He answered,
"Somebody has to do the work and somebody will. If it's not me, then it would be somebody who is more brutal and less conciliatory than I am."

Two days later my diarrhea was over and I was boarding the bus for Belize, a tiny country bordered by Guatemala on the west, the Caribbean sea on the east and Mexico`s Yucatan on the north. It was to be a three day rest period before going home. My main activity was a snorkling excursion on the barrier reef, the second largest in the world. Twenty-five years previously, I had observed an extremely rich marine life and 200 feet of visibility on the coral reef at the south of Cayo Largo, Cuba. I've never seen anything like it since. I was hoping that the Belize reef would be just as splendid. However, whereas I saw some large and many small fish, the coral was in bad condition, much of it either broken or dead. Since many species of fish depend on coral reefs for their spawning ground, this doesn't augur well for the oceans' chance of feeding humanity in the future.

The day after this dive, I woke up with pain in my right eye, which was tearing so much that the tears were coming out of my nose. The following day the pain was worse still and furthermore, I could not tolerate light. I consulted a doctor who diagnosed my condition as island conjunctivitis and prescribed antibiotic-prednizone drops, which, as it turned out, did more harm than good.

Monday was the day of my flight back home. Micheline was waiting for me at the airport upon my arrival late in the evening. What a joy, to come home into a country that is organized and rich! The following day presented me with glorious sunshine. Nature was extruding leaves of a tender green shade and the apple trees and lilacs were in bloom. We went for lunch at Dow's Lake with my mother-in-law and Micheline's brother André, her sister Louise and brother-in-law Nigel. The air was pure and fresh and it was so good to be wearing a light sweater instead of enduring the crushing heat. What fortune to live in the beautiful Ottawa region, with its walkways and its driveways decorated with hundreds of thousands of colorful tulips, its rivers, its Gatineau Park.

For the next few days I will be nursing my bruised rump and my eye infection, but I will revel in the thought that I'm so lucky to have been born in this wonderful country where you don't see armed guards on every corner, where there is opportunity for everybody and where there is toleration and respect. The day when I took my first breath in Ottawa 67 years ago, I won the lottery!

End of dispatch.

"Mr. Bériault, I'm afraid the situation is very serious. The infection has invaded the entire cornea and may have crossed over to the anterior chamber."

The news Dr. Bhargava, my cornea specialist was announcing was shocking. In plain English it meant that the difficult to treat fungal infection had overgrown the entire cornea, the transparent window to the eye, and may have crossed over and invaded the fluid inside the eyeball.

The first day I arrived in Canada I contacted Bruce, an ophthalmologist, a friend of the family. He asked me what I had been doing and I told him that I'd recently been in Central America and partook in some snorkeling in Belize. I didn't think of telling him about the branches that had struck my face in the jungle. He noted structures on the surface of the cornea that looked like what he had seen in patients many times before, a herpes simplex viral infection. The prednisone the Belize doctor had prescribed was effective in reducing the pain, but lowered the local immunity of the eye, which favoured the spread of the infection. Bruce put me on antiviral eye drops. After five days there was no improvement, so in addition to the drops, he had me take another antiviral drug in the form of capsules by mouth. At the end of two weeks the pain was very intense and the infection had spread to the stroma, the inside layer of the cornea. My friend could not do anything more for me at this stage and referred me to a colleague, a cornea specialist, Dr. Bhargava.

The specialist examined my eye under the slit lamp and asked me if I had been struck by vegetable matter during the trip in Central America. I remembered that night on horseback, being repeatedly struck in the face by branches, and one in particular that had bent my eyeglasses out of shape. This was an "Ah Ha" moment. Combining this information, with the wisdom of hindsight of two weeks of unsuccessful antiviral treatment, he recalled cases he had seen when he did his fellowship in a New York hospital, a referral centre for patients from around the world. He suspected that it must be a fungal infection, an extremely rare condition in northern latitudes, which Canadian doctors never have the chance to see, but a fairly common ailment closer to the Equator. Before starting treatment he had to confirm his diagnosis by culture. Scrapings of the cornea were sent to Bacteriology for culture and two days later a diagnosis of fusarium keratitis was confirmed. Unfortunately, the intervening two days allowed the infection to spread further.

Dr. Bhargava immediately put me on antifungal eye drops to be taken every half hour for the first day then every hour for the next week. Unfortunately that drug wasn't working as hoped and 8 days later he changed my treatment for a double drug regimen. One of the drugs, Natacin, was not licenced in Canada and required Health Canada approval to be brought into the country. In addition, to kill any fungus that might have progressed further back into the eye, he arranged for Dr. Hurley, a retina expert to give me an intra-vitreal injection of a powerful antifungal chemical, that is, straight into the eyeball! Dr. Hurley said that they had never treated this kind of infection at the Ottawa Eye Institute and that they were going by textbook. Not a good day.

The Natacin would take two days to get regulatory approval and be shipped to Ottawa. It was supposed to arrive at the Eye Institute by courier on a Saturday morning, but the driver couldn't find the loading dock at the hospital so he took the shipment back to the warehouse. Dr. Bhargava was upset with this, so he drove to the warehouse himself and met me there to hand me the medicine. The shipping company would not accept anybody else's signature except the doctor's whose name was on the package. How many doctors would go to that extent to treat their patients?

For three days and nights I took the two medications every hour, which meant one or the other of the meds every half hour for three days and down to every hour for the next two weeks. Since I was blind of that eye and couldn't see the eyedropper, I had to have someone instill the drops for me. Micheline patiently got up for me throughout the nights and went to work during the days. My son Philippe and my daughter Natalie acted as nurse during the daytime.

The pain was excruciating. I would wake up in the middle of the night, sit in my lounge chair with a cold compress on my eye, waiting for the pain to subside so I could catch a few more winks. During the day I had to keep all the curtains drawn, and I could not go outside, as the light was too intense for my photophobic eye. The region of the eye was too painful to allow me to wear an eyepatch. Fortunately, this treatment worked and the infection appeared to have cleared away. After a month, my vision had improved, but the pain was still very intense. During this course, there were three other medications I had to take. One served to keep the iris from seizing up, another to lower the intra-ocular pressure and one to prevent a secondary infection from settling in.

Then 47 days after the onset of treatment, the unthinkable happened. The infection recurred – with a vengeance! This time it had crossed the cornea into the anterior chamber, behind the cornea. Since the epithelium, the transparent skin on the outside of the cornea had completely healed, the medication would not be well absorbed. So to counter this problem, the doctor debrided my eye. This consists of scraping away the 4 to 5 layers of epithelial cells (skin cells) on the cornea, along with thousands of nerve endings, opening a circle of denuded cornea about 6 millimetres in diametre. That wasn't all for that fateful day. To kill whatever might have crossed into the anterior chamber, I was given another intra-vitreal injection! That was a bad day.

The naked cornea was very sensitive for the next two months, creating the sensation of having sharp, pointy stones in the eye. You know what it's like to have a bit of dust in the eye. Well just imagine sharp, pointy stones! By October I wasn't having pain, only discomfort and the need to continue applying drops eight times a day until the end of the year. The application of toxic drugs for such a long time has caused a cataract and the trauma has left a large scar on the surface of my cornea. The cataract operation failed to improve my vision because that darned scar causes extensive diffusion of light, leaving me unable to read with my affected eye. However, 20/100 vision is enormously better than no vision at all.

My extreme sensitivity to light prevented me from going outside all summer, but it gave me much time to think about my sailing experiences. If there's a silver lining in this terrible affliction, it's that it forced me into tranquility and gave me the opportunity to begin writing this book.

Perhaps the adventure was destined for failure right from the start. It is important, before initiating a long passage on an OPY, to make sure that the vessel be seaworthy, that its safety equipment be up-to-snuff, that all the charts and navigation equipment be up-to-date and that the provisioning and water supply be adequate. Those things are the *physical* needs for a successful crossing. But, how do you examine the captain's and crewmembers' inner selves? How can you predict whether their relationships will negatively influence the course of the trip?

I've been asked if I regret my last adventure. What happened, the missed Pacific crossing and the partial loss of an eye resulted from a confluence of circumstances. Had there been wind during our first two weeks into our passage, we would have completed the objective of reaching the Marquesas. Had Sami and Jennie fallen out of love halfway across the ocean instead of three days before leaving Acapulco, we would have completed the project. Had I not met the two Russian doctors in the jungle, I wouldn't have had the advice to get out on horseback, I would have recovered from my food poisoning the next day, I would have never ridden a horse at night in the jungle and I would still have perfect vision in both eyes.

So the answer to that question is no, I don't have any regrets. I enjoyed spending time in a beautiful anchorage with all the advantages of a luxurious resort in Bahía del Sol, I enjoyed the sailing on the Pacific, when we were actually sailing that is, and I discovered a part of the world I would have probably never known otherwise. And if the eye infection had not occurred I never would have stayed in place long enough to write this book.

If there is anything useful *you, the reader* will get out of this book, it's this: If ever you are in the Guatemalan jungle and you get the urge to ride on horseback at night, you'll know you have to *wear a full face mask*!

I've been asked whether, in view of all that has happened, I'm thinking of quitting sailing. Nothing can be further from my mind. I'm still sailing, I still enjoy teaching and I continue to educate myself through courses and seminars on nautical subjects.

However, I still hadn't resolved the question of whether or not I would want to sail around the world. I still needed to experience crossing a whole ocean before making up my mind on this issue.

Across the Atlantic on a racing machine!

Chapter 12

Transatlantic on an Open 60!

I was putting the final touches on this book when a totally unexpected sailing opportunity presented itself. Six weeks after ending all treatments for my eye infection, an email came in from Dolores. She was forwarding to NCSS members a message that had been sent to all sailing clubs in Canada.

> 10th February, 2010
>
> Spirit of Canada Ocean Challenges today announced that a number of training sessions with Derek Hatfield on the ECO 60 Spirit of Canada will be offered to individual crewmembers during the summer of 2010 as Derek trains for the upcoming Velux 5 Oceans starting in October 2010. Crewmembers will be able to experience a full blown Open 60 first hand in open ocean conditions. The sessions will include transatlantic voyages between France and Canada...

Canada's most famous long-distance sailor was born in 1952, grew up in rural New Brunswick and spent his youth near the water and around boats. After completing a BAdmin at York University in Toronto, Derek joined the Royal Canadian Mounted Police (RCMP). It wasn't until his early 20s that he set foot on a sailboat for the first time: While in the RCMP a neighbour took him sailing on Lake Ontario. He was immediately hooked and got enamoured with racing. At first he raced as a member of a team and learned much by sailing with people who were better than he was. He honed his long-distance racing skills through a number of transatlantic races and became interested in solo racing. After ten years of police work as a commercial fraud investigator he worked for the Toronto Stock Exchange as Manager of the Compliance Department and later he joined National Bank Financial where he was responsible for regulatory requirements. For years he juggled between a demanding career, a first marriage that produced two boys who are currently in their thirties and his love of racing. Ultimately, he decided to retire from conventional jobs and took up a full time career in racing sailboats. Later he remarried and is now the father of two pre-school children.

His web site lists many of his sailing accomplishments before getting into round-the-world racing:

Rolex Sailor of the Year 2003;
Gerry Roufs Offshore Sailing Award 2003;
Ontario sailor of the Year 2003;
2nd place 1999 Bermuda One Two;
2nd place 1997 Bermuda One Two;
1st place and Overall Winner of the 1996 Legend Cup Transatlantic Race;
7th place 1996 Europe One Single-handed Transatlantic Race;
1st place 1994 Labatt's Single-handed Race Series.

His first single-handed circumnavigation race was the 2002 Around Alone on an Open 40 racing yacht which he built himself. Off the coast of Cape Horn huge seas pitchpoled and dismasted his first *Spirit of Canada*. He was able to repair the damage in Ushuaia, Argentina and completed the race at the age of 50, winning 3rd place in his class and becoming the 126th person in history to finish a single-handed race around the world. He then built another boat, an Open 60 in which he participated in the prestigious Vendée Globe race in 2008-9. Unfortunately, he was forced to retire after 50 days at sea when a large breaking wave caused the boat to capsize and break two of his mast spreaders. He had spent four years building the boat, but ended up having to sell her to pay off his debts.

I had attended Derek's seminar when he visited Ottawa on a motivational speaking tour, after his 2002 Around Alone race. He gave a fascinating account of his preparations, of his harrowing experiences at sea and of the difficulties Canadian racers have in obtaining sponsors.

Derek's offer of training sessions sparked my interest in long-distance solo races. Thereupon, I began my research into this intriguing human activity. I discovered that the defining event that brought solo circumnavigation into the public eye took place in 1967, when Sir Francis Chichester became the first to sail around the world by the clipper route and with only one stop. Furthermore, he had accomplished this heroic feat in record time, nine months and one day. Prior to this, 22 sailors had completed a solo voyage around the globe, but via the less dangerous route through Panama and/or Suez Canals, but also with multiple stops along their route and some of them over a period of several years.

The clipper route was adopted by large, very fast, square rigged commercial sailing ships in the 19th century. It allowed them to make use of the strong westerly winds of the Roaring Forties on the route from Europe, around Cape of Good Hope, Australia, New Zealand and Cape Horn before returning home. Their purpose for sailing this route was to exchange goods between Europe and the main trading centres along the route. Sailing for sport or glory didn't exist in those days. When Chichester arrived home at the end of his journey he was acclaimed by a crowd of 100,000 cheering fans. People began looking for what was the new challenge, what was the next frontier. Chichester had been forced to stop half-way to make extensive repairs. So there remained one sailing challenge that was yet to be explored: sailing around the world single-handed *but non-stop*. The general public was very excited about this type of adventure and got into the spirit of it. So did the media. Hence, the British Sunday Times came up with the idea of subsidizing the first non-stop, single-handed, round-the-world yacht *race* in 1968-1969, which they termed the Golden Globe Race.

Donald Kerr, a journalist of the epoch explains it this way:

> "There could be no greater challenge. The first part down to the South Atlantic was fairly kind, but then your troubles started. Once you rounded the Cape of Good Hope you were into the Roaring Forties that endless band of storms that circle the world. Then, thousands of miles later, you pass south of Australia, New Zealand and across the rest of the Pacific to Cape Horn. The seas become narrow there and as they funnel together they grow wilder. Then up past the Falkland Islands, across the Equator and back into the North Atlantic and you're on your way home."

Nine contestants started the race and only Robin Knox Johnston completed it, becoming the first person ever to have sailed around the world solo, non-stop and unassisted. Another racer, Bernard Moitessier could have won the race, as he was ahead of the pack. But after rounding treacherous Cape Horn and having spent seven months at sea and finding himself barely six weeks from home, instead of sailing up the Atlantic to kiss his wife and children and gather the trophy, he did something completely unexpected. He turned toward Cape of Good Hope at the bottom of South Africa, sailed yet halfway across the world again to end up in Tahiti after covering 45,000 miles. In his logbook he justifies his bizarre decision this way,

"I didn't know how to explain to Françoise and the children my need to continue towards the Pacific. To be at peace. I know I'm right. I feel it deeply. I know exactly where I'm going. How could they understand that? It is so simple, but it can't be explained in words."

When interviewed for the documentary *Deep Water*, his wife Françoise provides an insight into the mind of a man consumed by his passion for the sea,

"He was happy at sea, he was content. He found himself...I couldn't stop him. Bernard always did whatever he wanted. I couldn't say no. It was impossible, unthinkable... When a man decides to race a car or to go to the moon, you can't stop him. You can't stop a seagull from flying."

Deep Water underlines the difficulties racers have in finding good sponsors and good contracts. Donald Crowhurst, a contender in the Sunday Times Race, had locked himself into a contract that put him between a rock and a hard place, a deadly Hobson's choice, which forced him to start the race when his boat was still far from ready to sail.

Since then, other organizations have sponsored *fully crewed* round the world races, such as the Volvo Ocean Race, the Clipper Round the World, the Jules Verne Trophy and the BT Global Challenge. Then there is the Barcelona World Race, a race done with crews of only two sailors, which is pretty close to being single handed, but not quite. Probably the most challenging of all circumnavigation races are the single handed races of which there is the Velux Five Oceans (formerly the Around Alone) and the famous Vendée Globe, created in 1989.

When the 2008 Vendée Globe took place, I viewed many of the videos racers posted on the race's official web site. Some of the clips pictured the participants' daily progress, some bore witness to the skippers battling fierce storms, some filmed them describing the way they lived from day to day, some had them baring their souls as they described their inner feelings and some even recounted their lighter moments, such as when Samantha Davies offered her libation of Champagne to Neptune as she crossed the Equator. Never did I entertain the idea of emulating these heroines and heroes of the sea, but I felt that they were part of an interesting breed of the human species.

Mind you, I had never given any thought to crossing an ocean on a racing boat either. I'm basically a cruiser at heart. To date, and I think it will always be the case, sailing has been for pleasure and for sharing the pleasure with others. A sailboat is notably a very useful tool for visiting new places, an ideal transportation vehicle for the water, which can double as a part-time hotel or residence.

I've occasionally participated in the Wednesday night races on Lake Deschênes and discovered that racing can add an entirely different dimension to the activity of yachting. The technical aspect can be challenging, interesting and satisfying. The International Sailing Federation's rules place limits and boundaries on what the skipper can and cannot do in a race. And there are strategies to allow placing oneself ahead, while working within these limits and boundaries. Racing is also an excellent way to refine one's abilities in trimming the sails. When you are sailing for pleasure it doesn't matter whether the boat is "chugging along" at 6 knots or "barrelling through" at 7 knots. You'll get to your destination just the same. But when you are racing the whole objective resides in squeezing the most speed out of the sails and the rigging. Sailing with an expert like Derek would be an ideal opportunity for me to hone my sail trim skills.

I've witnessed that some racers take the sport too seriously for my taste. Some go as far as yelling curses at opponents who've crossed them on the water. Getting upset defeats the entire purpose of sailing, an activity that is fun and that promotes camaraderie and friendship. I didn't know any professional racers, but I suspected that if some amateurs take the sport too seriously, then professionals whose livelihood depends on their placing well might do so too. Nevertheless, there was no harm in inquiring about the offer that Dolores informed me about.

The training sessions Derek was offering would be an exceptional adventure that very few people in the world would ever have the chance of experiencing. I had no illusions that there would be a substantial cost to the courses being offered. These purpose-built racing boats themselves are worth millions of dollars, so just the interest on the investment would justify a fee of thousands of dollars for an Atlantic crossing. Furthermore, the experience of the expert and the rareness of the occasion would command almost any price. If I were to be accepted as crew, I would enjoy the incredible chance of spending two weeks sailing, working, living, talking with and learning from one of Canada's greatest sailing legends, a superstar, a celebrity!

I didn't think I'd have a snowball's chance in hell of being accepted, but I nevertheless sent an email message indicating my interest. Shortly after, I received the following information from Derek Hatfield's wife Patianne, his official communications representative:

> Thanks for the inquiry about the offshore training sessions. There are no specific skills required to be aboard, so all are welcome. The sessions are outlined below and are split into three different durations; 3, 7 and 15 days. We are asking that a donation be made to "Derek Hatfield".
>
> Currently the donation levels are as follows:
> 3 day training session: $2,500
> 7 day training session: $4,000
> 15 day transatlantic session: $7,500

As mentioned in the email today, we will endeavour to cover a number of areas relating to shorthanded sailing and give everyone an excellent experience on an Open 60. Each session will be limited to four people.

1. France to Halifax – May 1st to May 15th – 15 days
2. Halifax to Saint-Pierre Miquelon – June 5th to 7th – 3 days
3. Saint-Pierre Miquelon to Halifax – June 9th to 11th – 3 days
4. Bermuda to Halifax – July 1st to 7th – 7 days
5. Saint-Pierre Miquelon to Halifax – July 15th – 3 days
6. Halifax to La Rochelle, France – Sept 12th – 26th – 15 days

Derek was accepting four crewmembers on a first come first serve basis and to my surprise, racing experience wasn't a prerequisite. In fact, it appeared that experience of any kind wasn't required and that the only criterion for acceptance was the ability to dish out the big bucks. What I wanted was one of the Atlantic crossings and since I would be sailing with Anthony in May, I applied for the 6th session, the passage from Halifax to La Rochelle in September. Within a few days I got an answer. I was the fourth person to apply and thus I was to be part of the crew!

As I suspected, the cost for this trip was steep, but like most members of my species, I'm an expert at rationalization. I was able to justify the expense this way: If I had bought a forty foot boat ten years ago she would have cost me $75,000 in storage, docking and maintenance fees over the years. So now after ten years of frugality, I find myself with a large sum of money to spend. Viewed in this light, this extraordinary offshore experience cost less than owning a boat for one year – an irresistible bargain! Now, if ever you need financial advice, come and see me.

When I announced my good fortune to my friend David, he responded,

"Are you sure you want to submit yourself to a captain who will rule every aspect of your life for two long weeks? A guy who has spent six months alone at sea without seeing a single human being has got to be schizoid or obsessive compulsive! He'll be a slave driver: *'Bériault, up the mast! ... Bériault, scrub the decks!'"*

My ever cynical brother-in-law Nigel had a similar reaction,

"So you're going to cross the whole Atlantic Ocean with a nautical hermit! How do you know he won't be a captain Bligh? Have you lost your marbles, Robert?"

My friend Don, the one with whom I've sailed on several live-aboard cruises, "You'd never catch me crossing the Atlantic on that boat! Hatfield would have to pay ME, Robert."

I decided that it wouldn't really matter if my friends were right about the attitude of the captain. I figured that for two weeks, I could put up with whatever I'm handed. It was a risk I had to take.

My mother in law's reaction was, "Oh mon Dieu! That will be dangerous. Atlantic storms and hurricanes. You worry me so much, Robert."

Micheline was more supportive, "There are advantages to doing it this way. For one thing, because the boat is so fast, the passage will take half as long as it would in a standard sailboat. You'll be sailing with a man of great experience and the boat is unsinkable, so it will be safe."

Furthermore, it was going to be a learning experience, as the training would comprise several elements according to the *Spirit of Canada* web site:

> ...Crewmembers can expect to learn about aspects of preparing for shorthanded cruising and racing including the setup of the boat, nutrition, sleep patterns, weather analysis, safety at sea, shorthanded sail selection, medical emergency procedures, navigation and communications.

As a sailing teacher myself, I was interested in observing his pedagogical techniques and the organization of his curriculum and teaching materials. One of the difficulties that I encounter when teaching the Basic Cruising Standard is the lack of time, since I'm limited to 28 hours all told for the practical and theoretical components of the course. I just can't afford the luxury of using techniques like guided discovery or role playing. I have to restrict myself to lectures, demonstrations and flash cards. In two weeks Derek would have plenty of time to teach each subject in depth. The difficulty he would encounter would be how to deal with trainees of greatly differing experience levels. Regardless of how much or how little actual teaching there would be, even if there were to be none at all, I figured that I would be getting my money's worth.

As for the objections of my friends and my dear brother-in-law, I reasoned that they had to be wrong. The organization of a round-the-world race like Derek was preparing takes an enormous amount of work, much of which is carried out by volunteers. He had so far amassed donations from more than 7000 admirers who ponied up $100 or more to have their names printed on the hull of his boat. To motivate people to donate their time would require a respectful and considerate leader, which Derek had to be. This kind of endeavour also requires an extraordinary amount of funding. Whereas for the 2008 Vendée Globe race, Derek had to skimp by with little more than $3 million, several of the European racers, whose countries are much more supportive of sailing than is Canada, have enjoyed budgets of $6-7 million. In order to amass the necessary funding, a racer has to be good at selling himself and his sport, which would require excellent interpersonal skills, or so I reasoned.

I've always been fascinated by individuals who have pushed the limits of human endurance and achievement, whether it be explorers extending the geographical frontiers or athletes defying the impossible. As an observer of human nature, I'm intrigued by these extreme behaviours and interested in learning what drives them.

Although sailing is an activity that dates back thousands of years, it is only recently in its history that sailors have attempted the almost impossible feat of circumnavigating the world alone, and sometimes up the ante by doing it non-stop and unassisted. The difficulties in achieving this have been compared to climbing Mount Everest. Whereas more than 4000 people have ascended the world's highest mountain, fewer than 175 have sailed around the world alone in a race. Single-handed racers have to face the physical demands of handling the large and cumbersome rigging and complex manoeuvres of a high performance racing machine without help, watch the weather and update their navigation continually, be on watch 24 hours a day for several months at a time, withstand long periods without sleep during emergencies, put up with extremes of temperatures from the beating tropical sun to the icy waters of the southern seas, contend with solitude, content themselves with bland freeze-dried food and with periods of fasting during storms and other emergencies.

On this trip I would have the unique opportunity to spend two weeks with Canada's most famous long-distance sailor; I was looking forward to having interesting discussions with him.

Over the subsequent months communication with Patianne sometimes left me confounded and uncertain about how the trip would pan out. For example, Derek's web site announced the completion of his passage from La Rochelle to Halifax, mentioning that he was accompanied by three crewmembers. I asked Patianne for the email addresses of the crewmembers in order to better prepare myself for my trip but never received their names and coordinates. When I spoke to her on the phone in February after having paid my deposit she mentioned that she would email the crew a list of gear to bring on board with us. After reminding her three times about the list, I finally received the following five days before departure:

Personal Transatlantic Equipment
Outer Layer	X1
Mid Layer	X2
Primary Layer	X2
Gloves, warm	X1
Cap, warm	X1
Boots	X1
Socks	X1

sleeping bag
Water Bottle if have preference
Sunglasses
sunscreen
Passport valid for 6 months
Health Card

Items that will be on the boat and utilized by the crew
saftety gear for the boat, liferafts, etc
utensils
bowls
water bottles
babywipes
recycling bags
paper towels
PFD with light, whistle
Harness & tether

If you look at Annex 2 "Checklist for sailing on an OPY" you'll understand that I wasn't overly enlightened by the sparse list. The useful bit of information that I deduced was that Baby Wipes would be the only way to bathe, as there obviously wouldn't be room to hang towels to dry in a cabin designed for one person.

At the end of August Patianne informed me that Derek had still not secured a major sponsor to pay for a new set of sails. The future of the entire race hung in the balance, as there was no other way to fund the $95,000 that new sails would cost and it was not possible for the old ones to withstand the 30,000 miles of the race. It was only September 6th, six days before his departure for La Rochelle that Derek announced that Active House, an ecological building company had agreed to become his title sponsor and provide the funding. It was a scramble to apply the new logo to the hull of the boat, which was then renamed *Active House* instead of *Spirit of Canada*. I don't know how this strikes you, but to me the new name just isn't as evocative as "*Spirit of Canada*". But so be it.

Active House was to be berthed in Lunenburg, about 95 km west of Halifax. Since our short-sighted Federal government has eliminated most railway routes in the Maritimes, there is virtually no way to get around Nova Scotia without an automobile. I emailed Patianne asking her for information about public transportation from the Halifax airport to Lunenburg but didn't receive a reply. There are no car rental agencies in this small town and no bus service either. Then I sent her another message, asking for the email addresses of the other crewmembers, so we could arrange to share a taxi. I added that if Derek and Patianne had time we could all meet for supper at a restaurant the eve of the departure to get acquainted. She didn't reply. I ended up hiring a taxi at the cost of $165 plus tip, ironically, costing more than my 954 km flight from Ottawa to Halifax! In the end, two of us each had to pay for the long taxi ride. This paucity of communication was not reassuring, but then I rationalized that Derek's people had a lot on their minds and were simply swamped with work.

This is the essence of an email I received on September 5:

> "...the boat will be leaving the dock at 10.00am, everyone to meet at 9.30am in front of the Fisheries Museum of the Atlantic. The mast is blue with 2 white furling jibs, the waterfront is not very big so you will find it."

When I told David about the half hour of briefing, his reaction was,

"Half an hour of briefing? That's madness! I wish you luck, Robert, but remember that once you're away from the dock you can't mutiny."

Then on September 8, after I had reserved my room in Lunenburg, a change of plans, from Patianne:

> "We have a small curve ball thrown at us. The docks in Lunenburg where the boat normally would berth were removed for the hurricane [Earl] and they have not been re-installed so we will be departing from East River Marine in Chester, Nova Scotia. Which means that from the airport one could either stay in Halifax and come to the boat on Sunday morning by taxi or stay in Lunenburg, Mahone Bay or Chester and I will pick you up on Sunday morning from your accommodation and take you to the boat."

"Are you worried about the trip, dear?" Micheline asked, as I was taciturnly drying the dishes that she was placing in the drip tray.

I answered that I wasn't worried for my safety, as the boat was built to withstand severe weather and Derek would undoubtedly want to arrive in France with an intact boat, which means he wouldn't be taking any chances. What concerned me, I confided, was how the relationship with the captain would transpire. So far, the few exchanges I'd had with Derek's communications representative were impersonal and actually made me feel irrelevant. In a confined space you have to learn to give and take. I'm flexible, so I get along with everybody, even if sometimes I feel that I need to give more than take. I added that the skipper has special powers that the crewmembers don't have, so we're pretty much at his mercy.

To this, Micheline responded, "Everything will be alright as long as you keep in mind this man's focus – he must do everything possible to win the race, to the exclusion of things that get in his way. You are not important to him, except for the dollars you will provide towards his objective. Don't expect to have fun like you do with Anthony. That wouldn't help him achieve his goal. You're just going for the ride. He can operate his boat without you, so you and the other crewmembers are there for financing his race. That's his focus."

Micheline is much more perspicacious than I when it comes to reading people. I decided to adopt her view of the situation and with this in mind, my expectations would be more realistic.

After the taxi dropped me off at the Maplebird B&B I decided to walk the streets of Lunenburg. What struck me as most remarkable about this historic little town of 2400 souls is the originality of its architecture. The houses are built with wood siding and richly carved wood trim, sometimes painted with contrasting colours. Many of the older houses as well as the renowned Lunenburg Academy are of Second Empire style, which displays ornate wooden towers and mansard roofs. The majority of the older houses feature the five-sided Scottish dormer that looks like a bay window, called a Lunenburg Bump. A three story house would have three of these windows one above the other. The town has been designated a UNESCO World Heritage Site in 1995, which ensures that much of the town's unique architecture will be preserved – for at least as long as wood can be kept from rotting, if my understanding is correct.

Lunenburg is renowned as the birthplace of the famous schooner *Bluenose*, Canada's most famous racing boat and her reincarnation *Bluenose II*, which remains a tourist attraction today. Unfortunately, she was on drydock in Halifax being restored when I was in Lunenburg. Fishing and shipbuilding have taken second place to the tourism industry, an observation that is supported by the large number of hotels, B&Bs, arts and crafts shops and restaurants. I enjoyed good pub grub in an establishment known as the Knot Pub, which, at two o'clock in the afternoon still teemed with loyal patrons.

The "must-see" attraction in Lunenburg is the Fisheries Museum of the Atlantic, which depicts the history of fishing on Nova Scotia's south coast. A plethora of ancient artefacts, tools, equipment and models of fishing boats were displayed. Fishing used to be the most dangerous of occupations and so death at sea was a very common occurrence. This sad fact is illustrated in a special memorial room where the walls are covered with alphabetical lists of the names of local fishermen who died at sea. Often several men from the same family suffered the tragic fate. Today the job is made much safer, but still remains one of the most dangerous ways to earn a living. Another exhibit that drew my attention was the revival of an ancient craft, the carding and spinning of flax. Two elderly ladies wearing early settlers' dresses demonstrated the technique with their old spinning wheels. I think that this is one of the skills that young people should learn, as it will be essential, when oil becomes rare, that manual methods of making clothes be reintroduced. Outside, at the museum's dock, was moored a diesel powered fishing boat that was withdrawn from service in 1965 when technology changed from hook and line fishing to trawler fishing. A retired fisherman who volunteered for the museum showed us around and entertained the visitors with stories of his days at sea.

I was later to learn that one of my crewmates, Garry, was in Lunenburg at the same time as I was. Patianne had told him that if he wanted to arrive a day or two ahead of time they could review the layout and rigging and go out for a sail to get him familiarized with the boat. When he tried to make contact upon arriving in town, she said they were busy having a family day, and that he would be picked up on the morning of departure!

Day 0: On the morning of September 12, Patianne collected me at my B&B. She was a tall, thin, athletic-looking woman in her thirties. She wore her sandy brown hair in a boy's haircut and exhibited the confident stance of a person in charge. As we drove to Chester, she spoke:

"Derek will be very tired for the next few days, so don't ask him too many questions. Never sit in his cabin chair. Don't be late for your watches. You will be responsible for being in the cockpit on time. Always clean up after yourselves. Don't leave personal effects hanging around. You're going to need to wear your foul weather gear before boarding the boat. There will be only three of you, since one of the four won't be joining the crew. There won't be time for briefing before casting off, but that will be done as time permits once you're underway."

As Derek's wife was bombarding me with these instructions I was wondering if the man himself was going to be as intense as his principal organiser. When the van pulled into the harbour, the newly named *Active House* came into view, her very high mast setting her apart from the other boats. There were a dozen or so of Derek's supporters at the dock, along with his two children, Sarah, 5 and Ben, 2½.

Patianne instructed me to be at the boat in half an hour. I walked around the marina, explored the shoreline and took a few pictures before changing into my yellow rain jacket and pants. I met my other two crewmembers, Ian and Garry. Ian was the younger of the two in his mid thirties, a tall man whose oval face wore a dark, short, well tended moustache and beard. He is an audiologist who runs his own hearing aid clinic in Parry Sound on Georgian Bay. Garry, a slim framed man whose bespectacled face is more triangular was sporting a greying beard. He was 54 years old, worked as a naval architect consultant and lived in Grimsby on

Lake Ontario. Ian's wife had flown to Halifax with him, rented a car and driven him to Chester to see him off. Her first words to me were,

"All summer we didn't know if there was going to be a trip – not until two days ago. After Ian paid his fee we hardly ever heard from Patianne again."

Derek's children were climbing in and out of the cockpit, turned the winches, tested the captain's seat, opened and closed cleats and played with the rigging, just as children always do on a boat. Derek was in discussion with his wife and some of the men I had seen on the dock. Patianne directed me and the two other crewmembers to step aboard and showed us where to stow our bags in one of the watertight compartments. She stepped off the boat and conducted the process of casting off the docklines.

Derek started the engine, but was faced with a problem. A strong beam wind was squeezing *Active House* against the dock. He couldn't motor against a bow dockline because he feared that the bowsprit could have gotten damaged against the dock. A power boat was tied to *Active House*'s side to pull her away, but with little success. The solution resided in the production of brute muscle power. A number of us pushed *Active House* away and walked her backwards to the end of the dock to set her free, while Derek steered her with the engine in reverse. Once the boat was clear of the dock, we waved at the crowd of well-wishers and headed for the open water.

We were at last committed to the 3,000-mile crossing. No sooner had we gone a few miles from shore than Derek discovered a problem with the battery charging system. Halifax was on our route, 60 miles away, so he decided to make a small detour to have the electrical system verified by an electrician.

It was dark by the time we berthed at the Royal Nova Scotia Yacht Squadron in Halifax. Patianne and her daughter were there to meet us, along with two electricians from Chester. After a couple of hours of prodding the entrails of the ship, they determined that the most likely cause of the charging problem resided with the heavy duty autohelm. This boat was equipped with two separate automatic steering devices. A heavy duty one that demanded a lot of electrical power and a light duty one that was more frugal in its power consumption. Derek was advised not to use the heavy duty autohelm on this trip and have the entire electrical system examined by a nautical electrical expert in La Rochelle. I suspect that the addition of a wind charger the previous week had something to do with the charging problem, as this was the first time the boat was used since the installation.

After we had munched down a hamburger and fries that Patianne brought us, Derek decided to wait till morning to cast off. We spent our first night on the boat at the dock. Garry kindly volunteered to bed down on a pile of sails in the windowless forward storage compartment leaving the two cabin bunks for Ian and me. I was pleasantly surprised with the comfort of the mattress since in the weeks prior to the trip I had nightmares that we'd be sleeping in hammocks. So it was a relief to know that I'd be able to slumber in comfort.

At this point, I might as well tell you about the physical arrangements of a 60-foot racing boat made to be operated singlehandedly. To begin with, all these vessels are planing hulls as opposed to displacement hulls, which means they can glide on the surface of the water. *Active House* weighs only 17,000 pounds, and half of this weight consists of the keel. This is light for a boat her size. For comparison, a 60-foot cruising monohull weighs in at 50,000 to 70,000 pounds. In order to make it easier for one person to handle the operation of the boat, all the lines come into the cockpit. On *Active House* I counted 34 lines that are accessible from the safety of the cockpit, almost eliminating any need to venture onto the deck. The deck itself is flat, is surrounded by strong, triple lifelines and has jacklines along both sides onto which one can clip one's harness.

The cabin is very different from that of a cruising sailboat since it's designed for only one person. The entrance can be closed with a watertight hatch and is protected by a two foot extension of the cabin roof, under which are two crash chairs facing each other. The chairs, which face the centreline of the boat are angled about ten degrees to compensate for the degree of heel of the boat, making the windward one almost level and the leeward one much too inclined for comfort. When the skipper is seated in the windward one, he's protected against wind and splashes. Inside the cabin at the front is a console with all the electronic instruments, including a shelf that holds the computer's keyboard and writing supplies. Aft of the console is the captain's seat which doubles as a bed. This is where the skipper spends all his time when he is inside. On either side of the cabin are two large storage compartments that each house a single bed on hinges that can be levelled with a set of pulleys to compensate for the heeling angle. Against the wall on the port side of the cabin is the galley, measuring no more than one foot deep by three feet wide. In the middle is a small sink with salt and fresh water faucets, both of which are activated by foot pumps. Just to the left of the sink when you are facing it, is the countertop, one foot deep by about a foot wide. To the right of the sink is a single burner gimballed stove that can accommodate a small pot that is used for all the cooking. The water supply is produced by a water maker that feeds a large storage tank. For the training sessions there was exceptionally enough cups, plates and cutlery to accommodate as many as five people, whereas for the race Derek would have to get rid of all surplus dinnerware to save weight. Ahead of the cabin is the engine room where the mechanism for canting the keel is situated. There are several storage compartments, some of which open from the engine room and some of which are available only from the deck. All are sealed with watertight hatches. All told there are six watertight compartments. Should one of them ever get punctured, the boat would stay afloat and might even be able to go on sailing. Even if all six compartments should fill up with water the boat still wouldn't sink, as the hull is made with enough floatation material to support the entire weight of the boat. All Open 60 boats are designed to be self-righting in case of capsize. However, should the keel ever break off, then their most stable position would be upside down! In such a case, the skipper could get out through an escape hatch at the stern.

In the way of sails, *Active House* is a sloop rigged as a cutter, like *Ventus*. But unlike the 39-foot Hallberg Rassy, this boat's sails are absolutely huge, the mast being 85 feet tall. The old mainsail alone weighs 200 kilograms and is entirely raised by human power. There are five big winches in the cockpit, three of which are operated through a coffee grinder mechanism. The mast is kept from falling forward with a pair of running backstays. I will explain how they work later in my story. Everything on the boat is big and all the operations are cumbersome and time consuming. In order to come about or to take or shake a reef, you have to go through numerous steps, all accomplished in the right sequence. Everything about the boat has been designed to make her go fast, and that comes at the expense of manoeuvrability and personal comfort. The designers have chosen tiller steering as opposed to wheel steering because its simplicity reduces the chances of failure. The tiller is connected to a pair of rudders placed in the aft corners of the hull to ensure that one of the rudders remains in the water when the boat heels. There is a large daggerboard that can be lowered for upwind sailing, which serves for reducing leeway. There are also two water ballast tanks, one on either side, for levelling the boat.

Day 1, 0630: Without an alarm clock and without previous agreement, everybody was awake and dressed. Time for coffee. On Derek's racing boat, for the sake of saving a few minutes per day (Derek's focus), it was to be the instant version of coffee. Ian tried to light the burner to boil the water, but the knob on the French-made stove would not budge. Derek took the burner apart, attempted to work the knob loose, but the brittle plastic broke under the pressure of the pliers. He rummaged through his parts storage and found a spare valve and knob assembly, which was actually a used one, which was also jammed. He had a spare stove, an American built model that worked on propane, not on the butane that the French stove ran on. When Patianne came back to meet us at the boat in the morning, she went to Tim Horton's to get us coffee and muffins to sustain us until Canadian Tire opened. My last cup of real coffee for the next two weeks! She then made a beeline for the store and came back with a package of one-pound cylinders of propane. We tested the stove and thanked our lucky stars that Derek hadn't decided to have breakfast only once underway, otherwise we would have had to eat cold food for two weeks!

At last, at 1035 on this fine morning of September 13th we cast off for good. Once again, we waved goodbye to the handful of well wishers on the dock. As we were motoring past the port facilities, I was reminded of the last time I motored in this direction on *Tulip One* ten years ago (already!)

This time I had a better idea of what to expect of the great ocean that lay before me. I held no fear of the sea and of the challenges she might impose upon the vessel that was carrying me. I felt perfectly at ease with finding myself in the middle of the vast ocean, a thousand miles from the nearest parcel of land. The ocean to me is like a steel beam at the top of a highrise under construction to a seasoned steelworker. It is a place to respect but not to fear. Some say that fear is essential for remaining alert and for reacting appropriately in case of emergency. They say that the man who knows not fear risks facing his demise. To date I've survived without fear of the sea to effect the appropriate survival response. One should never allow oneself to become smug about risk and danger, as danger is with us at all times. Yesterday a girl in my granddaughter's school got run over by a car while crossing the street. She will survive, but will be marked by the accident for life. We never know what awaits around the corner. It might be paradise or it might be hell. But we shouldn't deprive ourselves of enjoying life because of fear. With regard to that emotion, I tend to side with FDR, in his first inaugural address, March 4, 1933,

> "The only thing we have to fear is fear itself - nameless, unreasoning, unjustified, terror which paralyzes needed efforts to convert retreat into advance."

Once out of the Halifax harbour we hoisted the sails and set our heading for our long voyage. It took what seemed like ten minutes and many calories of muscle power to get the head of the enormous mainsail to its place at the top of the soaring mast. As we were moving away from shore, the wind became increasingly a head wind, which forced us to beat our way south. On an Eco 60, in the interest of saving weight, the diesel engine is very small, at 27 hp. This is just powerful enough to run the heavy duty alternator or propel the boat at its cruising speed of 4.5 knots, but not both at the same time.

During the day we tacked several times, as the wind was coming directly from where we were headed for. We sailed close hauled all day at 6 to 8 knots and made headway very slowly.

Transatlantic on an Open 60!

When nightfall came, I discovered a peculiar fault with this boat. All sailboats navigating under sail between sunset and sunrise must display, in addition to a white stern light, a red light on the port side and a green one on the starboard side. Usually the coloured lights are placed near the bow. But because this boat creates so much salt water spray at the front, its sidelights were placed at the transom, behind the cockpit to save them from corrosion. Since they are angled to be seen from the front and the sides of the boat, they illuminated the entire cockpit and part of the sails, completely ruining our night vision. It was impossible to see anything at all ahead of the boat. There was a trilight at the top of the mast, a unit that combines the red, green and white lights in one unit illuminated by a single bulb. However, the bulb was burned out, which is why Derek switched on the annoying side lights. After a while, our skipper decided that it was unsafe to navigate with these lights blinding the helmsman, so he turned them off. This brought back memories of my trip on *Tulip One* when we navigated for eight nights without lights after leaving Burmuda with dead batteries. The only times Derek turned them on again were when we met a ship and when we approached the French coast at the end of the passage.

Day 2: If you recall, inside a standard displacement hull there is a space between the floor and the bottom of the boat called the bilge. Not so with an Eco 60. Because the bottom of a planing hull is flat, the floor inside the cabin is also flat and mostly level. When you're standing in the cabin there is only half an inch of carbon fibre that separates your feet from the deep ocean below.

On our first day, when we were only minutes out of Chester I noticed that *Active House* was very susceptible to wave slap, much more so than displacement hull boats I've sailed. On larger waves, lets say in the six-foot range, she would slam down with a resounding BANGGGG! When I was standing in the cabin I could sometimes feel a wave rippling towards the stern under my feet! When the boat fell off an especially large wave the entire vessel trembled and shook as though a giant hand had picked her up and dropped her. The sensation was rather unsettling. This boat had competed in four round-the-world races and was now committed to clocking another 30,000 miles. I was wondering how many times the hull can be subjected to this kind of stress before it weakens and falls apart.

All this slamming reminded me of a cruising couple I met in Cuba who had a harrowing experience on their way to Curacao in a heavy chop. It was late at night, halfway across the Caribbean Sea when their 48' Cheoy Lee crashed down a wave with an exceptionally severe bang and started taking on water. They immediately put a spare electric bilge pump at work to supplement the automatic one. They discovered that a three-foot long crack had formed in the hull through which seawater was gushing in. They managed to jury rig a makeshift patch from the inside by screwing a piece of plywood lathered with caulking inside the bilge. They survived this life-threatening ordeal because they carried an inordinately large amount of scrap material, spare parts and tools, which a racing boat can't afford to haul because of weight constraints. A three-foot crack wouldn't cause an Eco 60 to sink, but a compartment filled with water could take it out of the race. Upon searching the Internet, I found no credible reports of boats sinking because of fibreglass fatigue, so perhaps the Cheoy Lee had suffered from a construction defect and Derek has nothing to worry about.

On this second day, as we were approaching Sable Island, the breeze subsided, then died down, reminding me of my attempted Pacific crossing. Derek could not afford to wait for the wind to resume, so he turned on the engine to motor sail. Then the wind picked up, then died down again. Each time there was a change in wind speed our skipper would have us take a reef or shake a reef, operations that require many steps and much time and physical effort.

Derek's proficiency really impressed me. Without a moment of hesitation, he could wrap the correct line around the corresponding winch, open and close cleats in the right sequence and either harden lines by cranking a winch or easing them out. This is exhausting work on a high performance racing yacht of this size. His years of heavy winching have developed his body (5'10" – 185 lbs) into a solid mass of muscle. Every now and then, when he sensed a slight change in the wind, he would take a good look at the sails. He would then either ease or harden a sheet, or maybe lower or raise the traveller, and then the reading of the GPS would show the boat speed increase by half or three quarters of a knot. This kind of focus is what would make Derek place well in a race. Another example of Derek's intent focus is what he revealed in an interview with Yachtpals. He explained why he does not take books or music on his races:

> "I don't get bored or anything, I'm just focusing on little edges and trims and little movements."

Not all racers are this focused. On his Golden Globe race Robin Knox Johnson took 52 books with him, including heavyweights such as War and Peace and the complete works of William Shakespeare.

During one of our discussions about *Active House*'s rigging, rope lashings and knots, Derek commented that the only knot that he bothered to learn was the bowline, (the basic knot that every sailor learns) as it is the only one he needed to master. I know he was exaggerating, but I'd guess he was articulating that he preferred to concentrate on learning the skills that were essential to his success and not to clutter his brain with unnecessary information. Derek's focus.

So far, our captain had been preoccupied with our slow progress and had not yet started the training sessions. It would come once we settle into a routine, I presumed.

I should mention Derek's communication system, as you will discover its significance on day 12 of the trip. He had on board, in addition to the regular VHF radio, a satellite phone. Several times a day he would place business calls or he would call home. His wife Patianne looks after keeping him abreast of the weather. From her home computer she monitors the weather stations, analyses weather patterns and relates to her racing husband the expected weather. Although I tried not to eavesdrop, it was difficult not to notice that he would invariably ask to speak to the children before ending a phone call home. When *YachtPals* asked what he likes doing when not sailing, he answered,

> "The family is the only thing you know. I enjoy the young ones, because they have kind of given me a second lease on life. I'm 56 years old [in 2008] you know... So, it's different. The first family, I was working, and doing all kinds of things, and missed the whole raising of the family. So, now I'm really enjoying that.

That night I slept very well, even if my sleep had been severed into four stages. Derek decided that his three crewmembers would be responsible for the watches, whereas he would always be available for sail changes and emergencies. The crewmembers would take turns doing one hour watches and then would take two hours off, around the clock. I would have preferred two hour watches with four hours off, as it would have allowed longer periods of sleep. But the captain felt that we would be more alert with short watch periods – and naval custom dictates that it's the captain who calls the shots. The following schedule is what I observed during the entire trip. My first watch of the evening started at 2000, so at 2100 I would prepare for bed. First I would remove my gloves, my PFD and harness, my rubber boots, my socks, my foul weather gear, my toque, my long-sleeved shirt, my two woollen sweaters and my trousers. I would keep my long johns top and bottom on. I would then brush my teeth, and roll out my sleeping bag liner and my backpacker's pillow. I didn't need my sleeping bag, as I discovered the first nights that it was sufficiently warm in the cabin to be comfortable with just my cotton sleeping bag liner. I would fall asleep as soon as my head touched the pillow and when my PDA sounded its alarm it would take me fifteen minutes to put away my bedding, go to the toilet and get dressed for the next shift. That might seem like a lot of trouble for an hour and a half of sleep, but I found that the psychological effect of getting undressed and having my own bedding and pillow made for good, sound sleep. I was able to get four sleep periods this way. My next night watches started at 2300, 0200 and 0500. After my last sleep period of the night I would get up at 0730, have a cup of instant coffee and a bowl of cereal and was ready by 0800 for my next watch. Those 6 hours of broken up sleep along with rest periods during the day, by and large sufficed to keep me feeling fresh.

On *Day 3* we turned off the engine but very soon had to put it back into service for another five hours. It was a glorious day, which allowed us to spend a few hours of the afternoon in shorts and T-shirts. Evenings and most days were typically cold enough to warrant all the clothes I mentioned in the previous paragraph. During the race Derek would have to spend a fair bit of time in the cold waters of the Southern Ocean, the Roaring Forties, so he needed the most high-tech clothing on the market, supplied by one of his sponsors.

The Velux Five Oceans race has been running every four years since 1982. The race was to take place over a period of about seven months and would comprise four stopovers to allow the participants to make repairs and resupply. I had obtained the following from the Velux web site:

> The race will start and finish [sic] from La Rochelle (France) on October 17, 2010, and will encompass 5 Ocean Sprints:
>
> 1. Cape Town Ocean Sprint: 7,500 nautical miles from La Rochelle (France) to Cape Town (South Africa)
> 2. Wellington Ocean Sprint: 7,000 nautical miles from Cape Town (South Africa) to Wellington (New Zealand)
> 3. Salvador Ocean Sprint: 7,400 nautical miles from Wellington (New Zealand) to Salvador (Brazil)
> 4. Charleston Ocean Sprint: 4,000 nautical miles from Salvador (Brazil) to Charleston (USA)
> 5. La Rochelle Ocean Sprint: 3,600 nautical miles from Charleston (USA) to La Rochelle (France)

Derek explained that for the race the skippers must make as much use of renewable energy as possible. They are allowed to use a set amount of diesel fuel for charging their batteries, but any use beyond that results in loss of points. Each team is limited to two professional shore crew, one of whom can be a manager or liaison person. They are also allowed a PR and/or media person, but this individual is not allowed to work on the boat in stopovers. All sails are measured and stamped before the race begins and these are the only ones allowed for the entire race. The propeller is locked with a seal to ensure that a skipper doesn't use the engine for moving the boat. If the seal is found to be broken upon inspection at the end of the race, the boat is disqualified. The racer isn't allowed to haul the boat out of the water at either of the four stopovers except for safety reasons, and only with the race committee's permission. The committee provides each team with a shipping container in which boat parts, supplies, tools and food are shipped free of charge from one stopover port to the next.

You might be wondering where the "Eco" fits into the name "Eco 60". With the famous Vendée Globe race which takes place every four years, many participants have a new boat purpose-built to take advantage of marginal technological improvements. Every time a new race takes place the specially built boats are a few percentage points faster than the previous cohort and form what is termed a "new generation" of boats. The organizers of the Velux Five Oceans decided that the emphasis on new generation boats was not only wasteful of natural resources, but placed too much emphasis on technology instead of on the skill and endurance of the participants. Furthermore, the law of diminishing returns was at play and the skyrocketing cost of each new generation excluded good sailors who are less financially endowed. So they decided that for this race they would create the Eco 60 category. To qualify, a participating boat has to be of the Open 60 class, have been built before 2003 and must have some alternate means of generating her electricity in addition to her diesel-run alternator. The purpose, we are told, is to reduce the boat's reliance on fossil fuels during the race.

All things considered, this reduction would have minimal impact on the total greenhouse gas emissions produced by running this race. The ground crew, their friends and race organizers would need to fly from home to each of the stopovers and back in airplanes that burn jet fuel. Collectively, they would have travelled hundreds of thousands of miles over the course of the race. Additionally, the supplies container for each team would be carried by cargo ships that run on bunker fuel. These days anything "green" will attract admiration, no matter how inconsequential. So from that perspective, you might say that Velux Five Oceans organisers were savvy to incorporate this touch of environmentalism into their racing programme.

Active House was built in 1999 by Bernard Nivelt, a French architect and was first named *Solidaires*. She changed owners and names twice before Derek bought her from Rich Wilson, an American racer who sailed her to 9th place in the last Vendée Globe.

Now I hear you asking, "What's open about an Open 60?" Even as far back as the very first round-the-world race, the Golden Globe, some racers died at sea in their pursuit of the finish line. In that pioneering race, one of the boats sank and one racer disappeared at sea. Subsequently there have been many sinkings and many losses of life. It's essential that some racers should perish once in a while, in order to maintain the interest of the public! But until the safety rules were put in place, the number of fatal accidents was getting out of hand. That is why the International Monohull Open Classes Association sat down and set out safety rules with regards to the design of racing yachts. The word "open" means that the participating boats can be of any design, as long as they meet a long list of safety restrictions. Here are some examples of safety items that are mandatory in addition to the ones I told you about earlier: a maximum size of sail plan (to limit the amount of power moving the boat), a torsion test of the keel's strength to reduce the chances of it breaking off, the time it takes for the cockpit to drain out when filled with seawater (maximum of 3 minutes), the size and strength of stanchions and lifelines to prevent falling overboard and a long list of safety equipment to be carried on board.

Now lets get back to renewable energy sources. There are three kinds that can be used on a sailboat. The most common is photovoltaics, or solar panels. These are flat boards encrusted with solar cells that convert the energy of sunlight directly into electricity, which is then stored in the boat's battery bank. They work silently, have no moving parts and require almost no maintenance aside from occasional washing. However they are not a panacea, as there are several factors that can limit their output.

The most obvious one is the physical size of the array of solar panels that can be placed on a boat. There are basically two types of solar panels: The rigid, flat, glass-encased panels that are mounted in aluminum frames and the flexible ones that can be glued onto moderately curved surfaces of the deck and that can endure a certain amount of being walked upon. The drawback with the latter is that they produce only half as much electricity per square foot and they are twice as expensive as the rigid ones. There are just so many places on a sailboat where you could install flat, glass encased solar panels and the same could be said about the flexible ones.

Another limitation resides in shading. There are a lot of things on a sailboat that can create shadows and any shadow on a solar panel blocks out the light. Another source of loss is cloud cover. There is a common myth that asserts that solar panels work on overcast days. With ultraviolet (UV) light, your skin can burn on cloudy days if you don't apply sunblock, as it is well documented that UV rays penetrate through clouds. Solar panels don't run on UV but on the longer wavelengths of the electromagnetic spectrum. The sad truth is that on overcast days up to 98 percent of the light energy from the sun is absorbed by the clouds, rendering the panels almost useless. Photographers have known this for a long time.

If you've ever spread yourself out on a towel on a beach in the tropics you've noticed how powerful the sun is when it is directly overhead. The same is true for solar panels. They produce their peak power when the sun's rays strike them at 90 degrees, in other words, at noon. Near sunrise and sunset and at winter solstice in the higher latitudes, photovoltaic panels produce virtually no electricity.

Because we hear so much about its virtues these days, wind power is the next obvious source of renewable energy for a sailboat. Typically, a wind charger is mounted on a post at the boat's transom. It usually takes a minimum of five knots of wind to get the blades spinning, but the unit produces very little power at that speed. What is important to realize is that wind power increases with the cube of its speed. This means that when the wind speed doubles (2^2) the power increases by a factor of eight (2^3) and vice versa. An important point to consider is capacity factor. Another drawback with wind power is that windmills have to be stopped when the wind is above thirty knots, otherwise they would spin so fast that they would break apart. Because the wind doesn't always blow hard enough and because it often does so in gusts, a generator with a capacity of one hundred watts will actually generate only 30 watts averaged over the course of a year.

The third method of producing electric power on a sailboat, which I have no experience with, is a hydrogenerator. It consists of a small turbine that is towed on a rope behind the vessel. It uses the movement of the boat through the water to provide the energy to spin the turbine. As long as the boat is moving through the effort of the wind, the electricity produced is entirely free from hydrocarbons. From my research into this device, I discovered that it has two disadvantages. First, the bulk of the system causes drag, which can slow down the boat. If it only slows the boat down, say one twentieth of a knot, that would still make a significant difference over a distance of 30,000 miles. The other drawback is that the turbine can get snagged on floating debris. In spite of its inconveniences, it sounds like a brilliant idea, and it would be especially efficient behind a fast boat like an Eco 60. The invention has been around for a long time, but I'm at a loss to explain why it hasn't caught on.

On *Active House*, there were five of the stick-on solar panels and one small wind charger. The limitations I just mentioned explain why at times during our Atlantic crossing Derek had to run the engine for several hours at a time to recharge the batteries. Later I was to learn that Chris Stanmore-Major almost ran out of fuel on the second leg of the Velux Five Oceans race because of electrical charging problems.

Day 4: In the afternoon the wind freshened, propelling us along at 14 knots. Derek asked us to steer by hand, fearing that the light duty autohelm might overheat under the strain and pack it up. This is when I discovered a maintenance issue with the boat. There was a lot of play in the steering mechanism, which I found distracting and annoying. Even though it didn't seem to bother anybody else, this is a minor flaw that I have no patience for. I pointed it out to Derek and he responded that this was on the "to-do" list for his ground crew in La Rochelle.

This is a racing boat, so the builders designed everything with weight reduction in mind. The mast, boom and hull were made of carbon fiber instead of fibreglass, all metal turnbuckles and shackles had been replaced by rope lashings, storage containers were lightweight bags suspended along the hull, cupboard "doors" in the galley were plastic curtains that could be zippered shut. There were no settees and no salon table where one could sit. There was no wine cellar for keeping that special vintage, no refrigerator or freezer for the preservation of food nor any ice for a rum and soda. There was no insulation or fancy liner decorating the walls and ceiling and no wood trim. They even thought about how to deal with bodily wastes. Instead of a head, there were two buckets. A blue bucket was dedicated to #1 productions. After you were done you would simply chuck the golden contents overboard. For #2 performances, you'd line the black bucket with an "ecological", compostable plastic garbage bag and retreat to the privacy of the engine room just ahead of the cabin. It was good etiquette to warn everybody in advance in case they would need to go into the cabin for the next half hour, as for that long the air would be heavy with the olfactory reminders of your visit to the engine room. Once your production was complete, you'd clean up with Baby Wipes (no toilet paper on board), tie a knot in the bag and throw it into the sea. Each time, with pangs of guilt, I would then watch the bag recede in the distance as the boat sped away, hoping that the corn-based plastic it was made of would decompose *real fast* so that no unsuspecting leatherback turtle would mistake my little present for a luscious jellyfish! Why not simply rinse out the bucket after use instead of using a plastic bag? Well, it isn't that simple. Since the boat is speeding along at 10+ knots, you can't dip the bucket into the sea to clean it because either the force of the water would just yank it out of your hands or the handle would get ripped off. And stopping such a fast boat by heaving to or going into irons is just too complicated and time consuming. This isn't an issue on cruising sailboats, since they are equipped with a head, which can be flushed directly into the sea.

Day 5 began with another sunny sky and a moderate wind driving us at 12 knots. Derek had become more talkative and relaxed but so far he offered nothing resembling training classes. It had now become evident that any learning would have to be through observation and questioning.

During the first two or three days he had been quiet and withdrawn, not speaking unless necessary and not responding to attempts at humour on the part of the crew. However, over the past day or two he was progressively loosening up. We engaged in interesting conversations about long-distance single-handed racing and even social or political topics. To my great relief and contrary to the predictions of my cynical friends, Derek was soft-spoken, polite and considerate. He never used coarse or profane language, nor did he have unrealistic expectations of the performance of his crewmembers.

At one point in our conversation we were talking about his previous training sessions of the summer. On one of those sessions there was a landlubber who had always dreamed of sailing around the world, like me, but had never been on a sailboat. He joined Derek to find out what sailing is all about. After a few days of fighting heavy seas and of being seasick nonstop, he swore that he would never set foot in a sailboat again! Derek confided that on another one of the sessions he got so angry at one of his crewmembers that he later had to apologize for the way he had yelled at him. I didn't know how to interpret this disclosure and how much importance to attribute to it.

There was a tiny splash of water far out in the distance near the horizon and an object resembling a miniature canoe paddle rose out of the water and disappeared below the surface. Derek said that what we had just seen was a right whale breaching. A sad fact, he related, was the disappearance of these giant animals. When he crossed the Atlantic for the first time in 1986 he could see whales every day, but in recent years he would only see one or two specimens during the entire crossing. And this time, on Derek's sixteenth trans-Atlantic crossing, this lone individual would be the only whale we would spot. The International Whaling Commission imposed a moratorium on whaling in 1986 to allow stocks to recover, but according to anecdotal observations by seafarers like Derek, populations are continuing to decline.

On *Day 6* the wind veered to the south, allowing us to bear away and aim closer to our destination. I was surprised to see that the water temperature gauge indicated 21.8 degrees C. We were into the Gulf Stream. One of my worries before the trip was that of being cold. After seasickness, being cold is probably the worst sensation one can be subjected to on the water.

I remembered a commercial whale watching tour Micheline and I joined out of Halifax many years ago. It was a warm June day, with a light, refreshing breeze. Many of the 30 tourists on board were dressed in T-shirts and shorts and had not even as much as a jacket. Micheline and I had outdoors experience and thus prepared for cold air on the open waters. As an excess of precaution we had brought a sleeping bag as a cover, just in case. Once we had reached a few miles from shore it felt as though our vessel had steamed into a giant open air freezer. We pulled on our sweaters and jackets. That was still not sufficient protection against the cold, damp breeze that permeated our flesh, right through to our bones. We snuggled up under the sleeping bag and were amongst the few who were warm enough to enjoy the tour. We pitied the poor hypothermic underdressed bunch, but there was nothing we could do for them. It would have been up to the tour company to take care of its passengers. On this day 6 of my trans-Atlantic voyage, I was able to strip down to a T-shirt again for a few hours.

There were cirrus clouds above, the thin, wispy telltale horsetail clouds that foretell bad weather. This was in line with the low pressure area coming from the north that Patianne had predicted for tomorrow.

At 1330, I was standing in the galley shaving, when suddenly, there was a muffled boom! and the boat lurched backwards and vibrated and I had to steady myself to regain my balance. I rushed to the companionway. Derek was taken aback and waited for the next shock. But the boat just continued sailing, without any further disturbance. He postulated that the keel must have struck a large sea animal, perhaps a whale or a shark. His ground crew would have to examine the hull carefully once the boat reaches La Rochelle.

Derek had us helming by hand again, as the wind picked up. By midnight the wind was blowing 30 knots from the north-west, resulting from the low pressure system that Patianne's weather gurus had forecasted as 20 knots. A dark sky heavy with thick clouds dumped a heavy downpour upon us throughout the night.

Day 7, 0445. Ian was steering by hand and Derek was lying in his cockpit chair, having spent the night in the cockpit. I was getting ready for my 0500 watch and I asked Ian how things were going. We exchanged a few comments about the heavy seas, then I raised my voice a decibel to make myself heard above the noise of the wind,

"Would you guys like a hot cup of soup before I come up?"

And then to my dismay, Derek replied in a loud voice, *"Would you guys SHUT UP? I'm trying to sleep. You guys are comfortable in your warm beds. I'm just trying to survive here."*

I was bewildered by this unexpected outburst. I could easily have retorted that for him it is a lifestyle choice and that I needed feel no guilt in sleeping comfortably since I had paid big dollars for the privilege, but thought the better of it. I responded that I was just trying to be helpful. I chose to put the event aside and never gave it any thought until my twelfth night at sea. I reasoned that I probably woke Derek up suddenly and maybe he was too groggy with sleep to make the connection between the sound of my voice and the friendly meaning of my words.

The wind had reached 35 knots and the swell grew in size. We were sailing on a broad reach and were constantly being splashed by waves smashing the side of the boat or flying over the cabin. We steered by hand all day, with Derek replacing us occasionally to give us a rest. By supper time we were navigating in 20 foot waves. The tiller on this boat has a removable angled extension so it can be flipped over and used on either side of the cockpit with the helmsman in a standing position and with his fanny pressed against the edge of the deck. When a large wave caused the boat to yaw windward, the helmsman had to steer very hard to bear away to prevent the boat from being knocked down, which required a large effort due to the awkward angle of his arm. To make it easier on the helmsman's arm, an assistant helped by pushing the tiller while the helmsman pulled on it. We formed two teams with four hands on the helm, Derek assisted by Ian and Garry assisted by me, with pairs replacing each other every half hour, and later every hour. Sometimes when I was helping Garry with the tiller, Ian would push on Garry's chest to hold him in place. On other occasions we were knocked down completely and struggled to get to our feet to grab the tiller again before the boat broached. Broaching means to lose control of steering in following seas and the ship turns broadside to the waves. An extremely dangerous situation in steep seas since the ship may trip on the keel and be rolled over into a capsize.

Our feet would sometimes slide out from under us as the boat heeled and we were leaning on the tiller. This lasted all night and the following day. Hour by hour the sea grew. Derek estimated that at its maximum, the wind peaked above 40 knots and the waves reached ten metres in height!

At one point in the middle of the night, Derek and Ian were alone in the cockpit and I was dozing in my bunk. I was bruskly awakened by a loud bang and a scream. The wind direction had forced us to sail south of our great circle course all day and time had come to make a change of direction by executing a controlled gybe. As per normal procedure, they had sheeted the (triple-reefed) mainsail to the centreline, but one of the cleats locking the traveller had been forgotten in the open position. So when the stern turned across the path of the wind and the mainsail presented its other side to the wind, it was blown violently to leeward, to the limit of its course, causing two luff cars to break near the top of the mainsail. On very large sailboats the front edge of the mainsail is equipped with cars instead of slides, and these run along a track built into the aft side of the mast. It could have been worse. In heavier air, the mast might have broken! Believe me, that's the kind of excitement I can live without!

When a yacht is sailing downwind, you have to let the mainsail out to the side of the boat, outside the lifelines, so that the wind hits it more or less perpendicularly. On ordinary sailing yachts there is nothing to interfere with the swinging of the boom from one side to the other. That's because the boom is short and has room to swing within the space between the mast and the backstay. But *Active House* has a long boom that sticks out beyond the back of the boat, made to accommodate a much larger mainsail. That is why she needs two running backstays, one that attaches to each of her aft corners – but only one at a time is secured to hold the mast up. In order for the long boom not to get snagged in the backstay when you want to let it out to the side of the boat, the leeward backstay has to be slackened and temporarily tied forward to get it out of the way. Each time you tack or gybe, you have to secure the windward one and slacken the leeward one. Having to deal with securing and releasing backstays is one more thing Derek has to think about each time he tacks or gybes. One more thing that makes this boat so cumbersome to operate. One more thing that could put the boat out of the race should he be absent-minded or mind-numbed with fatigue.

On another occasion Derek and Ian were helming and I was keeping them company in the cockpit while Garry was catching a few minutes of shut-eye in the cabin. Suddenly a huge wave knocked the boat down. Derek and Ian came tumbling down on me while they were trying to hang on to the tiller. I pushed on Ian with all my might to prop him up, so he could continue help pushing on the helm. When the boat levelled off another large wave came over the deck and filled the cockpit with seawater. It took almost ten minutes for the water to drain out. I was surprised that the designers hadn't foreseen larger drains.

Day 8: We kept up the two-per-team steering routine all day. By the end of the afternoon the wind had subsided and we unfurled the staysail and went back to steering with the autohelm. Soon after, however, we realized that there was too much canvass up, so we rolled up the staysail to travel with only the mainsail. At 2000 we unfurled the smaller headsail again and continued with the autohelm. The mainsail still had three reefs in it, and we could not shake a reef until calmer seas would allow Derek to climb the mast to repair the two defective cars.

Now that the storm was over we were in a more relaxed state and had resumed normal conversation. Derek told Garry that the steepness of the waves and the height of the seas during the storm were worse than the seas that put him out in the last race in the southern ocean, and that he was quite concerned. In fact, he said, the seas we encountered on this trip were the worst he had ever experienced on the Atlantic.

Day 9: We maintained a speed of 9 to 12 knots under a blue sky. Spirits were high because with the storm behind us and good winds on our beam, our ETA promised to be in time for Derek's meeting with the Race Committee Sunday and Garry would be in time to catch his flight home the next day.

We resumed cooking hot meals. During the storm we were limited to sandwiches, but now we could go back to preparing more elaborate "dishes". Patianne had looked after provisioning for the crewed Atlantic crossing. Whereas on my sailing, canoeing and hiking trips we plan our food carefully to eat well, I wasn't going on this trip with the expectation of gourmet cuisine. She had thrown in four litres of soup, which was very much appreciated. For lunches she had provided enough bread for the first eight days (as bread doesn't keep much longer without refrigeration). In the way of sandwich varieties, she had provided sliced mozzarella, turkey, ham and Dijon mustard in quantities to match the bread, but to the chagrin of my fussy palate, no butter or margarine. Suppers for the first two nights were spaghetti and tomato sauce from a jar, then for the rest of the trip it was either Minute Rice or noodles mixed with a can of Irish stew. To supplement the stew's reformed meat protein we threw in either fresh pepperoni slices, or canned chicken or tuna. As a token vegetable we enjoyed a generous quantity of canned corn added to the mixture.

Since everything had to be prepared in the one pot, we typically would cook the rice or pasta first, then add the Irish stew and protein supplement and return the creation to the burner to bring it back to a simmer. We would then divvy up the chow amongst four large cups, which acted as non-tipping plates. Dessert consisted of chocolate pudding in single serve containers or double-stuff and chocolate chip cookies. The days started with an apple or an orange, followed by a breakfast of multigrain cereal with UHT milk. Peanut butter and jam could be spread on crackers or bread. Between meals our snacks could be either granola or chocolate bars. We were still alive and in good health upon reaching France.

You might be asking yourself how a gourmet like me can be so philosophical about enduring two weeks of simple fare like this. Mind you, I've not always been a gourmet. I was raised on healthy but simple cooking like most of my peers. Then I was sent for two years to Collège St-Alexandre, a boarding school where the Grey Nuns served grub that was so horrible that I often left my plate untouched. It was only after I married Micheline that together we developed an interest in cooking and good food. Often when travelling I'm inescapably limited to a greasy spoon restaurant that serves gravy *made from a mix!* Since I always try to look for a silver lining, whenever I'm not pleased with the quality of the food, I need only think of the poor people from Central America or Cuba who live mostly off rice and beans, and who would delight in eating what I'm being offered. I then quickly revert to counting my blessings.

In the interest of saving weight during a race, Derek dines only on freeze-dried meals. He needs only bring water to a boil in his pot, add the contents of the envelope and let the mixture steep. Five minutes later he can enjoy a passably good tasting, nutritious meal. This system produces only one dirty pot, a reflection of Derek's focus. While racing, meal preparation is kept to its simplest, out of necessity. It is very difficult for a skipper to absorb as many calories as needed to maintain body condition. Our racer doesn't take vitamin and mineral supplements, and he typically loses twenty-five pounds of body weight when he does a circumnavigation.

Day 10: In the morning the wind and seas abated sufficiently for Derek to climb the mast to repair the two defective luff cars. At last, we could raise full main. However, we were only able to achieve 6.5 knots with the light wind, then 4, then 3. This is when Derek started the engine again and we motor sailed for the next 20 hours at only 4.5 to 6.5 knots.

One of the main challenges I was facing on this trip was to find a place to put myself. In the cockpit there was usually only the uncomfortable leeward crash chair crew could use, as the windward one was often occupied by the captain. Elsewhere in the cockpit there were places where you could hoist yourself up to sit on the deck between two winches, with legs dangling into the cockpit space. Although the front deck was huge, it was unsafe and usually too wet to use as a seating area. There were no seats for the crew in the cabin, only the two lateral bunks to lie down in, but which provided no headroom. You could prop yourself up on an elbow, with your head pressed against the net above if you wanted to write or read. Much of the time the boat's movement would shake us like on a Midway ride, which precluded writing anything more than a few scribbled lines. I read from a book on my PDA once in a while, but found the movement annoying and difficult to contend with. I welcomed the periods when we had to helm by hand, as it gave me something to do, albeit standing up.

However, back at home, when I read Chris Stanmore-Major's blog after he started the third leg of the race, it made me feel like somewhat of a wimp:

> I relished returning to my carbon cave after too many nights in soft-sprung, immobile, hotel beds. You think I'm joking? I'm really not. The first night in the hotel I had to work very hard not to run back to the 'comfort' of the boat, and on the last two nights of the stopover I happily once again huddled up under my fleece blanket in the familiar shape of my V-shaped nav seat and fell into the fitful half waking sleep I have grown so

accustomed to. Constantly waking every thirty minutes to freak out at the speedo reading zero as we bobbed alongside the dock!

Sailboats are like people. There are persons you like the first time you meet them, there are some you get to like after having known them for a while and others who leave you indifferent right from the start. Likewise with sailing yachts. Even though I was becoming increasingly at ease with *Active House*'s complex rigging, after ten days she still hadn't tugged at my heartstrings. A high tech racing boat like this one is akin to a Formula One racing car. Just as the average street driver wouldn't be able to operate the racecar proficiently, the average cruising sailor like me couldn't hope to get the best out of an Open 60.

If there is one great quality of the Eco 60 with respect to offshore sailing, it is its safety. Because it is unsinkable it is far safer than the majority of displacement monohull boats. Should an Eco 60 strike an iceberg or get dismasted and its mast puncture holes in the hull, the skipper would just have to lock himself in his cabin, set off his emergency position indicating radio beacon and wait for rescue, even if he's a thousand miles from nowhere. The damaged boat would never sink. Furthermore, *Active House* was equipped with two liferafts and all the safety equipment required by the racing rules.

This brings up an interesting question: When undertaking extreme sports like sailing the Roaring Forties, or kayaking across the Tasman Sea, or walking to the South Pole or climbing Mount Everest, is it OK to expect others to go through the expense of search and rescue and for the rescuers to risk their lives to save you if you get yourself in trouble? A difficult moral dilemma, because if the answer is no, then what about the hiker who gets lost in the Adirondacks, just doing what thousands of others do each year? What about the hunter who breaks a leg far into the forest? What about the sailor who took every precaution but through no negligence of his own got caught in a storm and needs rescue? What level of risk is society ready to tolerate of its risk takers? Should the victim of one's foolish adventures be made to pay for his own search and rescue operation? Would it be morally acceptable for a society to ignore the call for help from a risk taker just because he is the author of his own disaster? The Canada Shipping Act is clear on this, boaters are obligated to render assistance. And the international convention states:

> "Every qualified person who is the master of a vessel in any waters, on receiving a signal from any source that a person, a vessel or an aircraft is in distress, shall proceed with all speed to render assistance and shall, if possible, inform the persons in distress or the sender of the signal.

In Canada the maximum fine for ignoring this law is one million dollars! And the law doesn't differentiate between a victim who got himself in trouble through his own negligence or not.

Day 11, 0625: After 20 hours of motorsailing, the wind grew and we were at last able to kill the engine and enjoy freedom from mechanical noise. Derek judged that the wind direction and strength were just right to enable us to deploy the spinnaker. With Garry helping, he pulled the furling spinnaker out of the forward hatch and raised it. It is incredible that Derek can manage to put this enormous sail up and take it down all by himself! Half an hour later a change in wind direction forced us to undo all the work that had been put into raising the special sail. We were grateful that the wind strength kept up, allowing us to glide along at 10 to 12 knots all day.

I was enjoying a unique experience, unlike what most humans would ever know. And I enjoyed the company of my shipmates and the team work that got us this far. I was back on the sea again, inhaling the salt air, carried by the gentle swell and wind and the power in the sails, surrounded by the unending horizon in all directions. I was filled with the sense that time had stopped and I savoured being more alive than ever. These were the things that counted the most.

Day 12: The approaching day had not yet finished washing away the darkness of night than the pelagic birds appeared out of nowhere to begin fishing. I'm forever astonished when I think that these tiny birds live in the middle of the ocean 24/7 with nothing solid to land on for the greater part of their lives. The wind maintained its strength and we sailed all day in 8 to 10 foot seas at 12 to 14 knots and sometimes a gust would drive us at 16 knots for a few minutes and once we hit 18 knots. With the brightly shining sun filtering through the water splashing over the bow, a succession of mini rainbows came and went. Our heading was taking us directly to our destination on a port tack with a beam wind. Dolphins appeared on both sides of our boat, then mocked our slow speed by criss-crossing ahead of the bowsprit. After entertaining us for a few minutes they vanished just as mysteriously as they had come into sight.

I felt happy and contented, in spite of the discomfort of being the fourth person on a boat designed to take only one, of having no way to bathe except with Baby Wipes, of having no place to sit comfortably and of being deprived of home cooking, of brewed coffee and of my daily glass of wine. As for my captain, my friends back home had been completely wrong. He wasn't a self-centered egomaniac, nor a Captain Bligh. True, on the first day I can't say he and his wife had given us a warm welcome on the boat but

Transatlantic on an Open 60!

our racing skipper was civil and gentlemanly and I couldn't expect more from a man who was so driven by his passion.

It was dark, just after supper, when Ian and I were in the cockpit. Garry was in the cabin washing the dishes while Derek was at the console on the satellite phone. Garry appeared at the companionway and pitched a teabag overboard. Almost miraculously the innocent teabag got snagged on a lifeline and stayed suspended there like a pair of underwear on a clothes line! We all burst out laughing and joked that Garry had found a new way to economize on teabags by hanging them up to dry.

Just then, Derek came to the companionway, shoved Garry aside and exclaimed at the top of his lungs, *"Shut the fuck up, you guys. I'm on the phone trying to make a fucking call. You're acting like a bunch of children. I'm paying five fucking dollars a minute to use this phone,* he bellowed, *and I can't hear a thing!*

He was livid. He screamed:

"When I'm on the phone I want you to shut the fuck up!"

We were all stunned by this unexpected invective and became very silent. I had never experienced anything like this on a boat before. The first thought that came to mind as he was berating us was, "This will be an interesting story to tell when I get back home!"

Derek went back to his phone and Garry to his dishwashing. It is not possible to wash dishes without making at least small rattling noises. And a carbon fiber sink is particularly noisy. Well, these unavoidable sounds raised the wrath of our angry captain again.

Dropping his phone, he made for Garry and at the top of his lungs yelled, *"And Garry, get the fuck out of my cabin! I don't want to see you in here again!"*

Garry precipitated himself out of the cabin and joined the silence that reigned in the cockpit.

Later, when he was finished with his calls, Derek appeared at the door of the companionway, more subdued.

"I apologize for yelling at you fellas. You have to understand that when I'm on the phone it costs me a lot and you have to keep quiet. Sometimes the connection is very bad."

We were having fun. That was disrupting his focus.

Day 13: On Saturday September 25, the winds were variable and during the day the waves diminished from eight feet to a calm four feet. Later in the evening we had arrived in the Bay of Biscay, known for its strong winds, rough waves and large storms. An untold number of ships have perished in these waters. As was predictable, the wind freshened, forcing us to take three reefs in the mainsail.

Everything was back to normal on the boat. Nobody was to refer to the previous evening's unfortunate outburst for the rest of the trip and we all acted as though nothing had happened. It was the civil thing to do.

Day 14: It was midnight when we finally reached the waypoint Derek had placed on the chart plotter at the beginning of the trip. One particularity of the inner La Rochelle pleasure craft port is that it can only be entered at high tide because at low tide the main channel is only a few feet deep. From that point on, the chart plotter wasn't equipped with a large scale chart of the entrance, and we didn't have back-up paper charts, so we navigated very slowly, eyes rivetted to the depth sounder, conscious of *Active House*'s fifteen foot draft. At one point there were only two feet of water below the keel, an uncomfortably small margin. By 0600 local time we had reached the entrance to the Bassin des Chalutiers. A boat carrying Patianne and three of Derek's supporters joined *Active House* to escort us into the basin. The drawbridge was raised to let us in past the lock that holds the water in the basin and at 0630 we made fast to the dock. It was still dark as night.

The previous evening I had organized all my personal effects, ready to pack everything as soon as the boat docked. It always feels good to arrive at the destination after a long passage. And this time I was particularly anxious to get off the boat. After watching Derek's wife direct the docking and tying up procedures I returned to the cabin to finish packing my bag. Patianne stepped into the cockpit and through the companionway hatch she called out to me,

"Robert if you need any help to get your bags off the boat, let me know and I'll find somebody to assist you. We want everybody off the boat as soon as possible so that Derek can get his rest."

I may be a little naïve, but to be summarily dismissed in such a manner was not the expression of gratitude that I was expecting.

Ian had phoned his inlaws from offshore to arrange for them to join him at the dock when he arrived. They were taking a few weeks' holiday in France and had arranged to meet and spend some time with him in La Rochelle.

A representative of the Race Committee was at the dock to greet Derek. She arranged for me to secure a room at the Hotel Mercure, which was within sight of our dock. Patianne had one of her assistants drive Garry and me to the hotel with our baggage.

When I stepped out of the car in front of the hotel the ground rocked and I felt dizzy. This is a remarkable sensation that one often feels after having been on a boat in heavy seas. I had not experienced this feeling in a long time, since in the Caribbean you don't get thirty foot waves.

Interestingly, some of my students experience this sensation after an afternoon on lake Deschênes!

Garry had to catch a train to Paris in a few hours, in view of flying home the following morning. I had offered him the use of my room for a badly needed shower, which was gratefully accepted.

After we had made ourselves presentable and smelling civilized we went for a coffee while waiting for Garry's train. He commented that with respect to ocean passages, he would do one again, but unlike myself, only in a fast boat, not a slow cruiser. As you would correctly have guessed, he wouldn't do it with the same skipper again. He raised the unfortunate teabag rage incident and confided that he had been afraid that Derek would punch him. In spite of the negatives, he didn't regret his decision to undertake this adventure. In an email he sent me after returning home, he was philosophical about the whole thing,

> "I enjoyed the trip despite the outburst at the end. Like you it spoilt the experience at the time, but when I look back on it now I find that I do not think about the outburst, but I think about the actual sailing and the experience through the storm and the teamwork in getting through the storm, with more than one pair of hands on the tiller."

Garry and I bade farewell and resolved to keep in touch. I was now alone and free to explore this ancient sea port city and to ponder my future plans. I started by treating myself to a hearty breakfast that included scrambled egg, sausage, French pastries, fresh fruit and real café au lait.

The city of La Rochelle dates back to the 12th century when it was the most important commercial harbour serving western France. Today it boasts of a large commercial port for the shipping of grain, forestry products and petroleum and of the largest pleasure craft marina in Europe. The latter consists of several interconnected basins, which together can hold nearly 4,000 boats, soon to be enlarged to 5,000 – big by any standard.

If it wasn't for the modern sailboats in full view of rue Quai Duperré, you might think that you've stepped out of a time machine and find yourself perambulating an 18th century city. The entrance to the main harbour is guarded by a pair of stone towers that were built in the 14th century to control access to the basin. The town centre consists of three to four story stone buildings lining narrow streets that intersect each other at odd angles and that somehow manage to accommodate one-way automobile traffic – proof that you didn't step off a time machine. Along the waterfront and at every corner there are cafés filled with patrons chatting away or reading their newspaper or just watching other people walk by. When you ask for a coffee in France, you're served an ounce of dynamite, an espresso presented in a tiny cup. If you want something closer to a Tim Horton's, then you have to ask for *un café américain*, which is actually a diluted espresso, *un allongé*. If black coffee isn't your cup of tea, then you can either choose between a Capuccino or a *café au lait*. The former consists of a third espresso, a third steamed milk and a third whipped milk froth topped with a sprinkling of either powdered chocolate or cinnamon. The latter is a mixture of half coffee and half hot milk. The proper way of serving *café au lait* is to pour the coffee and the hot milk into a bowl-sized cup from their respective decanters simultaneously with the streams of contrasting colours intermingling on their descent into the cup.

This first day in La Rochelle I spent aimlessly walking around, taking in the sights, checking the pulse of this lively city and relishing the advantages of moving around freely in large spaces, eating delicious food, sitting in comfortable chairs, taking a shower and sleeping in a large bed that doesn't move. Invariably, when walking downtown, I would end up near one of the basins filled with sailboats moored to the docks. For any boat lover, strolling along the La Rochelle docks with its innumerable, gleaming sailing vessels, presents an unending supply of eye candy. Although I've never owned a sailboat, I can appreciate what is a beautiful boat and what is a dud in the same way as being or not being married doesn't preclude one from admiring the young and beautiful of the opposite sex. For many sailors, the simple act of oogling such a vast number of beautiful boats would incite them to trade up to a larger vessel.

So far I've resisted the temptation of buying a sailboat of my own. There would be some attractive advantages in owning my own boat. I would be able to leave anytime I want, sail on any body of water I want, choose my crewmates, set the rules on my boat, equip her to my taste with the amenities that suit me. Also, I wouldn't ever have to risk crewing for a temperamental captain. However, over the years I've observed that boat ownership isn't necessarily a bed of roses. The boat owner, for one thing is faced with many inescapable costs. On average, every year a boat can set him back between 10 and 20 percent of its value in maintenance, operating, dockage, storage and insurance costs. More importantly, he has to spend endless hours taking her out of storage in the spring, stepping the mast and adjusting the rigging, scrubbing and polishing the hull, scrubbing the deck, polishing the stainless steel parts, making repairs from a never ending list and hauling her out of the water and winterizing her in the fall. Furthermore, unless he's a hermit, he is constantly seeking compatible people to join him as crew. To boot, owning a boat can actually *reduce* your sailing venues and opportunities, since to justify all the money and work you've invested in your treasured yacht, you have to make use of her. The rational thing to do then, is to pass up opportunities to bareboat in other waters farther afield, and by the same token, it doesn't make sense to accept an invitation to join a

Transatlantic on an Open 60!

friend on *his* boat while *yours* stays unused at the dock. After thirteen years of sailing without a boat, I'm quite content. This wouldn't work if everybody did as I do, of course.

After my first day of just bumming around town, I headed for the Mercure dining room to treat myself to a fine dinner. Their breakfast had been excellent and I was impressed with the menu, which had the variety and sophistication of a first-rate French restaurant. Moreover, from the top floor of the hotel, the tables by the windows afforded a delightful view of the harbor. After two weeks without vegetables, I felt the need to top up with greens. So I started with a mixed green salad, tastefully presented with filaments of orange rind, fresh strawberries and a sprinkling of pine nuts. I bypassed the soup, although I'm sure it would have been superb, and went directly for the *plat de résistance*. It was a delectable seafood dish anointed with an unctuous sauce served with roasted potatoes and steamed vegetables. A meal is never complete without dessert, so the chocoholic in me opted for a Dark Chocolate Terrine with white chocolate slivers and orange scented English cream.

It was early when I decided to call it a day. Sleep came with ease and I slept like a log for ten hours. I woke up refreshed the next morning, still feeling the room tilt and rock during my first steps. I made a rough plan for the coming days and my return home. After eating, I went online with my laptop and the hotel's WiFi, pronounced VeeFee in French. I looked up the Velux Five Oceans news to see what was being said about the coming race. There was an article on Sail-World that left me puzzled:

> Canadian ocean racer Derek Hatfield arrived in Velux 5 Oceans home port La Rochelle this morning after sailing more than 3,000 miles **solo** (my emphasis) across the Atlantic. Derek's arrival marks the end of a two-week voyage from Nova Scotia, Canada, on his Eco 60 *Active House*. Derek slipped on to the berth in the Bassin des Chalutiers in the city's Vieux Port under the cover of darkness shortly after 6.30am...

This report was repeated almost word for word on at least eight web sites. I closed the sailing web site and then stayed on-line to reserve my flight from Paris to Ottawa and a hotel room near the Charles de Gaulle airport. Then I walked a few blocks to the train station to inquire about schedules to Paris and reserved my trip on the TGV (Train grande vitesse). By the way, for a city of 80,000 citizens, La Rochelle has a train station that would put any major Canadian railway station to shame, and what's more, it has trains running every half hour. My plan was that I would spend the next two days roaming around this great port city, on the third day I would take the TGV to Paris and on the fourth I would fly home.

I visited the La Rochelle aquarium, an impressive collection of 12,000 fish and coral species from all parts of the world, distributed amongst dozens of huge aquariums holding millions of litres of water.

With its flat topography, and its dedicated bicycle lanes, La Rochelle is the perfect place to visit on two wheels. To encourage visitors to use this means of transportation, the City rents bikes at no charge for the first two hours, then only one Euro per subsequent hour. I spent a whole day liesurely rolling along, taking in the sights of the city's ancient streets, its beautiful parks and its shorelines.

Now that I'm back in the familiar setting of my home and I reflect on the experience, like Garry, I think of the good moments on the boat. Admittedly, for several days after the adventure, I would mull over the captain's lack of appreciation for his crew and his lady's lack of sensitivity. But I no longer let this bother me. What Derek's behaviour reveals is that even our models, our champions, those who have reached the peak of perfection in their field, have human frailties. A bad temper is not uniquely the domain of a great sailor, but a foible that is frequently found in men and women in all walks of life. The fact that Derek offered an apology, even if somewhat imperfect, shows that he recognised his wrong and that he is not mean spirited.

At the time of this writing the Velux Five Oceans race is now over. Derek safely completed the race and placed overall third amongst the four contenders to reach the finish line. Moments after completing the race, this is what he had to say:

> "It's a fantastic feeling to be in. This was a huge project, two years in preparation and then nine months of sailing and to get it all done is amazing. The sense of accomplishment is huge..."

When I undertook to do this trip, I thought the experience would provide the answer to the question of whether or not I would want to sail around the world. I love being out at sea, I enjoy the smell of salt air, the commanding sunrises and sunsets, the visits by pods of dolphins, the spectacle of seabirds and their feats of flight, the awe-inspiring immensity of a star studded sky, the sound of the bow wave that ripples along the sides of the hull, the humbling immensity of the infinite horizon, the freshening breezes that swell the seas, the spray that invigorates.

My thinking now is that I can enjoy those things, but it doesn't have to be for years at a time. I may choose to direct my attention toward less ascetic ways of enjoying the sea than making thirty-day passages. One thing for sure, is that Open 60s are out of the question. Been there, done that.

An ideal way for a young man or woman of modest means to see the world is by hitchhiking their way by crewing on OPYs. But I'm becoming more and more chronologically-challenged. When I met the mayoress of Iqaluit on my way to the start of my trek across Baffin Island at the age of 63, she exclaimed,

"You're no spring chicken, to be doing that!"

That was very true at the time and now at the ripe age of 69, spring is a long way behind! There is less time ahead, so I have to concentrate on cramming as much activity as possible per unit of time. And for me there is not only sailing in my life. There is canoeing, hiking, skiing and cycling, all of which require that shrinking element, *time*. And there is my family, which occupies a big place in my life, and my granddaughter who is growing too fast to leave behind for a period of years.

There is also my commitment to society to which I owe a great debt. I see our civilization on the brink of collapse as we are blindly heading for the resources cliff at full speed, in pursuit of economic growth. I have some ideas as to how we should, if we are indeed an intelligent species, take measures to mitigate its ultimate collapse. Since the launching of my web site www.peakoilandhumanity.com in 2005 my thinking has evolved and I'm ready to put my unconventional ideas on paper in the form of a book, a project that will take all of my spare time for the next few years.

I can relish being at sea without leaving shore for weeks at a time by limiting my offshore passages to a few days and spend more time island hopping and coastal navigating. I still want to see French Polynesia and there are many more places I would like to explore by sea: the Azores, the Canaries, Croatia, Thailand, New Zealand, the Gulf Islands and I'd go back to Desolation Sound at the drop of a hat. Flying is still affordable and I could fly to those places and bareboat, couldn't I?

Next time you go to one of these places you may see on the terrace of a local watering hole, a mature man with thinning white hair, wearing a Tilley hat, a polo shirt and Crocs in his feet, sitting at a table with his laptop, and it will be me. Tap me on the shoulder and tell me you've read my book. I'll buy you a drink and we'll talk sailing. In the meantime, FAIR WINDS!

ANNEX 1

Advice for Finding an OPY

Experience: Whatever your level of experience, there should be some formal training in your background. If you have learned to sail from a friend or on your own, there are invariably important concepts that you have failed to grasp and you would benefit from taking a formal course with an accredited school either with the Canadian Yachting Association (CYA) or the American Sailing Association (ASA). Both associations allow an experienced sailor to challenge the lower level exams without having to take the basic courses. This way, you could take a course at your entry level without having to go through all the basic levels.

If you have never sailed, you should obtain the Basic Cruising Standard with the CYA or the Basic Coastal Cruising Standard with the ASA. This knowledge will open the doors to finding an interesting experience on an OPY and will give you the upper hand over a competing boatseeker with no formal training. If you have no experience at all, this won't necessarily exclude you, as some captains may already have enough experienced crew and might be ready to train you as you go. Regardless of your level of expertise, everybody has something they can contribute to the adventure. You might take some recipes aboard and attain a reputation as a galley star, or if you play the harmonica you might become the boat's entertainer, or if you have mechanical skills, you will soon become the boat's grease monkey, as repairs will come sooner rather than later.

First communication with captain: Your first communication with the skipper will probably be by email, at which time you will send him your sailing credentials (it could be a her, of course, but very few ladies advertise for crew). This will include any courses you've taken, how much you have sailed (how many days or miles), on what kind of boats and on which bodies of water. You will have to include some personal background such as sex, age, and special abilities, such as cooking, playing a musical instrument, ability to speak the language of the places you are going to visit, your swimming ability, handiwork, woodworking, mechanics, electronics or scuba diving. Be up front about your experience for your own safety and the safety of others. If you exaggerate your level of knowledge the cat will get out of the bag very soon, but perhaps at an inopportune time. It is a good idea to put together a sailing résumé, which will be useful to the captain in his selection of crew and later if you want to bareboat. You should also expect the skipper to provide you with information about his own level of experience, details about the boat and how long he has owned it. Look for a skipper who has had several years experience in the type of sailing he is offering (offshore or coastal). Then you should try to talk to him over the phone, although in the absence of body language, voice is not much better than writing. It's no guarantee you'll be able to detect all of the red flags, so if things don't feel right, drop him like a hot potato.

Meeting first time: When you meet for the first time, be yourself. Within little time, you will need to assess whether or not this trip is for you. Don't be afraid to ask questions relating to safety and the proposed itinerary. If the skipper doesn't offer a familiarization session, tell him you feel it is important that you be familiar with all safety aspects of the boat and ask him to show you where are the safety items listed in Annex 5, Checklists for Successful Bareboating. With the captain's permission, perform all the checks mentioned in the list.

Testing the boat and crew: A shakedown cruise in home waters would be very helpful if you're engaging in a long passage. If the boat is one the captain has just bought and wants to take across an ocean, then he should of necessity embark on a weeklong shakedown cruise before heading out for the great blue yonder. There are many things that can go wrong with a used boat, so it takes a lot of sea miles to discover them all. If it's a used boat the captain is not familiar with, you might find yourself many weeks in a foreign port waiting for the captain to receive boat parts and to make the necessary repairs.

Female crew request: Ladies, when a captain specifies that he is looking for female crew, take that as a warning that he may not want you just for your winching and cooking abilities.

Ladies versus men: Some women fear taking up sailing because they think that their limited physical strength will be a handicap. Everybody has certain limitations that he or she must overcome. The trick is to learn to work within one's limits. The sailing manoeuvres required for operating a sailboat don't require exceptional strength. Large boats are usually equipped with an electric windlass, which takes most of the muscle work out of anchoring; they often have a furling mainsail, which facilitates putting up sail. What women lack in strength they usually make up with brains. I'm not saying women are more intelligent than men, but when a woman needs to accomplish a physical chore, she uses her head rather than brute force. Furthermore, in situations that require endurance over a long period of time, women have an advantage over men, as their greater amount of body fat provides them with a long lasting source of energy that can help pull them through long stretches of hardship. Remember that Samantha Davis, who arrived third in the 2008 Vendée Globe sailed her 60-foot boat single-handedly around the world non-stop and unassisted – and she's undoubtedly a woman!

Schedule: Keep in mind that on the ocean it is not possible to adhere to a schedule. A safe captain won't venture into force seven winds if he has the chance to wait out the weather for a day or two. Furthermore, the boat can be held up for repairs somewhere other than the departure point of your flight home. So book your return flight at least 3 or 4 days after the planned arrival at your destination or wait until arrival before booking.

Money: It's always a tossup between having enough cash to serve your needs and insufficient enough to render a loss inconsequential. In the past you could stock up on travellers' cheques, which procured peace of mind, as they were insured against loss. In their heyday most stores would accept American Express cheques in lieu of cash. But with the advent of the ATM travellers' cheques are rapidly going the way of the dodo. Today, pretty well anywhere in the world your banking card is accepted and will permit you to withdraw money from your home bank account in the form of local currency. When you go to an ATM in Grenada the machine will produce East Caribbean dollars. Your bank will charge you an exchange rate for the currency and a hefty, fixed service charge. So it makes sense to withdraw enough money for several days at a time and hide some of it in a hard-to-find place on the boat. Bear in mind one important caution. In some countries your four-digit code won't work and in others a six-digit code won't work. Do your homework in advance and have your home bank supply you with a code accepted in the host country. You can carry out cash withdrawals on your credit card, but at a high price, since interest will be charged from the day of withdrawal at the usual usurious rate. This does not mean that you can't use your credit card however. You can avoid interest charges by depositing enough money into your credit card account before leaving home to provide funds for all that you intend to spend during the entire trip. You're better to borrow from your line of credit and put that money in your credit card account than to give the banks the chance to rip you off. Finally, you can use your credit card directly to pay for purchases or meals. But cruiser beware, the wolf is at the

Advice for Finding an OPY

door! For every credit card transaction abroad your dear bank will charge you an exchange rate, which is OK, but it may also charge you a 2½ percent service fee on top of that. However, if you are using a card that gives you a 1% dividend, you might rationalize that the 1½ % difference might be worth your while for the convenience of not having to deal with cash. And if you pay off your balance before the due date, you avoid interest charges.

What can you expect to pay? In a nutshell:
Travel insurance
Your flights to the point of departure and back home
Entry visas
Airport taxes
Exit fees
Taxi between airport and marina
Your personal expenses
Your share of the food and drink
Usually: Your share of the fuel and dock fees
Sometimes a daily stipend of $10 to $15

Health concerns: I can't insist too much on your visiting your local travel health clinic to get the vaccinations that are required for the places you will be visiting. Do so at least three months before your trip, as some vaccines, such as hepatitis, require two boosters. For the Caribbean, the main concern is hepatitis, a potentially fatal liver disease. You may be required to be immunized against both hepatitis A and B. You will be more at risk of sustaining an open wound, so you should get a tetanus booster. You might be advised to get vaccinated for diphtheria and typhoid depending on where you are going and what you will be doing. In many parts of the world malaria, which is spread by the Anopheles mosquito, is endemic. There is no vaccine for this deadly disease. If you are going to be visiting areas where your risk is high, you might have to take antimalarial drugs such as chloroquine continuously before, during and after the trip, which are not without side-effects. Malaria transmission can be reduced by preventing mosquito bites with mosquito nets and insect repellents. The little critters come out after sundown, so if you limit your excursions on land to daylight hours, you will be reducing your risk. Usually your boat will be anchored away from shore where the mosquitoes will be less abundant. If you are walking through the jungle, remember that there are fungal spores on every piece of vegetation. It is important to wear goggles or wraparound glasses to protect your eyes from an injury that could result in blindness. I know. It is a good idea on a boat for all members of the crew to be familiar with first aid and CPR. It's well worth the one hundred bucks it costs every three years to keep current. Finally, being away from home and responsibilities can lead to tempting romantic occasions. Remember that a one-night stand is risky with regards to contracting STDs. You'd be advised to practice safe sex, but abstinence, even if boring, might be the wiser option.

Keeping fit: One of the great advantages of life at sea is that even though you might eat like a king or queen, you will likely lose weight. The diet will be different from your normal fare and you will likely consume fewer calories all told. Sailing manoeuvres require use of your muscles, whether it be through raising and lowering sails, taking or shaking a reef, trimming the sails with the winch, handling the ground tackle or digging to the bottom of very full lockers to retrieve what you are looking for. The constant movement of the vessel renders displacing yourself around the boat a form of exercise that will keep your muscles toned up and keep you fit.

The digestive system: You may find that for a few days your digestive system might work on the "IN" mode while the "OUT" mode is out of service. It is unlikely that you will need to take a laxative, as everything should start working normally after a few days. The opposite problem might occur and this could be from microorganisms your immune system hasn't been exposed to before. Wash vegetables in seawater and rinse in fresh. Be mindful about refrigerator temperature. It's important to run the engine sufficiently long and frequently to maintain a temperature of 2 to 6 degrees C (36 to 42 F). If the captain neglects this aspect of health, then you will have to be doubly careful of what you eat. One easy precaution to take is to avoid sharing your water bottle with other members of the crew.

<u>Seasickness</u>: You won't know how motion sickness affects you until you've experienced heavy sea conditions. To recapitulate, to avoid seasickness, the night before casting off, take your seasickness pills, don't eat a heavy meal or drink alcohol or coffee and go to bed early. You can either take Gravol 12 hours before the trip by mouth or scopolamine by transdermal (skin) patch 4 hours before casting off. You should not take Gravol if you have bronchitis, emphysema, an enlarged prostate or glaucoma. You should not wear the patch if you are a child, pregnant, elderly, or if you suffer from glaucoma or urinary obstruction. If you have faith in this kind of hocus-pocus, you can use acupressure bands or a copper bracelet, which don't bestow any of the unpleasant side effects of the medications. Besides these precautions, there isn't much you can do. In my case, after my third trip on the open sea I had become an old salt, able to withstand sticking my head into a smelly engine compartment during a gale. Not all are so lucky.

<u>Potable water:</u> Water, water, everywhere and not a drop to drink...well, your captain will have seen to provisioning the boat with plenty of drinking water. Often the quality of the water that is supplied at third world marinas is of doubtful quality. Furthermore, even good water can become foul when it's been confined for an extended period of time in dark tanks in hot weather. Slime grows in the tanks and it's almost impossible to get rid of it all. There are generally two ways to obtain water that is potable. One is to boil it. When there are only two or three people on board this can be done reasonably easily if everybody cooperates. It's a matter of dedicating two large plastic bottles or carboys to the position of boiled water holders. Whenever you boil water to make coffee or tea you heat up a whole kettle full and let the unused portion cool, then pour it into the bottle that's not in use; you drink the water from the other bottle. At night before going to bed you boil a kettle full and maybe also a couple of potfuls, leave it to cool overnight and by the next morning you can pour your potable water into the carboys. It's safe, but not always good tasting. You can enjoy better tasting water by storing a bottle of it in the refrigerator. The second way is simply to buy bottled water. Of course there is a third way, the watermaker, but most cruisers have not undertaken that expense.

<u>Hydration:</u> Now that we're on the subject of H_2O: You can lead a horse to water but you can't make him drink. Which means that although the captain may have seen to providing the boat with an adequate supply, it's up to you to remember to drink plenty of it, especially when you're underway and exposed to the warm wind. It's surprising how much you can lose in perspiration. So drink 3 to 4 litres a day (including your coffee and other drinks).

<u>Bathing:</u> On a long passage you will have to limit your bathing to sponge baths. Never, never let the fresh water run. You might need to do as we did on *Three's Company* during our passage on the Pacific and bathe in the cockpit. For lathering with seawater, use sea soap or the green camp soap sold in camping equipment stores. Once the boat is at anchor, you have access to Mother Nature's giant bathtub and you can rinse off with fresh water from the transom shower.

Advice for Finding an OPY

<u>At the airport</u>: Arrive at the airport three hours ahead of time for an international flight. I discovered that for a 0600 flight out of Ottawa, there was no point in submitting to this rule, as the only moving creatures at the airport at 0300 were the dust bunnies. Remember that some airlines will charge a hefty surplus if a bag weighs more than 22 kg. So anything over that weight has to be taken with your carryon or shared amongst two pieces of checked luggage. But then, some airlines charge a fee for a second bag. Your airline can provide you with information about what is permitted on the aircraft and which dangerous weapons such as nail clippers are prohibited. All my life I've carried a pocketknife on me and every time I take a flight I have my terrorist weapon confiscated. I've just never learned to leave it in my checked luggage. Make sure your laptop's battery is fully charged in case the security people ask you to turn it on. Dump your drinking water into the nearest planter if you don't want your favourite water bottle confiscated. Submit graciously to our quasi totalitarian government's ridiculous requirement to go through the full body scanner. You have no choice if you want to travel, unless you prefer to have your private parts fondled by strangers. The slight health risk from the radiation is worth taking for the pleasure of sailing in a distant paradise. Dress neatly and take all metal out of your lips and nose. Be polite and cheerful with security and border personnel. And don't make any jokes, as they have no sense of humour.

<u>What to take on the boat with you:</u> On a sailboat space is at a premium. If you want to rub the captain the wrong way, come aboard his boat with a large, solid suitcase! He will make you sleep with it! Or *in* it! First thing then, is to pack everything in a soft suitcase or duffle bag that can be tucked into a small space. The choice of clothing depends on whether you are sailing in northern or southern latitudes. In northern latitudes you can expect the air above the sea to be cold at all times of the year, so you will want cold weather clothes including foul weather gear consisting of a heavy rain suit, with bib pants, a toque and rubberized gloves, plenty of woollen sweaters and long johns. A towel to put around your neck can be useful for absorbing splashes. You will also want a baseball cap to put under your hood, as its bill causes the hood to turn with your head. Below you will find lists of personal items to include in your baggage. In the tropics, you will be comfortable with just a pair of jogging shorts, T-shirt, hat and sunglasses. Make sure you get a tether for the sunglasses and prescription glasses, otherwise they will eventually get projected into the sea by a wayward line or flogging sail. Uncovered parts of the body should be protected with sunblock. If you're coming from the north in the winter, limit your solar exposure to ten minutes the first day and increase gradually. If your skin is very fair, you might need U-V blocking lip balm. And don't forget to protect your nose and ears.

<u>Relaxation:</u> Unless you end up with a slave driver as captain, you will have time on your hands occasionally. Take with you all the books you haven't yet had time to read. Better still, you can load as many as you want on a Kindle, which can be used in bright sunshine. You might want to take DVDs to watch, subject to prior discussion with the captain. You could save weight by transferring all your movies onto a memory stick. With the advent of the Ipod, there is no point in carrying music in the form of CDs anymore. Check with the captain as to which of your electronic gadgets he will allow you to operate on the boat's electric system. If you don't take a laptop with you, take a writing pad to keep notes of the places you've been to. If you like taking photographs take your camera along, but don't forget an extra battery, the charger and the data transfer cord. If you're so inclined, you might want to upload your pictures daily and create a PowerPoint presentation as-you-go while the events of the day are fresh in your mind. Keep in mind that salt spray is deadly for electronic equipment.

<u>Communication with home</u>:

Writing: The days of the personal letter by mail are pretty well over, as we now have instant communication by email. Almost every town now has Internet cafés where you can get online if you don't have your own computer. If you have access to an on board computer, you will find WiFi connections on just about every town's shoreline. This service is increasing exponentially, so within a few years, you will be able to connect from almost anywhere in the world. You can buy a range booster to increase your computer's range, allowing you to go online from the comfort of your boat's anchorage (Alfa Network AWUS036H works well). Finally, some boats, such as *Ventus* are equipped with satellite communication (Skymate) that allows sending and receiving emails offshore, as well as receiving weather faxes. There is a cost to this, so your captain might place restrictions on its use. Postcards are still in vogue, but not for long, as Facebook, which allows you to post pictures for your friends to see has dealt them a death blow.

Voice: Nothing equals hearing the voice of a friend or a loved one when you're far away in a foreign country. There are two inexpensive ways of phoning. One is to buy a phone card in the country you are calling from. This way you are certain you will not be exposed to highway robbery as I was once at the Newark airport. My flight was delayed and I used my Bell Canada calling card to phone Micheline, thinking that I would only be charged 7 cents a minute. The flight was postponed four times and each time I made a one minute call home. When I got my telephone bill, I almost fell to the floor! The local telephone carrier charged me $20 per call, for a total of $80. Better still than a telephone card is to use your computer and Skype. With this online service you can call computer-to-computer for free or from computer-to-telephone for about 2 cents per minute, anywhere in the world. There are two other ways of communicating by voice. One is by satellite phone at about $4 per minute; the advantage is that you can call from anywhere on the globe, even from the middle of the Pacific! Finally, if the boat is equipped with a Single Side Band short wave radio and the captain has made arrangements with a communication centre near home, you could phone home for free, subject to weather conditions and availability of a frequency.

Sleeping on the boat: It's not likely that the captain will give you the choice of berth. When underway the V berth will be unusable, as I explained in my story, but it is often the most comfortable one at anchor because of the position of its wind-grabbing hatch. Second in comfort, in my opinion is the main salon settee, because of the airyness of the space. Least comfortable are the "coffins" that are usually situated in the quarters. Here's a hint if you have qualms about hygiene with regards to hot bunking. Buy yourself a zippered, cotton sleeping bag liner. Sleeping bags are simply too hot for the tropics. Bring a pillowcase with a distinct pattern from home and when you organize your personal effects on the boat, slip one of the boat's pillows into the pillowcase and it will stand out as your personal pillow for the duration of the trip. If the boat doesn't supply a pillow, then you can buy a tiny down-filled camping pillow from a camping equipment store. When comes your turn to sleep, roll out your liner, plop down your pillow and enjoy sleeping in your own bedding. When your turn comes to rise and shine, just roll up the liner and put it away with your personalized pillow. To mitigate the sound of snoring in the next berth, you might have to wear earplugs. When at anchor avoid walking on the deck above sleeping crew.

Hiking and trekking: What about walking through the jungle in tropical and semitropical regions? You will need a pair of solid walking boots or shoes to protect yourself against a twisted ankle. You'll need to wear long pants and a long sleeve shirt to avoid being injured by prickly plants or by the toxic sap of young manchineel trees, which are found along coastal beaches in Florida, the Caribbean and Central and South America. Never sit under a manchineel tree when it's raining. The poison leaching from its leaves could leave serious burns all over your body, and it stands to reason, never succumb to the temptation of eating its little fruit that resembles an apple. If you encounter biting insects, an insect repellent would be of use. Wear a wide-brimmed hat and put on sunblock, to protect yourself from the sun. If you are doing a lot of trekking, a pair of collapsible walking sticks would be useful for securing your footing. You might want to take a pair of binoculars to get a closer look at wildlife. You'll find yourself perspiring a lot and the body's lost water has to be replaced; so bring along a couple of litres of water per half day. You'll find it nice to have munchies such as gorp (Good Old Raisins and Peanuts). Chocolate is not very practical in the tropical heat, but in northern latitudes it makes a good source of energy. But if you are a chocoholic like myself, you'll enjoy heat resistant Smarties or M&Ms. Other items that you might want to carry in case of emergency are rain gear, a pocket knife, matches, a compass, a whistle, a flashlight, water purification tablets, string or light rope and a first aid kit.

Yelling is normal: It's quite normal for the captain to yell orders, especially when the crew are upwind of him and the engine is making its normal noise or the wind is whistling through the rigging. However, if he yells for no good reason, or gets angry for no good reason, then have a Plan B and put it in effect. Yelling for attention is normal; yelling out of anger is not. Keep in mind that the skipper is the boss. A considerate captain will consult his crew about issues of daily life but will always have the last word.

Modesty: We all have different sensibilities with regard to nudity. It is quite possible that once you are out on the bluewater you will witness one or more crew removing more pieces of clothing than you are used to seeing, especially if they are European. It is generally harmless to the observer. Ladies, don't be shocked if you see gentlemen standing at the pushpit and a jet of yellow liquid is streaming into the ocean. It is a very common, if dangerous practice that I don't encourage on a boat that is underway.

Using the head: The captain will give you a demonstration on how to use and flush the head, as the head on a boat is very different from the toilet you are used to at home. He will probably warn you against putting toilet paper in the bowl. Don't cheat, ever! Always put your used paper in the container supplied for that purpose. And gentlemen, for the sake of hygiene and spray avoidance, remember that when you have to go to the head you should be *seated for all your performances*.

Footwear: Don't board the boat with the same shoes you wore on land. In the Caribbean the usual footwear is what you were born with. The risk of walking barefoot on a yacht is that you will inevitably smash a little toe on one of the many pieces of rigging at little toe level. If you prefer not to take that chance, or if you are sailing in colder climates, or if the captain has a rule against bare feet, reserve a pair of deck shoes or a pair of Crocks to wear solely on the boat. Deck shoes have non-scuffing, anti slip soles and are sold in chandleries. For cold weather sailing, you will have to wear rubber sailing boots over woollen socks and pass your foul weather pant legs over the tops of the boots.

Safety on board: Remember the old adage: "One hand for you and one hand for the boat." When walking on the deck of a boat underway, keep one hand free to hold onto the boat. Remember the safe parts to hold onto: the handholds, the pushpit and pulpit, the mast, the shrouds and the stays. Don't rely on the lifelines as they aren't strong enough to hold you if the boat gives a sudden lurch. In heavy seas, clip your harness onto the jackline on the windward side of the boat (the high side). Once you've reached the portion of the boat where you want to work, you can unclip from the jackline and clip onto one of the parts previously mentioned. A double tether system is best, as you can ensure there is always one of your tethers attached to the boat. Keep in mind that the only safe way to go down the companionway stairs is backwards whilst holding onto the handholds.

Liability: As for the question of responsibility, the captain might have you sign a waiver relieving him of any responsibility in case of accident or injury. He might want to see your return ticket home and ascertain that you have the funds to repatriate yourself from any distant port, should that be necessary. Remember that the captain is responsible if any of his crew jumps ship in a foreign country with the intention of immigrating. He will indubitably keep your passport with his boat papers for the duration of the passage as he will have to present all of his crews' passports whenever he clears in and clears out a country. He might want to see proof that you have travel insurance, as he wouldn't want to be stuck for paying your medical bills should you get injured on his boat.

Travel insurance: When you buy travel insurance, be sure that the period extends beyond your intended stay abroad, in case there is a change of plans. You must also ensure that the contract contains a repatriation clause that pays for flying you back home on a stretcher. I know a woman who was seriously injured in a car accident in France. She had to be flown back to Canada on a stretcher, which occupies three airplane seats. It cost her $8000 out of her own pocket, payable in advance – and this was back in the 1980s. Should you require medical attention abroad, your insurance company will likely want you to obtain preauthorization before you engage in any costs. If you are unable to do so yourself, ask another member of the crew to phone your insurance company in your place.

Float plan: An important precaution is to provide someone at home with the information about the captain, the boat, and the captain's email address. The captain should file a float plan with somebody who will alert the coast guard should the boat not show up within a reasonable time of its ETA. Make sure that if you expect to make landfall on a certain date that your loved ones at home waiting to hear from you understand that a long passage can take as much as 50% longer than average. Provide the captain with contact information of someone at home who can make decisions in your place in case of an incapacitating accident.

Safety inspection: Find out from the captain if there are any parts of the boat or any pieces of equipment that he considers "off limits" to the crew. If you see that he's too touchy about "his boat" to the point that he won't let you familiarize yourself with the safety aspects of the vessel, it might be better to put Plan B in effect.

Resolve issues before leaving: If there is anything that doesn't "feel right" about the boat, the crew, the food or whatever, discuss the matter with the captain and get resolution with him to allay any doubt or uncomfortable gut feeling. A boozing skipper or crew is a sign of trouble. A ration of rum or a beer per day is okay, but drinking to excess is not acceptable. If you have any doubt about the captain's competence or level of preparation or lack thereof, or if there are any sexual innuendos even before you're underway, remember your Plan B. Any misgivings on shore might turn out to be serious problems out at sea. Don't put yourself in the position of not having enough money to travel back home on your own.

Personal security: Wherever you go in the world, even if it's in your local neighbourhood there are dangers of some form or another. We tend to think of the criminal element as being the greatest threat to our safety, whereas the greatest risk to young people is that of dying in a car accident. If you're walking at night on a narrow Caribbean road, you will be in more danger of being struck by a car than being attacked by a robber. Keeping that in mind, obvious precautions would be to walk facing the traffic, wear light coloured clothing and wield a flashlight. It's important to know which parts of a city are safe and which are dangerous. If you must wait for a bus in a dangerous part of town, wear your knapsack in front of you and stand with your back against a wall. Don't wear a fanny pack in places that are known for having pickpockets. These scoundrels work in teams with an accomplice to distract you while the thief slices your fanny pack's belt. Don't wear jewellery and never wear earrings, as you might end up with torn earlobes. Carry a photocopy of your passport, your money and your credit cards in an undergarment pouch. In most popular sailing places there is no more danger than at home if you apply good old common sense. As for the danger of a pirate attack, read my musings on the subject in Annex 7.

Hitchhiking the seas: Many adventurers have gone around the world by hitching rides, one section of the globe at a time. Sailboats move around the world with the trade winds. These winds obey seasonal patterns, which govern the movement of the cruising community. If you wish to hitch a ride as crew on a yacht it is important to know these schedules in order to place yourself in the right place at the right time. Cruising yachts often take on extra crew to assist with sailing on long passages. The best way to find a berth on an OPY planning a passage is to be at one of the various points of departure and ready at the right time. Spend your days around the marinas and anchorages and offer all the sailboat captains help with boat maintenance and let them know that you are keen to join a yacht for an onward passage. Make yourself useful, reliable and likeable. Remember, cruisers are a close-knit community, so do what is necessary to be recommended for a crew position. Place notices of your availability at all of the marinas, boatyards, yacht clubs and chandleries in the area. Often cruisers take on sailing crew at the last minute due to a failure of prior arrangements, as in the case of Anthony when I first met him. Make sure that you are on hand, ready and available when crew is needed.

Making yourself useful: You don't necessarily need to have experience in navigation and meteorology to be useful to the captain. If you want to make an impression and be appreciated as good crew, these are some of the things you can do. First, "The way to a man's heart is through his stomach" is true of sailors as well as landlubbers. If you know how to cook, then you've got it made. There are, however many more ways you can endear yourself to the boat's captain and regular crew. There are always cleaning chores to do on a boat: scrubbing the hull before the barnacles take hold, scrubbing the white fibreglass deck, polishing the stainless steel rigging, polishing the woodwork, cleaning the head and the galley, cleaning behind the stove, cleaning and disinfecting the fridge as well as simply putting things back in their place. Furthermore, there are maintenance jobs like pumping the bilge every day (to clear it of propane gas), coiling and tidying up the lines, checking the rigging for missing screws, bolts, nuts, cotter pins and split rings, checking the lines for fraying, checking the sails for tears. Treat the captain, his boat and the other members of the crew with respect and they will reciprocate. Laziness will get you nowhere, so work hard and be creative and inventive. Be positive, cheerful, friendly, courteous and attentive to others' feelings. This way you'll have a great time on the OPY and you'll get invited again.

Keeping a record of your experience: As soon as you go on your first sailing outing, even if it's only one day, start keeping a log. The log should comprise the date, details about the boat, its make, length and name, the number of days of your outing or trip, the distance covered according to the GPS log, the number of hours spent underway at night, the name of the captain, even if it is yourself, the names of the crew, details about the places visited, anchored in and the track sailed and finally, the signature of the captain, instructor or boat rental manager. You can buy a ready-made logbook or create your own. On the next page you will find a sample personal log which you can reproduce on standard 8 ½ X 11" paper. You can make a number of copies and keep them in a loose-leaf binder. Better still, you can make yourself a logbook by photocopying a number of pages and have them spiral bound with a waterproof cover. If nothing else, your logbook will be an excellent memory bank in the future.

Advice for Finding an OPY

PRACTICAL EXPERIENCE LOG

Vessel		No. of days	Dist. (nm)	Night hours	Captain	Crew	Sailing ground	Certifying signature
Make & length	Name							

ANNEX 2
Checklist for Sailing on an OPY

Safety equipment	Self inflating personal floating device (PFD) with built-in harness (optional if the boat has other types)	
	Harness and tether (if boat not so equipped)	
	Pealess whistle (works when wet)	
	Strobe light for PFD	
	Sailing knife (you might need to cut yourself away if entangled in a rope)	
	Goggles or wraparound glasses in case of hail or heavy rain or walking through the jungle	
	#30 to #60 sunblock, Bug repellent, Lip balm	
	Warm rubber boots (cold weather sailing)	
Clothing	Woollen socks (cold weather sailing)	
	Heavy rain gear with bib pants, Velcro cuffs (cold weather sailing)	
	Light rain gear (warm weather sailing)	
	Toque and gloves (cold weather sailing)	
	Rubberized warm gloves (cold weather sailing)	
	Heavy long sleeved shirts (cold weather sailing)	
	Plenty of woollen sweaters (cold weather sailing)	
	Long johns, bottom and top (cold weather sailing)	
	Towel around the neck to absorb splashes (cold weather sailing)	
	Sailing gloves (purchase in chandleries)	
	Baseball cap to put under the hood, Tether for cap	
	Wide brimmed hat in addition to baseball cap	
	Bathing suit	
	Convertible pants with zip-off legs	

Clothing	At least one lightweight long-sleeve shirt for sun protection or walking through dense bush	
	Underwear, socks, T-shirts	
	Shoes dedicated to boat, with non-scuffing and non-skid soles	
	Street shoes or sneakers, Hiking boots or walking shoes	
	Tether for eyeglasses	
	Sunglasses	
	Prescription glasses (plus a spare pair)	
	Canoe water tight bags for clothing	
	Small pack sack for day outings	
Odds and ends	Under garment money pouch	
	Waterproof bag for wallet, passport, money, etc.	
	Water bottle	
	Sleeping bag (if bed sheets not supplied), Sleeping bag liner	
	Pillow (ask captain if necessary)	
	Pillow case if hot bunking	
	Headlamp (excellent as a reading lamp and useful for everything)	
	Mask, snorkel and fins	
	Fishing tackle if you're so inclined	

Checklist for sailing on an OPY

	A small travel sewing kit	
	Munchies to your taste	
	Light rope or string	
	Binoculars (ask captain if you can use boat's)	
	Laptop (with captain's permission), power cord, external mouse, USB drive	
	Camera, charger, spare battery, data transfer cord, instruction book	
	Extra batteries for everything run on batteries	
	Cheap watch	
	Small gifts	
	Ipod and earphones	
	Travel books, Reading material	
	A musical instrument if you play one (harmonica, flute)	
	Passport, with expiry date 6 months beyond longest possible stay	
	Give captain coordinates of a contact person at home	
	International driver's licence if intend to drive	
	Health insurance card (buy travel health insurance!)	
Papers	3 photocopies of passport (keep them separate from passport)	
	International Certificates of Vaccination booklet	
	Obtain a small amount of currency for each of the countries on your itinerary before leaving home ($50 minimum worth each)	
	Small bills for tipping porters, taxi driver	
	Return air ticket	
	Two different banking cards, One or two credit cards	
	Notebook and pen	
	Bring some of your favourite recipes	
	Sea soap (soap for salt water)	
	Towel and facecloth	
	Toothpaste	
	Toothbrush or electric toothbrush	
	Shaver or razor blades	
Toiletries	240V to 120V transformer if captain's boat or your hotels are on 240V	
	12V DC to 120V AC inverter if boat not so equipped (ask captain permission)	
	Tissues	
	Nail clipper	
	Ear plugs	
	Comb and/or hair brush	
	Band Aids, Gauze pads	
	Bunion or toe bandages	
	Disposable gloves	
	CPR mask (assuming you've taken the course)	
	Small scissors	
First aid and medication	Triangular bandage	
	Tweezers	
	Seasickness medication	
	Antacids (in case you overindulge in the delights of the table)	
	Immodium anti-diarrhoea pills	
	Broad spectrum antibiotic	
	Muscle relaxant	
	Mild laxative (not likely to need)	
	Spare screws and screwdriver for prescription eyeglasses	

ANNEX 3

OPY Search Web Sites

www.crewseekers.co.uk
In business since 1990, Crewseekers offer a wide variety of sailing yacht crew opportunities worldwide. These range from day sailing, offshore cruising and competitive yacht racing to blue water cruising, sailing yacht deliveries and professional sailing positions from deckhands to captains. There is no fee for the boater who is advertising a trip, but there is a £60.00 fee that allows those wanting to crew to obtain the contact information on any captain over a period of six months.

www.sailingnetworks.com
Multi function web site, includes nautical store, and boats for sale, with a large number of boaters looking for crew.
Click on the "Boating Register" button to find a boat or "Crew Finder" to leave your name. Free to register.

www.floatplan.com
This web site is dedicated to crew looking for OPYs or captains looking for crew. It offers other services namely, a "floatplan" page where sailors can post information about themselves and their trips. There are links for boat owners who want their yacht delivered, marine supplies, and post a listing for things they want to buy or sell. It is entirely free.

www.findacrew.net
You do not have to pay anything to see which OPYs are available, but once you have found a captain with whom you wish to communicate, you can upgrade to "Premium Membership" and exchange contact details with as many members as you like. Fees from A$75 for 30 days to A$375 per year, plus 20% extension discounts. (All payments are in Australian Dollars).

www.advantageboating.com

This is the school for which I work as instructor. It offers weeklong trips in different parts of the world during the northern hemisphere winter with excellent skippers at a reasonable cost.

www.cnbg.org

This sailing club organizes trips to various sailing venues in Canada such as the St. Lawrence River during summer months and unlimited sailing on its two boats out of Aylmer, Quebec. The club also offers the CYA Basic Cruising Standard to its members.

www.voile.org

"Affordable Yachting" has been functioning since 1994, For your first experience of a live-aboard sail, you might want to sail with qualified captains on the organized tours offered on this web site. If you're so qualified, this is an excellent resource for bareboating.

ANNEX 4

Canadian and American Sailing Standards

a) Canadian Yachting Association
www.sailing.ca

Basic Cruising covers the skills required to cruise safely in familiar waters as both skipper and crew of a sloop-rigged keelboat of 6 to 10 meters in moderate wind and sea conditions by day.

Basic Keelboat Racing Standard provides the knowledge necessary to compete in club & local races with a fundamental understanding of the racing rules, protest procedures and applying sailing and seamanship skills in winds up to 20 knots.

Intermediate Cruising Standard covers the skills required to safely cruise a keelboat of 8 - 12 metres in familiar waters. It is recommended as the minimum qualification for bareboat chartering. The recommended time for teaching and examining the standard is five days or two weekends.

Coastal Navigation Standard covers the theory required to navigate safely in coastal or inland waters. This theory is applied in the Advanced Cruising standard.

Advanced Cruising Standard covers the skills needed to skipper or crew a sailing cruiser of 8 - 15 metres, in both day and night conditions in coastal waters in any weather.

Offshore Cruising Standard covers the skills required to skipper or crew on offshore passages exceeding 500 miles in length and venturing more than 100 nautical miles from land.

b) American Sailing Association
www.asa.com

Basic Keelboat: Able to sail a boat of about 20 feet in length in light to moderate winds and sea conditions in familiar waters without supervision. A preparatory standard with no auxiliary power or navigation skills required.

Basic Coastal Cruising: Able to cruise safely in local and regional waters as both skipper and crew on an auxiliary powered sailboat of about 20 to 30 feet in length, in moderate winds and sea conditions.

Bareboat Chartering: An advanced cruising Standard for individuals with cruising experience. The individual can act as skipper or crew of a 30 - 50 foot boat sailing by day in coastal waters. The Standard includes
knowledge of boat systems and maintenance procedures.

Coastal Navigation: Able to demonstrate the navigational theory required to safely navigate a sailing vessel in coastal or inland waters. There is no Sailing Skills part to this Standard and practical application of this sailing knowledge is found in the Advanced Coastal Cruising Standard.

Advanced Coastal Cruising: Able to safely act as skipper and crew of a sailing vessel about 30 to 50 feet in length. This is a day and nighttime Standard in coastal and inland water, in any weather.

Offshore Passagemaking: The sailor is able to safely act as skipper or crew of a sailing vessel on offshore passages in any weather. The Celestial Navigation Standard is performed.

Canadian and American Sailing Standards

Organizations that Provide Classroom Instruction

In addition to the above which provide actual sailing experience, Power Squadrons in both Canada and the USA offer navigation and seamanship courses in a classroom environment:

a) Canadian Power and Sail Squadrons
www.cps-ecp.ca

Introductory Courses
Advanced Courses
Electronic Courses
Maritime Radio and Flares
Elective Courses

b) United States Power Squadrons
www.usps.org

Seamanship
Piloting
Advanced Piloting
Junior Navigation
Navigation
Cruise Planning
Engine Maintenance
Marine Communications Systems
Marine Electrical Systems
Electronic Navigation Systems
Sail
Weather

ANNEX 5.

Checklists for Successful Bareboat Chartering

      You want your vacation to be as trouble free as possible. It is wise therefore, to check that everything you need is on the boat and functions before you cast off the docklines. Below you will find a list of items to check prior to leaving with your rented boat, and things to check on a daily and weekly basis during your trip. Should you experience a breakdown in spite of all your precautions, reputable rental companies will come to your boat wherever it happens to be to make an emergency repair. But it's always preferable to serve an ounce of prevention to avoid having to carry out a pound of cure during your dream holiday.

      Share these lists with your first mate to save pre-departure time and to reduce chances of problems en route.

Pre-departure Bareboating Check List

Engine compartment	Check belts for proper tension and wear.	
	Check hoses.	
	Check fluid levels.	
	Battery fluid levels if not sealed.	
Electrical	Check starting and house battery voltage.	
	Activate and inspect all lights.	
	Check diesel fuel level.	
	Perform a radio signal check.	
Navigation	Obtain a long-range weather report for your sailing grounds.	
	Largest scale charts for area you will be sailing.	
	Dividers, pencil, eraser, plotter, calculator.	
	Depth gauge. Check calibration with weighted line.	
	GPS or electronic chart plotter.	
	Tide and current tables if applicable.	
	Sailing guide books if available.	
Aft	Check steering cable for wear.	
	Check pintles and gudgeons on boats with tiller steering.	
On the deck	Check all turnbuckles for tightness and make sure the split rings are all in place.	
	Check forestay(s) and backstay connections.	
	Take a look at each block to ensure it is not broken or loose.	
	Make sure that the sheet travellers slide and lock properly.	
	Check the gooseneck connection.	
	Spare propane tank is full.	
	Understand reefing system before casting off.	
	Check that jib unrolls and rolls freely.	
Anchors	Ensure that you have at least one spare anchor and location of second anchor.	
	Main anchor: check that shackles at the ends of the chain are wired in place.	
	Bitter end attached to the boat.	
	Check windlass works down and up.	
	Check or ask at what depth intervals the markers are placed on the rode.	
	Make sure you have a long mooring line for tying to shore (100 to 300 ft.)	

Checklists for Successful Bareboat Chartering

Cabin	Check head(s) function(s).	
	If you need to convert the salon table into a bed, set it up before leaving in case parts are missing.	
	Check that refrigerator cools.	
	Check propane flows to stove.	
	Bedding, blankets, pillows, towels.	
	Check that all hatches and portlights close and lock.	
Other	Check that all water tanks are full. Make sure you are given a hose.	
	Check operation of holding tank pumpout or dumping mechanism.	
	Shore power cable and adaptors	
	Companionway door panels and key for lock.	
	Deck brush and deck soap	
	Tool kit.	
	Boat manuals.	
Dinghy	Check condition of painter.	
	Start outboard engine to make sure it works, forward, neutral, reverse. Cooling water flows.	
	Know what oil-gas mixture if two cycle.	
	Location of spare shear pin.	
	Pump for re-inflating.	
	Oars.	
	Bailer.	
	Trilight for night travel	
	Padlock, key and chain.	
Safety equipment	Locate the emergency tiller and try it out. Sometimes they give you one from a different boat.	
	Boarding ladder (make sure it is tied up)	
	Check positions of the handholds and that they are secure (not loose).	
	Check manual bilge pump location and handle.	
	Know where electric bilge pumps are located	
	Check bilge water level. Pump dry.	
	Locate position of all thruhulls and make sure you have softwood plugs.	
	Check manual and electric water pumps.	
	Life jacket of right size for each person.	
	Heaving line or man overboard sling.	
	Life ring with 15 m floating line.	
	Fire extinguishers (10BC), one for engine plus one for each fuel burning apparatus. If boat is longer than 12 m, one at entrance of each cabin. Remember where they are.	
	1 Bucket. (Law requires 2 of more than 10 litres if boat is longer than 12 m).	
	Fog horn.	
	Waterproof flashlight.	
	12 flares, at least 6 of which are type A, B, or C.	
	If boat is longer than 12 m, an axe.	

Checklists During Your Bareboating Trip.

Daily checks	Check bilge and pump dry.	
	Water tank levels.	
	Holding tank(s). Plan when and where to pump them out.	

336

Checklists for Successful Bareboat Chartering

	Diesel and gasoline fuel level.	
	Engine oil level.	
	Coolant level.	
	Monitor weather channel.	
	Radio check.	
	Start engine, check cooling water discharge and gauges.	
	Note distance travelled during the day in log.	
Weekly checks	Transmission fluid level.	
	Inspect hoses and belts.	
	Inspect all rigging.	
	Obtain a long-term weather forecast.	
	Activate and inspect all lights.	
Daily post-sail checks	Check anchor swing of other boats arriving.	
	Check tidal range and water depth.	
	Check that battery is on proper setting (1 or 2).	
	Secure halyards to reduce noise.	
	Secure and coil all lines.	
	Check that anchor rode does not chafe.	
	Note longitude and latitude coordinates.	
When at anchor	Set anchor drag alarm	
	Record bearings on two objects on land	
	Turn on anchor light	
	Lock dinghy and/or raise it to deck level depending on level of danger of theft	
When moored to a dock	Secure all dock lines.	
	Secure halyards to reduce noise.	
	Secure and coil all lines.	
	Flake and cover mainsail.	
	Connect shore power.	
	Shut unused thruhulls.	
	Tidy up cockpit (winch handles, lines, etc.).	
	Close and lock hatches if leaving boat unattended.	
	Turn battery switch off.	
	Check fender heights, spring lines and dock lines.	

ANNEX 6

The Nautical Mile Explained as Best I Can

Where does this weird unit come from? Imagine drawing a line around the Earth from pole to pole. To calculate nautical miles this circumference is divided by 360 degrees of arc. There are 60 minutes of arc in a degree and by international agreement, it was decided that one minute would be equal to one nautical mile, which turns out to be 1,852 metres (6,076.12 feet).

This unit is very useful in aeronautic and marine navigation for measuring distances on a chart. Most charts are of Mercator projection, where the poles at top and bottom are as wide as the Equator, creating a distortion the further a point is from the equator.

Therefore, to measure distances between two points on a chart, you take a pair of dividers like the ones you used in geometry class, and apply one end on point A and the other on point B. Then you carry the open dividers over to one of the sides of the chart, which show the degrees of latitude on the latitude scale. You measure the number of minutes between the points of the dividers and voilà, you have the distance in nautical miles! The nautical mile, by the way, is the unit used in international treaties for delimiting territorial waters.

If you want to know more about navigation, you can take the on-line Coastal Navigation course at: http://www.coastalnavigation.com/home.htm.

ANNEX 7

Musings on Piracy

When I returned home after my frightful experience with pirates, a friend asked me if I'd ever want to cruise again. I have to say that the idea of quitting sailing had never crossed my mind. My thoughts were more geared to what to do to prevent a pirate attack. Once you're bitten by the sea bug, nothing short of the grave will keep you away. The many fond memories I had of sailing far outweighed the trauma I had experienced. I knew I would want to continue sailing. However, from then on I would have to keep in mind that the possible emergencies a sailor must be prepared for such as dismasting, a broken rudder, or springing a leak should also include boarding by pirates.

An experience like mine in Margarita, however, is cause for reflection. First and thankfully, we were lucky to have pulled through with only minor bruises, a bit of psychological trauma, a lost computer and a few scratches on the boat. It's easy to imagine worse possible outcomes.

What could we have done to prevent this? If we had been anchored in the company of other sailboats the bandits might have been less likely to attack. But isn't it one of the pleasures of cruising, to seek the peace and quiet of beautiful, isolated anchorages? If we had unceremoniously kicked Che off the boat with a stiff warning he might have perceived us as too tough to risk dealing with. On the other hand, if we had been even "nicer", and taken a picture of him with Jacqui, such a positive identification might have dissuaded an attack. Had the seas not been so rough outside the reef we could have anchored in full view of the poverty stricken village, which might possibly have discouraged boarding intentions.

On the other hand, our instinctive actions contributed to saving us. Had the companionway been open when the boarding took place, *Ventus* would have been the scene of a bloody battle between three old sailors and four strong young men in their prime of life. I shudder at the thought. Once we had succeeded in closing all the portlights and hatches we were less accessible and less vulnerable. Surrender would not have been a guarantee of survival, as pirates sometimes don't leave witnesses. When an older man commands a young, impressionable man in a loud, firm tone of voice, a situation of authority can sometimes be established and the younger man can be intimidated. This might explain why the two who attempted to enter through the hatches aborted their entry. In the end, calling for help on the VHF radio, and doing it loudly, with the volume turned up is what saved us. One might ask, however, if it is desirable to offer resistance when in the sight of a firearm and what would have transpired had the gun not jammed.

As a sailing instructor in Canada, I lead my students to reflect on what actions they could take in the event of an emergency such as dismasting, a broken tiller or running aground. The reasoning behind this is that by rehearsing the different actions mentally one has a better chance of reacting appropriately in a real-life situation.

But what should we advise a new sailor with regards to boarding by pirates? What would be sensible, preventative or mitigating measures? Once boarded, what actions would afford the best chances of survival?

First, some sailors equip their boat to ward off intruders. To restrict entry by intruders who have reached the deck, they install steel bars across the hatch openings. To scare them away they recommend equipping a sailboat with a burglar alarm and powerful deck lights. It is said that Joshua Slocum, the first person to sail around the world solo in 1895, spread carpet tacks on his deck when anchoring in hot spots.

Being aware of and avoiding danger zones is definitely a good strategy, but what if that's not possible? As Anthony mused in the aftermath, we never go to bed at home without locking the front door. Why forsake this basic precaution on a boat? Turning on all navigation lights might deliver a measure of surprise. One could amplify this effect by taking out the air horn and making a lot of noise. To repel the pirates you might have to muster effective resistance; this might involve using the weapons at hand, such as a monkey wrench or a crowbar. Anything that can inflict a bloodletting injury might be a deterrent by increasing the drama and the fright factor. All boats carry weapons in the galley cutlery drawer. You might want to supplement these with a spear gun. What about firearms? Had we killed one of the aggressors with a firearm we might still be in Porlamar, behind bars, waiting for Venezuelan justice to take its course...Finally, how does one ward off an attack by an approaching boat while underway? A sailor we met who regularly sails the coast of Venezuela boasted of keeping a couple of Molotov cocktails and a six-shooter flare gun in his cockpit. He claims that in one instance he transformed an approaching armed boat into a blazing pyre by simply throwing a bottle of gasoline into the boat, and igniting it with his flare gun!

There are probably no hard and fast rules for all cases of pirating. Each situation requires a different set of responses. I think the following are some important points to consider: 1) Be aware of the fact that this can happen to YOU, so rehearse in your mind what actions you would take to deter and repel a pirate encounter. 2) Before a passage in unfamiliar waters, inquire as to the danger zones and keep a safe distance from these. Along the coast of Columbia, for instance, sailors keep 100 miles away. 3) Equip your boat with means of being seen and heard in case of attack. 4) Lock your companionway at night. 5) Raise your dinghy to deck level and lock it. 6) Keep a reasonable amount of money "hidden" so you can retrieve it to pay off your attackers if the situation reaches that point. 7) Don't worry, be happy.

After all this, you might ask a perfectly reasonable question, «Was *Ventus*' experience in Margarita an isolated case?» This post on www.noonsite.com might provide some enlightenment on the subject:

Posted October 20, 2008

We knew before we arrived that there had been a few dinghy thefts and "petty" piracy in Porlamar as we were able to read all about these on numerous cruisers websites... We learned on our arrival, after talking with some of the boats that had been in the anchorage for awhile, that one boat with an older gentleman onboard had anchored in a no anchor zone (due to being piracy prone area) and woke up to several guns to his head and the pirates ransacked the boat and took everything electronic (laptop, vhf, etc.) and all of his cash, but not before pistol whipping him. Poor guy, he didn't have any money to replace anything and we felt terrible for him. Another boater got off a little easier, minus the pistol whipping, although he said later he still feared for his life because the robbers thought he must have had more money hidden somewhere and he wasn't telling them where it was. They finally left. Even still, another boat had gone in to shore for happy hour (famous time for theft is the cocktail hour) and came back to find that although they had locked their boat up tight (good for them) and the thieves could not get in they still took anything that was loose on deck, fenders, lines, life raft etc. Life rafts are very expensive to replace. Outside of all these instances, there were many dinghy thefts every nite. These thefts were so commonplace that they weren't being reported anymore.

GLOSSARY

This list doesn't pretend to be a complete glossary of nautical terms and acronyms, as it contains only terms found in this book.

Abeam: Something that is abeam to the boat is over to the boat's side.
About (to come about, to tack): To steer the vessel across the path of the wind to the opposite tack.
Aft: Rear or to the rear.
ASA: American Sailing Association
Backstay: A wire that joins the top of the mast to the aft deck, preventing the mast from falling forward.
Bareboat (verb): To rent a boat without a captain and taking charge of the boat and crew oneself.
Bare poles: Refers to a boat underway with all its sails down.
Beam: The vessel's width at its widest point.
Beam or abeam: 90 degrees to the side of the boat.
Beam reach: Sailing a course 90 degrees to the wind.
Beam wind: A wind at 90 degrees to the side of a vessel.
Bearing away: To turn away from the wind. Also known as "heading off" The contrary of heading up, turning into the wind.
Beat, beating: To sail against the wind, sailing close-hauled, by making multiple tacks from side to side.
Bend on, unbend: Bending on a sail is to attach it to the mast or the forestay. Unbending is to remove it.
Berth: A bed on a boat.
Bilge: The lowest part of the hull under the floorboards where water can accumulate. The engine bilge is a well under the engine designed to catch small spills.
Block: A pulley.
Boathook: A shaft with a hook on the end used to reach objects over the side of the boat.
Boltrope: A rope sewn into the fabric along the leading edge of a sail to reiforce it.
Boom: A horizontal pipe to which the foot (bottom side) of the mainsail is attached.
Bosun chair: A seat attached to a halyard used to hoist you up to the top of the mast.
Bow: The front part of a boat.
Bowsprit: A pole extending forward from the bow, to which the forestay is fastened.**Broad reach:** Sailing with the wind coming at a 45-degree angle to the boat from behind; you could say the wind is on your hip pocket.
Bow: Front part of the boat as opposed to the rear part, which is the stern.
Canting keel: A canting keel can be tilted to windward in order to counteract the heeling force of the wind in the sails.
Chain plate: A stout metal strap bolted to the hull so that the top protrudes above deck level, to which the shrouds are secured.
Chandlery: A store where nautical equipment is sold.
Chart: Navigators like to call a map a chart.
Chop: A chop is encountered when the distance between waves is short.
Close haul: A sailboat is on a close haul when it is sailing with the wind coming at a 45-degree angle from straight ahead.
Close reach: Any upwind angle between a close haul and a beam reach.
Cockpit: A sunken space in the deck of a boat, usually toward the stern for use by the helmsman. The part of the boat where most of the outdoors socializing is done.
Coffee grinder: A cranking system that resembles bicycle pedals operated with the hands for turning the winches.
Companionway: The entrance and stairway from the cockpit to the cabin. It is usually closed with a horizontal sliding hatch cover and a couple of vertical wooden panels called washboards.
Compass rose: The compass illustration printed on a chart indicating true and magnetic north and the 360 degrees of the compass.
CYA: Canadian Yachting Association

Glossary

Deck: The top part of the boat upon which one can walk.
Daggerboard: A daggerboard is a retractable keel on a sailboat.
Datum: Chart datum is a plane of reference for making soundings of depths of water.
Deliver: To move a vessel over water from one place to another, usually for a fee
Displacement hull: is usually round in shape and pushes the water ahead of it to the sides as it moves. A planing hull by contrast, has either a flat or V-shaped bottom and once enough power has been applied either by a motor or by the wind, it rises above the surface of the water and glides with little friction.
Draft: The vertical distance between the waterline and the deepest part of the keel, usually expressed in feet or metres.
Drydock: To put a boat on dry dock or on the hard is to take her out of the water to store her on land.
Dodger: A structure supporting a windshield and canvass to protect crew against spray.
ETA: Estimated time of arrival
Fender: A tire, inflated ball or cylinder which, when mounted or inserted between the vessel and another object, will absorb shock and prevent damage or chafing. On a sailboat it is usually a white elongated balloon. Called a bumper in the Caribbean.
Flake (verb): To flake a sail is to fold it accordion-like.
Flood tide, ebb tide: A flood tide is rising and an ebb tide is falling or receding.
Foil, headfoil: A spinning pipe through which the forestay passes. The foil has a groove along its whole length into which the luff (front) of the headsail is secured.
Footrail (toerail): A small rail, a few inches in height, around the deck of a boat. The toerail may have holes in it to attach lines or blocks and to let the water drain off the deck.
Forepeak: The part of a ship's interior in the angle of the bow.
Forestay: The wire cable in the standing rigging, which runs from the top of the mast to the foredeck at the bow.
Furling forestay: If the wind becomes too strong, you can reduce the size of the headsail by rolling up part of it onto a rotating forestay with a furling system. When you furl the jib the furling line causes the furling drum and foil to rotate, thus rolling the sail up around the forestay.
Freshen (ing): The wind is said to freshen when it grows in strength.
Galley: On a boat the area where food is prepared is called the galley.
Genoa: A large foresail that substantially overlaps the mainsail. In other words, it is larger than a jib.
GORP: Good old raisins and peanuts.
GPS: An electronic instrument that uses the Global Positioning System to provide the sailor with the precise position of his boat on the globe.
Great circle: The shortest distance between any two points on earth.
Gunwale: On a row boat, the gunwale is typically the widened edge at the top of the side of the boat, where the edge is reinforced with wood, plastic or aluminum.
Great circle: The shortest distance between two points on the surface of the globe.
Gybe: When going downwind, turning the boat so the stern crosses the path of the wind. An accidental gybe results in the boom swinging violently to the opposite side of the boat.
Halyard: A rope spliced onto a wire cable that is used for hoisting and lowering a sail.
Hatch: An opening in the deck of a boat, with a hinged closure, usually made of Plexiglass.
Head: On a ship the head refers either to the bathroom or the toilet. You say "I'm going to the head", not "to the toilet, the John, the loo, the can, etc.".
Heading: The heading is the direction in which the boat is moving
Heading up, bearing away: Heading up means steering the bow more into the wind and bearing away is the opposite.
Heel (heeling): A boat heels when it leans sideways due to the effect of the wind on the sails or to being improperly loaded.
Hook: Slang for anchor.
Hove to (to heave to): To bring the boat to a standstill by tacking with the foresail back-winded and the rudder secured to windward. The foresail tells the boat to turn one way and the rudder tells it to turn the other way, so she just stays put.
Hull speed: The maximum speed of a displacement hull dictated by the length of the boat at the waterline.
Iron genny: (Iron genoa) is running with the engine instead of the sails.
Jacklines: Strong lengths of webbing material stretched from bow to stern on either side along the surface of the deck used for clipping one's harness to the boat to prevent from falling overboard.

Glossary

Katabatic wind: From the Greek word katabatikos meaning "going downhill", is a drainage wind, a wind that carries high-density air from a higher elevation down a slope under the force of gravity. These winds can rush down elevated slopes at hurricane speeds, but many are on the order of 10 knots or less.
Keelboat: A sailboat with a fin-like protrusion on the bottom. It helps steer the boat in a straight line and reduces its tendency to drift sideways.
Ketch: A two-masted sailboat with the front mast being higher than the aft one (called a mizzen mast).
Leech: Not a bloodsucker. The leech is the hypotenuse of the triangular sail forming its aft side. The foot is the bottom side and the luff is the forward side.
Leeward: The side of the vessel away from the wind, the side not receiving the wind (also, alee) – the opposite of windward.
Leeway: Drifting sideways due to the wind, waves or current.
Lifelines: Fencing made of wire and stanchions (posts) arranged around the edge of the deck to protect people from falling overboard. Often used as clotheslines.
Luff: The front edge of the sail. The bottom is the foot and the rear side is the leech.
Make fast: To make fast is simply to tie up.
Nautical mile: The unit of distance used in navigation, which is equal to 1.85 kilometres or 1.15 statute miles, or road miles.
NCSS: North Channel Sailing School
On the hard: Another term for taking the boat out of the water and putting it on dry dock.
OPY: Other People's Yachts.
Pitchpole: To turn upside down by being thrown end over end in heavy seas.
Ponga: An open wooden boat with a high bow, with outboard engine, often used for small-scale fishing.
Poop (pooped): Suddenly overwhelmed by a sea breaking over the stern. A pooping sea is a wave coming over the stern.
Port: Left side of the boat when you're in it facing forward.
Portlight: A small side window. Also known as porthole.
Pushpit, pulpit: The pushpit is the railing at the rear (usually stainless steel) and the pulpit is the one at the front.
Quarter: The side-rear portion on the boat to one side or the other. You can talk of either the starboard quarter or the port quarter.
Rafting up: To raft up to another boat is to tie up to it by placing fenders between the two boats and securing them together with dock lines. You can do this at anchor or at a crowded dock. When you have to get to the dock you then have to step across the deck of the other boat.
Reef (to take a): To reduce the amount of sail exposed to the wind either by rolling it up or by folding it. To shake a reef is to let it out.
Rigging, standing, running: The standing rigging consists of the mast, the boom and all the wire stays and shrouds, whereas the running rigging consists of sails, halyards, sheets and their blocks.
Rode: Consists of the entire length of rope and/or chain joining the anchor to the boat.
Rudder and tiller: The rudder is the underwater part of the steering mechanism, whereas the tiller is the handle the helmsman uses to steer the boat with.
Settee: A couch in a boat, usually part the boat furniture.
Sheave: Pulley at the top of a mast.
Sheet: A rope that regulates the angle at which a sail is set in relation to the wind, by easing it away from, or pulling it more toward the centreline.
Shrouds: Wires that are attached to the mast and the side of the boat to hold the mast up. There can be two or more on each side.
Slides: Nylon or bronze attachments that are sewn in the front edge (luff) of the sail that slip into a groove in the mast, enabling the sail to slide up and down on the mast.
Sloop: A sailboat with a single mast and two sails: A mainsail attached to the aft side of the mast and a headsail attached to a forestay ahead of the mast.
Sole (cockpit): Floor of the cockpit.
Solenoid valve: An electric valve for turning the propane on or off, controlled by a switch near the stove.
Spinnaker: A large, very lightweight downwind racing sail resembling a colourful balloon.
Spit: A point of sand that extends into the sea from a beach.
Spreaders: A pair of horizontal bars that hold the shrouds away from the mast. On some larger boats there can be two or more sets of spreaders.
Starboard: The right side of the boat when you're in it facing forward.

Glossary

Stateroom: A private cabin on a ship.
Staysail: A smaller sail attached to a shorter stay at the front of the mast, making the boat a cutter rig.
Steerageway: The lowest speed of a vessel that provides sufficient movement of water over the rudder to control direction.
Stern: The back end of the boat (as opposed to the bow).
Storm sail: A very small headsail used instead of the jib in very high winds.
Sundowner: A drink taken at sundown. An important tradition with some cruisers.
Swell: Deep ocean waves with a very long distance between them.
Tack (verb) or to come about: To tack or to come about is to turn the boat across the path of the wind so that the sails are filled on the opposite side. In so doing, the bow turns about 90 degrees.
Tack (noun): 1) The front bottom corner of a sail. 2) The side of the main sail that receives the wind. 3) The turn one makes when coming about or tacking.
Tidal range: The tidal range is the difference in depth between high tide and the next low tide or between low tide and the next high tide.
Tide: Change in the depth of the water due to the gravitational effect of the moon and sun expressed in feet or metres.
Tide, flood or ebb: A flood tide is rising and an ebb tide is falling or receding.
Tiller: The horizontal stick, the part of the steering mechanism in the boat that controls the rudder in the water.
Toe rail : See footrail.
Traveller: A metal track mounted transversally on the cabin roof or on the aft deck under the boom to which the sheet block (pulley) can slide, allowing it to move to the lee side at each tack.
Trimming: To trim the sails is to adjust them so that their angle to the wind achieves the most power possible.
TTSA: Trinidad and Tobago Sailing Association
Turnbuckle: A mechanism with a threaded opening at both ends that connects to a shroud or stay, and by turning it, draws the ends together and puts tension on the cable.
VHF radio: A radio that works on the Very High Frequency bandwidth that is commonly used for communication between boats and between boats and land stations. They only work with line of sight transmissions and have a range of no more than 25 miles.
Weighing anchor: Raising the anchor.
Wind direction: Direction from where the wind is blowing.
Windage: The effect of wind on the course of a boat.
Windward: At or toward the side that is closest to the wind, or towards the wind. The opposite of leeward

Made in the USA
Charleston, SC
06 May 2015